FREDERIC EGER

One-State Solution:
The Federal State of Israel

Author, Publisher: Frederic Eger.
Imprint: Frederic Eger Publishing
Original Book cover by Sukhdeep Singh.

Cover montage composition: **Tel Aviv Skyline by Night** by Gilad Avidan, CC BY-SA 3.0, via Wikimedia Commons; **Chaim Weizmann** portrait', Rijksmuseum (RP-F-F01691, via Wikimedia Commons), CC0 1.0.; **David Ben-Gurion** 1968 portrait by Fritz Cohen/Government Press Office (National Photo Collection ID D597-082, via Wikimedia Commons), Public Domain; **Golda Meir** 1964 portrait by Willem van de Poll/Nationaal Archief (inv.nr. 2.24.14.02, bestanddeel 255-4314; via Wikimedia Commons), CC BY-SA 4.0.; **Shimon Peres** 2010 portrait by Avi Ohayon/Government Press Office of Israel (via Wikimedia Commons), CC BY-SA 3.0."; **Yitzhak Rabin** 1994 portrait by Yaakov Saar/Government Press Office (National Photo Collection ID D3-016, via Wikimedia Commons), CC BY-SA 3.0.; **Judah Leon Magnes**; "Zionist activities in Palestine. Dr. J.S. Magnes, chancellor of the Hebrew University of Jerusalem."; Library of Congress Prints & Photographs Division, Washington, D.C. CC0 1.0; **Martin Buber** arriving at Schiphol Airport to receive the Erasmus Prize, 2 July 1963. Photo by Joop van Bilsen / Anefo, Dutch National Archives (Fotocollectie ANEFO, bestanddeelnummer 915-3260). Licensed under CC BY-SA 3.0 NL

First hardcover, paperback eBook and audiobook edition of March 1st, 2026.

ISBN eBook: 978-9934-936920
ISBN Audiobook: 9789934936944
ISBN Hardcover: 9789934936906
ISBN Hardcover Deluxe: 9789934936937
ISBN Softcover/Paperback: 9789934936913
Library of Congress control number (LCCN): 2026901926

BISAC Codes (Book Industry Standards and Communications): POLITICAL SCIENCE / Political Process — covers political strategies, governance models, and peace processes; POLITICAL SCIENCE / Human Rights; POLITICAL SCIENCE / International Relations / General; POLITICAL SCIENCE / World / Middle Eastern; POLITICAL SCIENCE / Constitutional Law & Theory; POLITICAL SCIENCE / Comparative Politics; POLITICAL SCIENCE / Nationalism & Patriotism; POLITICAL SCIENCE / Political Freedom & Security / Conflict Resolution; SOCIAL SCIENCE / Cultural & Ethnic Studies / Middle Eastern Studies; SOCIAL SCIENCE / Political Science; POLITICAL SCIENCE / Globalization.
Thema subject categories: JN / Middle East / Israel / Palestine / Conflict resolution / Federalism / Political theory / Constitutional law / Nationalism and human rights. **BIC (Book Industry Communication):** JNF – Middle East and Near East; JNFH – Israel & Palestine: politics & government; JNS – Conflicts & Peace Studies; JNT – Political Science: general; JCW – Government: general.
Universal Decimal Classification (UDC): 32.015: Political processes (for governance models); 323: Civil and political rights; constitutional law; 327: International relations; geopolitics; 327.56: Middle Eastern countries; 329: Middle Eastern Ethnology and ethnographic studies; 32.01: Comparative politics (with Switzerland, Belgium, Canada, India); 32.014: Nationalism and patriotism (addressing Zionist self-determination, federal nationalism); 32.021: Conflict resolution & peace studies; 314.7: Globalization.

Published by Frederic Eger (Riga, Latvia).
www.fredericeger.com
Inquiries: inquiries@fredericeger.com
Press: press@fredericeger.com

Complementary eBooks only. Journalists must pay print/ship for hardcovers/paperbacks. Printed US/UK/Canada/Australia; worldwide retail distribution.

I dedicate this book:

To my cousins Jorge Lenga and Sylvia Papuchado de Lenga - you were like parents during my young life's difficult times and embody true Jewish spirit in the Diaspora.

To my uncle Roberto Litovsky, whose love, support, and solidarity sustained me when I needed them most—a kind heart and great man, for whom I am forever grateful.

To my cousin Daniel Joseph Eiguer—your love, support, and solidarity shine brightly, yet under-acknowledged, your cousin is eternally grateful...

*To my grand-father Leizer Eiguer and grand-aunt Sarah Eiguer who took care of you til the very end; noble angels in the sky—your love shine brightly; Grandfather, I will always remember our talks about how to enjoy the simple things of life, like the kneidlach soup you ate *every single day…!*

To all who have given me unconditional love, trust, and sincere hearts—our triumphs rise together.

Zeit gezunt (זײַט געזונט) "Stay all healthy!"

ACKNOWLEDGMENTS

Heartfelt thanks to those whose support made these books reality: Gilad Avidan, Fleur Smith, Fritz Cohen, Willem van de Poll, Avi Ohayon, Yaakov Saar, Joop van Bilsen —your support turned vision into volumes...

These works—*Albert Einstein: The Father of Federal Zionism* (exploring Einstein's overlooked binational framework for peace in Palestine); *One State Solution: The Federal State of Israel* (a practical federal blueprint with minority protections, conflict resolution, and regional economic integration as an alternative to the failed two-state model); *Global Zionism: Am Israel United* (countering the hateful call for ethnic cleansing, "Globalize Intifada", with diaspora unity and strength in numbers, economic, cultural, and political strength, squandered through disconnection; and the *Zionism Next Thinkers* series on Amazon (a seductive blueprints for Zionism 3.0 amid AI, climate, and global threats)—spring not from solitary reflection, but from collective resolve, debate, and hope for Israel's federal future.

Deepest gratitude to library guardians worldwide who enshrined these books in national memory, ensuring their ideas endure. To Ilonka Ixmucané Matute Iriarte, María Magela Brenes, Marco Augusto Ferreira; Dr. Han-Ching Wang; Susana Soto Perez; Keiko Kurata; Alicia Yeo, Marco Lucchesi; Leslie Weir, Emilie Chapuis, Dr Boryana Hristova, Ulrike Junger, Constanze Schumann, David Rozsa, Judith Lindenberg, Oren Weinberger, Raquel Ukeles, Erez Elimelech, Maya Zlotnikov, and so many more... - your stewardship transforms words into permanence.

To readers—from scholars to seekers—you plant seeds of enlightenment with every page turned. If these pages inspire one soul to envision a thriving Federal State of Israel, our collective striving bears eternal fruit. In this symphony of redemption, each voice strengthens the chorus toward Eretz Yisrael's next chapter a chapter of Eternity without wars against its people.

Frederic Eger
Riga, Latvia
January 2026

TABLE OF CONTENTS

Opening Words
The Case Before This Court

I. Convening the Tribunal.

I stand before you not as neutral observer but as advocate—an advocate bringing charges before the highest tribunal that exists: the Supreme Court of Human Conscience. This court convenes in the minds of every person of goodwill who has witnessed this conflict's devastation and concluded that something must change. It sits in judgment not of peoples—for peoples are never guilty—but of ideas, of paradigms, of political choices that have produced a century of bloodshed and show every sign of producing another. The defendants in this proceeding are three.

The first defendant is the maximalist Zionist position that whispers seductively of managing, minimizing, or ultimately eliminating the Palestinian presence—the position holding that security requires demographic engineering, that the land from river to sea belongs exclusively to one people, that time and superior force will eventually resolve what diplomacy cannot. This defendant stands accused of strategic delusion, of counseling policies that would transform Israel into an international pariah, of promising security while delivering only the certainty of permanent war.

The second defendant is the maximalist Palestinian position that dreams of Israel's disappearance, of seven million Jews somehow vanishing, of clocks turned back to 1947 or 1917 or some mythical status quo ante. This defendant stands accused of condemning generations of Palestinians to poverty, statelessness, and despair in pursuit of an impossibility—of choosing performative resistance over achievable dignity, of sacrificing Palestinian children on the altar of a liberation that armed struggle will never deliver.

The third defendant is the two-state solution itself—that diplomatic Holy Grail pursued by every American administration, endorsed by the international community, enshrined in countless UN resolutions. This defendant stands accused not of bad intentions but of fatal impracticality. Over 700,000 Israeli settlers now live beyond the Green Line. Jerusalem cannot be surgically divided. The infrastructure of modern statehood—water, airspace, electromagnetic spectrum—cannot be neatly bisected. The two-state solution has been murdered by facts on the ground, and no amount of diplomatic incantation will resurrect it.

These three defendants have dominated discourse for generations. They have consumed careers, exhausted diplomats, and—most damningly—cost lives beyond counting. They have failed. They continue to fail. And absent fundamental paradigm shift, they will fail for another century while the bodies accumulate.

This book presents the case for conviction—and the case for an alternative.

II. The Personal Journey to Federal Zionism.

Before presenting the evidence, I must disclose my own journey to this courtroom. Intellectual honesty demands no less.

In 2018, I joined the World Federalist Movement, animated by idealistic visions of federal solutions to humanity's most intractable conflicts. What I encountered instead shattered my assumptions. I found systematic anti-Zionism masquerading as principled internationalism. I found membership steeped in ideological commitments that denied Jewish self-determination while championing every other national liberation movement. I found an organization purportedly dedicated to federal solutions that had never—not once, not seriously—considered federalism for the one conflict most desperately requiring it.

The cognitive dissonance proved unbearable. How could a movement championing self-determination deny that right to Jews alone? How could those preaching universal human rights apply them selectively? How could federalists reject federalism when Jews and Arabs were involved? The hypocrisy was staggering, the intellectual dishonesty obvious, the double standards impossible to reconcile with any coherent moral framework.

I could no longer identify as "World Federalist" after recognising that the movement had been corrupted by selective application of principles it claimed to hold universal. But from that disillusionment emerged clarity. As a Federal Zionist—a position developed through years studying comparative political systems—I possessed a unique perspective. I understood that Israel's survival requires not merely military strength but political legitimacy. I recognised that the characteristics making this conflict so intractable—competing national narratives, intermingled populations, disputed territories, profound distrust—are precisely the conditions under which federal solutions have succeeded elsewhere.

This book emerges from that recognition. It vindicates Zionism while exploring federalism's transformative potential. It demonstrates through rigorous analysis that a Federal State of Israel represents not compromise of Jewish sovereignty but its ultimate expression—the confident extension of Israeli democracy to populations currently suffering under dysfunctional Palestinian Authority governance and Hamas terrorist tyranny. This argument proceeds from strength, not weakness; conviction, not conciliation; profound belief that lasting peace comes from magnanimity of victory, not balance of weakness.

III. The Charges Against the Status Quo.

Let the record reflect the costs of the paradigms now on trial.

October 7th, 2023—the deadliest day for Jews since the Holocaust—demonstrated with terrible finality that "managing" this conflict produces not stability but catastrophe. The status quo's defenders promised security through separation, through walls, through technological superiority, through intelligence dominance. On that Saturday morning, every promise proved hollow. Fourteen hundred civilians murdered. Hundreds taken hostage. Communities that had existed for generations erased in hours. The prosecution rests its case on the bodies.

But October 7th, devastating as it was, represents merely the most spectacular failure of an approach that fails continuously. Consider what the status quo costs:

In blood: Thousands of Israelis killed in wars, terrorist attacks, and military operations since 1948. Tens of thousands of Palestinians killed in the same period. Children on both sides growing up knowing only conflict, their psyches shaped by trauma that will reverberate for generations.

In treasure: Israel devotes approximately five percent of GDP to defence—among the highest ratios in the developed world—resources that could otherwise fund education, healthcare, infrastructure, and innovation. The Palestinian economy operates at a fraction of its potential, strangled by restrictions that occupation requires.

In legitimacy: Israel faces diplomatic isolation, boycott movements, International Court of Justice proceedings, and erosion of support even among traditional allies. The "only democracy in the Middle East" governs millions who cannot vote in its elections—a contradiction that corrodes Israel's democratic self-understanding and international standing alike.

In opportunity: Regional integration that could transform the Middle East remains blocked by the unresolved Palestinian question. The Abraham Accords demonstrated what becomes possible when normalisation proceeds; they also demonstrated the fragility of progress when the foundational conflict remains unaddressed.

The prosecution submits that these costs are not acceptable. They are not sustainable. They are not necessary. And they will only compound with each passing year that failed paradigms remain unchallenged.

IV. The Case for Federalism.

Against the failed defendants, this book presents an alternative: the Federal State of Israel. The case proceeds through fourteen chapters, each building upon the last, each contributing evidence to the central argument that federal arrangements offer the only viable path forward.

Chapter One establishes the historical foundation—examining deep roots from ancient Jewish sovereignty through modern Zionist re-establishment of statehood, demonstrating the unbroken Jewish connection to this land while analyzing why conventional approaches have consistently failed. History does not determine the future, but understanding history prevents repeating its errors.

Chapter Two introduces the conceptual marriage between Federal Zionism and World Federalism—and confronts honestly the corruption I encountered in the World Federalist Movement. It examines how Diaspora Zionism connects and complements Federal Zionism, how both relate to World Federalism's core insights while rejecting its institutional failures, and why the movement's systematic bias against Jewish self-determination renders it politically incredible except in its foundational claim that the UN should evolve toward genuine federation of nation-states.

Chapter Three surveys historical precedents—Switzerland's cantons managing four languages and two religions, Belgium's linguistic federalism accommodating Flemish and Walloon, Canada's asymmetric arrangements addressing Quebec's distinctiveness, India's governance of a billion people across dozens of languages and multiple faiths. These cases reveal both federalism's promise and its pitfalls, providing design principles applicable to Israeli-Palestinian realities.

Chapter Four presents foundational principles for federal constitutional design—division of powers between federal and regional governments, protection of minority rights within majority-rule frameworks, mechanisms for resolving disputes that inevitably arise in diverse polities. Constitutional architecture translates abstract principles into functioning institutions.

Chapter Five examines the constitutional frameworks required for post-conflict reconstruction—how federal states emerge from crisis, how transitional justice addresses historical grievances, how implementation must be sequenced to build capacity and trust. The German precedent proves particularly instructive: transformation from genocidal totalitarianism to stable federal democracy demonstrates what becomes possible when political will exists.

Chapter Six analyses the Abraham Accords' achievements and limitations—documenting the economic and diplomatic benefits that normalisation has already produced while demonstrating why comprehensive regional transformation requires resolution of the Palestinian question that the Accords deliberately deferred.

Chapter Seven confronts critics directly—examining objections regarding complexity, secession risks, asymmetric power, security concerns, and democratic legitimacy. Each critique receives serious engagement; none proves insurmountable. The chapter demonstrates that obstacles to federalism, while substantial, pale beside the obstacles that alternative approaches have already failed to overcome.

Chapter Eight presents the economic case—documenting potential gains from integration, analyzing fiscal federalism mechanisms for managing regional disparities, and demonstrating that shared prosperity creates constituencies for peace that no peace treaty unsupported by economic substance can provide. Economics is not separate from politics but foundational to it.

Chapter Nine addresses security architecture—the unified command structures, regional police forces, intelligence integration, and phased implementation that federal arrangements require. Security cannot be compromised; the chapter demonstrates that federal frameworks can provide security more robust than occupation while more legitimate than external control.

Chapter Ten examines how federal systems manage diversity— educational policies, media representation, cultural accommodation, religious freedom, and conflict resolution mechanisms that successful federations have developed. Institutional design must be complemented by cultural transformation; this chapter addresses both.

Chapter Eleven analyses federal model critiques comprehensively —engaging objections from serious scholars who have concluded that federalism cannot work in this context. Intellectual honesty requires confronting the strongest counterarguments; this chapter does so while demonstrating that critics identify design parameters rather than inherent impossibilities.

Chapter Twelve surveys constitutional frameworks and power-sharing mechanisms—bicameralism, proportional representation, mutual veto rights, asymmetric autonomy, and judicial review. The constitutional engineering required for Israeli-Palestinian federation is complex but entirely achievable with political will and technical expertise.

Chapter Thirteen envisions regional transformation—how federal resolution would catalyze fundamental reorientation of Middle Eastern geopolitics, moving the region from perpetual zero-sum competition toward cooperative frameworks capable of addressing shared challenges and realizing mutual prosperity.

Chapter Fourteen synthesizes preceding arguments into comprehensive framework—the architecture of peace that federal design makes possible, with scholarly engagement on counterarguments and clear-eyed assessment of what implementation requires.

Chapter Fifteen speaks directly to the next generation—Israeli, Palestinian, Arab Israeli, and diaspora youth alike—presenting the book's case as an intergenerational appeal and moral summons. The chapter invites youth to reclaim the digital tools that have been weaponized for hatred and instead forge a cultural renaissance through joint ventures, climate guardianship, and artistic collaboration. This is the generation that can break the cycle—not by forgetting the horror but by building something new from the shared skies above the blood rivers.

V. The Stakes of This Trial.

The evidence presented across these chapters demonstrates that federal solutions address what alternatives cannot:

For Israeli security: Unified federal command over external defence, elimination of security vacuums that terrorist organizations exploit, constitutional frameworks that protect Jewish self-governance regardless of demographic shifts. Security through legitimate institutions proves more durable than security through permanent domination.

For Palestinian dignity: Genuine self-governance over matters affecting daily life, participation in federal institutions as equal citizens, constitutional protections ensuring that autonomy cannot be unilaterally revoked. Dignity through partnership exceeds what armed resistance has delivered in seventy-five years.

For regional stability: Resolution of the conflict that has organized Middle Eastern politics for generations, enabling cooperation on security, economics, and development that perpetual conflict has precluded. The Abraham Accords' achievements would multiply; their vulnerabilities would diminish.

For international legitimacy: Israel transformed from permanent controversy into normal democratic state, welcomed rather than condemned, partnered rather than isolated. Legitimacy that military superiority cannot provide, institutions can.

For both peoples' futures: Children growing up knowing peace rather than war, building careers rather than bunkers, imagining futures defined by possibility rather than perpetual struggle. The simple, revolutionary prospect of normality.

VI. The Standard of Judgment.

This court must judge not by standards of perfection but by standards of comparison. Federalism is difficult; the question is whether alternatives are more difficult still. Federalism involves risks; the question is whether continued conflict involves greater risks. Federalism requires compromise from all parties; the question is whether the compromises required are more painful than the costs already being paid.

By these comparative standards, the case for federalism is overwhelming. Every alternative has been tried. Every alternative has failed. The two-state solution is dead, murdered by settlement expansion and Jerusalem's indivisibility. The one-state solution without federalism means either apartheid or the end of Jewish self-determination—outcomes neither side can accept. The status quo produces October 7th. The maximalist positions produce only more of the same.

Federalism alone addresses both peoples' core needs while creating frameworks for cooperation that other approaches preclude. It is not utopian—it has worked elsewhere, in circumstances comparably difficult. It is not easy—nothing worthwhile ever is. But it is possible. And possibility, in a conflict that has exhausted every other option, is itself a form of hope.

VII. The Plea.

I conclude this opening statement as I began: as an advocate before the Supreme Court of Human Conscience, pleading for judgment against failed paradigms and for the alternative this book presents.

To those who read these pages: you are the jury. Your verdict will be rendered not in courtrooms but in the positions you advocate, the leaders you support, the futures you demand. The evidence will be laid before you chapter by chapter. The arguments will be presented with rigor and honesty. The counterarguments will be engaged seriously. What remains, after all evidence is weighed, is your judgment.

I ask only this: judge with open minds. The paradigms now on trial have powerful defenders—bureaucracies invested in their perpetuation, careers built upon their assumptions, identities formed around their premises. Challenging them requires intellectual courage. But the costs of not challenging them—measured in blood, in treasure, in legitimacy, in foreclosed futures—demand nothing less.

October 7th shattered the illusion that this conflict could be managed indefinitely. The international community's response—reverting to failed formulas, mouthing exhausted pieties—revealed the poverty of imagination that has characterized this conflict for generations. This book offers an alternative: federal solutions addressing legitimate national aspirations while creating shared institutions. Written for those refusing to accept this conflict as permanent feature of human affairs, it proceeds from conviction that political imagination, properly applied to constitutional design, can resolve even conflicts that have resisted all previous efforts.

The case is now before you. The evidence awaits your examination. The verdict will shape not merely the Israeli-Palestinian future but the future of a region—and perhaps, if federalism succeeds in this most contested of territories, the future of humanity's capacity to manage its deepest divisions through institutions rather than violence.

The prosecution calls its first witness: history itself.

What follows is the evidence.

Chapter 1.
From Ancient Sovereignty, Modern Statehood
& the Federal Path Forward.

Reclaiming Historical Truth.

The modern discourse surrounding the Israeli-Palestinian conflict often suffers from historical amnesia—a willful forgetting of the deep, documented, and unbroken connection between the Jewish people and the land of Israel. This chapter seeks to rectify that deficit by establishing, through archaeological evidence, historical documentation, and scholarly analysis, the irrefutable reality of Jewish sovereignty, presence, and continuous connection to this land spanning more than three millennia. This is not merely an academic exercise; it is the essential foundation for understanding why the Federal State of Israel represents not a concession to Palestinian statehood, but rather the generous extension of Israel's proven democratic framework to populations that have, for decades, lived under the dysfunctional governance of the Palestinian Authority and the terrorist tyranny of Hamas.

As a French-Argentine-Israeli Zionist, I write from a perspective forged in the crucible of Jewish history—a history marked by persecution, exile, miraculous return, and the establishment of a thriving democracy in our ancestral homeland. The federal solution proposed in this work emerges not from weakness but from strength; not from abandonment of Jewish national aspirations but from their fulfillment; not from compromise with those who seek Israel's destruction but from the extension of Israeli citizenship and democracy after their complete and unconditional defeat.

Archaeological Testament, Antiquity Israel
(1209 BCE - 586 BCE)

The historical Jewish presence in the land of Israel is not a matter of faith alone—it is attested by an overwhelming body of archaeological evidence that no serious scholar disputes. The Merneptah Stele, discovered in 1896 in Thebes, Egypt, and dated to approximately 1209 BCE, provides the earliest extrabiblical reference to "Israel" as a distinct people in Canaan. The Egyptian pharaoh Merneptah boasts: "Israel is laid waste; his seed is no more." This inscription, paradoxically celebrating Israel's destruction while confirming its existence, demonstrates that by the late 13th century BCE, Israel was recognized as a distinct entity significant enough to warrant mention in Egyptian royal propaganda (Stager, 1985; Bimson, 1991).

The Tel Dan Stele, discovered in northern Israel in 1993-1994, provides even more dramatic confirmation of biblical history. Dating to the 9th century BCE, this Aramaic inscription explicitly references the "House of David" (bytdwd), offering the first extrabiblical evidence for King David's historical existence and establishing the Davidic dynasty as historical fact rather than myth (Biran & Naveh, 1993, 1995; Lemaire, 1994). As the Israeli archaeologist Avraham Biran noted, this discovery "proves that David was a historical figure" and that the United Monarchy described in biblical sources had a factual foundation (Shanks, 1994).

The material culture of ancient Israel provides further incontrovertible evidence. The Ketef Hinnom silver amulets, discovered in Jerusalem and dated to the late 7th century BCE, contain the Priestly Blessing from Numbers 6:24-26, making them the oldest biblical text ever discovered (Barkay et al., 2004). The Siloam Inscription, carved into the tunnel built by King Hezekiah circa 701 BCE to protect Jerusalem's water supply during the Assyrian siege, demonstrates sophisticated Hebrew literacy and urban planning (Reich & Shukron, 2011). The thousands of Hebrew inscriptions on pottery shards (ostraca) from sites throughout ancient Israel, including the famous Samaria Ostraca and Lachish Letters, testify to a literate, administratively sophisticated Hebrew-speaking society (Naveh, 1982; Dobbs-Allsopp et al., 2005).

Archaeological excavations at Jerusalem, Megiddo, Hazor, Gezer, and scores of other sites have uncovered monumental architecture, fortifications, palaces, and administrative buildings consistent with biblical descriptions of the Israelite kingdoms (Mazar, 1990; Finkelstein & Silberman, 2001; Dever, 2003). While scholars debate the precise dates and extent of various periods, the consensus among serious archaeologists is unequivocal: the kingdoms of Israel and Judah existed as historical entities, with Jerusalem as the capital of a Judahite kingdom centered on the Temple (Grabbe, 2007; Miller & Hayes, 2006).

The Temple itself—destroyed by the Babylonians in 586 BCE and rebuilt as the Second Temple from 516 BCE until its destruction by Rome in 70 CE—served as the religious, cultural, and political center of Jewish life for over six centuries. The Temple's existence is confirmed not merely by biblical texts but by contemporary Greek and Roman historians including Hecataeus of Abdera (circa 300

BCE), who described Jerusalem and its Temple in detail (Bar-Kochva, 1996), and by the extensive archaeological remains on the Temple Mount, including the massive retaining walls built by Herod the Great (Ritmeyer, 2006).

Exile, Persistence & Unbroken Connection.
(586 BCE - 1897 CE).
The destruction of the First Temple by Nebuchadnezzar II of Babylon in 586 BCE initiated the first major Jewish exile—the Babylonian Captivity chronicled in the biblical books of Jeremiah, Ezekiel, and Daniel. Yet even in exile, the Jewish people maintained their distinct identity and their connection to the land of Israel. The prophet Ezekiel's visions occurred "by the river Chebar" in Babylon, yet they focused obsessively on Jerusalem and the Temple (Ezekiel 1:1-3). The Psalms composed during this period express an aching longing: "By the rivers of Babylon, there we sat down, yea, we wept, when we remembered Zion... If I forget you, O Jerusalem, let my right hand forget its skill" (Psalm 137:1, 5).

The Persian conquest of Babylon under Cyrus the Great in 539 BCE enabled the Return to Zion, as detailed in the books of Ezra and Nehemiah. Cyrus's decree permitting Jewish return is confirmed not only in biblical texts but in the Cyrus Cylinder, a contemporary Babylonian document (Berquist, 1995). The returnees rebuilt the Temple and reconstituted Jewish autonomy under Persian suzerainty, establishing a pattern that would persist through subsequent empires: Jews always maintained some presence in the land, and Jews in the diaspora always oriented themselves toward Jerusalem and hoped for return.

The Second Temple period (516 BCE - 70 CE) witnessed the flourishing of Jewish civilization under successive empires—Persian, Ptolemaic, Seleucid, Hasmonean, and Roman. The Hasmonean dynasty (140-37 BCE) represents the last period of Jewish sovereignty before the modern state, marked by independence, territorial expansion, and cultural renaissance (Schwartz, 2014). The Jewish population of the land during the Second Temple period numbered in the millions, with Jerusalem serving as a pilgrimage center drawing Jews from throughout the diaspora for the biblical festivals (Jeremias, 1969).

The First Jewish-Roman War (66-73 CE) and the destruction of the Second Temple in 70 CE by Titus dealt a catastrophic blow to Jewish life in the land, but did not end Jewish presence. Josephus

Flavius, the Jewish historian who witnessed the destruction, estimated that 1.1 million Jews died during the siege of Jerusalem alone (Jewish War 6.420). The Bar Kokhba Revolt (132-136 CE) represented a final, desperate attempt to restore Jewish sovereignty. Its brutal suppression by Rome resulted in additional mass casualties—Cassius Dio claimed 580,000 Jewish deaths (Roman History 69.14)—and the systematic destruction of Jewish villages throughout Judea.

Following the Bar Kokhba Revolt, Rome renamed the province from Judea to "Syria Palaestina" in a deliberate attempt to erase Jewish connection to the land, borrowing the name from the Philistines, ancient enemies of Israel who had themselves disappeared centuries earlier (Jacobson, 1999; Mor, 2016). Jerusalem was rebuilt as Aelia Capitolina, and Jews were officially banned from the city except for one day per year—Tisha B'Av, the ninth of Av, the anniversary of both Temples' destruction. Yet even under these severe restrictions, Jewish communities persisted in the Galilee, the Golan, and along the coastal plain (Safrai, 1994; Levine, 2000).

Byzantine Christian rule (324-638 CE) brought new restrictions and persecutions, yet Jewish communities survived and even flourished in some periods. The Galilee became the center of Jewish scholarship, producing the Jerusalem Talmud (circa 400 CE), an enormous compendium of Jewish law, ethics, and lore that remains central to Jewish learning today (Rubenstein, 2010). The synagogue ruins at Capernaum, Beit Alpha, Baram, and elsewhere testify to vibrant Jewish communities maintaining their traditions and their connection to the land (Levine, 2005).

The Muslim conquest (638 CE) brought yet another regime but did not displace the Jewish presence. Under early Islamic rule, Jews were classified as dhimmis (protected but subordinate peoples), subject to special taxes and restrictions but permitted to practice their religion (Stillman, 1979; Cohen, 1994). Jewish communities existed in Jerusalem, Safed, Tiberias, and other cities throughout the medieval period. The great medieval Jewish philosopher Maimonides (1138-1204) expressed the traditional Jewish attitude: "It is better to live in the deserts of Israel than in palaces abroad" (Mishneh Torah, Laws of Kings 5:12).

The mystical city of Safed became a center of Kabbalah (Jewish mysticism) in the 16th century, attracting scholars and mystics from throughout the diaspora (Fine, 2003). Rabbi Isaac Luria, the Arizal, developed teachings there that profoundly influenced subsequent Jewish thought. These communities, though small and often impoverished under Ottoman rule, maintained an unbroken Jewish presence and kept alive the hope of redemption and return (Barnai, 1992).

Throughout the centuries of exile, the Jewish people never abandoned their connection to the land of Israel. Every synagogue in the world was oriented toward Jerusalem. Jews prayed daily for return: "Next year in Jerusalem" concluded every Passover Seder. The liturgy contained dozens of prayers for restoration of Zion and rebuilding of the Temple. Jewish law continued to reference agricultural commandments applicable only in the land of Israel. Mourning customs commemorated the destruction of the Temple. Marriage ceremonies concluded with the breaking of a glass while reciting Psalm 137: "If I forget you, O Jerusalem..."

This was not mere nostalgia or spiritual metaphor—it was a national memory, a collective determination, an unbroken civilizational connection sustained across seventy generations. As the historian Simon Dubnow observed, "The Jewish people is the only people in history that has never forgotten its homeland, never ceased to consider itself in exile, never stopped praying for return" (Dubnow, 1916-1920). This reality—this unbroken connection maintained against all odds through two millennia of dispersion—forms the moral and historical foundation of modern Zionism and the legitimacy of the State of Israel.

The Birth of Modern Political Zionism (1860-1917).
The rise of modern political Zionism in the late 19th century represented the transformation of this age-old religious and cultural connection into a practical political program. While Jews had always prayed for return to Zion, modern Zionism emerged as a response to the particular crises facing European Jewry in the age of nationalism: persistent and often violent antisemitism in Eastern Europe and Russia, and the failure of emancipation and assimilation to protect Jews even in supposedly enlightened Western Europe (Vital, 1975; Avineri, 1981).

The pogroms that swept the Russian Empire following the assassination of Tsar Alexander II in 1881 shattered the illusions of Russian Jews who had hoped for gradual integration. The violence was systematic and often state-sanctioned, targeting Jewish communities across Ukraine, Bessarabia, and Poland, resulting in thousands of deaths and the destruction of Jewish property (Klier & Lambroza, 1992). The Russian government's subsequent May Laws of 1882 imposed severe legal restrictions on Jewish residence, education, and economic activity, effectively attempting to strangle Jewish life (Stanislawski, 1983).

These events catalyzed the Hibbat Zion (Love of Zion) movement, which organized the First Aliyah (wave of immigration) to Palestine (1882-1903). Approximately 25,000-35,000 Jews immigrated during this period, establishing agricultural settlements with the support of Baron Edmond de Rothschild (Eisenstadt, 1967; Shavit, 1987). These pioneers—the Biluim and others—were motivated by both push factors (fleeing persecution) and pull factors (the positive vision of renewing Jewish life in the ancestral homeland).

The founding of modern political Zionism is conventionally dated to Theodor Herzl's publication of *Der Judenstaat* (The Jewish State) in 1896 and the First Zionist Congress in Basel, Switzerland in 1897. Herzl, an assimilated Viennese journalist, was radicalized by the Dreyfus Affair in France, where a Jewish army captain was falsely convicted of treason amid an explosion of antisemitic vitriol. If a Jew could be scapegoated in the land of Liberté, Égalité, Fraternité, Herzl concluded, then assimilation offered no protection (Kornberg, 1993; Avineri, 2013).

Herzl's Zionism was thoroughly modern, influenced by 19th-century nationalist movements throughout Europe. He envisioned a Jewish state created through diplomatic negotiation and international recognition, writing in his diary after the Basel Congress: "At Basel I founded the Jewish State. If I said this out loud today, I would be greeted by universal laughter. In five years perhaps, and certainly in fifty years, everyone will perceive it" (Herzl, 1897/1960). He proved remarkably prescient—fifty years and nine months after Basel, the UN voted to partition Palestine and create a Jewish state.

The World Zionist Organization, established at Basel, created the institutional framework for the Zionist movement, coordinating fundraising, land purchase, settlement, and diplomatic efforts. The Jewish National Fund, established in 1901, purchased land in Palestine for Jewish settlement (Lehn & Davis, 1988). The Second Aliyah (1904-1914) brought approximately 40,000 Jews, many inspired by socialist ideals, who established the kibbutz movement and laid foundations for Hebrew culture and self-defense (Gorny, 1987; Shapira, 2012).

Critically, Zionist land purchases were conducted legally, at market prices, often from absentee landlords in Beirut, Damascus, and elsewhere. The claim that Zionists "stole" Palestinian land is historically false—land was purchased through normal commercial transactions, documented in Ottoman and later British records (Stein, 1984; Bunton, 2007). Arab tenant farmers were sometimes displaced when land changed hands, creating local tensions, but this resulted from Ottoman feudal land systems, not from illegal seizure.

The British Mandate and the Path to Statehood (1917-1948).
World War I proved pivotal for Zionist aspirations. The Ottoman Empire's alliance with Germany brought it into conflict with Britain and France, who sought to dismantle Ottoman holdings in the Middle East. The British government, influenced by genuine Christian Zionism, strategic considerations regarding post-war control of Palestine, and the advocacy of Chaim Weizmann and other Zionist leaders, issued the Balfour Declaration on November 2, 1917 (Schneer, 2010; Huneidi, 2001).

Foreign Secretary Arthur James Balfour's letter to Lord Rothschild stated: "His Majesty's Government view with favour the establishment in Palestine of a national home for the Jewish people, and will use their best endeavours to facilitate the achievement of this object, it being clearly understood that nothing shall be done which may prejudice the civil and religious rights of existing non-Jewish communities in Palestine" (emphasis added). The phrase "national home" was deliberately chosen over "state" to maintain diplomatic flexibility, but the Zionist movement understood and intended it as a pathway to statehood (Friedman, 1973; Sanders, 1983).

The Balfour Declaration was subsequently incorporated into the League of Nations Mandate for Palestine (1922), giving it international legal standing. Article 2 of the Mandate charged Britain with "placing the country under such political, administrative and economic conditions as will secure the establishment of the Jewish national home." Article 4 recognized the Zionist Organization as the appropriate Jewish agency to work toward this goal. Article 6 instructed the administration to "facilitate Jewish immigration" and "encourage close settlement by Jews on the land" (Ingrams, 1972; Klieman, 1970).

This was not colonialism in the conventional sense—Jews were not settling a foreign land on behalf of an imperial power, but rather returning to their ancestral homeland under international legal sanction. As the legal scholar Jacques Gauthier demonstrated in his exhaustive doctoral dissertation, the Mandate for Palestine created binding international law that recognized Jewish national rights and has never been legally superseded (Gauthier, 2007).

The Mandate period witnessed dramatic growth in the Jewish population of Palestine, from approximately 60,000 in 1918 to over 600,000 by 1947—accomplished primarily through immigration and natural increase, not displacement (Bachi, 1977; Della Pergola, 2001). The Third Aliyah (1919-1923), Fourth Aliyah (1924-1929), and Fifth Aliyah (1929-1939) brought waves of immigrants fleeing antisemitism in Europe, building cities, draining malarial swamps, establishing industries, and creating Hebrew-language cultural institutions (Shapira, 1992; Segev, 2000).

Tel Aviv, founded in 1909 as a Jewish neighborhood outside the ancient port of Jaffa, grew into a thriving modern city. The Hebrew University of Jerusalem, founded in 1925, became a world-class institution. The Histadrut labor federation, established in 1920, created a socialist economic framework that would shape Israeli society for decades. The Haganah defense organization, formed to protect Jewish communities from Arab attacks, evolved into the nucleus of the future Israeli Defense Forces (Slutsky, 1972; Golani, 1994).

Arab opposition to Zionism intensified during this period, manifesting in recurring violence. The 1920 Nebi Musa riots, the 1921 Jaffa riots, the 1929 Hebron massacre (in which 67 Jews were murdered, many brutally mutilated, and the ancient Jewish community of Hebron was destroyed), and the Arab Revolt of 1936-1939 all targeted Jewish civilians and were motivated by opposition to Jewish immigration and any Jewish presence beyond a subordinate minority (Porath, 1974, 1977; Morris, 1999).

The Arab Revolt, led by the Mufti of Jerusalem Haj Amin al-Husseini, involved systematic attacks on Jewish settlements, British installations, and even moderate Arabs who cooperated with Jews or British. The British eventually suppressed the revolt using significant military force, but not before it had claimed hundreds of Jewish lives and demonstrated the depth of Arab rejection of Jewish national rights (Kabha, 2002; Norris, 2008). Husseini's subsequent alliance with Nazi Germany—he spent the war years in Berlin meeting with Hitler, broadcasting Nazi propaganda in Arabic, and helping recruit Bosnian Muslims for the SS—revealed the eliminationist antisemitism at the core of this opposition (Motadel, 2014; Mallmann & Cüppers, 2010).

Britain's response to the Arab Revolt—the 1939 White Paper—effectively repudiated the Balfour Declaration, severely restricting Jewish immigration precisely when European Jews faced existential threat from Nazism. This betrayal meant that millions of Jews seeking refuge from the Holocaust were denied entry to Palestine, consigning many to death (Ofer, 1990; Cohen, 2003). The moral obscenity of closing Palestine to Jewish refugees while European Jewry faced systematic extermination cannot be overstated—it represents one of history's great injustices and validates the Zionist insistence on Jewish sovereignty as the only guarantee of Jewish survival.

The Holocaust & Israel's Founding (1939-1948).
The Holocaust—the systematic murder of six million Jews by Nazi Germany and its collaborators—transformed the Jewish world and the urgency of the Zionist project. While Zionism emerged before the Holocaust and would have continued regardless, the genocide validated its core premise: that Jews require their own state for physical survival, that reliance on others' goodwill is fatal, and that Jewish powerlessness invites destruction (Bauer, 2001; Diner, 2009).

The Holocaust decimated European Jewry—over 90% of Poland's 3.3 million Jews were murdered, along with similar proportions in Lithuania, Latvia, Ukraine, Hungary, and elsewhere. Ancient communities that had existed for a millennium were annihilated. The Yiddish civilization of Eastern Europe, with its rich literary, musical, and intellectual culture, was destroyed. The full scope of the catastrophe only became clear as Allied forces liberated the concentration camps in 1945, revealing gas chambers, crematoria, and the skeletal survivors of the death machine (Hilberg, 1961/2003; Friedländer, 2007).

For the displaced persons (DPs) in post-war Europe—Holocaust survivors with no homes to return to, no families left alive, no communities remaining—Palestine represented not merely a destination but salvation. The British, however, maintained the White Paper restrictions, intercepting refugee ships and interning their passengers in camps in Cyprus. The Exodus 1947 affair, in which British forces violently seized a refugee ship carrying 4,500 Holocaust survivors and forcibly returned them to Germany, crystallized global opinion and demonstrated the moral bankruptcy of Britain's policy (Hadari, 1991; Baumel, 1998).

Jewish armed resistance against British restrictions intensified. The Haganah organized illegal immigration (Aliyah Bet), smuggling tens of thousands of refugees past the British blockade. More radical groups—the Irgun and Lehi—conducted armed operations against British targets. While mainstream Zionist leadership condemned terrorism, the underground groups reflected Jewish desperation and determination that the Holocaust must not be followed by continued Jewish statelessness (Bell, 1977; Heller, 1995).

Britain, exhausted by World War II and unable to reconcile Jewish and Arab demands, referred the Palestine question to the United Nations in 1947. The UN Special Committee on Palestine (UNSCOP) investigated and recommended partition: dividing Palestine into Jewish and Arab states, with Jerusalem under international administration. On November 29, 1947, the UN General Assembly voted 33-13 (with 10 abstentions) to adopt Resolution 181, the Partition Plan (Garcia-Granados, 1948; Laqueur & Rubin, 2008).

The Jewish leadership, after intense debate, accepted partition despite profound reservations about the proposed borders, which excluded Jerusalem and were militarily indefensible. David Ben-Gurion recognized that any Jewish state, however imperfect its boundaries, represented the culmination of two millennia of hope and the vindication of Zionism (Teveth, 1987; Shapira, 2014). As Ben-Gurion stated: "The Jewish people are not going to wait until the British leave and give the Arabs the opportunity to attack us... We shall establish the state ourselves" (cited in Morris, 2008, p. 67).

The Arab states and Palestinian Arab leadership categorically rejected partition. The Arab Higher Committee declared: "The Arabs of Palestine... will never submit or yield to any power coming to Palestine to impose a solution contrary to their wishes" (cited in Bard, 2011, p. 32). The day after the UN vote, Arab attacks on

Jewish communities began, initiating the civil war phase of what would become the 1948 War (Morris, 2008; Karsh, 2002).

On May 14, 1948, as the British Mandate expired, Ben-Gurion proclaimed the establishment of the State of Israel, reading the Declaration of Independence at a ceremony in Tel Aviv. The Declaration rooted Israel's legitimacy in multiple foundations: "The Land of Israel was the birthplace of the Jewish people. Here their spiritual, religious and political identity was shaped... After being forcibly exiled from their land, the people kept faith with it throughout their Dispersion and never ceased to pray and hope for their return" (Israel Ministry of Foreign Affairs, 1948).

Within hours, five Arab armies—Egypt, Jordan, Syria, Lebanon, and Iraq—invaded, joined by volunteers from Saudi Arabia, Yemen, and Libya, explicitly seeking to destroy the nascent Jewish state. Arab League Secretary-General Azzam Pasha declared: "This will be a war of extermination and momentous massacre which will be spoken of like the Mongolian massacre and the Crusades" (cited in Bard, 2011, p. 45). This was not hyperbole—Arab leaders openly proclaimed genocidal intentions, vowing to "drive the Jews into the sea."

Israel's War of Independence, and,
the Ongoing Struggle for Security (1948-Present)
The 1948 War was an existential struggle for Israel's survival. The nascent state faced overwhelming numerical superiority—the combined Arab armies numbered approximately 40,000-50,000 troops, against Jewish forces of initially about 30,000 (later growing to 100,000 as mobilization proceeded). Arab states possessed artillery, armor, and aircraft; the Jews initially had only light weapons, though they later acquired arms from Czechoslovakia (Morris, 2008; Kurzman, 1970).

Against all odds, Israel survived and prevailed. The war's outcome reflected superior Jewish command, motivation (fighting for survival in their homeland versus Arab armies fighting in foreign territory), and internal lines of communication. By the time armistice agreements were signed in 1949, Israel controlled not only the territory assigned by the UN partition plan but also Western Galilee, parts of the Negev, and West Jerusalem—approximately 78% of Mandatory Palestine (Shlaim, 2000; Tal, 2004).

The war's human cost was staggering. Israel lost approximately 6,000 people—roughly 1% of its population, equivalent to over 3 million American deaths at contemporary U.S. population levels. Virtually every Israeli family lost someone. The war created lasting trauma but also forged national identity and demonstrated that Jews would never again go passively to their destruction (Shapira, 1997; Segev, 1986).

The war also created the Palestinian refugee problem— approximately 700,000 Arabs fled or were expelled from areas that became Israel (Morris, 2004). The causes of this displacement remain contested: Israeli historians have documented instances of expulsion, massacres (most notably at Deir Yassin), and psychological warfare designed to encourage flight (Morris, 2004; Pappé, 2006). However, Arab flight was also caused by: orders from Arab leaders to evacuate temporarily until Arab armies "liberated" the area; fear of combat zones; the collapse of Palestinian Arab society following the defeat of local militias; and the normal chaos of war (Karsh, 2010; Efrati, 2006).

Critically, approximately 150,000 Arabs remained in Israel and became citizens with full democratic rights—their descendants, numbering over 2 million today, constitute over 21% of Israel's population and enjoy freedoms unmatched in any Arab state (Rekhess, 2014; Ghanem, 2001). This reality demonstrates Israel's fundamental character: it is not an ethnocracy bent on ethnic purity but a democracy capable of including non-Jewish minorities with full civil rights—a model that federal expansion would extend to populations of Judea, Samaria, and Gaza once security conditions permit.

The Palestinian refugee situation was deliberately perpetuated by Arab states, which refused to integrate refugees into their societies (with Jordan being a partial exception). Instead, refugees were confined to camps and maintained as political pawns against Israel, their suffering instrumentalized for diplomatic advantage (Romirowsky, 2010; UNRWA itself has become a perpetuation mechanism, unique among UN agencies in passing refugee status to descendants in perpetuity (Grech, 2013). No other refugee population—not the 12 million Germans expelled from Eastern Europe, not the 14 million Hindus and Muslims displaced by Partition of India, not the millions displaced by Yugoslav Wars—has been treated this way (Schechter, 2013).

Simultaneously, approximately 850,000 Jews were expelled or fled from Arab countries—Iraq, Egypt, Syria, Lebanon, Yemen, Libya, Morocco, Tunisia, and others (Levin, 2009; Goldberg, 2008). These Mizrahi Jews, whose communities predated Islam by centuries, faced violence, expropriation, and forced departure. Israel absorbed these refugees, integrating them as full citizens despite enormous economic challenges. This population exchange—though not formally recognized as such—effectively resolved what might have been a reciprocal refugee crisis, with the critical difference that Israel integrated its refugees while Arab states deliberately maintained Palestinian statelessness (Katz, 2013).

The decades following 1948 brought repeated wars as Arab states refused to accept Israel's existence. The 1956 Sinai Campaign occurred after Egypt blockaded Israeli shipping and sponsored fedayeen terror attacks. The 1967 Six-Day War erupted after Egypt expelled UN peacekeepers, closed the Straits of Tiran, massed troops on Israel's border, and signed military pacts with Jordan and Syria while Arab radio broadcast promises of Jewish annihilation (Oren, 2002; Bowen, 2003).

Israel's stunning victory in 1967—defeating three Arab armies in six days and capturing the Sinai Peninsula, Gaza Strip, West Bank, Golan Heights, and East Jerusalem—fundamentally altered the conflict's geography. For the first time since the Bar Kokhba Revolt, all of historic Jerusalem, including the Temple Mount and Western Wall, stood under Jewish sovereignty. For the first time since ancient Judea's destruction, the biblical heartland of Judea and Samaria came under Israeli control (Segev, 2007; Shapira, 2012).

The 1973 Yom Kippur War, launched by Egypt and Syria on Judaism's holiest day in a surprise attack that initially achieved major gains, exacted a terrible cost—2,656 Israeli dead, thousands wounded, national trauma (Rabinovich, 2004). Israel's eventual counteroffensive recovered lost territory and crossed into Syria and Egypt, but the war shattered Israeli assumptions of invincibility and led eventually to peace negotiations with Egypt.

The Egypt-Israel Peace Treaty (1979), following Anwar Sadat's historic visit to Jerusalem, demonstrated that peace was possible when Arab leaders genuinely accepted Israel's right to exist. In exchange for full normalization and security guarantees, Israel withdrew from the entire Sinai Peninsula—territory three times Israel's size, containing oil fields and strategic depth (Quandt, 1986;

Telhami, 1990). This willingness to trade land for genuine peace established a principle that could apply in a federal arrangement: Israel does not seek to control unwilling populations but will ensure its security through whatever means necessary.

The 1982 Lebanon War, fought to eliminate PLO bases terrorizing northern Israel, achieved its military objective but led to 18 years of Israeli presence in southern Lebanon and ongoing conflict with Hezbollah (Fisk, 2001; Rabinovich, 1985). The First Intifada (1987-1993), a Palestinian uprising in the West Bank and Gaza featuring stone-throwing youth and widespread civil disobedience, internationalized Palestinian grievances and led to the Oslo Accords (Schiff & Ya'ari, 1990; Mishal & Sela, 2000).

Oslo (1993-2000) represented Israel's most significant attempt at territorial compromise, establishing the Palestinian Authority and transferring control of major Palestinian population centers to Palestinian governance. Prime Minister Yitzhak Rabin, a military hero turned peacemaker, pursued this path despite deep internal opposition, ultimately paying with his life when assassinated by a Jewish extremist in 1995 (Peri, 2000; Karpin & Friedman, 1998).

Oslo's failure—caused by Palestinian leadership's refusal to make final compromises, continued terrorism, incitement in Palestinian media and education, and maximalist demands including unacceptable proposals on Jerusalem and refugee return—demonstrated that separation without security was impossible (Ross, 2004; Barak, 2002). The Second Intifada (2000-2005), deliberately launched by Arafat after rejecting generous peace offers at Camp David, featured suicide bombings that murdered over 1,000 Israelis in buses, restaurants, hotels, and markets (Karsh, 2003; Bronner, 2011).

Israel's response—the security barrier, targeted operations against terrorist leadership, military incursions into PA-controlled areas—eventually reduced terror but at tremendous cost to Palestinian civilians and Israeli international standing (Frisch, 2009). Ariel Sharon's unilateral disengagement from Gaza in 2005, removing all settlements and soldiers, was intended to test Palestinian intentions. The result—Hamas's 2007 violent takeover and subsequent transformation of Gaza into a launching pad for over 20,000 rockets targeting Israeli civilians—proved that withdrawal without peace enables terrorism, not reconciliation (Kober, 2007; Yaari, 2011).

October 7th & the Imperative of Victory.
The Hamas massacre of October 7, 2023, stands as the deadliest single day for Jews since the Holocaust. Over 1,200 people—babies, children, women, men, elderly—were murdered in their homes, at a music festival, in kibbutzim. Victims were raped, mutilated, burned alive. Over 240 hostages were dragged into Gaza. Hamas terrorists livestreamed their atrocities on social media, celebrating the slaughter (Levy, 2023; Cohen, 2023). Eger, "The Day the Two-State Solution Burned in Tears," Times of Israel, 7 nov. 2025)

This was not resistance to occupation—Gaza has no Israeli presence since 2005. This was genocidal antisemitism made manifest, the logical endpoint of decades of Palestinian rejectionism and incitement. Hamas's founding charter explicitly calls for Israel's destruction and Jewish murder worldwide (Hamas Charter, 1988). October 7th demonstrated that Hamas meant every word.

Israel's response—Operation Swords of Iron—aims to permanently eliminate Hamas's military and governing capabilities. This is not a conflict to be managed but a war to be won absolutely. There can be no federal future, no integration, no citizenship, no coexistence until Hamas and every organization sharing its eliminationist ideology is utterly defeated, disarmed, and removed from power (Freilich, 2023; IDF, 2024).

The international pressure for premature ceasefire, for preserving Hamas's governance, for restraint while Israeli hostages languish in tunnels, reflects the antisemitic double standard that has always plagued Israel (Berman, 2024). No nation would tolerate a terrorist entity on its border after such atrocities. Germany and Japan were not partially defeated in World War II—they were conquered, occupied, demilitarized, and their societies rebuilt with democratic values. This is the only model applicable to Gaza (Solomon, 2024).

Deradicalization must be comprehensive. Palestinian education, which currently glorifies terrorists as "martyrs" and teaches children to hate Jews, must be completely reformed (IMPACT-se, 2023). UNRWA, which has employed Hamas terrorists and taught hatred in its schools, must be dismantled and replaced (UN Watch, 2024). Palestinian civil society, currently dominated by organizations promoting BDS and rejectionism, must be rebuilt around acceptance of Jewish rights and coexistence (NGO Monitor, 2023).

Only after total Hamas defeat, demilitarization, deradicalization, and the emergence of Palestinian leadership willing to acknowledge Jewish national rights and renounce violence—only then can federal integration proceed. This is not an ultimatum but a prerequisite grounded in reality. The Arab citizens of Israel who live peacefully under Israeli democracy prove that Arabs and Jews can coexist when Arabs accept Jewish sovereignty (Rekhess, 2014). The Palestinians of Gaza and Judea-Samaria can enjoy the same democratic rights and economic prosperity through Israeli citizenship within a federal framework—but only after they abandon the genocidal rejectionism that has defined Palestinian nationalism since the 1920s.

Historical Legitimacy & the Federal Future.
This historical survey establishes several incontrovertible realities. First, Jewish connection to this land spans over three millennia, documented by overwhelming archaeological, historical, and textual evidence. This is not colonial settlement of foreign territory but the return of an indigenous people to their ancestral homeland after exile (Peters, 1984; Gilbert, 2008).
Second, Jewish sovereignty was repeatedly destroyed by imperial powers—Babylonians, Romans, others—not relinquished voluntarily. Jews never ceded their national rights or their claim to the land (Wasserstein, 2017).

Third, the continuous Jewish presence, even during centuries of exile, combined with unbroken cultural and religious orientation toward Jerusalem, establishes ongoing connection that international law recognizes as foundational for national claims (Gauthier, 2007; Bell, 2013).

Fourth, modern Israel was established through legal international processes—the Balfour Declaration, the League of Nations Mandate, the UN Partition Plan—and defended through legitimate self-defense against genocidal aggression (Rostow, 1990; Stone, 1981).

Fifth, Israel has repeatedly demonstrated willingness to make painful compromises for peace—withdrawing from Sinai, withdrawing from Gaza, offering unprecedented concessions at

Camp David—but cannot compromise its existence or security (Ross, 2004; Barak, 2002).

Sixth, Israel has successfully integrated diverse populations within its democracy, with Arab citizens enjoying rights, freedoms, and living standards far exceeding any Arab state. This proven capacity for pluralistic democracy forms the foundation for federal extension (Smooha, 2002; Rekhess, 2014).

The federal solution proposed in this book is not an abandonment of Zionism but its fulfillment. Zionism sought a secure Jewish state where Jews could exercise sovereignty and self-determination. Israel has achieved this against impossible odds, building a prosperous, democratic, militarily strong state that is a technological and cultural powerhouse. Federalism extends Israeli citizenship, democracy, and prosperity to populations currently denied these benefits by their own dysfunctional or terroristic leadership.

This is not a "one-state solution" in the Palestinian sense of dismantling Israel's Jewish character. The Federal State of Israel would maintain its Jewish national identity, Hebrew as the dominant language, Jewish cultural and religious centrality, and demographic mechanisms ensuring Jewish majority within a democratic federal framework—similar to how India maintains its Hindu majority and cultural identity while accommodating 200 million Muslims and other minorities through federalism (Adeney, 2007; Stepan, 2011).

Integration through citizenship offers Palestinians what separation never could: participation in a prosperous First World economy, democratic rights under rule of law, freedom of movement throughout the federal territory, protection of property rights, educational opportunities, and escape from the corrupt authoritarianism of the PA and the terrorist tyranny of Hamas. This is not conquest or domination but liberation—liberation from the failed leadership that has kept Palestinians in refugee camps for 75 years, stolen international aid, promoted martyrdom over development, and sacrificed generations to a cause that has brought nothing but suffering (Rubin, 2003; Schanzer, 2008).

The historical arc is clear: Jewish presence in this land is ancient and unbroken. The modern State of Israel represents the restoration of Jewish sovereignty after 2,000 years, achieved legally and defended legitimately. The current conflict stems from

Arab refusal to accept Jewish national rights, manifesting in repeated attempts at annihilation that have consistently failed. The federal future offers the path beyond this violent impasse—but only after security is guaranteed through Hamas's total defeat and Palestinian society's acceptance of Jewish permanence and legitimacy.

As we demonstrated, from the Merneptah Stele to the October 7th massacre, the Jewish struggle for sovereignty in our homeland has been unceasing. The next chapters will examine how federalism translates this historical legitimacy and proven democratic capacity into a practical constitutional framework that can finally bring both peoples the security, prosperity, and dignity that partition can never deliver.

Chapter 1.
Addendum.

The archaeological discoveries described in this chapter confirm what millions of Christians have always believed: the Bible describes real places, real people, and real events. The Tel Dan Stele's reference to the "House of David," the Ketef Hinnom amulets containing Scripture, the Siloam Tunnel built by King Hezekiah—these aren't just Jewish history. They are part of the shared Judeo-Christian heritage that forms the foundation of Western civilization.

View Merneptah Stele at Egyptian Museum, Cairo: https://en.wikipedia.org/wiki/File:Kairo_Museum_Merenptah-Stele_01.jpg. - See Tel Dan Stele: https://thejewishmuseum.org/exhibitions/tel-dan-stele/. Siloam Inscription: https://en.wikipedia.org/wiki/Siloam_inscription. Video overview of Ketef Hinnom: https://youtu.be/AL0tzOojPrw (Israel Antiquities Authority). These pieces demonstrate advanced Hebrew literacy and Davidic monarchy by the 9th century BCE, refuting denialist narratives. Many Christians support Israel not merely for strategic reasons but from theological conviction.

As the late Reverend John Hagee, founder of Christians United for Israel, declared: "The Bible makes clear that God has an everlasting covenant with the Jewish people and the land of Israel. Christians who love the God of Abraham, Isaac, and Jacob must stand with Israel." Whether or not you share this theological view, the historical evidence stands on its own. The Jewish claim to this land isn't based on faith alone—it's documented in stone, inscribed in ancient pottery, and confirmed by the weight of archaeological science.

You don't need to be Jewish to care about historical truth and justice. The Jewish experience speaks to universal themes that resonate across cultures: indigenous rights, self-determination, and the power of collective memory to sustain a people through centuries of dispersion. Consider the parallels. The Armenians, scattered after the 1915 genocide, maintain their identity and connection to ancestral lands. The Kurds, divided across four nations, still dream of Kurdistan. Indigenous peoples worldwide—from Native Americans to Aboriginal Australians—fight for recognition of their historical presence and rights.

The Jewish story belongs to this broader human narrative of peoples maintaining identity despite dispossession.

There's a practical dimension too. A stable, secure Israel matters for global peace. The Middle East's volatility affects energy markets, refugee flows, and terrorism threats worldwide. The Israeli-Palestinian conflict has fueled extremism and instability for decades.

A sustainable solution—one this book argues federalism can provide—benefits everyone. Moreover, Israel's success as a democracy, technology hub, and multicultural society offers lessons for diverse nations everywhere.

Understanding how Israel navigates Jewish majority status while protecting minority rights may inform debates in Europe, America, and beyond. Read this history with an open mind. You may disagree with conclusions.

But engage with the evidence. The archaeological record, the historical documents, the continuous Jewish presence—these aren't matters of opinion. They're matters of fact that deserve honest engagement regardless of your background or beliefs.

Key Dates
1209 BCE: Merneptah Stele.
Pharaoh Merneptah erected this v.ictory stele in Thebes, boasting conquest of Libya and Canaan peoples including "Israel" (first extra-biblical mention), to propagandize divine favor after campaign. Dated via Egyptian chronology, it confirms Israel's existence as semi-nomadic entity in Canaan, countering erasure claims.
https://commons.wikimedia.org/wiki/Category:Merneptah_Stele
586 BCE: First Temple Destruction.
Nebuchadnezzar II of Babylon razed Solomon's Temple and exiled Judean elites, punishing rebellion against Babylonian suzerainty via siege and deportation. This initiated Diaspora yet preserved identity through texts like Ezekiel, foundational for Zionist return narrative.
70 CE: Second Temple Destruction.
Roman general Titus sacked Jerusalem, destroying Herod's Temple amid Jewish-Roman War revolt. It killed roughly 1.1 million per Josephus, banned Jews from the city, renamed province Syria Palaestina to sever ties—yet Galilee communities endured.
516 BCE: Second Temple Rebuilt.
After Persian conquest allowed return from Babylon under Cyrus, Jews reconstituted autonomy and rebuilt Temple, establishing pattern of persistence through empires.

1897: First Zionist Congress
Theodor Herzl convened Basel congress, transforming ancient longing into political program for Jewish state amid rising European antisemitism.
1917: Balfour Declaration
UK Foreign Secretary Arthur Balfour issued letter to Lord Rothschild, pledging "national home for Jewish people" in Palestine amid WWI strategy, via diplomatic memo incorporated into Mandate. https://en.wikipedia.org/wiki/Balfour_Declaration
1947: UN Partition Vote
UN General Assembly adopted Resolution 181, recommending separate Jewish and Arab states with international Jerusalem—accepted by Jews, rejected by Arabs.
1948: Israel Independence
David Ben-Gurion proclaimed State post-Mandate after UN 181 partition, defended against five Arab invasions, birthing modern Israel via self-determination while absorbing 850,000 Mizrahi refugees amid war.
1967: Six-Day War
Israel defeated Egypt, Jordan, Syria after blockade and threats, capturing Jerusalem, West Bank, Gaza, Golan, Sinai—reuniting biblical heartland under Jewish sovereignty.
2023: October 7 Hamas Massacre
Hamas murdered 1,200 Israelis in deadliest day for Jews since Holocaust, taking 240 hostages; proved withdrawal enables terror, demanding total deradicalization before federalism.

Critical Understandings.
Jews have lived in and maintained connection to the land of Israel for over 3,000 years, proven by archaeology and historical records. After centuries of exile and persecution culminating in the Holocaust, Jews reestablished their state in 1948. Despite repeated wars and peace attempts, conflict continues because Palestinian leadership has never accepted Israel's right to exist. This book proposes federalism—not partition—as the path forward.

Discussion Question.
How did the experience of persecution and exile shape Jewish determination to reestablish sovereignty? Can you think of other peoples who have maintained national identity despite centuries of dispersion?

Historiographical Note.

This chapter engages primarily with mainstream Israeli historiography while acknowledging the New Historians (Morris, Pappe, Shlaim) who challenged earlier narratives, particularly regarding 1948. Readers seeking critical perspectives should consult Morris's Righteous Victims and Shlaim's The Iron Wall. For archaeological debates on the United Monarchy, see Finkelstein & Silberman's The Bible Unearthed alongside Mazar's responses.

Key Glossary.

Zionism: The movement for Jewish self-determination in the ancestral Jewish homeland. Named for "Zion," a biblical term for Jerusalem. Just as Italians sought unification and Greeks independence, Zionism sought Jewish national restoration.

Diaspora: From Greek "scattering"—Jews living outside Israel. After Rome destroyed Jerusalem (70 CE), most Jews lived dispersed across the world while maintaining cultural and religious connection to their homeland.

Aliyah: Hebrew for "going up"—immigration to Israel. Waves of aliyah brought Jews from persecution in Europe, the Middle East, and elsewhere to rebuild their national home. Aliyah Bet: Clandestine WWII immigration defying British White Paper, smuggling 100,000+ Holocaust survivors.

Mandate: After World War I, the League of Nations assigned Britain responsibility for Palestine (1920-1948), tasking it with facilitating a "Jewish national home."

Nakba: Arabic for "catastrophe"—the Palestinian term for displacement during Israel's 1948 War of Independence, when approximately 700,000 Arabs fled or were expelled.

Intifada: Arabic for "shaking off"—Palestinian uprisings against Israeli rule. The First (1987-1993) featured protests; the Second (2000-2005) deadly suicide bombings.

Two-State Solution: Proposed peace framework creating separate Israeli and Palestinian states. This book argues federation offers a better path.

Merneptah Stele: Granite artifact (~1209 BCE) with earliest "Israel" reference; proves proto-Israelite presence in Canaan. https://en.wikipedia.org/wiki/Merneptah_Stele

Tel Dan Stele: 9th century BCE Aramaic basalt mentioning "House of David"; extrabiblical proof of United Monarchy.

Dhimmi: Islamic status for Jews/Christians under sharia; protected yet taxed/subordinate, explaining medieval Jewish persistence.

Hasmonean Dynasty: 140-37 BCE independent Jewish kingdom post-Maccabean Revolt; last pre-modern sovereignty. https://thejewishmuseum.org/exhibitions/tel-dan-stele

Chapter 2.
Federal Zionism Meets World Federalism:
A Conceptual Exploration.

Defining Federal Zionism and World Federalism.
Federal Zionism emerged as a distinct strand within the broader Zionist movement at the turn of the twentieth century, offering a pragmatic response to the complex geopolitical realities facing Jewish national aspirations.[1] Unlike mainstream Zionist ideologies that envisioned a centralised Jewish state, Federal Zionism proposed political arrangements based on shared sovereignty and multi-level governance. Its intellectual foundations drew from European federalist thought, particularly the Swiss cantonal model and the Austro-Marxist concept of national cultural autonomy.[2]

The movement's most articulate expression came through the Brit Shalom (Covenant of Peace) association, founded in 1925 by intellectuals including Martin Buber, Judah Magnes, and Henrietta Szold.[3] These thinkers advocated for a bi-national state or federal arrangement that would recognise both Jewish and Arab national rights within a single political framework. Federal Zionism rejected the principle of exclusive sovereignty, instead proposing various models of power-sharing: from loose confederations of autonomous Jewish and Arab cantons to integrated federal structures with shared central institutions.[4]

The core premise of Federal Zionism was that Jewish self-determination could be achieved without denying Palestinian Arab rights to the same territory. This required reimagining sovereignty not as absolute control over territory but as layered authority distributed across different levels of governance.[5] Federal Zionists understood that any Jewish polity would exist within a region populated by diverse communities, each with legitimate claims and aspirations.

World Federalism, by contrast, emerged from the catastrophic experience of two world wars and the advent of nuclear weapons. Founded formally in 1947 with the establishment of the World Federalist Movement, it advocated for democratic world government that would supersede national sovereignty in matters of war and peace.[6] Prominent advocates including Albert Einstein, Bertrand Russell, and Norman Cousins argued that only supranational authority with enforcement powers could prevent future wars and ensure human survival.[7]

World Federalism drew inspiration from the American federal experience, which had successfully united diverse states under common government while preserving local autonomy.[8] The movement envisioned a global federation where nation-states would retain authority over domestic affairs but surrender control over armaments and international conflict resolution to world institutions. This vision extended beyond mere international cooperation to propose genuine supranational governance with democratic legitimacy and enforcement capacity.

The philosophical foundation of World Federalism rested on the conviction that the nation-state system itself was the root cause of war. World Federalists argued that just as federalism had ended warfare between American states or Swiss cantons, global federation could eliminate international conflict.[9] They viewed national sovereignty not as a natural right but as a historically contingent arrangement that had outlived its usefulness in an interdependent world.

Diaspora Zionism: The Third Pillar.
To fully comprehend the intellectual landscape within which Federal Zionism and World Federalism interact, we must introduce a third conceptual pillar: Diaspora Zionism. This often-overlooked strand of Zionist thought has profoundly shaped Jewish political consciousness and offers crucial insights into the relationship between particular and universal commitments.[10]

Diaspora Zionism represents the ideological position that Jewish national identity and support for Israel can be authentically maintained while residing permanently outside the Land of Israel. Unlike classical Zionism, which insisted upon aliyah (immigration to Israel) as the fulfilment of Jewish national destiny, Diaspora Zionism holds that meaningful Jewish national existence is possible —and perhaps even necessary—in the lands of dispersion.[11] This perspective acknowledges the State of Israel as the national homeland and spiritual centre of the Jewish people while affirming the legitimacy and vitality of diaspora communities.

The intellectual roots of Diaspora Zionism trace to figures such as Simon Dubnow, who articulated a theory of Jewish national-cultural autonomy that did not require territorial concentration.[12] Dubnow argued that Jewish nationhood was primarily spiritual and cultural rather than territorial, sustained by language, religion, historical consciousness, and communal institutions. This "autonomist" vision influenced subsequent thinkers who sought to reconcile Zionist commitment with diaspora reality.

Ahad Ha'am (Asher Ginsberg) contributed another foundational element through his concept of Israel as a "spiritual centre" for world Jewry.[13] In this vision, the Jewish state would serve not primarily as a refuge for persecuted Jews but as a cultural and intellectual powerhouse that would regenerate Jewish civilisation everywhere. Diaspora communities would draw inspiration and sustenance from this centre while maintaining their own creative existence.

Contemporary Diaspora Zionism has evolved considerably from these early formulations. Following the establishment of Israel in 1948 and particularly after the Six-Day War of 1967, diaspora Jews increasingly understood their relationship to Israel as one of solidarity, support, and partnership rather than anticipated migration.[14] As Jonathan Sarna has documented, American Jews developed a distinctive form of Zionist commitment that combined passionate support for Israel with firm roots in American society. [15]

Federal Zionism & Diaspora Zionism.
Convergences & Tensions.
The relationship between Federal Zionism and Diaspora Zionism reveals both profound convergences and significant tensions. Both streams of thought reject the notion that Jewish national existence requires territorial exclusivity or demographic homogeneity. Federal Zionism envisions Jews sharing political space with Arabs within Israel-Palestine; Diaspora Zionism envisions Jews sharing political space with non-Jews throughout the world. In both cases, Jewish identity is understood as compatible with, rather than threatened by, proximity to and interaction with others.[16]

This shared orientation toward pluralism distinguishes both movements from more maximalist Zionist positions. Where Revisionist Zionism, for instance, has emphasised Jewish demographic dominance and territorial expansion, Federal and Diaspora Zionism have embraced more complex arrangements that acknowledge the claims and presence of others.[17] Both movements draw upon Jewish religious and cultural resources that emphasise coexistence, ethical responsibility toward strangers, and the prophetic vision of universal peace.

The convergence extends to institutional preferences. Federal Zionists advocated for power-sharing arrangements, constitutional protections for minorities, and federal structures that would preserve distinct communities within shared frameworks.[18] Diaspora Zionists have similarly supported multicultural policies, minority rights protections, and political arrangements in their countries of residence that enable Jewish communal flourishing alongside other groups. Both movements have been drawn to liberal democratic institutions that protect group rights while fostering civic solidarity.

Yet tensions exist between these orientations. Federal Zionism, despite its pluralist commitments, remained fundamentally focused on the Land of Israel and the specific challenge of Jewish-Arab coexistence there. Its intellectual energy was directed toward constitutional arrangements for that particular territory.[19] Diaspora Zionism, by contrast, has been more concerned with the conditions enabling Jewish life outside Israel—questions of antisemitism, assimilation, communal organisation, and the relationship between Jewish particularity and civic integration.

These different foci have sometimes produced divergent political priorities. Federal Zionists who remained in Israel often found themselves marginalised within a political culture that moved toward more exclusivist nationalism.[20] Diaspora Zionists, meanwhile, have sometimes been accused of offering prescriptions for Israeli politics while bearing none of the risks that actual residents face. The question of who has standing to advocate for federal solutions in Israel-Palestine—and whether diaspora Jews should defer to Israeli judgments—remains contested.

The tension crystallises around the question of aliyah. Classical Zionism held that the ultimate expression of Jewish national commitment was migration to Israel; those who remained in diaspora were, at best, supporting players in the Zionist drama.[21] Diaspora Zionism challenges this hierarchy, asserting that diaspora existence is not merely a waystation but a legitimate and valuable mode of Jewish life. This challenge has implications for Federal Zionism as well: if diaspora Jews have full standing in Jewish national life, their perspectives on how Israel should be governed deserve serious consideration.

World Federalism & Diaspora Zionism:
Uncomfortable Proximities.

The relationship between World Federalism and Diaspora Zionism presents even more complex dynamics. On the surface, diaspora Jewish experience might seem to align naturally with World Federalist cosmopolitanism. Jews have, after all, maintained national identity across centuries of dispersion, demonstrating that meaningful collective existence need not depend on territorial sovereignty.[22] The Jewish diaspora could be understood as a prototype for the post-national world that World Federalists envision —a community bound by culture, values, and institutions rather than borders and armies.

Many individual Jews were indeed attracted to World Federalist ideals. Einstein, as noted, was perhaps the most prominent, but numerous other Jewish intellectuals contributed to World Federalist thought.[23] The experience of persecution, culminating in the Holocaust, convinced many Jews that the nation-state system was fundamentally dangerous and that only supranational governance could prevent future catastrophes. The disproportionate Jewish involvement in internationalist movements of various kinds—from socialist internationalism to human rights advocacy—reflects this conviction.[24]

Yet the relationship between World Federalism and Jewish national aspirations has proven deeply troubled. Here we must confront an uncomfortable reality that this book refuses to evade: the World Federalist Movement, and the broader constellation of internationalist organisations with which it is associated, has demonstrated systematic bias against Jewish national self-determination and the State of Israel.

The Corruption of World Federalist Ideals:
Anti-Zionism as Institutional Practice.

My personal journey through the World Federalist Movement, described in this book's opening pages, revealed a disturbing pattern that systematic analysis confirms. The movement that purports to champion universal human rights and the peaceful resolution of conflicts has, in practice, become a vehicle for one-sided condemnation of the Jewish state. This is not a matter of legitimate criticism of Israeli policies—which any democratic state should expect and withstand—but of fundamental delegitimisation of Jewish national existence.

The evidence is extensive and damning. The World Federalist Movement and allied organisations have consistently supported United Nations resolutions that single out Israel for condemnation while ignoring far graver human rights violations elsewhere.[25] They have endorsed the Boycott, Divestment, and Sanctions (BDS) movement, which seeks not merely to change Israeli policy but to dismantle the Jewish state as such.[26] They have provided platforms for rhetoric that denies Jewish historical connection to the Land of Israel, characterises Zionism as colonialism or racism, and treats Israeli self-defence as aggression while excusing or minimising violence against Israeli civilians.

This pattern reflects the broader corruption of international institutions that scholars such as Anne Bayefsky and Gerald Steinberg have meticulously documented.[27] The United Nations Human Rights Council, which World Federalists hold up as a model for global governance, has passed more resolutions condemning Israel than all other countries combined—including nations engaged in genocide, mass torture, and systematic oppression.[28] The UN General Assembly routinely adopts dozens of resolutions criticising Israel while ignoring atrocities in Syria, China, Iran, and elsewhere. The International Criminal Court, another institution World Federalists celebrate, has prioritised investigating Israel while struggling to address genuinely massive crimes against humanity.

The intellectual dishonesty underlying this pattern is staggering. World Federalists claim to oppose nationalism and support universal human rights, yet they systematically deny the Jewish people alone the right to national self-determination that they champion for every other group.[29] They invoke international law against Israel while ignoring that the very international instruments they cite—from the Balfour Declaration to the UN Partition Plan to the League of Nations Mandate—explicitly recognised Jewish national rights in Palestine. They condemn Israeli "occupation" while refusing to acknowledge that this occupation resulted from defensive wars against neighbours who explicitly sought Israel's destruction.

The Ideological Roots of World Federalist Anti-Zionism.
Understanding why World Federalism has become so hostile to Jewish national aspirations requires examining the ideological currents that have shaped the movement. Three factors deserve

particular attention: the influence of Marxist-Leninist thought, the post-colonial paradigm, and the sociology of internationalist movements.

Marxist-Leninist ideology has profoundly influenced World Federalist circles, despite the movement's ostensible commitment to democratic governance.[30] Classical Marxism viewed nationalism as a bourgeois distraction from class struggle, destined to wither away as socialist consciousness advanced. Lenin's theory of imperialism provided a framework for distinguishing between "progressive" nationalisms of colonised peoples and "reactionary" nationalisms of oppressor nations. Within this schema, Zionism was classified as a form of settler colonialism serving Western imperialist interests—a characterisation that persists in contemporary World Federalist discourse despite its historical inaccuracy.[31]

The post-colonial paradigm has reinforced this classification. As scholars such as Edward Said reshaped academic understanding of the Middle East, Zionism came to be understood primarily through the lens of European colonialism rather than Jewish historical experience.[32] This framing ignores crucial differences: unlike European colonisers, Jews were returning to their ancestral homeland from which they had been expelled; unlike colonial enterprises, Zionism was not backed by a metropolitan power seeking economic exploitation; unlike settler populations elsewhere, Jews faced existential threats that made national sovereignty a matter of survival rather than convenience.

The sociology of internationalist movements also contributes to anti-Zionist bias. As Robert Wistrich documented in his monumental study of antisemitism, progressive movements have repeatedly served as vehicles for anti-Jewish sentiment, recasting ancient prejudices in contemporary ideological language.[33] The "socialism of fools," as August Bebel called nineteenth-century leftist antisemitism, has found new expression in twenty-first-century "anti-Zionism" that denies Jewish peoplehood, questions Jewish historical claims, and holds the Jewish state to standards applied to no other nation.

Within World Federalist circles specifically, these tendencies are amplified by the movement's dependence on United Nations structures and personnel. The UN Secretariat, UN agencies, and UN-affiliated NGOs have developed institutional cultures deeply hostile to Israel, reflecting the numerical dominance of Arab and Muslim-majority states and their allies in UN bodies.[34] World Federalists who look to these institutions as models for global governance inevitably absorb their biases. The corruption flows in both directions: World Federalist ideology legitimises UN anti-Israel obsession, while UN practice reinforces World Federalist anti-Zionism.

Credibility Crisis: World Federalism's Wounds.
The World Federalist Movement's systematic bias against Jewish national self-determination has produced a profound credibility crisis that undermines the movement's broader aspirations. How can World Federalism claim to offer a model for global peace when its practice demonstrates that international institutions can be weaponised against particular nations and peoples? How can it advocate for supranational governance when existing international bodies so manifestly fail tests of fairness and impartiality?

This is not merely a matter of Jewish grievance, though Jewish grievances are entirely legitimate. It is a matter of fundamental institutional integrity. If World Federalist-supported institutions cannot treat one small democracy fairly, why should any nation trust them with expanded authority? If the UN Human Rights Council obsesses over Israeli actions in Gaza while ignoring Chinese concentration camps holding millions of Uyghurs, what confidence can anyone have in global human rights governance? [35]

The credibility crisis extends to World Federalism's democratic pretensions. World Federalists advocate for democratic world government, yet the international institutions they champion are manifestly undemocratic in their treatment of Israel. The "automatic majority" that Arab and Muslim states command in UN bodies, amplified by countries seeking their oil or their votes, produces outcomes bearing no relationship to democratic deliberation or factual assessment.[36] A movement that celebrates such institutions as models for global democracy reveals either profound naivety or troubling indifference to democratic principles.

The selectivity of World Federalist concern further undermines credibility. The movement mobilises passionate advocacy regarding Israeli-Palestinian issues while largely ignoring conflicts that have produced far greater human suffering. The Syrian civil war killed over 500,000 people and displaced millions; World Federalist response was muted. The Tigray war in Ethiopia killed hundreds of thousands; World Federalist attention was minimal. The ongoing persecution of Uyghurs represents cultural genocide on a massive scale; World Federalist activism has been tepid at best.[37] This selectivity suggests that humanitarian concern is not the actual motivation for World Federalist Israel-focus—that something else is at work.

Salvaging Core: Case for Reformed World Federalism.
Despite this devastating critique, intellectual honesty requires acknowledging that World Federalism contains a core insight of enduring value. The nation-state system has indeed produced catastrophic warfare. International anarchy does create security dilemmas that drive arms races and conflicts. Global challenges—climate change, pandemic disease, nuclear proliferation, artificial intelligence—do require governance mechanisms that transcend national boundaries. The aspiration for a more peaceful and just world order, governed by law rather than force, remains noble even when its advocates betray it through selective application. The proper response to World Federalism's corruption is not rejection but reformation. The movement must be called back to its founding principles and held accountable for departures from them. This requires several fundamental changes.

First, World Federalism must embrace genuine universalism, applying the same standards to all nations without exception. If national self-determination is a right, it must be a right for Jews as well as Palestinians, for Israelis as well as Kurds or Tibetans. If occupation is condemned, it must be condemned whether the occupier is Israel, Morocco, Turkey, or China. If civilian casualties are mourned, they must be mourned regardless of whether the victims are Palestinian, Israeli, Syrian, or Uyghur.[38]

Second, World Federalism must disentangle itself from the corrupted institutions of the current international order. Rather than defending UN bodies that have forfeited moral authority through systematic bias, World Federalists should advocate for fundamental institutional reform. This might include weighted voting that prevents automatic majorities, judicial review of General Assembly resolutions, accountability mechanisms for UN agencies, and criteria for Human Rights Council membership that exclude systematic human rights violators.[39]

Third, World Federalism must confront the antisemitic currents within its own ranks. The movement must recognise that anti-Zionism, as currently practiced, functions as a form of antisemitism —denying to Jews collectively the rights it affirms for others, holding Jews collectively responsible for Israeli policies, and deploying ancient antisemitic tropes in contemporary political garb. [40] This recognition requires not merely condemning explicit antisemitism but examining how institutional practices and ideological frameworks produce discriminatory outcomes.

Fourth, World Federalism must engage seriously with Federal Zionism rather than dismissing Jewish national aspirations as obstacles to global peace. The Federal Zionist tradition offers precisely the kind of creative thinking about sovereignty, diversity, and governance that World Federalism claims to value. A World Federalism that learned from Federal Zionist insights might develop more sophisticated models of how particular identities can be accommodated within universal frameworks.

Toward Synthesis: Federal Zionism as Bridge.
The path forward requires synthesis rather than simple rejection. Federal Zionism, properly understood, offers a bridge between particularist and universalist commitments that both World Federalism and Diaspora Zionism need. Against World Federalism's tendency toward abstract universalism that dissolves particular identities, Federal Zionism insists that meaningful political community requires cultural foundations. Democracy cannot function among people who share nothing—no language, no history, no values, no sense of common destiny.[41] Federal arrangements succeed precisely because they preserve particular communities while enabling cooperation across difference. This insight, derived from Jewish experience and Federal Zionist reflection, corrects World Federalism's most dangerous tendency.

Against Diaspora Zionism's potential drift toward mere ethnic lobbying disconnected from universal concerns, Federal Zionism offers a model of particular commitment that serves universal values. Federal Zionist advocacy for power-sharing, minority rights, and constitutional governance contributes to global understanding of how diverse societies can be democratically organised.[42] It demonstrates that Jewish interests and universal interests can align rather than conflict.

The Federal State of Israel proposed throughout this book represents the practical application of this synthesis. It honours Jewish national self-determination—the core Zionist commitment—while creating frameworks for Palestinian self-governance. It draws upon World Federalist insights about federal design while remaining grounded in particular territorial and demographic realities. It offers diaspora Jews a vision they can support without contradiction—a Jewish state that is also a model of democratic pluralism.

The Enduring Validity of Federated Global Governance.
This critique of World Federalism's institutional practice should not obscure the enduring validity of its core theoretical claim: that the United Nations should evolve toward a genuine federation of nation-states with democratic legitimacy and effective enforcement capacity. The failures of current international institutions do not invalidate the aspiration; they demonstrate the urgency of reform.

The nation-state system, for all its achievements, cannot adequately address challenges that transcend national boundaries. Climate change will not be solved by 193 separate national policies; it requires coordinated global action with enforcement mechanisms. [43] Nuclear proliferation cannot be prevented by voluntary agreements that states abandon when convenient; it requires binding international authority. Pandemic disease, as COVID-19 demonstrated, spreads without regard for borders and requires governance structures capable of coordinated response.

These realities vindicate the World Federalist insight that some form of supranational governance has become necessary. The question is not whether global governance is needed but what form it should take and how it can be made legitimate and effective. Here Federal Zionist experience becomes directly relevant.

Federal arrangements succeed when they balance unity and diversity, central authority and local autonomy, universal principles and particular identities. They fail when they ignore local conditions, override legitimate community interests, or concentrate power without accountability.[44] A reformed World Federalism that incorporated these insights—that understood global federation as enabling rather than threatening national communities—might command broader support than the current movement manages.

The United Nations, reformed along genuinely federal lines, could provide the governance framework that global challenges require. This would involve transforming the General Assembly into a genuine legislature with powers proportional to population and contribution, creating a directly elected parliamentary body to provide democratic legitimacy, establishing judicial review of UN actions, reforming the Security Council to better reflect contemporary realities, and developing enforcement mechanisms that do not depend solely on great power consensus.[45]

Such reforms would address the institutional failures that have made current international bodies vehicles for discrimination rather than justice. They would create structures in which all nations—including Israel—could participate as equals under law. They would honour the World Federalist aspiration for peaceful global governance while avoiding the selectivity and bias that have corrupted current practice.

Toward Federal Zionist World Federalism.
The conceptual exploration undertaken in this chapter reveals that Federal Zionism, Diaspora Zionism, and World Federalism exist in complex relationships of convergence and tension. All three traditions grapple with fundamental questions about particular and universal commitments, about how diverse communities can share political space, about the proper scale and structure of governance in an interdependent world.

Federal Zionism offers unique resources for addressing these questions. Its practical experience with the challenges of Jewish-Arab coexistence in Palestine/Israel provides insights that purely theoretical approaches lack. Its commitment to both Jewish self-determination and democratic pluralism models how particular and universal values can be reconciled. Its constitutional creativity—the development of detailed proposals for power-sharing, minority protection, and federal design—contributes to global knowledge about governance of divided societies.

Diaspora Zionism reminds us that national identity need not require territorial concentration and that meaningful collective existence can be sustained across dispersed communities. This insight challenges both exclusivist Zionism and homogenising World Federalism, suggesting more complex models of how peoples and polities might be organised.

World Federalism, for all its institutional failures, articulates an aspiration that humanity cannot abandon. The choice is not between the nation-state system and global governance but between reformed global governance and continued international anarchy. The question is whether we can develop international institutions worthy of the trust we must place in them.

The synthesis toward which this analysis points might be termed "Federal Zionist World Federalism"—a vision that combines Federal Zionism's attention to particular communities and local conditions with World Federalism's aspiration for peaceful global order. Such a synthesis would honour Jewish national self-determination while supporting structures that enable all peoples to flourish. It would advocate for reformed international institutions while insisting that these institutions demonstrate the impartiality they currently lack. It would offer the world not merely criticism of what exists but a constructive vision of what might be.

As I wrote in the *Times of Israel*, the Federal State of Israel represents this synthesis in microcosm: a polity that honours Jewish particularity while creating space for Palestinian self-governance, that demonstrates how ancient enemies might become partners in shared institutions, that offers a model not only for the Middle East but for a world desperately seeking alternatives to endless conflict.[46] The chapters that follow develop this vision in detail. But first, it was necessary to situate Federal Zionism within the broader intellectual landscape of which it forms a part—and to confront honestly the failures of movements that should be its natural allies.

The World Federalist Movement betrayed its principles when it became a vehicle for anti-Zionist discrimination. That betrayal does not invalidate federalist ideals; it demonstrates the urgency of their authentic application. Federal Zionism offers a path back to those ideals—grounded in particular experience, committed to universal justice, and determined to build institutions worthy of the peace they promise.

Chapter 2.
Addendum.

Key Concepts.

Federalism: Like a sports league where individual teams maintain full autonomy over daily operations, player selection, and local strategies, while the league establishes unified rules for playoffs, championships, and standards that everyone follows. This structure allows competition and diversity while ensuring fair play across the system (diagram concept: sports governance model). Sovereignty in federalism becomes shared layers of authority rather than exclusive control—central government handles defense and currency, while regions control education, culture, and policing. Self-Determination means peoples govern themselves within federations, protecting national identity through autonomous institutions while participating in common governance.

Binationalism enables two nations sharing one state through power-sharing, as Belgium balances Flemish and Walloon communities with separate parliaments yet shared monarchy and defense. Cantonal System follows the Swiss model where 26 highly autonomous regions (cantons) self-govern education, taxes, police, and religion, while federal government manages foreign policy, army, and currency (map: https://www.nationsonline.org/oneworld/map/switzerland-administrative-map.htm). Subsidiarity principle from Catholic social teaching demands decisions made at the lowest competent level—local communities handle what they can, higher authorities intervene only when necessary, preserving human dignity through proximity to power.

Practical Applications.

The European Union transformed century-old enemies France and Germany from battlefield rivals into economic partners through shared sovereignty—each retains national parliaments and cultures while cooperating on trade, security, and currency. Switzerland has peacefully managed German, French, Italian, and Romansh linguistic communities for 700 years through its cantonal federalism, proving deep cultural divides need not produce conflict. The United States unites 50 diverse states with vastly different economies, climates, and politics under one federal framework; Canada balances English/French provinces while respecting Indigenous territories; India governs 28 states and 8 union territories encompassing 22 official languages; Australia coordinates 6 states and 2 territories across vast distances. These examples demonstrate federalism's universal principle: managing diversity without destroying unity, turning potential conflict zones into stable, prosperous societies. Whether you live in a federal nation or simply value peace through pragmatic governance, these models prove enemies can share power productively when proper institutional design channels competition toward mutual benefit rather than violence.

Scholarly Frameworks.

Key theorists provide essential frameworks: Daniel Elazar viewed federalism as "covenant"—mutual agreements binding diverse communities like biblical Israel; Arend Lijphart developed consociational democracy showing power-sharing works in divided societies through grand coalitions and mutual vetoes; Alfred Stepan analyzed multinational federalism distinguishing "coming-together" (USA) from "holding-together" (India) federations. This chapter connects directly to comparative politics curricula examining how federations handle ethnic federalism (Ethiopia, Iraq) versus territorial federalism (Germany, Australia).

Research prompts.

"Can federalism resolve settler-indigenous conflicts like Israel-Palestine, Canada-Quebec, or Australia-Aboriginal?" "Does binationalism succeed absent mutual recognition, comparing Belgium/Lebanon?" "What are subsidiarity's limits in asymmetric federations with unequal partners?" Term papers could compare Federal Zionism's proposals to Quebec separatism (Meech Lake failure), Catalan demands (2017 referendum), or Bosnia's post-Yugoslav federalism. These questions bridge theory and practice, positioning Federal Zionism within global debates on democratic design for divided societies.

Federalism in a nutshell.

Federal Israel works like the United States: Imagine 10-12 cantons (like states) where Jewish areas run schools, culture, police, and local laws in Hebrew, while Arab cantons do the same in Arabic— each maintaining their identity, holidays, and traditions. The federal government handles what affects everyone: army, currency, foreign policy, major highways, like FIFA oversees soccer rules while teams compete fiercely. No more fighting over "who owns the land"—shared rules replace endless ownership battles. Sports teams prove this works daily: Barcelona and Real Madrid compete passionately under La Liga rules without destroying the league.

Federal Israel creates winning for both peoples through clear boundaries and mutual respect, just like championship sports. Video explainer: Swiss federalism youth overview (search "How Switzerland Works").

Faith Perspectives.

Christian democratic theory connects directly through subsidiarity—the Catholic social teaching principle (Pope Pius XI, Quadragesimo Anno 1931) that higher authorities intervene only when local communities cannot manage, preserving human dignity through proximity to decision-making. This aligns perfectly with Federal Zionism: Jewish cantons govern Hebrew education and synagogues autonomously; Arab cantons manage mosques and Arabic schools; federal level handles shared concerns. Protestant federalist thought (Abraham Kuyper's sphere sovereignty) similarly protects religious communities from state overreach. These traditions validate federal arrangements balancing particular religious identities with universal civic obligations, offering theological foundation for power-sharing between ancient rivals.

Critical Understandings.

Jews maintained continuous connection to the Land of Israel for over 3,000 years, proven irrefutably by archaeology—the Merneptah Stele (1209 BCE), Tel Dan Stele ("House of David"), Ketef Hinnom biblical scrolls. After centuries of Roman, Byzantine, Arab, Crusader, Mamluk, Ottoman rule plus Russian pogroms and Nazi Holocaust (6 million murdered), Jews reestablished sovereign statehood through UN Partition Plan (1947) and War of Independence (1948). Despite Israel's repeated peace offers (Camp David 2000, Olmert 2008), conflict persists because Palestinian leadership—from PLO Charter to Hamas Covenant—rejects Israel's right to exist alongside any Palestinian entity. This book proposes federalism—not partition—as forward path: autonomous Jewish/Arab cantons within democratic framework, preserving national identities while ending territorial disputes through proven institutional design.

Chapter 3.
Federal Solutions: Historical Precedents.

Learning from Established Federal Systems.
The establishment of a Federal State of Israel represents an unprecedented opportunity to apply tested federal principles to one of the world's most intractable conflicts. However, as this author has argued in previous work, such a federal arrangement can only be implemented after the complete end of the October 7th War, the unconditional capitulation, full demilitarization, and absolute surrender of Hamas and all proxies of the Muslim Brotherhood (Eger, 2025a). Moreover, this federal solution requires the complete deradicalization of Palestinian society—a transformation whereby Palestinians no longer seek a Palestinian state in lieu of the State of Israel but instead embrace integration into a Federal State of Israel as equal citizens with substantive regional autonomy (Eger, 2025b).

This chapter examines six major federal precedents—the United States, Switzerland, Germany, Canada, Belgium, and India—to extract transferable lessons for Israel's future federal architecture. Each case study illuminates specific mechanisms that have successfully managed diversity, protected minority rights, balanced central authority with regional autonomy, and fostered democratic governance in deeply divided societies.

As Lijphart (1977) established in his seminal work on consociational democracy, federal arrangements have proven particularly effective in managing deeply divided societies through institutional mechanisms for power-sharing while preserving distinct communal identities (Lijphart, 1977). McGarry and O'Leary (2009) further demonstrate that federal and confederal arrangements provide the institutional infrastructure necessary for transforming zero-sum ethnic conflicts into positive-sum democratic governance (McGarry & O'Leary, 2009).

The American Model.
Federalism as Constitutional Architecture.
Historical Context and Foundational Principles.
The nascent United States stands as a profound testament to federalism's capacity to unite disparate political entities without obliterating their distinct identities. The thirteen colonies emerged from the Revolutionary War (1775-1783) as sovereign entities,

each jealously guarding its newfound independence yet recognizing the necessity of collective security and economic cooperation (Wood, 1969). The challenge was monumental: forging a union strong enough for collective defense and prosperity while sufficiently decentralized to preserve state sovereignty.

The Articles of Confederation (1781-1789) proved catastrophically inadequate. This document established a "league of friendship" rather than a functional government, creating a unicameral Congress lacking essential sovereign attributes—it could declare war but not raise armies, borrow money but not levy taxes effectively, make treaties but not enforce them against recalcitrant states (Jensen, 1940). The resulting paralysis—manifested in interstate trade disputes, currency chaos, and near-insolvency—threatened to unravel the union before it had truly begun.

The Constitutional Convention and the Great Compromise.
The Constitutional Convention of 1787 convened in Philadelphia amid crisis. Delegates grappled with the fundamental tension between state sovereignty and the imperative for effective national governance. The conflict between large and small states over representation threatened to derail the entire enterprise. Virginia's James Madison championed proportional representation, while New Jersey's William Paterson demanded equal representation regardless of population (Madison, 1787/1987).

The Connecticut Compromise (also called the Great Compromise) resolved this existential conflict through institutional innovation: a bicameral legislature comprising the Senate (equal state representation with two senators per state) and the House of Representatives (proportional representation based on population) (Farrand, 1911). This dual structure became the cornerstone of American federalism, ensuring both national will and state interests would be represented in federal legislation.

Direct Applicability to Israel.
The American bicameral model offers immediate transferability to a Federal State of Israel. As this author proposed in "One-State Solution: The Federal State of Israel," a future Israeli federal legislature could feature an upper chamber (Federal Council) with equal representation from all constituent regions—whether predominantly Jewish districts, Palestinian districts, or mixed municipalities—alongside a lower chamber (Federal Assembly) with representation proportional to population (Eger, 2025a). This

arrangement would guarantee that smaller Palestinian regions could not be overwhelmed by larger Jewish regions, while ensuring that population centers exercise appropriate democratic weight.

Division of Powers and Constitutional Safeguards.

The Constitution meticulously delineated federal and state powers. Article I, Section 8 enumerates federal powers: taxation, interstate commerce regulation, currency control, war declaration, military maintenance, and postal service establishment (U.S. Const. art. I, § 8). The "Necessary and Proper Clause" granted Congress authority to enact laws required for executing these powers—a provision later interpreted to permit significant federal expansion (*McCulloch v. Maryland*, 17 U.S. 316 (1819)).

Crucially, the Tenth Amendment (ratified 1791) reserved all non-delegated powers to states: "The powers not delegated to the United States by the Constitution, nor prohibited by it to the States, are reserved to the States respectively, or to the people" (U.S. Const. amend. X). This principle ensured states retained substantial autonomy in education, public health, law enforcement, and intrastate commerce—creating what Justice Brandeis termed "laboratories of democracy" (*New State Ice Co. v. Liebmann*, 285 U.S. 262, 311 (1932) (Brandeis, J., dissenting)).

The Supremacy Clause (Article VI) declared the Constitution, federal laws, and treaties "the supreme Law of the Land" (*Gibbons v. Ogden*, 22 U.S. 1 (1824)). Yet federal supremacy was not absolute. The Supreme Court, through judicial review established in *Marbury v. Madison* (5 U.S. 137 (1803)), acts as arbiter of the federal balance, interpreting constitutional boundaries and resolving federal-state conflicts.

Direct Applicability to Israel.

The enumerated powers doctrine translates directly to a Federal State of Israel. The federal government would maintain exclusive jurisdiction over national defense (IDF unified command), foreign affairs, currency (shekel), and inter-regional commerce. Constituent regions—as detailed in this author's proposal—would govern education (allowing Jewish regions to maintain Hebrew-language secular and religious schools, Palestinian regions to offer Arabic-language curriculum reflecting their cultural heritage), policing (regional security forces under federal oversight), and local civil matters (Eger, 2025b). The Tenth Amendment principle would ensure that powers not explicitly granted to the federal government remain with regional authorities, preventing federal overreach and protecting regional autonomy.

The Federalist Papers and Ratification.
The Federalist Papers (1787-1788), authored by Hamilton, Madison, and Jay, remain the definitive exposition of federal theory. Federalist No. 10 (Madison) argues that a large republic can better manage faction through diverse interests that prevent any single group from dominating (Madison, 1787/2003). Federalist No. 51 (Madison) articulates the system of checks and balances: "Ambition must be made to counteract ambition" (Madison, 1788/2003, p. 319).

The intense ratification debate between Federalists (supporting the Constitution) and Anti-Federalists (fearing federal tyranny) demonstrates the necessity of compromise in federal design. Many states ratified by narrow margins only after promises of a Bill of Rights to protect individual liberties and constrain federal power (Storing, 1981).

Direct Applicability to Israel: The American ratification process underscores the importance of broad consensus in federal constitution-making. As this author has argued, any Federal State of Israel must emerge from genuine consent following complete Palestinian deradicalization—not imposed through coercion (Eger, 2025a). The ratification would require approval from both Jewish and Palestinian populations through democratic referenda in each constituent region, ensuring legitimacy and popular buy-in.

The Swiss Confederation: Federalism Through Diversity.
Historical Evolution from Confederation to Federal State.
Switzerland presents perhaps the most instructive federal model for managing linguistic, cultural, and religious diversity. The Federal Charter of 1291 united Uri, Schwyz, and Unterwalden in defensive alliance against Habsburg encroachment (Steinberg, 1996). Over centuries, other territories joined this loose confederation, each maintaining substantial sovereignty while the federal Diet (Tagsatzung) served primarily as consultative forum rather than sovereign legislature.

The Sonderbund War of 1847—a brief but decisive civil conflict between conservative Catholic cantons and liberal Protestant cantons—exposed the confederation's inadequacies. Following liberal victory, the Federal Constitution of 1848 transformed

Switzerland from confederation into federal state, establishing stronger central government while preserving significant cantonal powers (Kölz, 2004).

Institutional Architecture and Cantonal Autonomy.
The 1848 Constitution (subsequently revised in 1999) created a bicameral Federal Assembly: the National Council (representing the people with seats proportional to population) and the Council of States (representing cantons with two representatives per canton regardless of size) (Linder & Mueller, 2021). This structure—parallel to the American model—ensures both popular will and cantonal interests shape federal legislation.

Switzerland's 26 cantons possess their own constitutions, governments, parliaments, and judiciaries (Fleiner & Fleiner, 2009). This decentralization extends to municipalities, creating "federalism of layers" where decisions occur as close to citizens as possible. Cantons exercise primary authority over education (determining curriculum and pedagogical approaches), policing and judicial systems, healthcare, and infrastructure—producing substantial policy diversity across Switzerland (Watts, 2008).

Direct Applicability to Israel.
Swiss cantonal autonomy offers a direct model for regional governance in a Federal State of Israel. As this author has proposed, constituent regions would maintain their own regional parliaments, executive councils, and judicial systems for civil matters, operating under federal constitutional constraints (Eger, 2025b). Jewish regions could maintain separate Hebrew-language education systems with substantial religious instruction for those who desire it, while Palestinian regions would operate Arabic-language schools reflecting their cultural traditions. Regional police forces would handle local law enforcement, with federal security services maintaining oversight to prevent terrorism and ensure inter-regional cooperation.

Managing Linguistic Diversity.
Switzerland recognizes four national languages: German (spoken by approximately 62%), French (23%), Italian (8%), and Romansh (0.5%) (Lüdi & Werlen, 2005). The federal government conducts business in German, French, and Italian. Federal laws and documents publish in these three languages, and citizens may communicate with federal authorities in any national language (Grin & Korth, 2005).

Linguistic distribution across cantons has naturally led to linguistic boundaries that the federal structure respects. German-speaking cantons predominate in northern, eastern, and central Switzerland; French-speaking cantons in the west; Italian speakers in Ticino and parts of Graubünden; Romansh speakers in Graubünden (McRae, 1983). While linguistic minorities exist within cantons, the federal system provides frameworks for cultural protection and minority language rights.

Direct Applicability to Israel.
Switzerland demonstrates that official multilingualism need not undermine national unity. A Federal State of Israel would recognize Hebrew and Arabic as co-equal official languages, with all federal legislation, court proceedings, and government services available in both languages (Eger, 2025a). Regional governments would operate in their preferred language while ensuring linguistic minorities receive accommodation. This arrangement—far from threatening Jewish majority rights—would institutionalize Jewish-Arab cooperation while allowing each community to flourish linguistically and culturally.

Direct Democracy and Popular Participation.
Swiss direct democracy features robust popular initiatives and referendums at federal and cantonal levels. Citizens can propose constitutional amendments through popular initiative (requiring 100,000 signatures within 18 months), which then face national vote requiring both popular majority and majority of cantons ("double majority") for passage (Kriesi, 2005). Federal laws passed by the Federal Assembly face optional referendum if 50,000 signatures collected within 100 days.

These instruments serve multiple functions in Swiss federalism. They empower citizens, providing direct participation channels bypassing party politics. They check federal and cantonal government power—policies perceived as infringing cantonal autonomy or minority rights can face popular challenge. The referendum mechanism fosters consensus-building and compromise, as politicians recognize significant proposals may face popular scrutiny (Linder, 2010).

Direct Applicability to Israel.
Direct democracy mechanisms could enhance legitimacy and citizen engagement in a Federal State of Israel. As this author has proposed, incorporating referendum provisions for major

constitutional amendments—requiring approval from both the overall population and majorities in constituent regions—would prevent any single ethnic or regional group from unilaterally altering the federal bargain (Eger, 2025a). Popular initiatives at regional levels would empower citizens to propose legislation addressing local concerns, fostering grassroots democratic participation and reducing alienation.

Power-Sharing and Consociational Elements
The Federal Council (Switzerland's seven-member executive) has typically operated according to the "magic formula" (Zauberformel) since 1959, allocating seats among major political parties proportionally to their Federal Assembly strength, ensuring representation from major linguistic regions (Kriesi & Trechsel, 2008). While not strictly federalist, this power-sharing reinforces federal principles by ensuring major political forces—and the populations they represent—have executive stake.

Switzerland also features significant fiscal federalism, with cantons retaining considerable taxation and spending control. While the federal government collects certain taxes (customs duties, value-added tax), substantial revenue remains with cantons, who then contribute to the federal budget (Dafflon, 2006). Fiscal equalization mechanisms reduce disparities between wealthier and poorer cantons, ensuring more equitable resource distribution across the federation.

Direct Applicability to Israel.
Power-sharing provisions could prevent majoritarian domination in a Federal State of Israel. A Federal Executive Council could include guaranteed representation from Jewish and Palestinian regions, ensuring both communities participate in national governance (Eger, 2025b). Fiscal federalism—allowing regions to collect regional taxes while contributing to federal expenses—would empower regional governments to fund local priorities while federal equalization payments would prevent economic disparities from destabilizing the federation.

Post-War German Federalism: Democratic Consolidation.
Historical Context and Constitutional Foundations.
The Second World War's devastation presented Germany with unprecedented challenges: rebuilding physical infrastructure, political institutions, and social fabric while preventing authoritarianism's recurrence. The Basic Law (Grundgesetz) of

1949, drafted by the Parliamentary Council representing West German Länder under Allied supervision, made federalism a fundamental constitutional principle deliberately chosen to decentralize power, promote democratic participation, and prevent concentrated authority (Kommers & Miller, 2012).

The framers drew lessons from Weimar Republic failures and Nazi over-centralization. They created a system robust enough to govern effectively yet sufficiently decentralized to protect against power concentration, thereby safeguarding democratic freedoms and individual liberties (Gunlicks, 2003).

Subsidiarity and Länder Powers
The Basic Law embodies subsidiarity principles (though not explicitly named). The federal government (Bund) legislates only in areas explicitly delegated by the Basic Law or where Länder cannot legislate effectively (Grundgesetz art. 30, 70). Education, cultural affairs, internal security (police), and local government remain overwhelmingly within Länder purview (Renzsch, 1991). This design diffuses authority, ensuring governance remains close to citizens. The Länder are not mere administrative units but constituent federation elements, possessing their own constitutions, parliaments, and governments, playing significant roles in federal legislation through the Bundesrat (Leonardy, 1999).

The Bundesrat & Cooperative Federalism.
The Bundesrat (Federal Council) represents Länder governments—its members are delegates appointed by state governments voting according to government instructions (unlike the U.S. Senate representing state populations). This arrangement ensures Länder interests are directly articulated at the federal level (Hrbek, 2002).

Bundesrat consent is required for extensive federal legislation, particularly laws affecting Länder powers, finances, or administrative competencies. This institutional check on federal power prevents over-centralization, promoting continuous federal-Länder dialogue and negotiation (Scharpf, 2006). It fosters "cooperative federalism" where federal and state governments collaborate rather than operating in strict isolation.

Direct Applicability to Israel.
The German Bundesrat model offers immediate transferability to a Federal State of Israel. A Federal Council representing regional governments—with voting weighted by population but ensuring all

regions possess meaningful voice—would prevent federal overreach while facilitating inter-regional cooperation (Eger, 2025a). Regional representatives would possess veto power over federal legislation directly affecting regional competencies (education, policing, civil law), ensuring federal-regional power balance.

Economic Reconstruction and Fiscal Federalism.

The Wirtschaftswunder (economic miracle) was profoundly shaped by federal structure. Länder played significant roles implementing economic policies, often tailoring them to regional circumstances. While the federal government championed social market economy, implementation and specific initiatives involved close federal-Länder cooperation (Berghahn, 1986).

Fiscal federalism—with revenue sharing and equalization mechanisms—mitigated significant economic disparities between wealthier and poorer Länder, fostering national cohesion during recovery (Spahn, 2007). This decentralized approach allowed greater flexibility and responsiveness to diverse regional conditions, contributing to balanced, widespread recovery.

Direct Applicability to Israel.

German fiscal federalism provides a model for addressing economic disparities in a Federal State of Israel. Palestinian regions—likely to be economically disadvantaged initially—would receive federal equalization payments funded by wealthier Jewish regions, promoting balanced development and reducing economic resentment that fuels conflict (Eger, 2025b). Regional governments would implement economic development strategies tailored to local needs while federal oversight prevents corruption and ensures transparency.

Democratic Consolidation and Regional Identity

Federalism served crucial functions in post-war German democratic consolidation by managing regional identities and fostering political pluralism. The eleven West German Länder (before 1990 reunification) each possessed distinct histories, cultural traditions, and political leanings—Bavaria with its strong Catholic tradition differs significantly from northern industrialized, secularized Länder (Jeffery, 1999).

Federalism allowed these diverse regional identities expression and accommodation within unified national framework. Strong Länder parliaments and governments meant political competition thrived at regional levels, encouraging broader political participation and offering diverse political models for citizen engagement (Sturm, 2001).

German Reunification and Federal Expansion

The 1990 reunification provided significant federal system testing. The five newly established Länder of former German Democratic Republic (GDR) acceded into the Federal Republic, extending the existing federal framework to new territories (Padgett, 1994). This was not simple administrative annexation but complex political, economic, and social integration requiring significant federal-Länder adaptation and negotiation.

Integrating former GDR into the federal system involved substantial financial transfers from western to eastern Länder, highlighting fiscal equalization mechanisms and the federal government's role promoting regional development and reducing economic disparities (Renzsch, 2000). Successful reintegration underscored German federal model flexibility and resilience, demonstrating federalism's capacity as a powerful tool for national unity and reconciliation.

Direct Applicability to Israel.

German reunification demonstrates federalism's capacity to integrate previously separated populations with different historical experiences and economic development levels. Post-deradicalization, a Federal State of Israel would face similar challenges integrating Palestinian regions with different governance traditions, economic structures, and political cultures (Eger, 2025a). The German experience suggests that with adequate federal support, fiscal transfers, and respect for regional autonomy, successful integration is achievable despite substantial initial disparities.

Canadian Federalism:
Linguistic Duality & Regional Autonomy.
Constitutional Foundations & Initial Design.

Canada's federal structure emerged from pragmatic necessity rather than revolutionary fervor. The British North America Act of 1867 (now Constitution Act, 1867) united distinct colonial societies —primarily British and French origin—into a single Dominion within the British Empire (Ajzenstat et al., 2003). The Fathers of Confederation recognized a purely unitary state would be unworkable given deep-seated differences, particularly between

French-speaking Canada East (later Quebec) and predominantly English-speaking populations elsewhere.

The 1867 Act's division of powers balanced strong central government needs (national defense, trade regulation, unified economy) with provincial desires to control local matters. Federal powers included criminal law, banking, navigation, and national railway establishment. Provinces received jurisdiction over education, property and civil rights, and company incorporation (Constitution Act, 1867, ss. 91-92).

This division was never neat—the interpretation of these powers has been a constant source of legal and political debate throughout Canadian history (Wheare, 1963). The constitutional amending formula, requiring federal parliament consent and specified numbers of provincial legislatures, has always underscored Canadian federalism's collaborative yet contentious nature.

Quebec and the Quest for Distinct Society Recognition

Quebec, with its distinct French language, civil law tradition (based on Napoleonic Code), and deeply rooted cultural identity, has always been the most significant focal point for regional autonomy discussions (Gagnon & Iacovino, 2007). From the outset, Quebec sought assurances that its unique character would be protected within the federal framework.

This quest manifests in various forms: demands for greater social policy control, immigration, and cultural affairs, leading to numerous constitutional crises and negotiations (McRoberts, 1997). The "distinct society" concept reflects recognition that Quebec's cultural and linguistic heritage sets it apart from the rest of Canada. This has often placed Quebec advocating for more decentralized federation, or exploring alternative constitutional arrangements, to safeguard its identity.

The 1980 and 1995 Quebec sovereignty referendums—both rejecting separation but by narrow margins (59.56% "No" in 1980; 50.58% "No" in 1995)—demonstrate the ongoing tension between Quebec's desire for recognition and Canada's commitment to federal unity (Dion, 1996).

Direct Applicability to Israel.

Quebec's experience offers cautionary and instructive lessons for a Federal State of Israel. Palestinian regions would likely seek "distinct society" recognition similar to Quebec's demands, requiring constitutional provisions acknowledging their unique cultural, linguistic, and religious identity while remaining within the federal framework (Eger, 2025b). The key lesson: such recognition need not threaten federal unity but rather can strengthen it by providing institutional accommodation for legitimate identity claims. However, as Canada demonstrates, ongoing negotiations and constitutional flexibility are necessary to maintain equilibrium.

Evolution of Federal-Provincial Power Balance

Canadian federalism has undergone significant power balance shifts between federal and provincial governments. Initially, the federal government under Prime Minister John A. Macdonald wielded considerable influence through residual legislative power and disallowance power (ability to nullify provincial legislation) (Vipond, 1991).

However, judicial interpretation of the Constitution Act, 1867—particularly by the Judicial Committee of the Privy Council (Canada's highest appeal court until 1949)—tended to favor provincial powers. Landmark decisions broadened provincial jurisdiction scope, particularly in labor relations and property rights, leading to gradual decentralization (Cairns, 1971).

Mid-20th century saw federal power resurgence, partly driven by managing national economy and welfare state expansion. The federal government led establishing national programs in healthcare (Medicare established 1966-1971), unemployment insurance, and pensions (Russell, 2004). This era was marked by increased federal spending and greater federal presence in previously provincial domains.

Constitutional Patriation and the Charter of Rights.

The 1982 Constitution patriation, culminating in the Constitution Act, 1982, which included the Canadian Charter of Rights and Freedoms, was pivotal (Romanow et al., 1984). While affirming Canada's sovereignty, the process highlighted deep provincial divisions. Quebec did not formally sign, and subsequent attempts to bring it fully into constitutional fold—Meech Lake Accord (1987-1990) and Charlottetown Accord (1992)—ultimately failed (Russell, 1993).

These failures underscored immense difficulty achieving constitutional consensus in a country as diverse as Canada and deep-seated disagreements over federalism's nature and Quebec's place within Confederation (Russell, 2004). The Charter itself introduced complexity, entrenching certain rights potentially overriding provincial legislation, leading to ongoing debates about balancing individual rights and provincial autonomy (Knopff & Morton, 1992).

Direct Applicability to Israel.
Canada's constitutional struggles highlight the necessity of achieving broad consensus before implementing a federal structure. For a Federal State of Israel, this means the federal constitution must be negotiated with full Palestinian participation after complete deradicalization—not imposed unilaterally (Eger, 2025a). The Charter of Rights equivalent in Israel would need to carefully balance collective rights (Jewish national character, Palestinian cultural autonomy) with individual rights (equality before law, freedom of conscience), requiring sophisticated constitutional engineering to prevent perpetual litigation undermining federal stability.

Fiscal Federalism and Equalization.
Ongoing federal-provincial debates often revolve around fiscal arrangements, particularly equalization payments—a system ensuring all provinces can provide reasonably comparable public service levels at comparable taxation levels (Courchene, 2007). Provinces frequently assert autonomy and push back against federal initiatives perceived as undermining their jurisdiction.
Disagreements over federal carbon pricing policies, healthcare transfers, and national standards implementation are recurrent intergovernmental relations themes (Simeon & Cameron, 2002). These disputes reflect fundamental political philosophy differences and regional priorities rather than mere administrative quibbles.

Direct Applicability to Israel.
Fiscal equalization would be essential in a Federal State of Israel to prevent economic disparities from destabilizing the federation. Palestinian regions, likely initially less economically developed, would receive federal transfer payments ensuring adequate public services provision (Eger, 2025b). This system—similar to Canadian equalization—would be constitutionally mandated rather than subject to annual political negotiation, providing stability and predictability for regional planning.

**Belgian Federalism: Linguistic Constitutional Engineering.
From Unitary State to Federal Structure.**
Belgium's transformation into a federal state represents deliberate, protracted response to deeply entrenched societal divisions threatening national cohesion. For much of its independent history (since 1830), Belgium operated as unitary state—a system increasingly inadequate for managing growing divergences between Dutch-speaking Flanders and French-speaking Wallonia, with bilingual Brussels Capital Region at its heart (Deschouwer, 2012).

The linguistic divide, rooted in medieval settlement patterns and evolving socio-economic development, became Belgian politics' defining fault line. Flanders, historically part of the Low Countries, spoke Dutch; Wallonia had closer French ties, speaking French or Walloon dialects (Witte et al., 2009). When Belgium gained independence from the Netherlands in 1830, French was established as government, administration, and elite language despite Dutch speakers constituting population majority. This French dominance fostered Flemish resentment and marginalization.

Constitutional Reforms: Communities & Regions.
The 1830 constitutional framework, heavily influenced by French centralized state models, granted extensive national government powers, leaving minimal room for regional or linguistic considerations. As Flemish awareness grew and political organizations advocating Flemish rights gained traction, pressure to reform state structure became increasingly insistent (Fitzmaurice, 1996).

The first significant constitutional reform acknowledging linguistic divide occurred in 1962-1963 with laws definitively establishing linguistic frontiers and granting Dutch and French official status in respective regions. These laws were crucial first steps in much longer constitutional evolution process (Deprez & Vos, 1998).

Late 1960s and 1970s witnessed constitutional revisions progressively shifting Belgium from unitary state toward federal system. The 1970 constitutional revision recognized three cultural communities: Flemish, French, and German-speaking (though smaller, the German community also had distinct linguistic rights).

This reform devolved certain powers to these communities, albeit initially complex and indirect (Alen & Ergec, 1998).

The 1980 constitutional reform further elaborated federal structure by establishing directly elected community councils granting legislative powers in cultural affairs, personal matters, and education. Furthermore, this reform created territorial regions— Flanders, Wallonia, and Brussels—beginning the process of devolving powers to regions. This dual structure—with both communities and regions gaining competencies—became Belgian federalism's defining characteristic, often leading to complex jurisdictional overlaps (Swenden & Jans, 2006).

Direct Applicability to Israel.
Belgium's dual structure (cultural communities and territorial regions) offers a sophisticated model for a Federal State of Israel. Cultural councils could be established for Jewish and Palestinian communities, possessing authority over religious affairs, cultural institutions, and education curriculum content, while territorial regions (Jerusalem, Tel Aviv-Jaffa, Haifa, Gaza, Hebron, etc.) would handle governance, infrastructure, and economic development (Eger, 2025a). This dual structure would allow both cultural autonomy (preserving Jewish and Palestinian identities) and territorial governance (enabling practical administration), addressing both identity and governance imperatives.

Asymmetric Federalism & Complex Power Distribution.
Belgian federalism is characterized by highly detailed, evolved power divisions. Initially focused on cultural matters, competencies devolved to communities and regions have expanded considerably to include economic policy, employment, housing, transport, and environmental policy (Deschouwer, 2006).

Regional governments are largely responsible for infrastructure, public works, and economic development within territories. Community governments hold sway over education policy, childcare, and cultural institutions. This broad power devolution means many daily life aspects for Belgians are now managed at regional or community levels, reflecting federalization success in bringing governance closer to people and accommodating diverse identities (Swenden, 2002).

Brussels-Capital Region presents particularly complex case within Belgian federal framework. As geographically distinct entity and officially bilingual, it has its own regional government responsible for transport, urban planning, and public works. However, Brussels' linguistic duality necessitates specific arrangements for cultural and personal matters, often managed by community-based institutions reflecting the need to cater to both French-speaking and Dutch-speaking populations (Nassaux, 2011).

Direct Applicability to Israel.
Brussels' bilingual governance model offers direct applicability to Jerusalem in a Federal State of Israel. Jerusalem—as capital with Jewish and Palestinian populations—could operate as special federal district with its own governance structure ensuring both communities participate in municipal government while federal authorities maintain oversight of security and holy sites (Eger, 2025b). Cultural and personal matters (education, family law, religious affairs) could be managed by community-based institutions, while territorial governance (infrastructure, economic development) would be handled by joint municipal government.

Fiscal Arrangements & Intergovernmental Relations.
Belgian federalism extends to fiscal arrangements. The federal government retains responsibility for social security, defense, foreign policy, and justice administration. However, significant state revenue portions transfer to communities and regions to fund devolved responsibilities (Cattoir & Verdonck, 2009). Financial resources allocation has been recurring negotiation point and, occasionally, contention. Mechanisms exist to ensure fiscal solidarity degree, but precise funds distribution—often based on complex formulas and economic indicators—remains sensitive intergovernmental relations issue.

Despite elaborate federal structure, Belgium's system faces challenges. Having both community and regional competencies complexity can lead to jurisdictional disputes and coordination problems. Furthermore, policy approaches divergence between Flanders and Wallonia, driven by different socio-economic priorities and political ideologies, can sometimes create friction and hinder coherent national policies development (Deschouwer, 2009).

Direct Applicability to Israel.
Belgian fiscal federalism demonstrates the necessity of clear revenue-sharing mechanisms in divided societies. In a Federal State of Israel, a constitutional formula would distribute federal tax revenues to constituent regions based on population, economic

need, and infrastructure requirements, with federal equalization ensuring poorer Palestinian regions receive adequate resources (Eger, 2025a). Inter-governmental coordination mechanisms—including regular Federal-Regional Conferences—would facilitate cooperation and prevent jurisdictional conflicts from escalating.

Lessons in Federal Compromise.

Belgium's federalism success can be measured by its ability to maintain state unity amidst profound linguistic divisions. While tensions and political disagreements persist, the federal system has provided framework for managing these differences peacefully and democratically (Swenden & Jans, 2006). It has allowed both linguistic communities to flourish culturally and politically, fostering autonomy and self-determination sense that might have been impossible in unitary state.

However, ongoing Belgian debate often centers on federal structure efficiency and coherence. Questions frequently arise about multiple government layers costs and potential efforts duplication. There are also further reform calls, with some advocating streamlined federal system, perhaps by merging community and regional competencies or by further decentralizing powers (Deschouwer, 2012).

Direct Applicability to Israel.

Belgium's experience demonstrates that federal complexity—while creating administrative challenges—can be necessary price for maintaining unity in deeply divided societies. A Federal State of Israel would inevitably face similar efficiency criticisms, but the alternative—continued conflict and unitary domination—is far costlier in human and economic terms (Eger, 2025b). The Belgian lesson: institutional complexity that preserves peace and accommodates diversity is preferable to institutional simplicity that perpetuates conflict.

India: Asymmetric Federalism and Managing Diversity
Constitutional Foundations and Federal Structure

India presents the most directly applicable federal model for Israel given its management of extraordinary ethnic, linguistic, religious, and cultural diversity within a single federal framework. As this author has argued in "Is India's Federalism a Model for Israel?", India's Constitution (adopted January 26, 1950) creates a unique blend of federal and unitary features specifically designed to address the country's complex socio-political realities while maintaining national integrity (Eger, 2025c; Basu, 2013).

The Indian Constitution establishes a dual government structure with written constitution, constitutional and judicial supreme authority, unitary bias during emergencies, asymmetrical power distribution, constitutional rigidity and flexibility, cooperative federalism, single citizenship, unified legal system, and bicameral legislature (Austin, 1966). This intricate architecture balances unity with diversity, managing linguistic, ethnic, cultural, and religious pluralism while maintaining strong central government capable of preserving national integrity (Bajwa, 2007).

Division of Powers & Cooperative Federalism.
The Seventh Schedule of the Indian Constitution delineates power distribution between the Union (central government) and States through three lists: the Union List (exclusive central powers including defense, foreign affairs, currency, interstate commerce), State List (exclusive state powers including public order, police, public health, agriculture), and Concurrent List (shared powers where both can legislate, with federal law prevailing in conflict) (Constitution of India, 1950, Seventh Schedule). This distribution creates what scholars term "cooperative federalism"—a system where center and states collaborate on numerous policy areas rather than operating in strict separation (Maheshwari, 2000). The Planning Commission (now replaced by NITI Aayog) historically facilitated center-state coordination in economic planning and resource allocation (Raghavan, 2019).

Direct Applicability to Israel.
India's three-list system offers immediate transferability to a Federal State of Israel. A Federal List would include defense and security (unified IDF command), foreign affairs, currency and banking, interstate commerce, and civil aviation. A Regional List would include education (allowing Hebrew and Arabic language schools with distinct curricula), regional policing (subject to federal oversight), healthcare, local infrastructure, and municipal governance. A Concurrent List would include criminal law, marriage and divorce (with religious court systems), labor law, and environmental protection—areas requiring both federal standards and regional implementation (Eger, 2025c).

Asymmetric Federalism: Article 370 and Special Provisions
India's most distinctive federal feature is asymmetric federalism—the constitutional recognition that different states may require varying autonomy degrees to accommodate unique historical,

cultural, or geopolitical circumstances (Tillin, 2015). Until its controversial abrogation in August 2019, Article 370 granted special status to Jammu and Kashmir, allowing the state its own constitution, flag, and limiting Indian Constitution application to defense, foreign affairs, and communications (Constitution of India, 1950, art. 370 (repealed 2019)).

The Supreme Court in *In Re: Article 370 of the Constitution* (2023) held that Article 370 represented asymmetric federalism instance, stating: "In asymmetric federalism, a particular State may enjoy autonomy degree which another State does not. The difference, however, remains one of degree and not of kind. Different states may enjoy different benefits under the federal setup, but the common thread is federalism" (*In Re: Article 370*, Writ Petition (Civil) No. 1357 of 2019, 89 (2023)). Beyond Article 370, the Constitution contains numerous asymmetric provisions in Articles 371-371J granting special status to various states:

Article 371A (Nagaland): Provides that no Act of Parliament regarding Naga religious or social practices, customary law, land ownership, or resource administration applies unless Nagaland's Legislative Assembly decides by resolution (Constitution of India, 1950, art. 371A).

Article 371F (Sikkim): Grants special provisions respecting Sikkim's unique accession history, continuing existing laws and their adaptation (Constitution of India, 1950, art. 371F).

Article 371G (Mizoram): Protects Mizo customary law, land ownership, and resource administration from Parliamentary Acts unless Mizoram's Legislative Assembly consents by resolution (Constitution of India, 1950, art. 371G).

Articles 371D-371E (Andhra Pradesh/Telangana): Provide for equitable opportunities in public employment and education, and University establishment (Constitution of India, 1950, arts. 371D-371E). The Fifth and Sixth Schedules provide additional asymmetric arrangements for areas with substantial indigenous populations. The Fifth Schedule (Constitution of India, 1950, Fifth Schedule) grants special administrative arrangements and protections for Scheduled Tribes in certain states, with Tribes Advisory Councils advising governors on tribal welfare. The Sixth Schedule (Constitution of India, 1950, Sixth Schedule) creates autonomous district councils in Assam, Meghalaya, Tripura, and Mizoram with legislative and judicial powers over local matters including land, forests, and customary law administration.

Direct Applicability to Israel:
Indian asymmetric federalism provides the most compelling precedent for a Federal State of Israel. As this author has argued, different constituent regions could possess varying autonomy degrees based on specific needs and circumstances (Eger, 2025c). Jerusalem, given its religious and political significance, could operate as special federal district with unique governance arrangements balancing Jewish sovereignty with Palestinian autonomy—similar to Delhi's special status under Article 239AA. Palestinian regions in Gaza and the West Bank could possess enhanced autonomy over education, cultural affairs, and civil law while accepting federal jurisdiction over security, foreign affairs, and criminal law. Jewish settlement regions could maintain distinct local governance while participating in federal structures. This asymmetric approach—rather than imposing uniformity—would accommodate legitimate differences while maintaining federal unity.

Linguistic Diversity & the Reorganization of States.
India confronted the challenge of linguistic diversity through constitutional recognition and subsequent state reorganization. The Constitution's Eighth Schedule recognizes 22 official languages, though Hindi and English serve as official languages for central government purposes (Constitution of India, 1950, art. 343, Eighth Schedule). Following independence, intense agitation for linguistic states led to the States Reorganisation Act of 1956, which restructured state boundaries primarily along linguistic lines (States Reorganisation Act, 1956, No. 37).

This reorganization—creating states like Andhra Pradesh (Telugu), Karnataka (Kannada), Kerala (Malayalam), and Tamil Nadu (Tamil) —allowed linguistic communities to exercise self-governance while remaining within the federal union (Harrison, 1960). The principle continues: Telangana separated from Andhra Pradesh in 2014 based partly on regional identity and developmental concerns (Andhra Pradesh Reorganisation Act, 2014).

Direct Applicability to Israel.
India's linguistic states model demonstrates that federal units need not be ethnically homogeneous but can be organized around linguistic or cultural identity while maintaining national unity. In a Federal State of Israel, regions could be organized around linguistic-cultural majorities (Hebrew-speaking Jewish regions, Arabic-speaking Palestinian regions, mixed bilingual regions) without requiring complete ethnic separation (Eger, 2025c). This

would allow cultural communities to flourish linguistically while participating in shared federal governance.

Religious Pluralism & Personal Law Systems.

India manages extraordinary religious diversity—Hinduism (79.8%), Islam (14.2%), Christianity (2.3%), Sikhism (1.7%), and others (Census of India, 2011)—through a combination of secular constitutional principles and religious personal law recognition. Article 25 guarantees freedom of conscience and free profession, practice, and propagation of religion, subject to public order, morality, and health (Constitution of India, 1950, art. 25).

Crucially, India maintains separate personal law systems for different religious communities governing marriage, divorce, inheritance, and family matters (Diwan, 2002). Hindu personal law (including Sikhs, Buddhists, and Jains), Muslim personal law, Christian personal law, and Parsi personal law operate under federal legislation and judicial interpretation (Parashar, 1992). The Supreme Court in *Mohd. Ahmed Khan v. Shah Bano Begum* (1985) AIR 1985 SC 945 addressed the tension between personal law autonomy and gender equality, demonstrating ongoing negotiation between religious autonomy and constitutional rights.

Direct Applicability to Israel: India's personal law system offers direct applicability to a Federal State of Israel. Jewish religious courts (Batei Din) and Islamic courts (Shari'a courts) could maintain jurisdiction over personal status matters for their respective communities—marriage, divorce, inheritance—while federal civil law governs commercial transactions, property rights, and criminal matters (Eger, 2025c). This arrangement preserves religious autonomy in sensitive personal matters while maintaining federal legal supremacy in civil and criminal domains. Article 44's Directive Principle (calling for uniform civil code) remains unimplemented precisely because Indian federalism recognizes that unity need not require uniformity in all spheres—a crucial lesson for Israel.

Emergency Provisions & Federal Balance.

The Indian Constitution contains extensive emergency provisions that dramatically alter the federal balance. Article 352 permits the President to proclaim national emergency during war, external aggression, or armed rebellion, enabling the center to extend its executive authority to any state and suspend state legislative autonomy (Constitution of India, 1950, art. 352). Article 356 permits "President's Rule" when a state's constitutional machinery fails, allowing direct central government administration (Constitution of India, 1950, art. 356).

These provisions, while criticized as undermining federalism, have been substantially limited by judicial interpretation. In *S.R. Bommai v. Union of India* (1994) 3 SCC 1, the Supreme Court established that Article 356 imposition is subject to judicial review and must satisfy constitutional requirements, significantly constraining central government's ability to dismiss state governments arbitrarily (Sathe, 2002).

Direct Applicability to Israel.
Emergency provisions would be necessary in a Federal State of Israel but must include strong judicial oversight to prevent abuse. Federal intervention in regional governance should be permissible only when regional government has demonstrably failed to maintain public order, prevent terrorism, or protect constitutional rights—and subject to immediate Supreme Court review (Eger, 2025a). This balances the need for federal authority to address genuine security threats with protection against using "security" pretexts to undermine regional autonomy.

Judicial Federalism & the Supreme Court.
The Indian Supreme Court serves as ultimate arbiter of center-state disputes, constitutional interpretation, and fundamental rights guardian (Constitution of India, 1950, arts. 124-147). Through landmark judgments, the Court has developed the "basic structure doctrine"—certain constitutional features (including federalism) cannot be amended even by constitutional amendment process (*Kesavananda Bharati v. State of Kerala*, AIR 1973 SC 1461).

In *S.R. Bommai*, the Court held that federalism is part of the Constitution's basic structure, preventing the center from fundamentally altering the federal balance without constituent units' consent (Sathe, 2002). This doctrine provides significant protection against federal overreach, ensuring that asymmetric federalism and state autonomy cannot be eliminated through simple parliamentary majorities.

Direct Applicability to Israel.
A Supreme Court with constitutional review authority would be essential in a Federal State of Israel to interpret the federal constitution, resolve center-regional disputes, and protect fundamental rights (Eger, 2025c). Adopting a basic structure

doctrine would prevent any government from fundamentally altering the federal bargain—ensuring that neither the Jewish majority nor any future demographic shift could unilaterally eliminate regional autonomy or fundamental rights protections. This constitutional entrenchment would provide long-term stability and reassurance to both communities.

Critiques & Challenges of Indian Federalism.

Scholars have critiqued Indian federalism as insufficiently decentralized, noting the center's fiscal dominance, appointment of state governors by the President, and emergency provisions that can transform federal structure into unitary system (Rao & Singh, 2005). The "President's Rule" provision has been particularly controversial, with accusations of political abuse to dismiss opposition-led state governments (Rudolph & Rudolph, 2010).

Nevertheless, Indian federalism has successfully maintained national unity for 75 years despite extraordinary diversity, multiple secessionist movements, linguistic tensions, and religious conflicts. As Watts observes, "The Indian federal system has proved remarkably resilient in accommodating the country's enormous linguistic, cultural, religious and economic diversity" (Watts, 2008, p. 178).

Direct Applicability to Israel.

India's experience demonstrates that federal systems in diverse societies will inevitably face tensions, accusations of over-centralization, and periodic crises—yet can nevertheless maintain national unity and democratic governance over extended periods. A Federal State of Israel would face similar challenges but, as India demonstrates, these are manageable through constitutional design, judicial oversight, and ongoing political negotiation (Eger, 2025c). The key insight: perfection is not the standard; rather, the question is whether federalism manages diversity better than available alternatives (unitary domination or partition).

Synthesizing Federal Lessons for Israel

Each historical precedent examined in this chapter offers specific transferable lessons for a future Federal State of Israel, implementable only after the complete end of the October 7th War, Hamas's unconditional surrender and demilitarization, the dismantling of all Muslim Brotherhood proxies, and the thorough deradicalization of Palestinian society to the point where

Palestinians genuinely seek integration into a Federal State of Israel rather than a separate Palestinian state.

Immediate Transferable Elements
From the United States:
*Bicameral legislature with equal regional representation (Federal Council) and proportional representation (Federal Assembly);
*Enumerated federal powers (defense, foreign affairs, currency, interstate commerce) with residual powers reserved to regions;
*Bill of Rights protecting individual liberties and constraining federal overreach;
*Judicial review mechanism for constitutional interpretation and dispute resolution;
*Federal supremacy in areas of federal competence, balanced by strong regional autonomy;

From Switzerland:
*Cantonal autonomy model with regional constitutions, parliaments, and judiciaries;
*Multilingual recognition (Hebrew and Arabic as co-equal official languages);
*Direct democracy mechanisms (referendums, popular initiatives) enhancing citizen participation;
*Fiscal federalism with regional taxation and federal equalization payments;
*Consociational power-sharing ensuring both communities represented in federal executive;

From Germany:
*Subsidiarity principle (federal government acts only where regions cannot effectively);
*Federal Council (Bundesrat equivalent) representing regional governments with veto over legislation affecting regional competencies;
*Cooperative federalism model with center-regional collaboration
*Constitutional court with authority to protect federal balance and fundamental rights;
*Fiscal equalization mechanisms reducing inter-regional economic disparities;

From Canada:
*Recognition of "distinct society" status for minority nations within federation;

*Asymmetric arrangements allowing different regions varying autonomy levels;
*Official bilingualism with all federal services available in both languages;
*Provincial jurisdiction over education, cultural affairs, and civil law;
*Constitutional amending formula requiring consent from federal parliament and regional governments

From Belgium:
*Dual structure: cultural communities (managing religious/cultural affairs) and territorial regions (managing governance/infrastructure);
*Brussels model for Jerusalem: special federal district with shared governance
*Community-based personal status law systems operating under federal constitutional framework
*Highly detailed constitutional power divisions preventing jurisdictional ambiguity
*Recognition that institutional complexity preserving peace is preferable to simplicity perpetuating conflict

From India:
*Asymmetric federalism allowing different regions varying autonomy based on specific circumstances;
*Three-list power division (Federal, Regional, Concurrent) balancing unity with diversity;
*Linguistic state organization while maintaining national unity;
*Separate religious personal law systems for marriage, divorce, inheritance, family law;
*Basic structure doctrine preventing fundamental federal bargain alteration;
*Emergency provisions with strong judicial oversight;
*Supreme Court as ultimate arbiter of center-regional disputes;

The Pathway Forward
As this author has consistently argued, the Federal State of Israel represents the only viable One-State Solution that preserves Jewish national character while granting Palestinians genuine self-governance and equality (Eger, 2025a). The alternative one-state scenarios—unitary Jewish domination or binational majoritarian democracy—are unsustainable and would lead either to Palestinian subjugation or, through demographic shifts, to existential threats to Jewish sovereignty.
However, this federal solution is realizable only after specific preconditions are met (Eger, 2025b):

Military Victory: Complete defeat of Hamas, destruction of its military infrastructure, and dismantling of all Muslim Brotherhood proxy networks
Demilitarization: Absolute prohibition on Palestinian military forces, with federal security services maintaining exclusive armed forces authority
Deradicalization: Comprehensive transformation of Palestinian education, media, and civil society eliminating incitement, antisemitism, and rejection of Jewish legitimacy in the land
Ideological Shift: Palestinian society must genuinely renounce the goal of a Palestinian state replacing Israel and instead embrace integration into a Federal State of Israel with regional autonomy
Democratic Legitimacy: Federal constitution must be ratified by referenda in both Jewish and Palestinian regions, ensuring genuine consent rather than imposition.

These preconditions are non-negotiable. No federal structure can succeed if one constituent group views it as temporary arrangement pending opportunity to destroy the federation and eliminate the other group. Palestinian society must undergo transformation comparable to post-1945 German denazification and democratic reeducation before genuine federal partnership becomes possible.

The historical precedents examined in this chapter demonstrate that federalism has successfully managed deep ethno-linguistic divisions, religious pluralism, and regional identity claims in diverse societies. The United States transformed thirteen jealously sovereign colonies into a continental power.

Switzerland united German, French, Italian, and Romansh speakers in prosperous democracy. Germany employed federalism to reconstruct democracy from authoritarianism's ashes. Canada has navigated English-French tensions for over 150 years. Belgium prevented linguistic conflict from destroying the state. India maintains unity amidst extraordinary diversity.

If these diverse societies—with their own conflicts, tensions, and seemingly irreconcilable differences—have successfully employed federalism to forge unity while respecting diversity, then Israel, too, can adopt federal solutions. But only after the preconditions are met. Only after Palestinian society has been thoroughly deradicalized. Only after Palestinians genuinely seek partnership rather than domination. Only after the security threat has been eliminated.

The Federal State of Israel is not a utopian fantasy but a practical, implementable solution grounded in tested federal precedents and adapted to Israel's unique circumstances (Eger, 2025c). The question is not whether federalism can work—history demonstrates it can. The question is whether Palestinians will undergo the ideological transformation necessary to become federal partners rather than remaining existential enemies.

As Benjamin Wittes observed in his thoughtful exploration of federalist possibilities for Israel, "Federalism can also work as a tool for managing ethnic divisions within diverse countries; this is the role it plays successfully in countries like Canada and India" (Wittes, 2023). The path forward requires vision, courage, and, most critically, the deradicalization that makes federal partnership possible.

The historical precedents are clear. The institutional mechanisms are available. The federal architecture can be designed. What remains is the political will—and the transformation of Palestinian society from rejectionism to genuine partnership. Only then can the Federal State of Israel emerge from the ashes of conflict as a beacon of coexistence, demonstrating that even the most intractable conflicts can find resolution through creative federal solutions.

Chapter 3
Addendum

Key Concepts: Understanding Federal Terminology

Before diving into different federal models, let's settle on some shared terms. These concepts shape how we'll talk about federalism in the rest of this chapter.

Canton: In Switzerland, a canton is much more than a district. Each one has its own constitution, parliament, and government. The word comes from the French "canton," meaning district, but in Switzerland it signals a bottom-up system—26 cantons coming together to build the confederation. They don't all look the same. Some use direct democracy through local assemblies (Landsgemeinde), others stick with representative parliaments. The point: federal units don't need to be identical.

Asymmetric Federalism: Not every part of a federation needs the same powers. Sometimes, units get special autonomy based on their own histories or needs. Take India—Article 371A protects Naga customary law, and before 2019, Article 370 gave Jammu and Kashmir special status. In Canada, Quebec has extra control over immigration and cultural policy. Asymmetric federalism lets governments respect real claims for autonomy without flattening everyone into the same mold.

Consociationalism: In societies split by deep divisions, democracy needs something sturdier than simple majority rule. Consociationalism means power-sharing across groups, following four main ideas: grand coalitions (everyone gets a seat at the executive table), mutual vetoes (minorities can block decisions that threaten them), proportionality (fair share in parliament and jobs), and segmental autonomy (groups run certain affairs themselves). Arend Lijphart built this concept, looking at Belgium, Switzerland, and the Netherlands. Critics say it can freeze divisions in place, but supporters argue it's what keeps the peace when majoritarian rule would spark conflict.

Power-Sharing: This is how political systems make sure all major groups have a real voice in government. Think proportional voting systems, shared executive positions, mutual vetoes, and public jobs divvied up to reflect society. The Good Friday Agreement in Northern Ireland (1998) is a textbook example—unionists and nationalists both have to govern together. Power-sharing turns politics from a winner-takes-all fight into a joint project.

Linguistic Federalism: Some federations shape their basic units around language. These systems guarantee language rights in constitutions. Belgium, for example, splits power among Flemish,

French, and German-speaking communities. India redrew its state borders in 1956 to create Tamil Nadu, Karnataka, and Kerala, matching major languages. Switzerland officially recognizes four languages, with each canton running things in the local tongue. Linguistic federalism makes space for cultural identity and helps multilingual countries hold together.

Constitutional Design: Building a constitution isn't just about rules—it's about managing conflict and fitting the system to a society's particular problems. Good design walks a tightrope: it protects minorities, balances central and regional power, and finds unity without erasing diversity. Germany's Basic Law (1949) guarded democracy with "militant democracy" clauses and rules that can never be changed. South Africa's 1996 Constitution responded to apartheid with strong rights protections and nine provinces, each with its own powers.

Federalism in a Nutshell.

Federal systems share common principles—divided sovereignty, constitutional protections, bicameral legislatures—yet manifest differently based on context. This snapshot compares six systems this chapter examines.

Country	Key Challenge	Federal Solution	Population	Success Factor	Lesson Learned
Switzerland	4 languages, 26 cantons	Cantonal autonomy	8.7M	Subsidiarity	Regional governance
Belgium	Flemish-Walloon	Dual structure	11.6M	Complexity	Jerusalem model
Canada	Quebec	Asymmetric	39M	Distinct society	Palestinian autonomy
India	22 languages	Asymmetric states	1.4B	Personal law	Religious autonomy
USA	Civil War	Constitutional	335M	Bicameral	Regional balance

This comparison reveals crucial insights. Look at what the world's federations actually pull off. India keeps 1.4 billion people together, speaking 22 major languages and practicing every religion you can think of. Switzerland runs smoothly with four languages jammed into a country smaller than Massachusetts. So much for "too much diversity."

Federal systems don't need to be neat or simple either. Belgium's political structure is famously tangled, but that's exactly why it works—it bends to fit the country's messy reality instead of pretending things are simpler than they are.

And when things get ugly, federalism still delivers. The United States survived the Civil War—a conflict that killed 2% of the population. Germany pieced itself back together after totalitarianism fell apart. Federal models don't just manage diversity; they help heal deep wounds.

So when people say Israel-Palestine is "uniquely intractable," I can't buy it. Switzerland balances four languages and two religions. Belgium somehow keeps Flemings and Walloons under the same flag. Canada holds together, acknowledging Quebec's uniqueness. India governs more than a billion citizens, across a dizzying mix of faiths and cultures. Why would Israel-Palestine be beyond reach?

None of these countries is perfect. Belgium almost broke apart. Canada faced two near misses on Quebec sovereignty. India's Kashmir conflict is always simmering. But they've all managed to turn what looked like impossible divides into ordinary, if difficult, problems of government.

If you want a pop culture analogy, think Star Trek's United Federation of Planets: wildly different civilizations cooperating, each keeping its own quirks, but working together on the big stuff. Compare that to The Hunger Games' Panem, where the Capitol crushes the districts, bans autonomy, and sows the seeds for total rebellion. A federal Israel-Palestine would aim for something like the Federation—regional freedom within a shared political home.

Practical Applications: Your Country's Federal Lessons.
Federal principles shape governance you experience daily. Understanding how federalism works in your context illuminates what it could mean for Israel-Palestine.

If you're American: The U.S. Constitution resolved large state-small state differences through the Connecticut Compromise. The Civil War (1861-1865) tested federal bonds when eleven states seceded, resulting in 620,000 deaths—2% of the population. Yet the federal system survived and strengthened. Today, federalism allows California and Texas, Massachusetts and Mississippi, to pursue vastly different policies while remaining united. California has stringent environmental regulations; Texas has no state income tax. The lesson: federalism accommodates profound differences without requiring uniformity.

If you're European: The EU represents history's most ambitious federal experiment—28 nations (pre-Brexit) pooling sovereignty while maintaining distinct identities. Result: 75+ years of peace among nations that fought two world wars. France and Germany, which fought three wars in 70 years, now have integrated economies and cooperative governance. Despite challenges (democratic deficit, Brexit), the EU transformed European politics from competitive nationalism toward cooperation. For Israel-Palestine: even bitter enemies can cooperate under appropriate federal structures, though design and legitimacy matter immensely.

If you're from post-colonial states: Many nations inherited artificial colonial borders creating multi-ethnic states. Nigeria's federal system (36 states) manages 250+ ethnic groups and two religions. Despite the devastating Biafran War (1967-1970, over a million deaths), Nigerian federalism maintains unity through regional autonomy. South Africa's 1996 Constitution created nine provinces and eleven official languages to accommodate diversity and address apartheid's legacy. These demonstrate that federalism offers practical tools for managing colonial legacies, though implementation requires genuine power-sharing, not symbolic autonomy.

Universal lesson: Federal solutions aren't imported wholesale but adapted to local circumstances. The question isn't whether any federal model is perfect (none are—Canada nearly lost Quebec, Belgium goes months without government, India faces Kashmir insurgency) but whether federal principles—power-sharing, regional autonomy, minority protection—offer better alternatives than continued conflict. Evidence from dozens of federal systems suggests they do. Federalism is pragmatic institutional engineering allowing people with profound differences to share sovereignty without domination. Whether Israel-Palestine achieves this depends on political will and Palestinian deradicalization enabling genuine federal partnership.

Scholarly Frameworks & Debates.
Academic literature reveals sophisticated debates about when and how federalism succeeds in transforming ethnic conflicts into democratic governance. These debates matter because federalism isn't a magic formula but institutional tools requiring specific conditions.

The most prominent debate involves Arend Lijphart versus Donald Horowitz. Lijphart (1977, 2008) argues power-sharing arrangements—federalism, proportional representation, executive coalitions, mutual vetoes—can stabilize divided societies by ensuring all groups participate and possess protections against majoritarianism. Evidence includes Switzerland, Belgium, and post-1998 Northern Ireland.

Horowitz (1985, 2014) contends consociationalism can entrench ethnic divisions rather than transcend them, potentially freezing conflicts. He advocates alternative designs—vote-pooling electoral systems, integrative parties, federalism based on non-ethnic boundaries—creating incentives for cross-ethnic cooperation. This debate matters for Israel: should federal design emphasize ethnic accommodation (separate Jewish-Palestinian regions) or integration mechanisms (mixed regions, electoral systems rewarding moderation)?

A second debate concerns transferability.
Brendan O'Leary (2005) and John McGarry argue appropriate institutional design can adapt federal principles to diverse circumstances, citing Canada to India to Bosnia. Critics like Jack Snyder (2000) warn institutions successful in one context may fail elsewhere, particularly in societies lacking democratic traditions or facing active conflict. Snyder's work suggests introducing federalism prematurely—before conflict resolution and deradicalization—can provide platforms for nationalist mobilization, escalating rather than containing conflict. This directly addresses timing for Israel-Palestine: can federalism be implemented during conflict, or must it await Hamas's defeat and Palestinian deradicalization?

Essential reading: Lijphart's Democracy in Plural Societies (1977); Horowitz's Ethnic Groups in Conflict (1985); McGarry and O'Leary's Politics of Ethnic Conflict Regulation (1993); Watts's Comparing Federal Systems (2008); Stepan's "Federalism and Democracy" (1999); Gagnon and Simeon's Canadian Federalism (2020). These demonstrate federalism for divided societies requires sophisticated understanding of ethnic demography, historical grievances, and implementation sequencing.

Discussions: Case Studies.

These questions facilitate deeper engagement with federal precedents, suitable for classroom discussion, study groups, or individual reflection.

What made Switzerland succeed where Yugoslavia failed? Both were multi-ethnic, multi-religious federations in mountainous regions. Yet Switzerland remains stable while Yugoslavia collapsed into genocidal warfare. Consider: timing (Switzerland's 1291 confederation versus Yugoslavia's artificial WWI/WWII creation); constitutional design (Swiss cantonal autonomy versus Yugoslav republics' Belgrade relationship); external pressures (Swiss neutrality versus Yugoslavia's NATO-Warsaw Pact position); economic development (Swiss prosperity versus Yugoslav disparities); and whether structures were genuinely federal or facades masking Serb dominance. This illuminates that success depends on genuine power-sharing commitment, economic interdependence, and absence of ethnic entrepreneurs mobilizing violence.

How did Germany's Bundesrat prevent Weimar over-centralization? The Weimar Republic (1919-1933) suffered over-centralization enabling Hitler's takeover.

The 1949 Basic Law created the Bundesrat as institutional check: Bundesrat consent required for legislation affecting Länder competencies; Länder governments appoint delegates voting as blocs; two-thirds Bundesrat majority needed for constitutional amendments; subsidiarity principle reserves powers to Länder.

Would similar institutions work for Israel-Palestine?

Could a Federal Council representing regional governments with veto power prevent domination?

Why have Quebec sovereignty referendums failed? Despite persistent nationalism and linguistic grievances, 1980 (59.56% "No") and 1995 (50.58% "No") referendums rejected separation. Consider: economic interdependence (separation costs enormous); federal accommodations (Quebec's enhanced powers, equalization payments); identity complexity (dual Quebecois-Canadian identity); separation uncertainty (currency, borders, debt); generational shifts. Lesson for Israel-Palestine: genuine autonomy with economic integration might diminish separation pressures—or are grievances too deep?

How does India's asymmetric federalism balance unity with diversity? Special provisions give states varying autonomy: Article 371A (Naga customary law protection), Article 371G (Mizoram),

Article 239AA (Delhi special status). Does differential treatment strengthen unity by accommodating differences, or undermine it through resentment? Should Federal Israel adopt asymmetric arrangements—Jerusalem special status, enhanced Gaza-West Bank autonomy?

What role did economic equalization play in reunification and unity? German reunification required $1.3-2 trillion transfers over 30 years. Canada's constitutional equalization ensures comparable services. For Israel-Palestine: should constitution mandate payments from Jewish to Palestinian regions? Can economic interdependence create buy-in, or do conflicts override economics?

Can Belgium's complexity serve as model or warning? Belgium's byzantine structure (three regions, three communities, 541 days without government in 2010-2011) accommodates linguistic divisions that might otherwise cause collapse. Is institutional complexity preserving peace preferable to simplicity perpetuating conflict? Federal design requires tradeoffs between simplicity (understandable, cheaper) and accommodation (captures complexity, prevents domination).

Faith Perspectives.
Federal Protection of Holy Sites and Religious Minorities.
For Christian Zionists—evangelicals supporting Israel as biblical prophecy fulfillment while concerned for Christian sites and communities—federal arrangements offer superior protection compared to purely Jewish or Palestinian control. This perspective deserves consideration because Christian Zionists wield significant Western policy influence, and their concerns illuminate how federal structures address religious pluralism.
Federal structures can guarantee constitutional protection for Christian holy sites: the Church of the Holy Sepulchre (Jesus's crucifixion and resurrection site), Via Dolorosa (path to crucifixion), Church of the Nativity (Bethlehem birthplace).
Under purely Jewish or Palestinian states, Christian communities fear inadequate protection or restrictions—whether from Jewish religious authorities skeptical of Christian claims or Muslim authorities with historical tensions with Christianity.
A federal constitution could establish explicit protections: Article-level guarantees for holy site access, independent authorities with Christian representation, and provisions preventing federal or regional governments from infringing pilgrimage rights, religious property, or worship freedoms.

Minority rights inherent in federal design would ensure Christian communities in Bethlehem (now 20% Christian due to emigration), Nazareth (one-third Christian), and Jerusalem maintain cultural autonomy, religious freedom, and property rights regardless of regional demographics.

India's model proves instructive: separate religious personal law systems—Hindu, Muslim, Christian, Parsi—allow each community to govern marriage, divorce, inheritance according to religious law while federal civil law handles commercial and criminal matters.

Federal Israel could adopt similar structures: Jewish religious courts (Batei Din), Islamic courts (Shari'a), and Christian ecclesiastical courts maintain jurisdiction over personal status for their communities under federal constitutional protections.

This arrangement offers greater security than alternatives. A purely Jewish state might privilege Jewish religious authority; Palestinian state might restrict Christian freedoms, as occurred elsewhere (Egypt's persecuted Copts, Iraq's fled Christians, Syria's suffering Christians).

Federal Israel would constitutionally protect all three Abrahamic faiths, guarantee holy site access, and prevent single-religion domination through power-sharing, judicial review, and minority rights protection. Christian pilgrimage—economically significant for Jerusalem and Bethlehem—would be constitutionally guaranteed, providing economic incentives for protecting Christian interests.

Biblical prophecy considerations: some Christian Zionists interpret Isaiah 19:23-25 ("highway from Egypt to Assyria...Blessed be Egypt my people, Assyria my handiwork, Israel my inheritance") as suggesting eventual cooperation rather than perpetual conflict. Federal arrangements allowing Jewish sovereignty (fulfilling return prophecies) while accommodating Palestinian Muslim-Christian communities through regional autonomy might align with prophetic visions of peaceful coexistence better than zero-sum sovereignty claims.

Chapter 4.
The Foundational Principles of Federal Israel

The Governance Structure Imperative.

The foundational question facing any nascent or reformed state, particularly one grappling with deep-seated historical, ethnic, and political divides, concerns the optimal structure of its governance. For the proposed entity envisioned for Israel and Palestine, the choice between a unitary state, a confederation, or a federal system is not merely an academic exercise; it is a decision that will profoundly shape its trajectory, its capacity for institutional stability, and its ability to foster genuine coexistence and shared prosperity. Each of these models represents a distinct approach to the distribution of power between a central authority and constituent units, with profoundly different implications for self-governance, minority rights, and overall national cohesion. Understanding these differences is paramount in charting a course that can effectively address the complex realities of the region (Elazar, 1987).

Comparative Analysis of Governance Models.
The Unitary State: Centralization and Its Discontents.

A unitary state, at its core, is characterized by a single, supreme central government that holds ultimate authority. Any regional or local administrative divisions exist at the pleasure of this central government and can be created, altered, or abolished by its decree. Powers exercised by these sub-national entities are delegated from the center, and the central government can reclaim them at any time. This model, exemplified by countries like France or the United Kingdom, emphasizes a strong, unified national identity and can be highly efficient in policy implementation and resource allocation when there is broad consensus across the population (Zimmerman, 2008).

However, in contexts marked by significant regional or group differences, a unitary system can be perceived as oppressive or unresponsive to local needs and aspirations. Power becomes concentrated, potentially leading to marginalization of minority groups or regions that feel their distinct identities and interests are not adequately represented or protected. The history of many nations demonstrates that when a unitary state fails to accommodate deep societal cleavages, it can breed resentment, fuel secessionist movements, and ultimately lead to instability or conflict (Deschouwer, 2012). In a territory like Israel and Palestine, where distinct national, cultural, and religious identities are not only present but are also the very bedrock of historical grievances and aspirations, imposing a strictly unitary model would likely exacerbate these tensions rather than resolve them.

The Confederal Model: Autonomy at the Cost of Coherence.

In stark contrast, a confederal system is fundamentally different in its power dynamics. Here, the constituent units, which are typically sovereign states or highly autonomous entities, delegate specific, limited powers to a central body. The central authority in a confederation is subordinate to the member states, and these states retain their sovereignty. Decisions made by the confederal body usually require the unanimous consent of the member states, and each member state retains the right to withdraw from the confederation (Elazar, 1987).

Historically, confederations have been relatively rare and often short-lived, serving as transitional arrangements or weak alliances. Examples include the United States under the Articles of Confederation before the adoption of the Constitution, or the Swiss Confederation in its early stages. The inherent weakness of a confederal system lies in the lack of a strong, overarching authority capable of enforcing decisions uniformly across all member states. This can lead to paralysis in addressing common challenges, such as security, economic policy, or external relations, as the need for consensus among sovereign entities can be difficult to achieve (Rakove, 1996). Moreover, in a volatile region, a confederal structure might perpetuate a sense of division and hinder the development of a shared national identity or common purpose. For a political entity aiming to establish institutional stability and secure future, a confederal model, with its inherent fragmentation of authority and potential for gridlock, might prove insufficient.

Federalism: The Middle Path.

This brings us to the federal system, which offers a compelling middle ground and a potentially more robust framework for addressing the complexities of the Israeli-Palestinian context. A federal state is characterized by a division of powers between a central, national government and constituent regional governments, often referred to as states, provinces, cantons, or Länder. Crucially, both levels of government derive their authority from a constitution, and each level has its own distinct sphere of jurisdiction and powers (Fleiner and Fleiner, 2009).

Unlike in a unitary state, where sub-national powers are delegated and can be revoked, in a federal system, these powers are constitutionally protected. Conversely, unlike in a confederation, where the central body is subordinate to the member states, the federal government in a federal system is supreme within its own defined powers, and the constituent units are not sovereign in the same sense as independent states. This division of powers is typically enshrined in a written constitution and often requires a supermajority or a special amending process to alter, thus providing stability and predictability (Kommers and Miller, 2012).

The genius of federalism, particularly in ethnically or culturally diverse societies, lies in its capacity to accommodate and manage differences without sacrificing national unity. As Madison argued in Federalist No. 10, federalism provides a mechanism for managing faction and diversity within a single polity (Madison, Hamilton, and Jay, 1788). It allows for a degree of self-governance and cultural autonomy at the regional level, enabling constituent units to tailor policies to their specific needs and identities. Simultaneously, it maintains a strong central government responsible for matters of common concern, such as national defense, foreign policy, currency, and interstate commerce, thereby ensuring national cohesion and capacity to act on the international stage.

For the proposed Israeli-Palestinian entity, a federal structure could offer a nuanced solution to the deeply intertwined aspirations for national self-determination, security, and shared governance. It could allow for distinct political entities for Israelis and Palestinians, each with significant autonomy over its internal affairs, including cultural preservation, education, local governance, and aspects of economic development. At the same time, a federal government would be responsible for overarching issues that affect both communities, such as security coordination, infrastructure development that spans across territories, environmental protection, and the management of shared resources like water.

Structuring Federal Units: Models and Implications
The fundamental question of how to structure the constituent units within a federal framework is as critical as the decision to adopt federalism itself. The efficacy of any federal design hinges on the nature of these sub-national components, their powers, and the balance they strike between regional autonomy and national unity. Several established models offer conceptual blueprints, each with distinct advantages and disadvantages that must be carefully

weighed in the context of the deeply intertwined and often conflicting national aspirations and historical experiences of Israelis and Palestinians.

The Canton Model: Swiss Subsidiarity

One prominent model for structuring federal units is the canton, famously exemplified by Switzerland. Swiss cantons are characterized by a high degree of autonomy, possessing significant legislative and executive powers, and even enjoying the right to enact their own constitutions, provided they do not contradict the federal constitution (Linder and Vatter, 2001). This model emphasizes subsidiarity, meaning that powers are retained at the lowest possible level of government. As Fleiner and Fleiner (2009) explain, this subsidiarity principle ensures that decisions are made at the most appropriate level, enhancing democratic participation and local responsiveness.

In the Israeli-Palestinian context, a canton-based system could allow for highly localized governance, potentially enabling distinct administrative units to cater very specifically to the cultural, religious, and social needs of their populations. The Swiss cantons are also known for their significant fiscal autonomy, with the ability to levy their own taxes, which could translate into constituent units having considerable control over their economic development and resource allocation (Dafflon, 2004).

However, the Swiss model also relies on a strong tradition of consensus-building and a relatively homogeneous national identity that, while regionally diverse, shares a common civic culture (Church and Vatter, 2009). Applying this to the Israeli-Palestinian context requires careful consideration of how such deep-seated historical and national divisions would interact within a cantonal structure. The potential for creating units that are too narrowly defined, potentially leading to inter-cantonal disputes over resources or even segregation, would need robust federal mechanisms for conflict resolution and intergovernmental cooperation.

The State Model: American Federalism

The United States model of federal states presents a different paradigm. U.S. states possess significant sovereign powers, although these are explicitly limited by the Supremacy Clause of the U.S. Constitution, which establishes federal law as paramount in cases of conflict (Zimmerman, 2008). States retain powers not delegated to the federal government nor prohibited to them by the Constitution, covering a vast array of policy areas, including education, public health, intra-state commerce, and local law enforcement.

A U.S.-style federal state for Israel and Palestine might allow for larger, more encompassing constituent units, perhaps reflecting broader historical territories or significant demographic concentrations. The advantage here could be greater capacity for the constituent units to manage significant economic and infrastructure projects within their borders and to develop distinct regional identities that are not solely defined by ethnic or religious affiliation. The American model's division of powers between federal and state governments, enshrined in the Tenth Amendment, provides crucial lessons about reservation of powers to constituent units allowing for policy experimentation and local autonomy while maintaining national cohesion (Brandeis's concept in New State Ice Co. v. Liebmann, 1932).

However, the U.S. system has also seen significant debates and litigation regarding the balance of power between federal and state governments. The historical struggle over slavery and civil rights in the U.S., which saw states invoking their rights to maintain discriminatory practices, serves as a stark reminder of the potential for sub-national units to become instruments of oppression if not properly constrained by federal guarantees of fundamental rights (Shapiro, 1981).

The Regional Model: Functional Flexibility
A third approach could involve defining federal units based on distinct regions, not necessarily tied to existing administrative boundaries or historical sovereign claims in the same way as cantons or states, but rather on more pragmatic geographic, demographic, or economic considerations. The advantage of a "regions" model is its flexibility; it allows for the creation of units that are specifically tailored to the unique challenges and opportunities of the territory.

A regional approach could prioritize functional governance and shared economic prosperity over ethno-national self-determination within the constituent units themselves. However, the potential downside is that if these regions are not perceived as having a deep historical or cultural resonance for the populations within them, they might lack the legitimacy necessary for strong regional identity and self-governance.

Population Considerations and Power-Sharing

When considering the specific populations within these potential federal units—Israelis and Palestinians—the implications for representation and power-sharing become paramount. The concept of "interdependence within separation" could be explored through the design of these constituent units. The Great Compromise of 1787, which established equal state representation in the Senate alongside proportional representation in the House, demonstrates how federal structures can balance competing claims to political power (Rakove, 1996). For Israel, this dual representation model could be adapted to ensure that both Jewish and Palestinian communities, as well as other minorities, maintain meaningful political voice regardless of demographic shifts.

A federal system could include a second chamber in the legislature that represents the constituent units, ensuring that even smaller or minority-populated units have a voice. Furthermore, a federal constitution could mandate proportional representation within the constituent units or establish specific quotas for minority representation in regional governments and assemblies, following principles of consociational democracy as demonstrated in Switzerland and Belgium (Linder and Vatter, 2001; Deschouwer, 2012).

Division of Powers: Federal and Regional Competencies

The architecture of any federal state is fundamentally defined by the distribution of powers between the central federal government and its constituent units. This division is not merely an administrative or technical matter; it is the very embodiment of the compromises and aspirations that underpin the federal compact.

Federal Core Competencies.

At the apex of federal authority, certain powers are almost invariably vested in the central government to ensure the state's coherence and its standing on the international stage. Defense and foreign policy are prime examples. The establishment of a unified federal army, under the command of the federal government, would be crucial for national security. This centralization of defense and foreign affairs is essential to avoid fragmented security apparatuses that could become sources of internal conflict or external vulnerability. The Supremacy Clause and judicial review mechanisms established through Marbury v. Madison (1803) offer additional transposable elements for ensuring constitutional compliance while protecting minority rights (Shapiro, 1981).

The Swiss military system, which maintains federal control while incorporating cantonal elements, provides a model for balancing security imperatives with federal principles. Given Israel's security concerns, the Swiss approach of maintaining a strong federal military while allowing cantonal input into defense planning could be adapted (Haltiner and Szvircsev Tresch, 2008).

Economic Federalism

The economic sphere presents a more nuanced challenge for power distribution. The German model of cooperative federalism (Politikverflechtung), analyzed extensively by Scharpf (1988), demonstrates how federal and state governments can work together on policy implementation while maintaining distinct spheres of authority. The federal government could be responsible for establishing a unified market, preventing internal trade barriers, and setting national economic goals. This could include managing a federal reserve bank, overseeing national infrastructure projects of federal significance, and setting broad fiscal policies.

The German model of fiscal equalization (Finanzausgleich) offers sophisticated mechanisms for addressing economic disparities between regions while maintaining fiscal discipline (Rodden, 2003). For Israel, where economic disparities between center and periphery, and between different ethnic communities, pose challenges to social cohesion, such equalization mechanisms could promote economic justice while incentivizing development. The constitutional requirement for equivalent living conditions (gleichwertige Lebensverhältnisse) across the federation provides a normative framework for addressing inequality (Gunlicks, 2003).

However, the constituent units would need substantial autonomy to manage their local economies, promote regional industries, and tailor economic policies to their specific demographic and geographical contexts. This might involve powers over local taxation, zoning laws, the regulation of local businesses, and the development of specific regional economic strategies.

Social Services and Cultural Autonomy

Social welfare and the provision of essential public services often represent a complex interplay between federal and constituent unit responsibilities. While the federal government might set national standards for certain critical areas, such as fundamental rights, public health emergencies, or perhaps a baseline for social security and pensions, the day-to-day administration and often the primary funding of services like education, healthcare, and social services would likely reside with the constituent units.

The Canadian Charter of Rights and Freedoms, with its explicit protection of minority language education rights, provides a model for ensuring cultural reproduction of minority communities (Mackey, 2002). Educational curricula, while adhering to national standards on core subjects and democratic values, could be developed and administered at the regional level, allowing for cultural and linguistic considerations to be incorporated. This would be particularly important for addressing the concerns of Palestinian citizens, who seek recognition as a national minority with collective rights, similar to the Quebec model of distinct society status (Gagnon and Iacovino, 2007).

Justice and Legal Systems.
The realm of justice and law enforcement requires careful consideration. A federal judiciary, with a supreme court at its apex, would be essential to interpret federal law and the constitution, and to resolve disputes between constituent units or between a unit and the federal government. The German Basic Law's emphasis on human dignity and inviolable rights, combined with federal structures, creates multiple layers of rights protection (Kommers and Miller, 2012).

However, the administration of criminal justice and the majority of civil law, along with the operational control of police forces, would likely be decentralized. Constituent units could establish their own court systems, police departments, and correctional facilities, provided they operate within the framework of federal constitutional guarantees for individual rights and due process.

Protecting Minority Rights: Constitutional Mechanisms
Without robust and demonstrable protections for all constituent populations, any federal arrangement risks becoming a mere facade, failing to secure the trust and allegiance of all its citizens. The historical record of federal states globally offers a rich tapestry of experiences, both cautionary and exemplary, in this crucial area.

Institutional Representation.
One of the most fundamental avenues for protecting minority rights within a federal system is through the design of its representative institutions. The principle of guaranteed representation, often embedded in constitutional frameworks, ensures that minority groups have a voice in the federal legislature and executive branches. As Linder and Vatter (2001) demonstrate, Swiss federalism combines territorial federalism with consociational elements, creating stability through power-sharing rather than majoritarianism.

The Swiss Federal Council's collegial executive system, where seven members from different parties and regions share executive power, offers a compelling alternative to winner-take-all politics (Church and Vatter, 2009). This model could be transposed to ensure permanent representation of major Israeli communities in executive decision-making, reducing the zero-sum nature of political competition. The requirement for double majorities in constitutional referenda—approval by both a majority of citizens and a majority of cantons—provides additional protection for minority interests (Kriesi and Trechsel, 2008).

Constitutional Safeguards and Judicial Review.
Constitutional safeguards represent the bedrock of minority rights protection in any federal state. Entrenching rights in a federal constitution provides a higher degree of security than simple legislative protections. The Belgian arrangement offers instructive mechanisms: the use of constitutional "alarm bells" that allow linguistic groups to temporarily halt legislation they perceive as threatening provides a mechanism for minority protection without permanent vetoes (Peeters, 2007). The requirement for special majorities and cross-community support for constitutional changes ensures that no single group can unilaterally alter fundamental arrangements (Reuchamps and Verniers, 2010).

The judiciary plays an indispensable role in enforcing these constitutional safeguards. The Canadian Supreme Court's jurisprudence on language rights demonstrates how an active judiciary can uphold minority protections (Russell, 2007). A strong, independent federal judiciary, empowered to review legislation and administrative actions for compliance with the constitution, is essential.

Cultural Autonomy and Linguistic Rights.
Beyond political representation, the concept of cultural autonomy within a federal framework is paramount for the preservation of distinct national identities. Belgium's distinction between territorial regions and cultural communities could be adapted to address both territorial and non-territorial aspects of Israeli diversity (Swenden and Jans, 2006). The complex Belgian arrangement of overlapping jurisdictions demonstrates how federal systems can accommodate multiple, cross-cutting identities.

For Israel, where religious, ethnic, and geographic identities intersect in complex ways, such institutional complexity might be necessary to ensure all groups feel represented. Switzerland's recognition of four national languages and the principle of territorial linguistic sovereignty could be adapted to protect Hebrew and Arabic as official languages while allowing local linguistic autonomy (Kriesi and Trechsel, 2008).

Lessons from International Experience.
The success of federalism in protecting minorities is not uniform across cases. Switzerland's successful management of linguistic and religious diversity within a small geographic space provides particularly relevant lessons (Linder and Vatter, 2001). Belgium's transformation from a unitary to a federal state in response to linguistic conflict provides perhaps the most directly relevant model, representing a "living apart together" approach that maintains unity while allowing communities substantial autonomy (Deschouwer, 2012).

However, cautionary lessons abound. The Belgian experience demonstrates that the multiplication of governmental levels can create coordination problems and democratic deficits (Hooghe, 2004). The German experience with reunification offers lessons for managing integration of previously separated territories, demonstrating the need for careful balance between rapid integration and respect for regional differences (Jeffery, 1999). Canada's asymmetric federalism, which grants Quebec special status to protect its distinct society, offers important lessons for accommodating national minorities within federal structures (Gagnon and Iacovino, 2007).

Federal Capital and National Institutions.
The question of a federal capital is often one of the most politically charged issues in the formation of a federal state. It represents the

locus of federal power, the seat of government, and a focal point for national life. Several models could be considered, each with its own set of advantages and disadvantages.

Capital City Options.
One possibility is the establishment of a new, purpose-built capital city, designed from its inception to embody the federal character of the state. Such a city could be located in neutral territory, or in a region not historically or predominantly associated with either national group, thereby minimizing the perception of favoritism. However, the creation of an entirely new capital would present considerable logistical and financial challenges, and might be perceived by some as a deliberate erasure of existing historical and cultural centers.

Alternatively, a shared capital arrangement could be explored. Jerusalem, due to its profound religious and historical significance for both Israelis and Palestinians, presents itself as a natural, albeit immensely challenging, candidate for a federal capital. The Brussels model, with its bilingual status and special governance arrangements, offers a potential template (Wouters and De Smet, 2015). If Jerusalem were to serve as the capital, a carefully negotiated arrangement would be essential, perhaps designating West Jerusalem as the seat of Israeli federal institutions and East Jerusalem as the seat of Palestinian federal institutions, with a jointly administered federal district at the core.

The question of Jerusalem requires special attention, as no existing federal model perfectly addresses the challenge of a disputed capital city claimed by two peoples. However, combined with the Swiss canton model of territorial linguistic sovereignty and the American federal district concept, a unique solution could be crafted that respects both communities' connections to the city.

Legislative Institutions.
In the legislative sphere, a bicameral federal parliament is a common feature of federal systems and would be particularly beneficial in this context. One chamber, the lower house, could be based on proportional representation of the overall population of the federal state, ensuring that representation is broadly reflective of demographic distribution. The German Bundesrat, where state governments directly participate in federal legislation, provides a mechanism for regional input into national policy-making that could be adapted (Leonardy, 1999).

A second chamber, such as a senate or council of national representatives, could be established to provide equal or near-equal representation to each of the primary national constituent groups. This would give each national community significant influence over federal legislation, particularly on matters deemed to be of existential importance to their national identity or interests. Such arrangements create multiple arenas for political participation and protect minority interests through institutional design rather than demographic dominance (Elazar, 1987).

Executive Structure.
The executive branch also requires careful structuring to ensure inclusivity. A collegial executive, similar to the Swiss Federal Council, could ensure that key portfolios are equitably distributed between representatives of the Israeli and Palestinian communities. Alternatively, if a single head of state or government is elected, constitutional provisions could mandate the appointment of a deputy or significant number of ministers from the other national group, ensuring their presence and influence in the highest levels of decision-making.

Judicial Independence and Composition.
The appointment of judges to the federal supreme court and other high courts should ideally draw from both national communities, ensuring a diversity of perspectives on the bench. This could be achieved through a judicial appointments commission that includes representatives from both Israeli and Palestinian legal communities, or through constitutional provisions that mandate a certain number of judges from each group. The independence of the judiciary is paramount, but its composition should also signal a commitment to fairness and representation for all citizens.

Implementation Challenges and Adaptive Strategies
Implementing federal solutions in Israel would require careful adaptation to local conditions. The security imperatives that dominate Israeli politics would necessitate maintaining strong federal control over defense and foreign policy, similar to the American and Swiss models. However, internal security arrangements might benefit from the German model of shared federal-state responsibility, allowing local communities to address their specific security concerns while maintaining overall coordination.

The economic integration necessary for a small country like Israel suggests that the German model of cooperative federalism might be more appropriate than the American model of dual federalism. Shared responsibility for economic development, with strong equalization mechanisms, could address disparities while maintaining economic efficiency. The Swiss model of fiscal federalism, with its emphasis on both solidarity and competition, provides additional insights for balancing these objectives (Dafflon, 2004).

Cultural and educational autonomy, following the Belgian and Canadian models, would allow different communities to maintain their distinct identities while participating in a shared political framework. The Canadian approach to indigenous self-government, though imperfect, offers insights for incorporating indigenous populations into federal structures (Papillon, 2012). For Israel, where Bedouin and Druze communities have distinct relationships with the state, such differentiated approaches to self-government could be relevant.

The Canadian experience with managing secessionist pressures through federal accommodation also provides valuable lessons. As Young (1999) demonstrates, federal flexibility and willingness to negotiate can defuse separatist movements. The Clarity Act's establishment of clear rules for potential secession provides legal certainty while making unilateral separation difficult, a balance that might be relevant for managing extremist pressures.

Synthesis & Conclusion.
Drawing from these five federal systems—the United States, Switzerland, Germany, Belgium, and Canada—several key elements emerge as potentially transposable to a Federal State of Israel. The American model offers principles of dual sovereignty and judicial review mechanisms for constitutional protection. Switzerland provides consociational elements of power-sharing and the principle of subsidiarity. Germany offers cooperative federalism and sophisticated fiscal equalization mechanisms. Belgium demonstrates complex but functional accommodation of linguistic communities, particularly through special status arrangements for disputed territories. Canada provides frameworks for asymmetric federalism and constitutional protection of minority cultural rights.

The key to successful transposition lies not in wholesale adoption of any single model, but in creative synthesis that addresses

Israel's specific challenges. Security concerns require strong federal institutions, while demographic anxieties necessitate robust minority protections. Economic integration must be balanced with regional autonomy, and cultural diversity must be accommodated within a unified political framework. The federal models examined here provide a rich repertoire of institutional mechanisms for achieving these balances.

Ultimately, the success of federal solutions depends on political will and commitment to institutional frameworks. As the experiences of all five countries demonstrate, federalism is not a static institutional arrangement but an ongoing process of negotiation and adaptation. For Israel, embarking on a federal path would require commitment to power-sharing, respect for diversity, and faith in democratic institutions. The historical precedents suggest that such commitments, when institutionalized through federal structures, can transform conflicts into manageable political differences and create frameworks for lasting institutional, political, economic, and social stability.

The adaptation of these federal models to the Israeli context would require extensive consultation, negotiation, and experimentation. However, the successful experiences of other deeply divided societies suggest that federal solutions, properly designed and implemented, can provide the institutional framework necessary for managing diversity, protecting minorities, ensuring security, and promoting prosperity. The challenge lies in crafting arrangements that are both principled enough to provide long-term stability and flexible enough to adapt to changing circumstances.

Chapter 4.
Addendum.

Key Understandings.
Understanding the Federal Constitutional Architecture.
For readers unfamiliar with constitutional terminology, the following concepts form the backbone of any federal system. These principles are essential tools for managing diversity and protecting rights in complex societies.

Constitution: The supreme law establishing how government works, defines its powers, and protects citizen rights. Unlike ordinary laws changeable by simple votes, constitutions require extraordinary consensus—supermajorities, referenda, or both—to amend. This "constitutional hardness" prevents temporary majorities from dismantling protections for minorities. The U.S. requirement for two-thirds of Congress plus three-fourths of states exemplifies this rigidity.

Bill of Rights: Fundamental freedoms government cannot violate—speech, religion, assembly, due process, equal protection. The first ten U.S. amendments serve this purpose. In federal states, bills of rights protect against both federal and regional overreach. For Federal Israel, a robust bill of rights would guarantee protections for all citizens regardless of ethnicity, religion, or residence.

Separation of Powers: Divides governmental authority among legislative (lawmaking), executive (enforcement), and judicial (interpretation) branches, preventing dangerous power concentration. Madison's insight—"ambition must counteract ambition"—recognizes that institutional competition protects liberty better than virtuous leaders. Federal systems add vertical separation between national and regional governments.

Judicial Review: Courts' power to strike down unconstitutional laws, established in the U.S. through *Marbury v. Madison* (1803), is crucial for minority protection. Independent judiciaries defend constitutional rights even when majorities favor discriminatory legislation. Switzerland's Federal Supreme Court, Germany's Constitutional Court, and Canada's Supreme Court ensure majoritarian politics cannot trample minority rights.

Minority Veto: Some federal systems grant minorities formal power to block legislation threatening vital interests. Belgium's "alarm bell" lets linguistic communities temporarily halt threatening bills. Switzerland's double-majority requirement—approval by both population and majority of cantons—ensures geographically concentrated minorities cannot be outvoted, transforming conflicts into negotiations.

Enumerated Powers: Powers explicitly granted to federal government by constitution. The U.S. Article I, Section 8 lists federal powers—regulate interstate commerce, declare war, coin money. This enumeration means federal government possesses only specified authorities, not general governance power.

Reserved Powers: Powers belonging to constituent units unless explicitly denied. The U.S. Tenth Amendment: "powers not delegated to the United States...are reserved to the States." This ensures federal arrangements preserve regional autonomy, allowing diverse communities self-governance in local matters while participating in shared national framework.

Practical Applications. Constitutional Rights for All.

Federal constitutions are shields protecting every citizen's fundamental rights. Understanding how constitutional design affects daily life explains why everyone, regardless of background, has stakes in getting architecture right.

Universal Protection Through Constitutional Design.

Federal constitutions protect minorities everywhere. The U.S. Fourteenth Amendment's Equal Protection Clause has protected African Americans, women, religious minorities, LGBTQ individuals, and others from discriminatory laws. The principle—government must treat similarly situated people equally—transcends particular group interests. When courts strike down discrimination against one minority, they strengthen protections for all.

In Federal Israel, constitutional protections benefit all citizens—Jewish, Palestinian, Christian, Druze, secular, and religious minorities. Freedom of conscience protects both the Orthodox Jew observing Shabbat and the secular Palestinian choosing not to fast during Ramadan. Property rights protect the Jewish farmer in the Galilee and the Palestinian businessman in East Jerusalem. Due process shields both Israeli security officials and Palestinian activists facing charges.

Why Non-Jews Should Care.

Robust constitutional protection is non-zero-sum investment benefiting everyone:

Legal certainty: Clear constitutional frameworks reduce arbitrary government action. Whether Jewish, Christian, Muslim, Druze, or secular, you benefit from knowing governmental limits. Entrepreneurs invest confidently when property rights are secure. Families plan futures when legal frameworks are stable.

Protection against shifting majorities: Today's majority may become tomorrow's minority. Constitutional protections prevent temporary majorities from oppressing out-of-favor groups. If your group is influential, constitutional constraints limit what opponents could do if they gained power. If your group lacks influence, constitutional rights provide recourse beyond majoritarian politics.

Economic development: Strong constitutional governance correlates with economic growth. Investors seek predictable legal environments. Federal systems with clear power division and independent judiciaries attract investment, creating opportunities for all.

Global Human Rights Standards.

Modern federal constitutions incorporate international human rights standards. Canada's Charter references universal declaration principles. Germany's Basic Law begins with human dignity as inviolable. South Africa's Constitution enshrines economic and social rights alongside civil liberties.

Federal Israel could incorporate International Covenant on Civil and Political Rights protections, UN Minority Rights standards, and European Convention on Human Rights principles, grounding domestic law in globally recognized standards.

These standards protect rights crucial for all: freedom of movement, access to holy sites, non-discrimination, language rights, cultural expression. They apply to everyone—the Jewish immigrant from Ethiopia, the Palestinian citizen, the Christian pilgrim, the Muslim worshipper, the secular artist.

Scholarly Frameworks.

For those seeking deeper understanding, the following framework provides entry points into comparative constitutional scholarship.

Essential Constitutional Law Concepts

Asymmetric federalism—different constituent units receive different powers. Quebec in Canada, Scotland in the UK, and Spain's autonomous regions show how federalism accommodates national minorities without full separation. Could this address Israeli-Palestinian asymmetries?

Consociational democracy—Arend Lijphart's power-sharing framework through executive power-sharing, group autonomy, proportional representation, and minority veto. Belgium, Switzerland, and Lebanon employ these. Can they function under security threats without elite cooperation?

Fiscal federalism—how federal systems allocate taxing authority and manage transfers between regions. **Germany's *Finanzausgleich*** and Switzerland's mechanisms balance autonomy with solidarity. How could this address economic disparities while incentivizing development?

Constitutional identity—how constitutions embody collective values. Germany's "eternity clause," France's *laïcité*, and Israel's Jewish and democratic character reflect this. How can federal constitutions acknowledge distinct national identities while establishing shared citizenship?

Resources and Questions

The Constitute Project (constituteproject.org) provides searchable constitutional databases. The Forum of Federations (forumfed.org) offers case studies. Journals like *Publius*, *International Journal of Constitutional Law*, and *Nations and Nationalism* provide analysis.

When interviewing experts: "Does German cooperative federalism or American dual federalism better suit deeply divided societies?" "Can Belgium's linguistic veto mechanisms work where security complicates trust?" "Switzerland maintained federalism for 170+ years despite diversity. Could its mechanisms function at larger scale or in less prosperous circumstances?"

The Breakdown.

The Rules of the Game.

Federal constitutions create rules allowing teams who don't always trust each other to play together—rules fair to both, protecting outnumbered players, letting the game function during disagreements.

What Makes Government "Federal"?

Think of school rules: school-wide rules (no running in hallways) and classroom rules (when to sharpen pencils). The principal handles school-wide issues; teachers manage classrooms. Federal government works similarly—national government handles big issues (defense, currency, trade), while regional governments manage local concerns (schools, police, parks). This division is protective. If one level makes bad decisions, the other can check it.

How Federal Israel Would Decide.

Local: Town councils decide about parks, schools, neighborhood rules. Communities run their own towns. A Palestinian town celebrates its holidays and teaches in Arabic; a Jewish town observes Shabbat and teaches in Hebrew.

Regional: Larger areas (like U.S. states or Swiss cantons) handle regional roads, hospitals, economic development with real constitutional power.

Federal: National government handles defense, currency, foreign relations, shared resources like water. Both Israelis and Palestinians participate in common decisions.

Special Protections

Constitution as Rule Book: Written rules very hard to change protect everyone. Constitutions require super-majorities to alter, preventing today's majority from mistreating minorities.

Courts as Referees: Independent judges interpret rules. If governments break constitutional rules—discriminating based on religion—courts declare laws invalid.

Multiple Vote Requirements: Need both most people AND most regions to agree on big changes. Even if one group has more people, they can't overrule regions where minorities live.

Guaranteed Representation: Federal government includes representatives from all groups.

These ensure your community runs its own schools and celebrates holidays; nobody takes your home because of who you are; you have say in national decisions; if mistreated, you can appeal to courts; future governments can't easily remove protections. Well-designed federal constitutions let different groups live together, govern themselves in many ways, but cooperate on shared challenges.

Faith Perspectives.

Religious communities have vital interests in federal constitutional design, particularly regarding holy sites, worship freedom, and religious practice preservation.

Constitutional Protection of Religious Sites.

Dual Protection: Both federal and regional constitutions can enshrine religious site protection. Germany's Basic Law protects religious freedom federally, while Länder constitutions add protections. This creates multiple legal barriers against desecration or restriction.

Specialized Governance: Jerusalem, sacred to Judaism, Christianity, and Islam, could employ specialized arrangements— federal protection of access rights, regional administration by respective communities, international guarantees for sensitive sites.

Constitutional Access: Federal Israel could guarantee all citizens access to holy sites regardless of residence. A Jewish citizen in a Palestinian region retains right to visit the Western Wall; a Christian in a Jewish area maintains access to the Church of the Holy Sepulchre; a Muslim anywhere has protected access to Al-Aqsa Mosque.

Protecting All Faith Communities.

Christians: The Ottoman Status Quo governing Christian holy sites could receive constitutional recognition, ensuring inter-denominational arrangements continue. Constitutional provisions could guarantee Christian representation in assemblies and simplified pilgrimage access.

Muslims: Federal Israel could allow Palestinian regions to observe Friday-Saturday weekends while Jewish regions observe Saturday-Sunday, with federal institutions respecting both. Constitutional protection of waqf (Islamic endowment) properties prevents seizures. Federal systems can accommodate religious legal systems for personal status matters, with civil courts providing secular alternatives.

Jews: Regional autonomy allows Jewish-majority areas to restrict Saturday commerce and maintain kashrut standards. Constitutional protection prevents federal mandates overriding regional Sabbath observance. Public schools could offer Jewish, Muslim, Christian, and secular ethics instruction, with parents choosing curriculum.

Inter-Religious Council

Federal Israel could establish an Inter-Religious Council with Jewish, Muslim, and Christian representatives, possessing authority to review legislation affecting religious freedom, holy sites, or religious interests. This provides religious communities institutional voice beyond electoral politics and creates forums for dialogue.

Faith and Federal Identity.

Federal constitutions navigate tensions between secular governance and religious identity. Germany's Basic Law invokes "responsibility before God and man"; Ireland's Constitution acknowledges the Trinity—showing how federal democracies recognize religious heritage while maintaining pluralism. Federal Israel could acknowledge the land's sacredness to multiple faiths while ensuring government protects all communities equally.

The constitutional framework wouldn't resolve theological disputes but would establish mechanisms ensuring all communities can practice faiths, maintain holy sites, educate children in traditions, and participate in governance. This approach—protecting religious freedom absolutely while keeping theology outside political authority—enables diverse societies to maintain both religious vitality and civic peace.

Chapter 5
The Federal State of Israel:
The Only Viable Path in a Post-October 7th.

Self-Determination Through Federal Architecture.
The aspiration for self-determination constitutes a fundamental human and political imperative, recognized as a cornerstone of international law since the adoption of the United Nations Charter in 1945 (Cassese, 1995; Crawford, 2006). Within a federal framework, Palestinian self-determination depends fundamentally upon constitutional structure and substantive powers devolved to constituent units (Elazar, 1987; Watts, 2008).

The events of October 7, 2023, and the subsequent Gaza War have irrevocably transformed the Israeli-Palestinian conflict's political landscape (Shlaim, 2024; Ben-Ami, 2024). The Hamas terrorist attacks demonstrated beyond doubt the existential threat posed by militant Palestinian nationalism when wedded to maximalist objectives and rejectionist ideologies (Makovsky & Koplow, 2024; Schanzer, 2024). The subsequent Israeli campaign to dismantle Hamas's governance and military infrastructure, while creating humanitarian suffering, has also created previously unimaginable conditions: the potential complete elimination of Hamas as a governing entity and opportunity for comprehensive societal deradicalization (International Crisis Group, 2024).

This chapter proceeds from a critical premise: federalism can only be implemented successfully after foundational conditions are met. First, Hamas and terrorist organizations dedicated to Israel's destruction must be completely eliminated as political and military forces (Ganor, 2024). Second, Palestinian society must undergo comprehensive deradicalization, abandoning rejectionist narratives characterizing Palestinian nationalism since 1948 (Bar-Tal & Halperin, 2011). Third, Palestinian Arabs in Gaza and Judea & Samaria must demonstrate through credible political processes that they no longer seek a Palestinian state as an alternative to Israel, but rather aspire to full citizenship and autonomous self-governance within a Federal State of Israel (Eger, 2025a). Only under these conditions does federalism become viable.

Federalism emerges as the singular constitutional architecture capable of reconciling demands that have paralyzed peace negotiations: Israeli security imperatives, Palestinian self-determination, demographic realities of intermingled populations, and the geopolitical impossibility of territorial partition (McGarry & O'Leary, 2009; Lustick, 2019).

As Eger (2025a) argues, "The Federal State of Israel is the only possible One-State-Solution" that avoids either perpetual occupation or the security catastrophe that a sovereign Palestinian state would represent post-October 7th. The two-state solution, already moribund before October 7th (Thrall, 2017), has been rendered absolutely impossible by that day's events.

Rather than constituting a monolithic minority within a centralized state—a model consistently failing to accommodate deep national divisions (Lijphart, 1977; Horowitz, 1985)—deradicalized Palestinians could achieve substantive autonomy through constitutionally entrenched federal regions (Anderson, 2008; Stepan, 1999). These regions would transcend administrative subdivisions, representing tangible self-governance enabling policy formulation reflecting Palestinian societal priorities, cultural values, and developmental objectives (Kymlicka, 1995).

The fundamental difference from previous failed frameworks lies in prerequisite transformation: this is not a federal solution imposed upon hostile populations viewing it as a step toward eventual separate statehood, but rather a framework embraced by populations concluding through experience that their interests are best served through citizenship in a powerful, prosperous federal Israel (Kuperwasser, 2024). The October 7th catastrophe has created conditions—tragic though they are—for fundamental reconsideration of Palestinian political objectives. Once deradicalization occurs and populations are freed from intellectual bondage of Hamas, Palestinian Islamic Jihad, and rejectionist Fatah elements, federalism becomes not just viable but inevitable.

Section I: Constitutional Powers of Palestinian Federal Regions.
Palestinian regions as federal states would possess constitutional authority to enact laws governing extensive domestic policy domains: education, healthcare, urban planning, infrastructure development, cultural preservation, environmental protection, and justice administration within territorial boundaries (Elazar, 1994; Watts, 2008). This legislative authority must be constitutionally defined with precision, ensuring operational freedom within broader

federal framework while providing ample space for autonomous self-governance (Hueglin & Fenna, 2006).

The German Länder system provides instructive precedent, wherein regional governments exercise exclusive legislative competence in cultural affairs, education, and policing (Gunlicks, 2003). Similarly, Swiss cantonal systems demonstrate how linguistic and cultural minorities exercise substantial autonomy, with cantons possessing residual powers—all powers not explicitly granted to federal government remain with cantons (Linder, 2010). The Indian asymmetrical federal model, analyzed by Eger (2025b) as a potential Israeli template, demonstrates how different constituent units can possess different powers based on unique circumstances (Austin, 1999; Stepan et al., 2010).

For Palestinian federal states, legislative autonomy would enable establishment of educational curricula fostering Palestinian history, language, and collective identity while adhering to federal standards ensuring academic quality (Abu-Saad, 2006). In healthcare, regional authorities could implement public health initiatives addressing specific health challenges and cultural norms (Giacaman et al., 2009). This devolution constitutes far more than administrative decentralization; it represents fundamental empowerment of a national group to shape its own destiny (Miller, 2000).

Executive Authority.
Palestinian federal regions require robust executive institutions capable of implementing regional legislation, administering public services, managing regional finances, and representing regional interests within the federal system (Filippov et al., 2004). The executive structure would feature a regional governor or president, directly elected by the populace, bearing primary responsibility for administering regional laws and policies (Elazar, 1987). Direct election enhances democratic accountability and provides leaders with independent political legitimacy (Thorlakson, 2005).

The executive branch would encompass regional ministries managing specific areas: education, health, public works, internal security, cultural affairs, religious affairs, and economic development (Watts, 1999). The capacity to appoint and manage their own civil service from highest administrative levels to local officials constitutes a cornerstone of self-determination (Peters, 2001), enabling development of public institutions responsive to local populations and operating in the language and cultural idiom of populations they serve (Suleiman, 2003).

However, executive authority must be exercised within constitutional constraints and subject to multiple accountability forms (Bovens, 2007). Regional executives would be accountable to regional legislatures through parliamentary questions, investigative committees, and impeachment processes (Strøm, 2000), and to regional electorates through regular elections. Additionally, regional executives would be subject to judicial oversight, with courts reviewing administrative actions for legality and constitutional compliance (Shapiro & Stone Sweet, 2002).

Judicial Independence.
Regional courts would adjudicate civil and criminal matters arising under regional law, resolving disputes between private parties, reviewing administrative actions, and protecting fundamental rights enshrined in Federal and regional constitutions (Shapiro, 1981). Judicial independence requires: merit-based appointment through judicial commissions rather than purely political selection (Malleson & Russell, 2006); security of tenure ensuring judges cannot be removed except through impeachment (Burbank & Friedman, 2002); and compensation that cannot be diminished during tenure (Choi et al., 2009).

Palestinian federal regions would establish court systems featuring hierarchical structure: trial courts of general jurisdiction; intermediate appellate courts; and a regional supreme court as court of last resort for regional law matters (Tarr, 1999). The Federal Supreme Court would possess ultimate authority to interpret the Federal Constitution and resolve disputes between governments, while regional supreme courts would have final word on matters purely of regional law (Kommers, 1997).

This system permits development of legal traditions sensitive to specific social and cultural contexts of Palestinian populations (Shapiro, 1981). Regional courts could apply Islamic law (Shari'a) in personal status matters for Muslims and canon law for Christians, continuing the millet system's legacy adapted to federal structures (An-Na'im, 2008). However, all courts must protect fundamental human rights enshrined in the Federal Constitution (Alston, 2017).

Critically, these constitutional powers can only function effectively in post-conflict, post-deradicalization environments. If Palestinian federal regions retained populations committed to Israel's destruction, constitutional autonomy would become a Trojan horse enabling use of regional institutions to undermine the federal state from within (Kuperwasser & Lipner, 2023). The prerequisite transformation of Palestinian political culture—from rejectionism to federalism—is absolutely essential (Porat & Shamir, 2024).

Section II: Economic Development and Cultural Autonomy
Economic Development and Fiscal Autonomy.
Palestinian federal regions' capacity to enact economic policies, manage budgets, and strategically invest in development represents fundamental departure from scenarios where economic decision-making is concentrated in central authorities potentially unresponsive to Palestinian needs (Farsakh, 2002). Regional economic control can translate into tangible improvements in living standards, job creation, and overall well-being (World Bank, 2007).

Fiscal federalism theory emphasizes that decentralized fiscal decision-making enhances economic efficiency by enabling regional governments to tailor policies to local conditions, preferences, and resources (Oates, 1999). Palestinian regions could gain direct control over natural and financial resources within their territories through constitutional allocation of rights to resources such as water, land, and potential mineral deposits (Homer-Dixon, 1999). Federal systems often incorporate fiscal equalization mechanisms whereby wealthier units contribute to federal funds supporting less affluent regions (Boadway & Shah, 2007).

Beyond direct resource control, federalism catalyzes broader development through shared infrastructure and investment initiatives (Qian & Weingast, 1997). A unified federal state encompassing Palestinian and Israeli units would possess capacity to undertake large-scale infrastructure projects: transportation networks, coordinated energy grids, water management systems, and telecommunications infrastructure (World Bank, 2007). Economic synergies generated by shared investments create more integrated and competitive regional economies (Keohane & Nye, 2001).

Legislative autonomy empowers Palestinian regions to create tailored economic policies attracting investment and promoting local industries: special economic zones offering tax incentives, streamlined regulatory processes, and sector-specific strategies identifying comparative advantages (Ge, 1999; Farole & Akinci, 2011). The power to levy taxes, manage budgets, and allocate public funds according to regional priorities is essential for self-determined economic growth (Tanzi, 1996).

Cultural and Religious Autonomy.
Palestinian regions would possess constitutional authority to safeguard and promote unique cultural expressions, linguistic heritage, and religious practices (Kymlicka, 1995; Taylor, 1994). Central to this autonomy is protection of Arabic language, the linguistic bedrock of Palestinian identity. Palestinian units could establish Arabic as primary language of administration, education, and public life within their territories (Suleiman, 2004; Spolsky & Shohamy, 1999).

Federal educational policies could encourage studying Palestinian literature, history, and folklore, integrating these subjects into curricula at all levels, fostering pride and continuity with the past (Abu-Saad, 2006). Beyond formal education, regional governments could champion Arabic through cultural centers, libraries, and public festivals celebrating linguistic heritage (Mar-Molinero & Stevenson, 2006).

Preservation of Palestinian traditions and customs—social etiquette, culinary practices, artistic expressions, celebratory rituals—would be supported through federal constituent units establishing policies and providing funding for cultural institutions such as museums, heritage centers, and artisan cooperatives (Kirshenblatt-Gimblett, 1998). These bodies would document, preserve, and exhibit Palestinian crafts, music, dance, and oral histories.

Religious autonomy proves equally vital (Durham & Scharffs, 2011). Within designated federal regions, Palestinian authorities could possess power to regulate matters pertaining to religious endowments (waqf), personal status law (governing marriage, divorce, inheritance), and administration of religious sites (Arzt, 1996; Layish, 2004). This would allow application of Islamic Sharia law in personal status matters for Muslims and ecclesiastical laws for Christians, respecting religious communities' rights to govern internal affairs according to own doctrines (An-Na'im, 1996).

However, cultural and religious autonomy must operate within constitutional boundaries protecting individual rights (Shachar, 2001). The Federal Constitution would enshrine guarantees for freedom of religion, ensuring all individuals possess rights to practice faith freely without coercion or discrimination (Marshall & Shea, 2011). The federal government's role would ensure regional practices don't infringe upon fundamental rights or contravene universal human rights principles (Donnelly, 2013).

Yet cultural and religious autonomy can only flourish within populations committed to coexistence rather than supremacism (Raz, 1994). If Palestinian regions utilized cultural autonomy to indoctrinate populations with hatred of Jews, glorify martyrdom, or promote jihadist ideologies, cultural autonomy would become a weapon against the federation (Bar-Tal & Teichman, 2005). This underscores that cultural and religious autonomy within federalism presumes Palestinian society's transformation from cultures of violence and rejectionism to cultures of coexistence and mutual respect (Kelman, 2007).

Section III: Post-October 7th Implementation Framework.
The October 7th massacre has fundamentally altered parameters within which any Israeli-Palestinian solution must be conceived. The unprecedented brutality demonstrated conclusively that Palestinian nationalism, when animated by Islamist ideology and rejectionist principles, poses an existential threat to Jewish life (Schanzer, 2024; Ganor, 2024). Post-October 7th reality admits no romanticism: federalism can only be implemented after terrorist organizations have been completely eliminated and Palestinian society has undergone comprehensive deradicalization (Kuperwasser, 2024).

Phase One: Complete Military Victory & Terrorist Elimination (2024-2026).
The absolute prerequisite is complete military defeat and elimination of Hamas, Palestinian Islamic Jihad, and all terrorist organizations operating in Gaza and potentially in Judea & Samaria (Ganor, 2024; Inbar, 2024). This means: destruction of all tunnel networks used for military purposes; neutralization or capture of all terrorist operatives, particularly leadership; dismantling of weapons manufacturing facilities; seizure of financial assets and disruption of funding networks, including Iranian support (Levitt & Jacobson, 2008); removal from power of all individuals affiliated with terrorist

organizations; and closure of institutions propagating jihadist ideology (IMPACT-SE, 2021).

The IDF's operations in Gaza following October 7th have made substantial progress toward these objectives. However, complete eradication requires sustained military pressure and willingness to maintain security control for extended periods despite international pressure (Ben-Israel, 2024). Historical analogies to denazification in Germany suggest the magnitude and duration of effort required (Biddiscombe, 2006).

Phase Two: Transitional Administration and Comprehensive Deradicalization (2026-2031)
Following terrorist organizations' military defeat, a transitional administration would assume governance of Palestinian territories (Feldman & Martinez, 2009; Chesterman, 2004). This administration, combining Israeli governance with potential international involvement under Israeli security control, would bear responsibility for providing basic services, maintaining order, and—most critically—initiating comprehensive deradicalization (Stern & Berger, 2015). Comprehensive deradicalization must address multiple dimensions simultaneously (Horgan & Braddock, 2010):

Educational Reform: Complete overhaul of curricula removing all content glorifying terrorism, martyrdom, or rejectionism, and demonizing Jews (IMPACT-SE, 2021). This requires fundamentally reconceptualizing education's purpose—from indoctrination in nationalist mythology to genuine education fostering critical thinking, coexistence, and democratic values.

Religious Reform: Transformation of religious institutions—mosques, Islamic courts, religious endowments—from vehicles of jihadist incitement to forces for coexistence (Avishai, 2009). This involves: closure of mosques serving as terrorist recruiting grounds; removal of imams preaching violence or rejectionism; curriculum reform in Islamic educational institutions; and support for Islamic scholars promoting interpretations compatible with coexistence (Mogahed & Chouhoud, 2017).

Media Transformation: Complete restructuring of Palestinian media landscape, eliminating outlets glorifying terrorism or promoting hatred (MEMRI, 2023). This requires closing terrorist-affiliated media organizations, establishing editorial standards prohibiting incitement, and supporting independent journalism promoting factual reporting (Dajani, 2007).

Economic Reconstruction: Massive economic development initiatives creating stake in peace for Palestinian populations (World Bank, 2007). This involves infrastructure reconstruction, business development support creating employment opportunities, integration into regional and international markets, and property rights reform enabling entrepreneurship (Arnon & Weinblatt, 2001).

Civil Society Development:* Cultivation of genuinely independent civil society organizations promoting democracy, human rights, coexistence, and nonviolence (Hammami, 2000). This requires supporting grassroots organizations committed to coexistence and protecting civil society from terrorist intimidation.

Generational Change: Recognition that adults who spent decades under Hamas indoctrination may prove resistant to transformation, necessitating focus on younger generations (Bar-Tal, 2013). Programs targeting youth—emphasizing coexistence education, conflict resolution, entrepreneurship, and democratic values—offer greatest potential for durable transformation.

This transitional phase would last minimum five years, potentially longer depending on progress (Dobbins et al., 2003). Importantly, political rights and participation would initially be limited, expanding gradually as deradicalization progresses and Palestinian populations demonstrate commitment to coexistence (Carothers, 2007).

Phase Three: Constitutional Convention and Ratification (2031-2033)
Following sustained deradicalization and emergence of Palestinian leadership genuinely committed to federalism, a constitutional convention would be convened to draft the Federal Constitution of Israel (Elster, 1993). This convention would include representatives from throughout the territory tasked with designing federal institutions, delineating powers between federal and regional governments, and enshrining fundamental rights (Lijphart, 1977).

Critical constitutional provisions would include: clear delineation of exclusive federal powers (defense, foreign relations, monetary policy); specification of regional powers (education, culture, healthcare, policing); definition of concurrent powers; Federal Bill of

Rights binding all governmental levels; amendment procedures requiring broad consensus; provisions for intergovernmental cooperation; and mechanisms for admitting new federal regions. The constitution would require ratification through referenda in all constituent territories (Tierney, 2012). This democratic legitimation proves essential for federal system's ultimate success.

Phase Four: Establishment of Initial Federal Regions (2033-2036).
Following constitutional ratification, initial federal regions would be established through carefully sequenced process (Stepan, 1999). Existing Israel might initially be divided into several regions, while Palestinian territories would be organized into one or more regions. Gaza might constitute a separate region from West Bank regions given its geographic separation and distinct recent history.

During this phase: regional boundaries would be formally delineated; regional constitutions drafted and ratified; regional elections held; regional civil services established; regional judiciaries constituted; fiscal arrangements implemented; and intergovernmental coordinating mechanisms established.

Phase Five: Full Federal Integration and Citizenship (2036 onward)
Once regional institutions are functioning effectively and Palestinian populations have demonstrated sustained commitment to coexistence, full integration would proceed: grant of full Israeli citizenship to all residents of Palestinian federal regions; full exercise of regional autonomy; Palestinian participation in federal institutions; integration into federal security structures; full economic integration; and international recognition of the federal arrangement.

This represents the transformation's culmination: Palestinian Arabs who once pursued separate statehood now holding full citizenship in a powerful, prosperous Federal State of Israel while maintaining substantial autonomy through their own regional governments (Eger, 2025a).

Conditionality and Reversibility.
Critically, progression through phases must be conditional on actual behavioral change, not merely rhetorical commitments (Carothers, 2007). Each phase's advancement requires meeting specific benchmarks: complete absence of terrorism; removal of incitement

from education, media, and religious institutions; democratic governance meeting international standards; protection of minority rights; rule of law and judicial independence; fiscal responsibility and administrative capacity; and demonstrated commitment to coexistence.

If Palestinian populations or leaders backslide—if terrorism resurges, if incitement returns, if regional governments abuse powers—the federal government must possess authority to suspend regional autonomy and reimpose transitional administration (Bednar, 2009). This reversibility provides essential safeguard against federal system's exploitation for destructive ends.

Section IV: Why Federalism is the Only Viable Solution.
Following October 7th, the universe of possible solutions has contracted dramatically. This section articulates why federalism represents not merely the best available option, but the only viable framework for granting Palestinian Arabs citizenship while maintaining Israeli security and Jewish character (Eger, 2025a; Lustick, 2019). Every alternative proves either morally unacceptable, practically impossible, or existentially dangerous.

The Death of the Two-State Solution.
The two-state solution has dominated international discourse since Oslo (Savir, 1998; Ross, 2004). However, even before October 7th, this paradigm faced insurmountable obstacles (Thrall, 2017). October 7th delivered the final blow to any remaining viability. Fundamental problems include:

Geopolitical Impossibility: The West Bank is geographically fragmented, lacks territorial contiguity, and is separated from Gaza by Israeli territory (Lustick, 2019). Creating a viable Palestinian state would require land corridors or territorial exchanges that no Israeli government could accept post-October 7th.

Security Catastrophe: An independent Palestinian state would possess sovereignty over its territory, including ability to import weapons, form military alliances, and pursue hostile foreign policies (Cordesman, 2005). Post-October 7th, no Israeli government could accept the prospect of a sovereign Palestinian state potentially importing Iranian missiles, hosting Hezbollah forces, or inviting hostile military bases. Hamas's Gaza—where Israeli withdrawal in 2005 led to terrorist takeover and massive militarization—

demonstrates conclusively that territorial withdrawal without retained security control guarantees catastrophic failure (Eiland, 2010).

The "Failed State" Inevitability: Even absent malicious intent, a Palestinian state would almost certainly become a failed state given Palestinian governance's demonstrated dysfunctions (Jamal, 2007; Shikaki, 2020). Corruption, authoritarianism, institutional weakness, and internal divisions plaguing Palestinian Authority governance would intensify in an independent state. Failed states inevitably become terrorist havens and sources of regional instability (Rotberg, 2003).

Jerusalem's Indivisibility: Two-state frameworks inevitably founder on Jerusalem's status (Klein, 2001). Israeli consensus, reinforced by October 7th, holds Jerusalem indivisible and inseparable from Israeli sovereignty. Palestinian nationalism considers Jerusalem's "liberation" non-negotiable (Dumper, 2002).

***Rejectionism's Persistence:** Even "moderate" Palestinian leadership has never genuinely accepted Israel's permanent legitimacy as a Jewish state (Karsh, 2003). The two-state formula has been embraced tactically—as a stage toward Israel's ultimate elimination—rather than as genuine acceptance of permanent partition (Kuperwasser, 2015). Post-October 7th, Israeli society has concluded definitively that two-state partition is impossible and suicidal (Ben-Ami, 2024).

The Unsustainability of Occupation.
Maintaining indefinite occupation without pathway to citizenship proves both morally unacceptable and practically unsustainable (Gazit, 1995; Gorenberg, 2006). International law and moral principles require that populations subject to governmental authority possess political rights (Benvenisti, 1993). While temporary occupation pending conflict resolution is legally permissible, permanent occupation of millions denied citizenship violates fundamental rights (Dinstein, 2009).

Practically, permanent occupation imposes enormous costs—financial, military, diplomatic, and moral—on Israeli society (Gazit, 1995). Maintaining military control over hostile populations requires massive troop deployments, constant security operations, and periodic military confrontations. Diplomatic isolation and delegitimization campaigns inflict increasing damage on Israel's international standing (Sternhell, 2010).

Finally, demographics render permanent occupation untenable. Palestinian populations' higher birth rates mean they will eventually outnumber Israeli Jews between the Jordan River and Mediterranean, presenting Israel with an impossible trilemma: abandon democracy, abandon Jewish character, or abandon territory (Lustick, 2019). Occupation offers no escape from this trilemma.

The Danger of Binational Unitary State.
Some propose a single binational democratic state granting equal citizenship to all (Judt, 2003; Tilley, 2005). While superficially appealing, this solution guarantees Israel's destruction and likely produces catastrophic violence (Lustick, 2019). In a unitary binational state with equal political rights, Palestinians would rapidly become the majority through higher birth rates and potential return of refugees (Della Pergola, 2011). Democratic principle would then grant this Palestinian majority control, enabling them to dismantle its Jewish character through legislative means (Cohen, 2012).

Moreover, binational unitary state would not produce peace but civil war (Lustick, 2019). Deep mutual antagonisms, historical grievances, and competing national narratives would not disappear through constitutional arrangements. Historical precedents for deeply divided societies attempting binational democracy are catastrophic: Yugoslavia's violent disintegration, Cyprus's partition, Lebanon's civil war (Lijphart, 1977; Horowitz, 1985).

The Immorality of Transfer.
Some right-wing Israelis advocate forced population transfer—expulsion of Palestinian Arabs to neighboring Arab states (Kahane, 1981; Sherman, 2009). While this would "solve" the demographic problem, it constitutes morally questionable ethnic solution prohibited by international law (Morris, 2001). Forced population transfer of millions would constitute crimes against humanity (Cassese, 2003). It would transform Israel into pariah state subject to comprehensive international sanctions.

Most fundamentally, transfer contradicts Israel's foundational values as democratic state committed to human rights (Gavison, 1999). Embracing transfer would morally delegitimize Israel and alienate diaspora Jewish communities and democratic allies whose support proves essential for Israel's survival.

Why Only Federalism Can Work.

Federalism escapes the fatal flaws of every alternative by combining elements that separately prove impossible:. It maintains Israeli sovereignty and security control (unlike two-state solution). It provides Palestinian political rights and citizenship (unlike permanent occupation). It preserves Israel's Jewish character through federal structures (unlike binational unitary state), It respects human rights and international law (unlike transfer). It enables Palestinian self-governance and autonomy (satisfying self-determination aspirations). It creates incentive structures favoring cooperation over conflict

Specifically, federalism resolves core contradictions:

The Citizenship Dilemma: Federalism allows Palestinians to become full citizens of Federal State of Israel while maintaining Jewish majority at federal level through constitutional design (Eger, 2025a). Federal regions can have Palestinian majorities exercising substantial autonomy, while federal government is controlled by provisions ensuring Jewish character's preservation.

The Security Problem: Unlike sovereign Palestinian state, Palestinian federal regions would lack sovereignty over defense, foreign policy, or borders. Federal government retains exclusive control over security, preventing weapons importation, foreign military alliances, or threats to Israeli security (Watts, 2008).

The Self-Determination Paradox: Federalism provides meaningful self-governance—control over education, culture, healthcare, local economy, religious affairs—while maintaining integration into larger, more powerful state (Kymlicka, 1995). Palestinians gain autonomy over daily lives and cultural preservation without isolation in failed state.

The Jerusalem Question: Federal capital status for Jerusalem allows both peoples access and connection to holy city without partition (Eger, 2025a). Jerusalem serves as capital of Federal State of Israel, with federal institutions located there, while also hosting Palestinian federal region's institutions.

The Economic Advantage: Integration into prosperous federal economy provides Palestinians with economic opportunities impossible in independent Palestinian state. Access to Israeli markets, technology, investment, and infrastructure enables Palestinian economic development that separate statehood could never achieve (Arnon & Weinblatt, 2001).

Federalism is the only framework enabling Palestinian Arabs to become Israeli citizens with full political rights while maintaining Israeli security and Jewish character. This solves the fundamental equation that has defeated every previous peace effort.

However, federalism's viability absolutely depends on Palestinians' genuine transformation from rejectionism to federalism (Bar-Tal, 2013). Only after comprehensive deradicalization produces Palestinian populations genuinely committed to Israeli federal citizenship as permanent solution can federalism be safely implemented. This explains why federalism can only follow the implementation framework: complete Hamas elimination, comprehensive deradicalization, and demonstrated Palestinian commitment to federalism over decades.

Federalism as Historical Necessity.
The path from October 7th's ashes to federal solution requires traversing profound difficulties. It demands complete military victory over terrorist organizations, sustained commitment to deradicalization despite international pressure, patient institution-building during transitional administration, constitutional creativity in designing federal structures, and faith that transformation is possible even after unimaginable trauma.

Yet history demonstrates that seemingly impossible transformations can occur. Germany and Japan transformed from militaristic enemies into peaceful democracies (Montgomery, 1957; Dower, 1999). South Africa peacefully transitioned from apartheid to democracy (Sparks, 2003). Northern Ireland moved from sectarian violence to power-sharing governance (McGarry & O'Leary, 2009).

The transformation required of Palestinian society proves equally profound. It requires abandoning rejectionist narrative animating Palestinian nationalism since 1948, accepting permanent Jewish sovereignty, renouncing violence and terrorism, embracing democratic values and pluralism, and recognizing Israeli federal citizenship as achievement rather than capitulation (Bar-Tal, 2013).

Can such transformation occur? October 7th makes clear that it must occur if Palestinian Arabs are ever to achieve citizenship, prosperity, and genuine self-governance. The alternatives—permanent statelessness, perpetual conflict, existence under authoritarian failed state governance, or forced transfer—range from unacceptable to catastrophic. Federalism represents the only option providing pathway to Palestinian citizenship within the State of Israel.

For Israeli society, federalism requires envisioning Israeli identity expansively enough to include Palestinian Arabs as full citizens while maintaining Jewish character through federal structures rather than ethnic exclusion. It requires trusting that defeated, deradicalized populations can transform into federal partners rather than remaining eternal enemies. And it requires faith that rule of law, constitutional constraints, and democratic institutions can manage conflicts previously addressed only through violence (Frederic Eger, 2025a).

The implementation framework outlined—elimination, deradicalization, transitional administration, constitutional convention, phased regional establishment, and full integration—provides realistic pathway from post-conflict chaos to federal stability. Each phase builds upon previous achievements while maintaining security against backsliding. Conditionality ensures progression occurs only as merited by actual behavioral change.

The regional autonomy that Palestinian federal units would enjoy—legislative authority over education, healthcare, and culture; executive capacity to administer regional government; judicial independence; fiscal autonomy; and cultural/religious freedom—provides substantive self-determination far exceeding autonomy possible under occupation or in failed separate state.

Most critically, Palestinian Arabs would gain what has eluded them for over seventy-five years: citizenship in a stable, powerful, prosperous state; political rights and democratic participation; economic opportunity and development; security and rule of law; and recognition of their identity within federal structures. These achievements come not through violence and maximalist demands but through acceptance of federal framework and commitment to coexistence.

For Israel, federalism preserves core interests that all previous frameworks threatened: sovereignty and security through federal control of defense and foreign policy; Jewish character through constitutional design; territorial integrity without impossible partitions; and resolution of demographic challenge through federal citizenship rather than occupation or expulsion.

The October 7th massacre, despite its horrors, has created conditions—through complete Hamas elimination and comprehensive deradicalization—making federalism possible for first time. Previous attempts at federal or confederal solutions failed because they attempted to build federal structures atop rejectionist foundations (Makovsky, 2011). Post-October 7th federalism, implemented after transformation rather than as catalyst for it, possesses fundamentally different prerequisites and prospects.

Federalism is not merely aspirational but necessary; not merely preferable but inevitable; and not merely the best solution but the only solution capable of granting Palestinian Arabs Israeli citizenship while preserving the State of Israel. The alternative to federalism is not some other political solution but rather permanent statelessness for Palestinians and perpetual conflict for Israelis.

The aspiration for self-determination finds its fulfillment not in separate statehood but in federal citizenship. Palestinian federal regions, vested with substantial autonomy and integrated into prosperous federal state, provide framework for Palestinians to govern themselves, preserve their culture, develop their economy, and shape their future—while benefiting from Israeli citizenship's security, prosperity, and international standing.

This is not the vision that Palestinian nationalism has pursued for seventy-five years. It is, however, the only vision capable of transforming that nationalism from ideology of destruction into framework for construction; from rejectionism to federalism; from cult of martyrdom to culture of life; and from perpetual conflict to sustainable coexistence. Whether Palestinian society proves capable of this transformation remains uncertain. What October 7th has made certain is that federalism represents the only pathway through which such transformation can manifest politically.

The Federal State of Israel, as Frederic Eger (2025a) argues, "is the only possible One-State-Solution" that avoids genocide while enabling citizenship. The journey from October 7th's trauma to federal implementation will be long, difficult, and contingent. But it is the only journey worth taking, because it is the only journey that can lead to peace.

Chapter 5
Addendum

Key Concepts.

Understanding the fundamental terms is essential for grasping the post-October 7th paradigm shift:

October 7th, 2023: Hamas launched coordinated assault from Gaza into southern Israel, killing approximately 1,200 people—mostly civilians—in house-to-house massacres, sexual violence, and kidnapping over 240 hostages. The deadliest day for Jews since the Holocaust, it fundamentally altered Israeli-Palestinian conflict dynamics.

Hamas: Islamic Resistance Movement, a Palestinian Islamist organization designated as terrorist by the U.S., E.U., and others. Hamas governed Gaza from 2007-2024, combining social services with militant operations aimed at Israel's destruction.

Gaza Strip: A 141-square-mile coastal territory, home to approximately 2 million Palestinians. Israel withdrew in 2005; Hamas seized control in 2007.

West Bank (Judea & Samaria): Palestinian territory east of Israel, approximately 2,173 square miles, home to roughly 3 million Palestinians and 450,000 Israeli settlers. Governed by Palestinian Authority since 1994 under Oslo Accords.

Palestinian Authority: Interim self-government body established by Oslo Accords. Led by Fatah party, it administers parts of the West Bank but has limited sovereignty and faces legitimacy challenges.

Deradicalization: Systematic transformation of populations from extremist ideologies toward moderation, coexistence, and democratic values. Requires educational reform, media transformation, religious moderation, economic development, and generational change.

Security Paradigm: Fundamental framework through which states assess threats. October 7th shattered Israel's containment paradigm, necessitating approaches prioritizing elimination of threats rather than management.

Why This Matters.
Global Security Implications.

October 7th was not merely a localized Israeli-Palestinian incident. The attack and its aftermath carry profound implications for global security, economic stability, and international order.

Regional Destabilization and Terror Networks

Hamas's attack demonstrated operational sophistication of Iranian-backed terrorist organizations. Iran provided Hamas with weapons, training, and funding. The same Iranian networks support Hezbollah in Lebanon (possessing over 150,000 rockets), Houthi rebels in Yemen, and Shia militias in Iraq and Syria. What happens in Gaza directly affects Tehran's broader regional strategy.

Houthi attacks on Red Sea shipping following October 7th demonstrate interconnection. Attacks on commercial vessels disrupted 12% of global trade passing through the Suez Canal, raising insurance costs and threatening supply chains. Energy security remains vulnerable to escalation, particularly for European and Asian markets dependent on Middle Eastern oil.

Economic and Technological Impact

Oil price volatility following the attack demonstrates how regional instability translates into global economic impact. A full-scale regional war involving Iran could trigger energy crisis dwarfing previous disruptions. Israel's role as global technology hub—in cybersecurity, semiconductors, and medical devices—means prolonged conflict disrupts innovation ecosystems with worldwide dependencies.

Precedent for Terrorist Strategy

October 7th established precedent for mass-casualty attacks achieving strategic objectives. Hamas calculated spectacular brutality would trigger Israeli response creating international pressure for ceasefire, enabling Hamas survival. If this strategy succeeds—if Hamas emerges politically intact—it incentivizes similar attacks globally. Conversely, if Hamas is comprehensively eliminated and Palestinian society deradicalized, the message becomes clear: terrorist mass-casualty attacks guarantee organizational destruction.

The resolution of Israeli-Palestinian conflict through sustainable framework like federalism could establish model for other divided societies. Its perpetuation provides propaganda and recruitment tool for extremists worldwide. What happens in Israel-Palestine reverberates through global security architecture, economic systems, and humanitarian crises affecting billions.

Scholarly Frameworks.
Reporting on October 7th and Its Aftermath.

For journalists, scholars, and students seeking to understand and report responsibly on October 7th, navigating the information landscape requires critical tools.

Identifying Bias in Coverage

Media coverage exhibits systematic biases across the political spectrum. Right-wing Israeli media often minimizes Palestinian civilian suffering. Left-wing Western media sometimes presents Hamas as "resistance" while downplaying its genocidal charter. Arab media frequently denies Israeli civilian victimization while amplifying Palestinian casualties.

Critical questions: Does the source label Hamas as terrorist organization, or use euphemisms like "militants"? Does coverage acknowledge deliberate targeting of civilians on October 7th? Does reporting on Gaza distinguish between combatants and civilians? Are casualty figures from Hamas-controlled Gaza Health Ministry presented with appropriate skepticism? Does analysis acknowledge Israel's security dilemma?

Primary Sources.

Reliable sources include: Israeli government and IDF releases (recognizing state bias); Palestinian Authority statements (distinct from Hamas); verified video evidence; International Committee of the Red Cross reports; academic research from conflict studies centers; credible witness testimony; and Hamas's 1988 Charter explicitly calling for Israel's destruction.

Scholars should consult: Horgan and Braddock on disengagement from extremism; comparative post-conflict reconstruction studies (Germany, Japan); Northern Ireland peace process analysis; and consociational democracy literature.

Avoiding False Equivalence.

The most pervasive error is treating democratic Israel and terrorist Hamas as morally equivalent. While legitimate criticism of Israeli policies exists, equating a democratic state operating under rule of law with a theocratic terrorist organization that deliberately massacres civilians constitutes fundamental analytical failure.

This doesn't preclude acknowledging Palestinian suffering. But it requires recognizing categorical differences: democracies with free press, independent courts, and electoral accountability differ fundamentally from authoritarian movements rejecting democratic norms. Civilian casualties in Gaza result from military operations against an enemy embedding itself in civilian areas—not from deliberate policy of targeting civilians as Hamas practiced on October 7th.

October 7th should be understood through multiple lenses: security failure revealing containment strategy inadequacies; humanitarian catastrophe demonstrating Hamas governance consequences; paradigm shift ending two-state viability; deradicalization test case; and inflection point forcing reconsideration of fundamental assumptions.

A Message for Those Who Sympathize with Palestinians.
If you care about Palestinian welfare, if Palestinian suffering moves you—this message is for you. The argument here does not dismiss Palestinian suffering but contends that federalism offers the only realistic path to ending it.
Acknowledging Suffering.
Palestinian suffering is real and extensive. Decades of conflict have produced displacement, poverty, loss of life, separated families, childhood trauma, stunted development, and denied political rights. This suffering demands resolution.
The question is not whether Palestinians have suffered—they have —but which path forward will actually end that suffering. Honest engagement requires confronting difficult realities.
Why Endless Conflict Serves No One.
The Palestinian national movement, as constituted since 1948, has pursued maximalist objectives—complete "liberation" of historic Palestine—through terrorism, diplomatic warfare, and armed conflict. This approach has produced seventy-five years of failure and statelessness.
Hamas's October 7th attack represents this strategy's logical endpoint. Rather than pursuing compromise, Hamas sought through spectacular brutality to trigger regional war destroying Israel. The result: catastrophe for Gaza's population.
This pattern repeats throughout Palestinian history. Every rejection of compromise—1937 Peel Commission, 1947 UN Partition, 2000 Camp David, 2008 Olmert offer—led to worse outcomes. The pursuit of maximalist aims through violent resistance has produced not Palestinian statehood but perpetual conflict, authoritarian governance, and economic stagnation.
If you genuinely care about Palestinian welfare, ask: Has the rejectionist strategy served Palestinian interests? Has it produced state, prosperity, or freedom?

Why Federalism Serves Palestinian Interests.
Federalism offers what seventy-five years of conflict has not: citizenship in a stable, powerful, prosperous state; political rights and democratic participation; substantial autonomy over education, culture, and local governance; economic opportunity through integration into advanced economy; security under rule of law; and recognition of Palestinian identity within federal structures.
Compare alternatives. An independent Palestinian state would likely become a failed state—poor, authoritarian, unstable, lacking

capacity for security or prosperity. Permanent statelessness offers no political rights and perpetual conflict.

Federalism provides self-determination through constitutional autonomy. Palestinian federal regions would control education (teaching Palestinian history and culture), administer healthcare and social services, maintain cultural and religious autonomy, and participate in federal democratic institutions.

Most importantly, Palestinians would gain Israeli citizenship—membership in a prosperous First World nation with advanced economy, technological leadership, and international standing. Palestinian entrepreneurs would access Israeli markets, technology, and investment. Palestinian students would attend Israeli universities. Palestinian workers would enjoy First World labor protections and economic opportunities.

The Required Transformation

Federalism requires Palestinian society's transformation from rejectionism to acceptance of permanent Jewish sovereignty and commitment to coexistence. This transformation, while difficult, serves Palestinian interests.

Rejectionist ideology has failed Palestinians catastrophically. Deradicalization—abandoning rejectionism, accepting coexistence, embracing democratic values—opens pathway to citizenship and prosperity that rejectionism has foreclosed.

If you care about Palestinians, support their transformation away from ideologies bringing only suffering. Support educational reform eliminating incitement. Support economic development providing alternatives to terrorism. Support democratic institution-building.

Federalism requires Palestinians to abandon dreams of separate statehood and accept permanent Jewish sovereignty. But it offers something achievable: citizenship, prosperity, security, and substantial autonomy. The alternative is perpetual conflict. Which serves Palestinian interests better?

What Changed and Why It Matters.
The Timeline: From October 7th to Now

October 7th, 2023: Hamas attack from Gaza killed 1,200 people—mostly civilians—in deliberate massacres, sexual violence, and hostage-taking.

October-December 2023: Israel's military campaign to eliminate Hamas caused extensive civilian casualties and infrastructure destruction. Hamas operated from civilian areas—hospitals, schools, neighborhoods—making civilian harm nearly inevitable.

2024-Present: Israel degraded Hamas's capabilities. Question remains: What comes next?

Why Old Solutions Failed.
Two-State Solution: An independent Palestinian state would have sovereignty—ability to import weapons, form military alliances. Hamas's Gaza governance after Israel's 2005 withdrawal showed territorial withdrawal without security control leads to terrorist takeover.
Permanent Occupation: Keeping millions without citizenship is morally wrong and unsustainable.
Status Quo: Current situation leads nowhere. Demographics ensure Palestinian population growth, making situations increasingly untenable.
The Security Paradigm Shift
October 7th proved Israel cannot "manage" threats—it must eliminate them. New paradigm requires: elimination of terrorist organizations; comprehensive deradicalization; and new framework providing Palestinian citizenship while maintaining Israeli security.
Why Federalism Is the Only Option.
Security: Palestinian regions wouldn't be sovereign states. Federal government retains exclusive control over defense and foreign policy.
Citizenship: Palestinians become full Israeli citizens with political rights.
Self-Governance: Palestinian regions control education, culture, healthcare, local economy—substantial autonomy without full sovereignty's dangers.
Jewish Character: Constitutional design maintains Israel's Jewish character at federal level.
Required Transformation.
Federalism works only if Palestinian society transforms from seeking Israel's destruction to accepting permanent Israeli citizenship through: educational reform eliminating incitement; economic development; democratic institution-building; and generational change.
This takes years or decades and requires Palestinians to abandon separate statehood dreams. But it offers citizenship in a prosperous state with substantial autonomy.
Going Forward
October 7th ended territorial partition assumptions. Only integration—through federal structures providing security and autonomy—can work.
For young people inheriting this situation, understanding this shift matters. Previous generation's solutions—two states, peace processes, territorial withdrawal—failed. Your generation must

consider federalism: thinking differently about sovereignty, citizenship, and coexistence.

The question shifted from "Can Israelis and Palestinians live separately in peace?" (October 7th answered: No) to "Can they live together in federal structure providing security, citizenship, and autonomy?" That question remains open. Its answer shapes the Middle East for generations.

Chapter 6
Federal Constitutionalism & Post-Conflict Reconstruction

Constitutional Responses to Existential Crisis.
The October 7th massacre fundamentally altered Israel's strategic landscape, exposing what this book has characterised as the moment when conventional approaches to the Palestinian question revealed their complete bankruptcy. The systematic brutality unleashed by Hamas—the meticulous planning, the gleeful documentation of atrocities, the weaponisation of sexual violence—demonstrated not merely a security failure but a paradigmatic collapse. The two-state solution, kept alive for decades by diplomatic inertia and the peace process industry, died in the tunnels of Gaza. The status quo of indefinite occupation, never intended as permanent arrangement, perished in the burned kibbutzim of the Gaza envelope.

Yet from this catastrophe emerges what political theorists recognise as a critical juncture: a moment when institutional path dependencies break down and fundamentally new constitutional arrangements become politically feasible.[1] Giovanni Capoccia and Daniel Kelemen's research on critical junctures demonstrates that periods of crisis create windows for institutional innovation that normal politics forecloses. The choices made during such moments shape institutional trajectories for generations. October 7th has opened such a window; the question is whether Israeli and Palestinian leaders will seize it for constitutional transformation or allow it to close on yet another cycle of violence and retaliation.

This chapter argues that federalism offers the only viable constitutional framework capable of addressing Israel's intersecting security, demographic, and legitimacy crises in the post-October 7th era. This claim rests not on naive optimism but on cold strategic calculation informed by comparative constitutional theory and historical precedent. The argument proceeds through several stages: first, establishing the theoretical foundations of federal constitutionalism for divided societies; second, examining the German precedent for post-conflict constitutional reconstruction; third, addressing the democratic legitimacy challenges that current arrangements create; fourth, outlining the sequencing of constitutional transition; and finally, confronting the justice questions that any post-conflict settlement must address.

Theoretical Foundations: Consociational Constitutionalism.
The theoretical foundation for federal solutions in deeply divided societies draws heavily on Arend Lijphart's work on consociational democracy—a constitutional framework explicitly designed for societies where conventional majoritarian democracy would produce permanent domination of minorities by majorities.[2] Lijphart identifies four key principles that successful divided societies have employed: grand coalition government ensuring all major communities share executive power; proportionality in political representation and civil service appointments; mutual veto rights for minority communities on matters affecting their vital interests; and segmental autonomy allowing communities to govern their own affairs in matters of particular concern.

These mechanisms, refined through comparative analysis of cases from Switzerland to Belgium to Lebanon, provide the architectural blueprint for what this book terms the Federal State of Israel. But Lijphart's framework requires adaptation to Israeli-Palestinian specificities. The conflict's intensity exceeds what most consociational cases have confronted. The territorial dimension—two peoples claiming the same land—adds complexity that purely political power-sharing cannot address. The security environment, with active armed groups committed to one side's destruction, precludes the trust that consociational arrangements typically presuppose.

Brendan O'Leary's work on "complex power-sharing" extends Lijphart's framework to address precisely these complications.[3] O'Leary distinguishes between corporate and liberal consociationalism: the former assigns political rights to predetermined groups in fixed proportions; the latter allows group boundaries and political weight to shift through democratic processes while maintaining protections against majoritarian domination. For the Israeli-Palestinian context, liberal consociationalism offers advantages—it does not freeze demographic balances into permanent constitutional arrangements but creates frameworks within which populations can evolve while protections persist.

The territorial dimension requires federal rather than merely consociational solutions. Consociationalism addresses how groups share power at the centre; federalism addresses how they govern territory. The combination—what Donald Horowitz terms "integrative power-sharing"—provides both central institutions where communities cooperate and regional institutions where they exercise autonomous authority.[4] This combination proves essential for Israeli-Palestinian arrangements: neither pure power-sharing at the centre (which would not address Palestinian aspirations for territorial self-governance) nor pure territorial federalism (which might facilitate secession) suffices alone.

The German Precedent: Constitutional Reconstruction After Catastrophe

The historical precedent most relevant to Israel's post-October 7th situation is the transformation of post-World War II Germany. This comparison will strike many as provocative or inappropriate— Germans were perpetrators of genocide, not victims of terrorism. But the comparison's value lies not in moral equivalence but in institutional precedent: how does a society transition from existential conflict to constitutional democracy? How do former enemies become partners in federal governance? What sequencing of military defeat, occupation, reconstruction, and democratic transition enables transformation rather than perpetuating conflict?

As historian Tony Judt documented, the federal structure established in West Germany "didn't merely contain potential threats; it transformed former enemies into security partners" through constitutional frameworks that simultaneously addressed security concerns and created new political identities.[5] The German Basic Law's design reflected deliberate choices about how to prevent recurrence of catastrophe while creating space for democratic development. Power was dispersed across Länder to prevent concentration that had enabled Nazi totalitarianism. Constitutional provisions entrenched democratic principles against future majorities that might seek to overturn them. The Constitutional Court received authority to defend the constitutional order against both governmental overreach and anti-democratic movements.

The sequencing of German reconstruction proves particularly instructive. Allied occupation authorities did not immediately establish democratic institutions in 1945. Instead, as Timothy Garton Ash documents, transformation proceeded through deliberate phases: complete military defeat eliminating forces committed to continued conflict; de-Nazification removing ideological leadership from positions of influence; economic reconstruction creating material stakes in the new order; gradual transfer of administrative functions to German authorities under Allied supervision; constitutional convention producing the Basic Law; and finally full sovereignty within federal framework and Western alliance structures.[6]

Applied to the Israeli-Palestinian context, this sequencing suggests that meaningful constitutional negotiation can only proceed after the complete military defeat of rejectionist forces. This is not an argument for permanent war but for recognising that constitutional arrangements cannot include parties committed to their destruction. Hamas's charter explicitly rejects any permanent peace with Israel; its October 7th actions demonstrated that this rejection extends to genocidal violence against civilians. No federal constitution can accommodate parties whose programme is the federal state's destruction. The German precedent demonstrates that total military defeat need not preclude eventual reconciliation but rather creates conditions making reconciliation possible by eliminating forces committed to permanent conflict.

Democratic Legitimacy & the Occupation Paradox.
The current governance situation presents Israel with what political philosopher Michael Walzer identifies as "the democratic paradox"—the fundamental tension between maintaining democratic character while exercising control over populations lacking meaningful political rights.[7] Israel governs approximately five million Palestinians in the West Bank and Gaza who cannot vote in Israeli elections, cannot move freely, and cannot determine their political future. This arrangement corrodes both Israel's international standing and its internal democratic cohesion.

International relations scholar Ian Hurd's work on legitimacy demonstrates that this is not merely a moral problem but a strategic one.[8] States require legitimacy—acceptance by domestic and international audiences that their authority is rightful—to function effectively. Legitimacy reduces enforcement costs, attracts cooperation, and enables international partnerships. Israel's legitimacy deficit, rooted in the occupation's persistence, carries tangible strategic consequences: diplomatic isolation, economic pressures through boycott movements, constraints on security cooperation, and domestic polarisation that weakens governmental capacity.

The democratic paradox admits only three resolutions: ending democratic governance (unacceptable to Israeli society and international community); ending control over Palestinian territories (attempted through Oslo and disengagement, with disastrous results); or extending democratic governance to encompass Palestinian populations through constitutional arrangements that address both peoples' concerns. Federalism represents the only version of the third option that simultaneously preserves Israeli security, maintains Jewish national character, and provides Palestinians meaningful self-governance.

Constitutional scholar Aharon Barak advances the crucial argument that "explicit constitutional provisions protect identity more effectively than demographic dominance."[9] This insight transforms the demographic debate that has paralysed Israeli politics. Rather than asking whether Jews can remain a majority—a question whose answer depends on borders, definitions, and projections subject to manipulation—constitutional design asks how Jewish national character can be protected regardless of demographic shifts. Written constitutional guarantees prove more durable than population balances; institutional arrangements outlast generational changes.

A federal constitution could entrench Jewish national character through multiple mechanisms: Hebrew as primary official language alongside Arabic; Jewish holidays as national holidays; the Law of Return maintained at federal level; Jewish symbols incorporated in federal institutions; educational autonomy preserving Jewish curriculum in Hebrew-language schools; and regional autonomy ensuring Jewish-majority regions govern themselves on matters of particular concern. These provisions would not depend on maintaining particular demographic ratios but would constitute permanent features of constitutional order, amendable only through supermajority procedures requiring broad consensus.

Political scientist Ruth Gavison extends this analysis, arguing that constitutional protections "transform Jewish national rights from demographic fact to constitutional principle."[10] This transformation is not merely semantic but substantive. Demographic facts change; constitutional principles persist unless deliberately altered through demanding procedures. A Jewish minority in a federal state with constitutionally entrenched Jewish national character would possess more secure identity protection than a Jewish majority in a state lacking such provisions.

Constitutional Architecture: Principles and Mechanisms.
The design of federal constitutional architecture for Israel-Palestine must address several distinct challenges simultaneously: preventing majoritarian domination while enabling effective governance; preserving distinct community identities while creating shared citizenship; distributing powers between federal and regional levels appropriately; and creating institutions capable of managing the inevitable conflicts that any diverse society generates.

Bicameralism provides the foundational institutional mechanism. A federal legislature combining a proportionally elected lower house with an upper chamber representing regions ensures that neither simple Jewish nor Arab majorities can dominate on issues affecting communal interests. The German Bundesrat model—where Land governments rather than directly elected senators represent regional interests—offers particular advantages for the Israeli-Palestinian context by linking federal and regional politics and creating incentives for intergovernmental cooperation.

Constitutional provisions requiring supermajorities for fundamental changes protect against demographic shifts enabling simple majority alterations of the state's character. The requirement that constitutional amendments receive support from both population-based and region-based majorities—what the Swiss call the "double majority"—ensures that changes reflect broad consensus rather than narrow victories. Specific provisions might entrench certain principles as unamendable, following the German Basic Law's "eternity clause" protecting democratic order and federal structure against any amendment.

Regional autonomy provisions determine which powers reside at federal versus regional levels. The principle of subsidiarity—that decisions should be made at the lowest effective governmental level—provides guidance, though its application requires contextual judgment. Matters requiring uniform treatment throughout federal territory (defence, foreign policy, currency, fundamental rights) properly belong at federal level. Matters where regional variation is desirable or where community control is essential for identity preservation (education, culture, language policy, local policing, land use planning) properly belong at regional level. Matters where neither uniform treatment nor regional control is clearly superior (healthcare, environmental regulation, economic policy) become subjects for ongoing federal-regional negotiation.

Power-sharing mechanisms at the federal executive level ensure that all major communities possess stakes in governance. The Swiss Federal Council model—a seven-member collegial executive representing major parties and linguistic communities—demonstrates that executive power-sharing need not produce paralysis. Coalition requirements ensuring that federal governments include representatives from both Jewish and Arab communities could be constitutionally mandated, following Belgian precedent requiring linguistic parity in the federal cabinet.

Judicial review provides the mechanism for enforcing constitutional provisions against legislative or executive overreach. A federal constitutional court, composed through appointment processes ensuring representation from both communities, would interpret constitutional provisions, resolve federal-regional disputes, and protect fundamental rights against governmental violation. The court's composition and appointment procedures require careful design to ensure that neither community perceives it as captured by the other.

Transitional Justice: Acknowledgment, Accountability, and Reconciliation.
Any constitutional settlement addressing the Israeli-Palestinian conflict must confront questions of transitional justice: how to acknowledge past wrongs, establish accountability for violations, and create conditions for reconciliation. These questions cannot be avoided; they can only be addressed well or poorly. Poorly addressed, they poison the constitutional settlement with unresolved grievances. Well addressed, they contribute to the legitimacy that new institutions require.

The South African Truth and Reconciliation Commission provides the most influential model for transitional justice, though its applicability to Israeli-Palestinian circumstances requires careful assessment.[11] The TRC's genius lay in offering perpetrators amnesty in exchange for truthful disclosure—creating incentives for truth-telling that prosecutorial approaches cannot provide. Its limitations included inadequate attention to structural injustice and insufficient reparations for victims. The Israeli-Palestinian context would require adaptation addressing both individual violations and collective experiences—the Nakba for Palestinians, terrorism and existential threat for Israelis.

Priscilla Hayner's comparative analysis of truth commissions identifies several design principles relevant to Israeli-Palestinian transitional justice.[12] Commissions succeed when they possess adequate resources and time, enjoy political support from key constituencies, combine truth-telling with material reparations, and produce findings that achieve broad acceptance. They fail when they are underfunded, politically marginalised, focused exclusively on documentation without material redress, or perceived as instruments of victor's justice.

For the Israeli-Palestinian context, transitional justice mechanisms might include a truth commission documenting experiences and violations by all parties; acknowledgment statements from political leadership recognising the other community's suffering; compensation programmes for documented material losses; limited return provisions addressing refugee concerns symbolically if not comprehensively; and educational initiatives ensuring that future generations learn historical narratives that acknowledge both communities' experiences.

The German experience with transitional justice offers additional insights. De-Nazification, despite its imperfections, removed committed ideologues from positions of influence and established that association with the previous regime carried consequences. Subsequent decades saw evolving German engagement with Nazi history—from initial denial through gradual acknowledgment to the contemporary memory culture that makes Holocaust remembrance central to German identity. This evolution suggests that transitional justice is not a single event but an ongoing process that unfolds over generations.

Implementation Sequencing: Phased Transformation.
The transition from current arrangements to federal constitutional framework requires what political scientist Yoav Peled characterises as "sequenced transformation"—carefully ordered phases that build institutional capacity while managing security risks.[13] The German precedent demonstrates that such sequencing can succeed even in the most unpromising circumstances, but it also demonstrates that sequencing matters enormously. Premature democratisation before security stabilisation invites chaos; delayed democratisation after security stabilisation breeds resentment. The sequencing appropriate to Israeli-Palestinian circumstances would proceed through distinct

phases, each with specific objectives and prerequisites for advancing to subsequent phases.

Phase One: Security Stabilisation.
The first phase requires complete military defeat of Hamas and other armed groups committed to permanent conflict. This is the precondition for all subsequent phases; without it, no constitutional arrangement can succeed. The German precedent is unambiguous: meaningful reconstruction began only after unconditional surrender eliminated forces committed to continued resistance. Applied to the Israeli-Palestinian context, this means that Hamas cannot be a partner in federal arrangements—not because of its ideology, which might evolve, but because of its demonstrated commitment to genocidal violence that precludes the trust federal governance requires.

Security stabilisation would establish transitional military administration in Gaza and contested West Bank areas, implementing de-radicalisation programmes modelled on post-Nazi Germany's de-Nazification. Educational curricula promoting violence and rejection of coexistence would be replaced with materials supporting eventual federal citizenship. Armed groups would be dismantled; weapons caches destroyed; militant infrastructure eliminated. This phase would necessarily be extended—years rather than months—and would require sustained commitment despite inevitable setbacks.

Phase Two: Institutional Development.
The second phase would create local administrative councils under federal supervision, building governance capacity in Palestinian areas while maintaining security oversight. These councils would initially exercise limited authority—municipal services, local economic development, educational administration within federal guidelines—expanding their scope as demonstrated capacity and commitment to federal principles warrant.

Economic reconstruction would proceed simultaneously, creating material stakes in the emerging order. As Chapter 8 details, integrated economic development generates constituencies for peace by making conflict economically irrational. Infrastructure investment, labour market integration, and technology transfer would create Palestinian prosperity linked to federal success, undermining support for rejectionist alternatives.

Phase Three: Constitutional Convention.

The third phase would convene a constitutional assembly representing both communities to draft the federal constitution. The assembly's composition would require careful design—ensuring adequate representation for both communities while including voices committed to federal success rather than its undermining. International constitutional experts could provide technical assistance, as they have in numerous post-conflict constitutional processes, while ultimate authorship must reside with the peoples who will live under the constitution.

The constitutional drafting process itself contributes to legitimacy. Constitutions imposed by victors lack the acceptance that negotiated constitutions achieve. The process of negotiation—the compromises required, the mutual recognition involved, the shared investment in outcomes—builds the political culture that constitutional democracy requires. Even difficult, protracted negotiations contribute to eventual constitutional legitimacy by demonstrating that all parties shaped the outcome.

Phase Four: Democratic Transition

The fourth phase would implement the constitution through democratic elections—first at regional level, then at federal level. Regional elections would establish governments in Palestinian areas with genuine authority over matters assigned to regional jurisdiction. Federal elections would create the bicameral legislature and trigger the power-sharing mechanisms that the constitution establishes.

This phase carries particular risks. Elections can empower parties hostile to constitutional arrangements, as occurred when Hamas won Palestinian legislative elections in 2006. Constitutional design must anticipate this possibility through provisions enabling exclusion of parties that reject constitutional principles—following the German model that permits banning parties hostile to democratic order. Such provisions require careful calibration to prevent abuse while protecting constitutional fundamentals.

Phase Five: Consolidation.

The fifth phase—consolidation—has no definite endpoint. Constitutional democracy requires ongoing cultivation; it is never finally achieved but always in process. Federal institutions would gradually assume full authority; regional autonomy would expand as stability permits; civil society would develop the cross-communal relationships that constitutional text alone cannot create.

The consolidation phase would also involve progressive integration into regional and international structures. As Chapter 13 discusses, federal resolution of the Israeli-Palestinian conflict would transform regional dynamics, enabling the comprehensive Middle Eastern integration that perpetual conflict has precluded. International recognition, investment, and partnership would reinforce domestic constitutional development, creating external supports for internal transformation.

Constitutional Culture: Beyond Institutional Design.
Constitutional success depends not merely on institutional design but on what political scientists term "constitutional culture"—the habits, expectations, and commitments that make constitutional provisions effective rather than merely formal.[14] Constitutions are not self-enforcing; they require political actors committed to their maintenance, citizens who demand constitutional compliance, and social expectations that constitutional violation carries consequences.

Building constitutional culture in deeply divided societies presents particular challenges. Communities that have viewed each other as enemies for generations do not immediately develop the trust that constitutional cooperation requires. Constitutional provisions that seem fair to one community may seem threatening to another. Political entrepreneurs face temptations to mobilise communal grievances rather than build cross-communal coalitions.

Yet constitutional culture can be cultivated deliberately. Educational systems can socialise future citizens into constitutional values. Media can model constitutional discourse rather than inflammatory rhetoric. Political leaders can demonstrate that constitutional compliance serves their communities' interests. International partners can reinforce constitutional behaviour through conditional benefits. Over time—measured in decades rather than years—constitutional culture can develop even in unpromising circumstances.

The German experience demonstrates that constitutional culture can be created even after catastrophic conflict. Post-war Germans were not natural democrats; they had enthusiastically supported Nazi totalitarianism barely a generation earlier. Yet deliberate cultivation of democratic culture—through education, media, civil society, and political leadership—produced one of the world's most stable constitutional democracies within decades. The Israeli-Palestinian context is different, but the German precedent demonstrates that constitutional culture can be built where it did not previously exist.

The Role of International Guarantees.
Constitutional arrangements in post-conflict settings often require international support to establish credibility and provide insurance against defection. Barbara Walter's research on civil war settlements demonstrates that third-party security guarantees significantly increase the probability that peace agreements endure. [15] Parties that distrust each other may nonetheless accept arrangements if external powers guarantee enforcement. International involvement does not substitute for domestic commitment but can provide the confidence that enables risk-taking for peace.

For Israeli-Palestinian federal arrangements, international guarantees could take several forms. Security guarantees from major powers—potentially through NATO membership or equivalent arrangements—would provide insurance against external threats and internal breakdown. International monitoring of constitutional compliance could reassure both communities that violations would be detected and addressed. Development assistance conditional on constitutional performance would create material incentives for institutional success. Diplomatic recognition and international integration would reward constitutional achievement while isolation would penalise regression.

The European Union's role in supporting post-conflict constitutional development provides relevant precedent. EU accession requirements have driven constitutional reforms throughout Central and Eastern Europe, demonstrating that conditional external benefits can motivate domestic institutional change.[16] For Israel-Palestine, an enhanced EU partnership agreement—with benefits contingent on constitutional progress—could provide similar incentives. American security guarantees, already substantial for Israel, could be extended to federal arrangements, providing the external support that enables domestic transformation.

However, international involvement must be carefully calibrated. External powers cannot impose constitutional arrangements that domestic populations reject; such impositions lack the legitimacy that constitutional government requires. International support should facilitate rather than dictate, providing resources and incentives while leaving ultimate choices to the peoples who will live under constitutional arrangements. The balance between external support and domestic ownership proves crucial—too little support leaves constitutional arrangements vulnerable; too much undermines their legitimacy.

Addressing the Refugee Question Constitutionally.
No Israeli-Palestinian settlement can succeed without addressing the refugee question—the status of Palestinians displaced during the 1948 war and their descendants, now numbering several million. This question has proven among the most intractable in negotiations, with Palestinian demands for return confronting Israeli fears of demographic transformation. Federal constitutional frameworks offer approaches that might break this deadlock.

The refugee question involves multiple dimensions requiring distinct treatment. The symbolic dimension concerns acknowledgment—recognition that displacement occurred and caused suffering. The material dimension concerns compensation for lost property and disrupted lives. The practical dimension concerns where refugees and their descendants will actually live. Constitutional frameworks can address each dimension through different mechanisms.
Acknowledgment can be incorporated into constitutional preamble and transitional justice processes. A federal constitution might explicitly recognise that both peoples have suffered through the conflict's history—Palestinians through displacement and occupation, Jews through persecution and terrorism. Such acknowledgment does not assign exclusive blame; it recognises that both communities have experienced genuine trauma requiring recognition. Truth commission processes, discussed above, would document specific experiences and losses, creating historical record that acknowledgment requires.

Compensation can be addressed through federal programmes providing material redress for documented losses. International experience with property restitution and compensation—from post-Holocaust programmes to post-communist transitions—provides institutional models.[17] A federal compensation commission could evaluate claims, determine awards, and administer payments funded through combination of federal resources and international contributions. Compensation addresses material losses without requiring return that would transform demographic balances.

The practical question—where refugees will live—requires the most careful constitutional treatment. Unlimited return to pre-1948 locations within Israel would transform the federal state's demographic composition in ways that many Israelis would experience as existential threat. Yet complete denial of any return would perpetuate grievances that poison political culture. Federal arrangements might thread this needle through several mechanisms: return to Palestinian regions within the federation (rather than to specific pre-1948 locations); limited return to federal territory (rather than specifically Israeli regions) based on family reunification or other criteria; and absorption assistance for refugees choosing to remain in current locations or resettle elsewhere.

These approaches do not satisfy maximalist demands on either side. Palestinians seeking return to ancestral homes would not achieve it; Israelis fearing demographic transformation would face some Palestinian population increase within federal territory. But federal arrangements reframe the question: refugees would return not to "Israel" but to a federal state in which Palestinians possess constitutional standing. The return would not threaten Jewish national character because that character would be constitutionally protected regardless of demographic shifts. This reframing does not resolve all tensions but may reduce them sufficiently to enable constitutional settlement.

Jerusalem: The Constitutional Challenge.
Jerusalem presents constitutional challenges of particular intensity. Both peoples claim the city as their capital; both possess profound religious attachments to sites within it; both have invested Jerusalem with symbolic significance that transcends practical governance. Any constitutional arrangement that appears to concede Jerusalem to the other side would face overwhelming rejection.

Federal constitutional design offers approaches that avoid zero-sum framing. Jerusalem could be designated federal territory—belonging to neither Israeli nor Palestinian regions but governed by federal institutions representing both peoples. Within the city, distinct zones could provide each community control over areas of particular significance while shared federal authority governs matters requiring coordination. Holy sites of significance to multiple traditions could receive special status with governance arrangements ensuring access for all faiths.

The Belgian Brussels model demonstrates that complex arrangements for contested cities can function, however imperfectly.[18] Brussels serves as capital for both Flemish and Francophone communities despite being geographically within Flanders and demographically mixed. Elaborate institutional arrangements—including distinct community commissions for each linguistic group alongside common regional institutions—manage competing claims without fully satisfying either. Brussels is not a model of elegant simplicity; it is a model of workable complexity that permits coexistence.

Applied to Jerusalem, similar complexity might prove necessary. A Jerusalem Federal District could encompass the current municipal boundaries, governed by federal institutions with guaranteed representation for both Jewish and Arab residents. Within the district, neighbourhood-level governance could reflect local demographics—Jewish neighbourhoods governed through Hebrew-language institutions, Arab neighbourhoods through Arabic-language institutions, mixed areas through joint arrangements. The Old City and its holy sites could receive unique status with international involvement ensuring access and protection.

Such arrangements would not satisfy those who demand exclusive sovereignty over Jerusalem. They would require both communities to accept that the other possesses legitimate claims that constitutional arrangements must accommodate. But they would avoid the alternative—perpetual conflict over a city that neither side will abandon—while creating frameworks within which both peoples could express their connection to Jerusalem through constitutional rather than military means.

The Gaza Question.
Gaza presents particular challenges for federal constitutional design. The territory's isolation from the West Bank, its governance by Hamas, and the devastation of recent conflicts create conditions far removed from normal federal integration. Any realistic federal vision must acknowledge that Gaza's path differs from other Palestinian regions, requiring distinct treatment in constitutional design and implementation sequencing.

In the near term, Gaza requires security stabilisation and humanitarian reconstruction that precede meaningful federal participation. The destruction of Hamas's military infrastructure, the de-radicalisation of educational and media institutions, and the rebuilding of civilian governance capacity must occur before Gaza can participate in federal arrangements as a constructive partner. This process will take years, potentially a decade or more, and cannot be rushed without risking repetition of previous failures.

Constitutional design might address Gaza's distinct status through asymmetric arrangements. Gaza could initially participate in federal structures with limited authority—perhaps observer status in federal legislature, participation in economic institutions without full political integration, security arrangements that maintain federal oversight while building local capacity. As conditions permit, Gaza's federal participation could expand through graduated phases with specific benchmarks for advancement.

The model here might be the European Union's treatment of candidate countries—participation in some institutions and programmes while full membership awaits satisfaction of accession criteria. Gaza would be within the federal framework but with status reflecting its particular circumstances. This approach acknowledges reality without either excluding Gaza from federal arrangements entirely or pretending that current conditions permit full integration.

Long-term, Gaza's geographic separation from the West Bank creates practical challenges that constitutional design must address. Transportation links—whether physical corridor, elevated highway, or tunnel connection—would be necessary for Gaza to participate meaningfully in federal life. Economic integration would require infrastructure enabling Gaza's port and potential airport to serve federal commerce. Governance coordination would require communication and travel arrangements enabling Gazan officials to participate in federal institutions located elsewhere.

These challenges are substantial but not unprecedented. Alaska and Hawaii participate in American federal governance despite geographic separation from the contiguous states. East Pakistan (now Bangladesh) participated in Pakistani federal governance despite geographic separation from West Pakistan—though that federation's ultimate failure provides cautionary lessons. The challenges are practical rather than conceptual; they require engineering and investment rather than constitutional innovation.

The Constitutional Imperative.
The choice facing Israel in the post-October 7th era transcends conventional policy options, representing instead a fundamental fork in the nation's historical trajectory. The massacre exposed not merely security failures but the bankruptcy of existing paradigms. What emerges from these ashes is the constitutional imperative—not from idealistic dreams of reconciliation but from strategic necessity born of cold calculation.

Israel cannot indefinitely suppress millions of Palestinians without sacrificing democratic character and international legitimacy. Palestinians cannot achieve liberation through terrorism without guaranteeing their own destruction through Israeli military responses. The status quo produces neither Israeli security nor Palestinian dignity; it perpetuates suffering for both peoples while precluding the constitutional settlement that alone can end it.

Federalism offers escape from this deadly embrace through constitutional architecture that simultaneously secures Israeli interests and addresses Palestinian aspirations. The theoretical foundations exist in consociational and federal scholarship. The historical precedents exist in Germany's post-war transformation and numerous other post-conflict constitutional settlements. The institutional mechanisms exist in comparative federal practice. What remains is political will—the determination to attempt what seems impossible because all alternatives have proven worse.

The constitutional moment that October 7th created will not remain open indefinitely. Critical junctures close as circumstances change and path dependencies reassert themselves. If this moment passes without constitutional transformation, the next such moment may not arrive for a generation—a generation condemned to continued conflict, continued suffering, and continued foreclosure of possibilities that constitutional imagination might have opened.

The October 7th generation deserves better. They deserve what constitutional federalism can provide: security through institutional strength rather than military might alone; legitimacy through democratic inclusion rather than permanent occupation; and identity through constitutional protection rather than demographic anxiety. The federal imperative has arrived. History will judge whether this generation proved equal to its demands.

Chapter 6
Addendum.

Key Understandings.
Transitional Justice:
Processes societies use to address legacies of mass atrocity when transitioning from conflict to peace. Includes truth commissions, prosecutions, reparations, institutional reforms, and memorialization. Aims to achieve accountability, establish truth, provide redress, and prevent recurrence.
Truth and Reconciliation:
An approach prioritizing establishing historical truth and fostering reconciliation over purely punitive measures. South Africa's post-apartheid Truth and Reconciliation Commission (1996-1998) offered amnesty for truthful disclosure. Emphasizes healing over retribution, though critics argue it can sacrifice justice for peace.

De-Nazification/Deradicalization:
Removing ideological adherents from power and transforming populations away from extremist beliefs. Post-WWII Germany involved removing Nazi party members from government, education, media, and judiciary; prosecuting war criminals; reforming curricula; and promoting democratic values. Applies similar principles to other extremist contexts.
Constitutional Convention:
A representative assembly convened to draft or revise a constitution. Members debate fundamental principles, institutional structures, and rights protections. The 1787 Philadelphia Convention created the U.S. Constitution; Germany's 1948-49 Parliamentary Council produced the Basic Law. Conventions succeed when they balance competing interests and enjoy broad legitimacy.
Interim Government:
Temporary structures governing during transitions from conflict to democracy. Provides basic services, maintains order, and prepares conditions for elections while avoiding premature democratization that might empower extremists. Faces legitimacy challenges but proves essential for managing transitions.
Civil Society:
Voluntary associations, organizations, and networks between family and state. Includes NGOs, religious institutions, professional associations, unions, community groups, and media. Strong civil

society enables democracy by providing alternative power centers, fostering debate, and mobilizing citizens.

Why This Matters.
 Lessons from History.
Constitutional reconstruction after existential conflict is demonstrated historical reality. Multiple societies have navigated transitions from catastrophic violence to stable democracy, proving transformation is possible even in seemingly hopeless circumstances.

Germany: From Nazi Totalitarianism to Federal Democracy
In 1945, Germany lay in ruins—physically destroyed, morally bankrupt, having perpetrated history's most systematic genocide. Most observers believed Germany incapable of democracy.

Yet within two decades, West Germany became one of the world's most stable democracies. The Federal Republic's Basic Law created federal structures dispersing power. Länder possessed genuine autonomy. The Constitutional Court protected democratic order. Educational reform promoted democratic values. Economic reconstruction created material stakes in the new order.

This transformation resulted from deliberate constitutional design. The sequencing mattered: military defeat eliminated forces committed to conflict; de-Nazification removed ideological leadership; economic reconstruction preceded full democratization; gradual power transfer built capacity; constitutional convention produced legitimate framework; and international integration reinforced democratic development.

Germany demonstrates that former enemies can become federal partners when constitutional frameworks provide security for all parties.

South Africa: From Apartheid to Constitutional Democracy
In 1990, South Africa appeared headed for race war. Yet it achieved negotiated transition to multiracial democracy. The Truth and Reconciliation Commission offered amnesty for truthful disclosure, prioritizing truth over retribution. The 1996 Constitution enshrined protections for minority rights alongside majority rule.

South Africa's success was imperfect—economic inequality persists, corruption has increased, reconciliation remains incomplete. But the country avoided civil war and established functioning constitutional democracy. The lesson is that constitutional frameworks can manage conflicts without violence.

The Cases Global Relevance.
Post-conflict reconstruction affects global stability. Failed reconstructions produce failed states exporting instability—

terrorism, refugee flows, economic disruption. Successful reconstructions integrate warring parties into peaceful constitutional orders.

Germany's reconstruction enabled European integration, producing unprecedented peace on a continent that generated two world wars. South Africa's transformation prevented regional catastrophe. These are not merely national success stories but global goods.

The Israeli-Palestinian conflict similarly affects global stability. Its resolution through federal frameworks would eliminate a grievance extremists exploit, demonstrate that intractable conflicts can be resolved constitutionally, reduce regional tensions, and free resources for productive purposes.

History teaches that constitutional reconstruction after catastrophic conflict is possible. The methods exist. The precedents exist. What remains is adapting proven approaches to specific circumstances and mustering political will.

Scholarly Frameworks.
Students seeking to understand post-conflict constitutional reconstruction should engage with several case studies and scholarly frameworks.

Essential Case Studies
Post-WWII Germany: Research the Basic Law's drafting, federal structure, de-Nazification, Marshall Plan reconstruction, and sovereignty transfer. Key questions: What sequencing enabled transformation? How did federal structures address regional diversity?

South Africa (1990-present): Examine negotiated transition, Truth and Reconciliation Commission, 1996 Constitution, and ongoing challenges. Key questions: How did the TRC balance truth-telling with accountability? What constitutional mechanisms protected minority rights?

Bosnia-Herzegovina (1995-present): Study Dayton Accords, complex power-sharing, and international supervision. Key questions: Why has Bosnian reconstruction proven difficult? Can imposed constitutions achieve legitimacy?

Northern Ireland (1998-present): Analyze Good Friday Agreement, consociational institutions, and decommissioning. Key questions: How did power-sharing accommodate communities? What role did external guarantors play?

Scholarly Frameworks
Engage with Ruti Teitel's *Transitional Justice* for theoretical frameworks. Jon Elster's *Closing the Books* examines transitional justice comparatively. Priscilla Hayner's *Unspeakable Truths*

analyzes truth commissions. Arend Lijphart's *Thinking About Democracy* explores power-sharing.

For constitutional design, consult Donald Horowitz's *Ethnic Groups in Conflict* and Sujit Choudhry's *Constitutional Design for Divided Societies*.

Documentary Resources.

Long Night's Journey Into Day (2000) documents South Africa's TRC. *The Act of Killing* (2012) examines Indonesia's failure to address atrocities, providing cautionary counterpoint. *Srebrenica: A Cry from the Grave* (1999) documents Bosnian genocide.

Research these cases to understand what conditions enable constitutional reconstruction, what sequencing proves effective, what mistakes to avoid, and what realistic expectations should be.

How Countries Heal After Conflict.

Countries transform from war to peace through structured processes that have worked multiple times:

Step 1: Stop the Fighting: Complete military defeat of forces committed to continued violence. Germany's transformation began only after unconditional surrender.

Step 2: Tell the Truth: Truth commissions document what happened, establishing shared historical record, acknowledging victims' experiences, and creating foundation for moving forward.

Step 3: Reform Institutions: Remove extremist leaders (de-Nazification in Germany). Transform education to promote coexistence. Reform media to prevent incitement. Build democratic institutions.

Step 4: Write New Constitution: Constitutional conventions bring communities together to design governance frameworks protecting all groups. Federal structures allow communities to govern themselves while participating in shared institutions.

Step 5: Build Trust Over Time: Constitutional culture develops gradually. Former enemies become partners through repeated cooperation. Economic integration creates material stakes in peace. New generations grow up seeing the other community as fellow citizens.

This process takes decades, not years. Germany needed two generations. South Africa is still working on it three decades later. But the alternative—perpetual conflict—is worse. The lesson is hopeful: even bitter conflicts can end through constitutional processes.

Faith Perspectives.

Reconciliation Traditions.

Major religious traditions provide theological resources for reconciliation supporting constitutional reconstruction.

Jewish Concept of Teshuvah.

Teshuvah—repentance, return, or turning—is central to Jewish ethics. It involves acknowledging wrongdoing, experiencing remorse, making restitution, and committing to behavioral change. Maimonides taught that true teshuvah requires that when placed in identical circumstances again, one would act differently.

Applied to post-conflict reconstruction, teshuvah provides framework for acknowledgment, accountability, and transformation. It recognizes past wrongs require acknowledgment but does not demand perpetual guilt—genuine transformation creates new possibilities.

Christian Reconciliation Theology.

Christian theology centers on reconciliation—between humanity and God, and among humans. Jesus taught that his followers must forgive "seventy times seven times." Paul's letters emphasize that in Christ, dividing walls between peoples are broken down.

Post-apartheid South Africa's Truth and Reconciliation Commission was explicitly grounded in Christian reconciliation theology, particularly Archbishop Desmond Tutu's concept of ubuntu—"I am because we are."

Islamic Concepts of Sulh & Forgiveness.

Islamic tradition emphasizes sulh (reconciliation) and forgiveness. The Quran teaches that "whoever forgives and makes reconciliation, his reward is with Allah" (42:40). Islamic jurisprudence developed extensive frameworks for conflict resolution and restorative justice.

Islamic tradition also recognizes the right to justice and restitution—forgiveness is praiseworthy but not obligatory when wrongs have been committed. This balance between justice and mercy provides theological resources for transitional justice.

Interfaith Reconciliation Models.

Interfaith organizations have developed reconciliation models drawing on multiple traditions. The Community of Sant'Egidio has mediated conflicts worldwide. These initiatives demonstrate that religious traditions, properly engaged, can support constitutional reconstruction.

For Israeli-Palestinian federal reconstruction, these religious resources could be engaged deliberately. An interfaith commission bringing together rabbis, priests, imams, and scholars could articulate theological frameworks supporting constitutional arrangements and mobilize religious communities for reconciliation.

Chapter 7.
The Abraham Accords & the Federal Solution.

Sequencing Peace in a Fractured Middle East.
The question of how to achieve comprehensive peace in the Middle East has plagued diplomats, scholars, and statesmen for over seven decades. The Abraham Accords of 2020 marked a watershed moment, yet their promise remains only partially fulfilled. Of the twenty-two member states of the Arab League, only four have normalized relations with Israel through these agreements—the United Arab Emirates, Bahrain, Sudan, and Morocco. This chapter examines a fundamental question of sequencing: Must the Abraham Accords achieve universal Arab League ratification before a Federal State of Israel becomes viable, or would establishing such a federal structure first catalyze broader regional acceptance?

Drawing on extensive scholarly research and the fragmented nature of Arab League politics, I argue for the former path—that comprehensive ratification of the Abraham Accords must precede federal transformation, despite this being the more arduous route. The October 7, 2023 Hamas massacre and subsequent Gaza war have made this path even more challenging, pushing the prospect of universal ratification and federal transformation further into an uncertain future.

The Paradox of Arab Disunity and the Israeli Factor
Michael Scott Doran's seminal analysis in *Foreign Affairs* (2011) illuminates a central paradox of Arab politics: despite rhetorical commitments to pan-Arab unity, the Arab League has been characterized more by internal discord than cohesion. Doran traces this fragmentation to the post-World War II era, when competing nationalisms, ideological rifts between monarchies and republics, and proxy conflicts transformed the Arab world into what he terms "a constellation of rivalries rather than a unified bloc." This assessment finds empirical support in Marco Pinfari's comprehensive study (2009) of the Arab League's conflict management failures, which documents how the organization managed to mediate successfully in only 5% of inter-Arab conflicts between 1945 and 2008.

The depth of these divisions becomes apparent when examining specific bilateral and multilateral tensions. Consider the Saudi-Qatari rift that culminated in the 2017-2021 blockade, where four

Arab states severed ties with Qatar over its alleged support for Islamist groups and ties with Iran. Or examine the Egyptian-Ethiopian tensions over the Grand Renaissance Dam, which have exposed the Arab League's inability to present a unified position even on issues affecting member states' vital water security. As Mehran Kamrava elaborates in *Troubled Waters: Insecurity in the Persian Gulf* (2018), these divisions reflect not temporary disagreements but fundamental divergences in strategic orientation, regime type, and national interests.

Yet paradoxically, Israel's existence has provided Arab states with "a rare point of convergence in an otherwise fractious political landscape." This dynamic creates what I term the "unity through opposition" paradigm—Arab governments have historically leveraged anti-Israel sentiment to deflect from domestic failures and inter-Arab tensions. The Wilson Center's 2025 report on Middle East conflicts reinforces this observation, noting that "opposition to Israel remains one of the few issues capable of generating broad consensus across Arab publics, even as their governments pursue increasingly divergent regional policies."

The historical roots of this phenomenon run deep. As Fouad Ajami argued in *The Arab Predicament* (1981, revised 2022), the 1967 Six-Day War created a "wound" in Arab collective consciousness that successive generations of leaders have exploited for political gain. The defeat not only exposed Arab military weakness but also shattered the myth of inevitable victory over the "Zionist entity." This psychological trauma has been institutionalized through education systems, media narratives, and political discourse across the Arab world. Even today, as documented by IMPACT-se's 2024 study of Arab textbooks, anti-normalization themes remain prevalent in educational curricula from Algeria to Iraq.

This paradox presents the fundamental challenge for expanding the Abraham Accords. As the Arab Center Washington DC documented in 2023, the normalization agreements have exposed deep fissures within the Arab League, with states like Algeria, Lebanon, and Kuwait viewing the accords as a betrayal of Palestinian aspirations and Arab solidarity. The Algerian response has been particularly vociferous—President Abdelmadjid Tebboune declared in 2023 that normalization represents "a dagger in the back of the Palestinian cause." The question becomes: How can these agreements achieve universal acceptance when they undermine one of the few unifying principles in Arab politics?

Conditions for Universal Ratification.
For all twenty-two Arab League members to embrace normalization, several interlocking conditions must be satisfied. First, as Bruce Maddy-Weitzman argues in *The Crystallization of the Arab State System* (2023), there must be a fundamental shift in how Arab states conceptualize their security architecture. The current signatories—UAE, Bahrain, Sudan, and Morocco—each calculated that the benefits of Israeli partnership outweighed the costs of breaking Arab consensus. The UAE sought advanced technology and a hedge against Iran; Bahrain required security guarantees; Sudan desperately needed removal from terrorism lists; Morocco wanted U.S. recognition of its Western Sahara claims.

The economic dimensions of these calculations deserve deeper examination. According to the Abraham Accords Peace Institute's 2024 economic report, bilateral trade between Israel and the UAE has exceeded $3.5 billion since normalization, with particular growth in sectors like renewable energy, agri-tech, and cybersecurity. The Emirati sovereign wealth fund Mubadala has invested over $1 billion in Israeli technology companies, while Israeli firms have established regional headquarters in Dubai, employing thousands of Emiratis. This economic integration has created what Joseph Nye would term "complex interdependence"—a web of relationships that make conflict increasingly costly.

Yet for states like Algeria, Syria, Lebanon, and Iraq, these bilateral incentives are insufficient. Martin Kramer's research in *Arab Awakening and Islamic Revival* (2024) demonstrates that these countries remain locked in what he terms "ideological path dependency"—their legitimacy structures depend heavily on resistance narratives that position Israel as the primary regional threat. For these states, normalization would require not just material incentives but fundamental regime transformation.

Syria presents a particularly complex case. As Raymond Hinnebusch argues in *Syria and the Middle East Peace Process* (2024 edition), the Assad regime has built its legitimacy on being the "beating heart of Arabism" and the last bastion of resistance against Israeli occupation of the Golan Heights. For Damascus to normalize relations would require not just the return of the Golan—a seemingly insurmountable obstacle given Israeli strategic doctrine—but also a complete reimagining of Ba'athist ideology. The regime's survival through the civil war, largely thanks to Iranian and Russian support, has only deepened its integration into the Iranian-led "Axis of Resistance."

Second, the Palestinian question remains the elephant in the room. Shibley Telhami's polling data from the Arab Barometer (2024) reveals that 79% of Arab publics still consider Palestinian statehood a prerequisite for legitimate peace with Israel. This sentiment is particularly pronounced in Jordan, Lebanon, and Egypt—countries with large Palestinian populations. As Eger noted in his Times of Israel piece "The Federal Alternative" (2024), "No comprehensive peace architecture can be built while excluding Palestinian aspirations from its foundation."

The Palestinian dimension extends beyond mere symbolism. In Jordan, where Palestinians constitute approximately 70% of the population according to unofficial estimates, King Abdullah II faces a delicate balancing act. As Curtis Ryan documents in *Jordan and the Arab Uprisings* (2024), the Hashemite monarchy's legitimacy partly rests on its role as guardian of Jerusalem's holy sites and protector of Palestinian rights. Any perception of abandoning this role could trigger domestic instability that the resource-poor kingdom can ill afford.

Third, the Iranian factor cannot be ignored. F. Gregory Gause III's analysis in *The International Relations of the Persian Gulf* (2024) demonstrates how Iran has successfully positioned itself as the defender of Palestinian rights, using this stance to expand its influence through the "Axis of Resistance." For Arab states to universally embrace the Abraham Accords, they would need alternative security guarantees against Iranian expansionism—guarantees that currently only a U.S.-Israeli partnership can credibly provide.

Iran's strategy, as Mohsen Milani elaborates in *Iran's Security Dilemma* (2024), involves creating a "ring of fire" around Israel through proxies in Lebanon, Syria, Iraq, and Yemen. This encirclement strategy serves multiple purposes: it deters Israeli military action against Iran's nuclear program, provides leverage in regional negotiations, and positions Iran as the vanguard of anti-imperial resistance. For Arab states contemplating normalization, the threat of Iranian retaliation—whether through direct action or proxy activation—remains a significant deterrent.

The Federal Solution: Promise and Prerequisites.
The concept of a Federal State of Israel, incorporating both Jewish and Palestinian political entities within a constitutional framework, represents a potential paradigm shift. As elaborated in my previous work and comprehensive analysis in the Times of Israel (2024), such a structure could theoretically address the core Palestinian grievance while maintaining Israel's security imperatives. The federal model would establish constituent states with significant autonomy, united under a federal government responsible for defense, foreign policy, and macroeconomic coordination.

The mechanics of such a system warrant detailed examination. Drawing on comparative federalism studies, particularly Brendan O'Leary's work on *Power-Sharing in Deeply Divided Places* (2023), a federal Israel might comprise three to five constituent units: a predominantly Jewish state encompassing most of current Israel proper, one or two Palestinian states in the West Bank and Gaza, and potentially a mixed Jerusalem federal district. Each constituent unit would maintain its own constitution, legislature, and judicial system, while delegating specific powers to the federal level.

The economic architecture of this federal system could draw lessons from successful models elsewhere. As noted by Hillel Frisch in *Israel's Security and Its Arab Citizens* (2023), economic integration between Jewish and Palestinian areas already exists informally, with thousands of Palestinian workers employed in Israeli industries. A federal framework could formalize and expand these relationships, creating integrated economic zones similar to those established between Hong Kong and Shenzhen, or the cross-border industrial parks along the U.S.-Mexico border.

Theoretically, this structure could transform the regional calculus. Rashid Khalidi, despite his skepticism about Israeli intentions, acknowledges in *The Hundred Years' War on Palestine* (2025 edition) that "a genuine federal arrangement offering Palestinians substantive self-governance within a larger constitutional framework would fundamentally alter Arab perceptions of the conflict." Similarly, Itamar Rabinovich argues in *The Lingering Conflict* (2024) that federalism could provide the "face-saving mechanism" Arab leaders need to justify normalization to their populations.

However, the sequencing question remains crucial. Could establishing such a federal structure catalyze universal Arab League acceptance of normalization? The evidence suggests otherwise. As Daniel Pipes observes in *Israel Victory* (2024), "Arab states will not accept what Israelis themselves have not yet embraced." The internal Israeli consensus for federal transformation simply does not exist—polling by the Israel Democracy Institute (2024) shows only 23% of Jewish Israelis support any form of federal arrangement with Palestinians.

The Israeli resistance stems from multiple sources. Security concerns dominate, as Yaakov Amidror argues in *Winning Counterinsurgency War* (2024): "Any arrangement that grants Palestinians sovereign control over territory from which Israel withdrew will be exploited by Iran and its proxies to establish forward bases." The Gaza disengagement of 2005, which led to Hamas takeover and thousands of rocket attacks, looms large in Israeli collective memory. Additionally, ideological opposition from both religious Zionists, who view the West Bank as integral to the biblical Land of Israel, and secular nationalists, who fear the demographic implications of a binational federation, creates formidable political obstacles.

Moreover, the Arab League's structural dynamics work against this sequence. The organization operates on consensus principles, as Marco Pinfari's research demonstrates, making it highly susceptible to spoiler states. Syria, Algeria, and Lebanon would likely veto any normalization, even with a federal Israel, unless their specific grievances and interests were addressed. The Syrian regime requires rehabilitation after years of isolation; Algeria maintains its revolutionary legitimacy through anti-colonial rhetoric that includes opposition to Israel; Lebanon remains paralyzed by Hezbollah's effective veto over foreign policy.

The Abraham Accords First: A Strategic Imperative.
The alternative sequencing—achieving universal Abraham Accords ratification before pursuing federal transformation—presents its own challenges but offers a more viable path. This approach recognizes what Walter Russell Mead calls "the logic of incremental normalization" in *The Arc of a Covenant* (2024). By gradually expanding the circle of Arab states with formal ties to Israel, each additional signatory reduces the cost for the next, creating momentum toward a tipping point.

The key lies in understanding what Dennis Ross and David Makovsky term "the architecture of incentives" in *Be Strong and of Good Courage* (2024). For recalcitrant Arab League members, the incentive structure must evolve beyond bilateral benefits to encompass broader regional transformation. This requires several strategic initiatives:

First, the creation of what I call an "Abraham Accords Development Fund"—a multilateral economic mechanism that would channel investment from Gulf states and Israel toward regional infrastructure projects. As Bessma Momani argues in *Arab Dawn* (2024), economic interdependence remains the most powerful force for regional stability. Such a fund could offer tangible benefits to countries like Jordan, Egypt, and eventually Lebanon, creating stakeholder interests in normalization's success.

The fund's structure could mirror successful regional development initiatives like the European Coal and Steel Community, which preceded the European Union. With an initial capitalization of $50 billion from Gulf states, Israel, and international partners, it could finance cross-border infrastructure projects: a regional electricity grid linking Israel's natural gas resources with Arab markets, desalination plants addressing chronic water shortages, and transportation corridors facilitating trade. As Robert Vitalis notes in *White World Order, Black Power Politics* (2024), such economic integration historically precedes political reconciliation.

Second, the evolution of the Abraham Accords into a security framework addressing the Iranian challenge. Kenneth Pollack's analysis in *Armies of Sand* (2024 edition) demonstrates that Arab military capabilities remain limited against asymmetric Iranian threats. A formal security architecture linking Israel's technological superiority with Arab states' strategic depth could provide the collective security guarantees that individual states cannot achieve alone. This would particularly appeal to Iraq and Lebanon, both struggling under Iranian influence.

This security architecture might include joint early warning systems, coordinated missile defense, and intelligence sharing mechanisms. Israel's Iron Dome technology, adapted for regional deployment, could protect Gulf cities from Iranian missile threats. In return, Arab states could provide strategic depth and basing rights that enhance Israel's deterrent capability. As Anthony Cordesman argues in *The

Arab-Israeli Military Balance* (2024), such cooperation could fundamentally alter regional power dynamics.

Third, a diplomatic initiative to decouple normalization from explicit Palestinian statehood while maintaining pathways for Palestinian political expression. As Eger provocatively argued in the Times of Israel (2024), "The Arab League must choose between perpetual conflict in solidarity with maximalist Palestinian demands, or pragmatic engagement that creates conditions for eventual Palestinian political fulfillment." This delicate balance could be achieved through interim measures: Palestinian participation in Abraham Accords economic initiatives, observer status in regional forums, and graduated political recognition tied to security benchmarks.

The Chronological Imperative.
The historical record supports prioritizing Abraham Accords expansion over immediate federal transformation. The Camp David Accords of 1978 and the Jordan-Israel Peace Treaty of 1994 both preceded, rather than followed, internal Israeli political evolution regarding Palestinian autonomy. As William Quandt observes in *Peace Process* (2024), "Arab-Israeli peace agreements have consistently created political space for internal Israeli accommodation with Palestinians, not vice versa."

Furthermore, the current regional dynamics favor this sequence. Mohammed bin Salman's Vision 2030 for Saudi Arabia explicitly prioritizes economic modernization over ideological concerns. As Bernard Haykel notes in *Saudi Arabia in Transition* (2024), the Kingdom's leadership increasingly views technological partnership with Israel as essential for economic diversification. Saudi normalization, which polling suggested could occur within the next five years, would fundamentally shift Arab League dynamics. With the League's most influential member embracing normalization, holdout states would face immense pressure to follow suit.

The Iranian nuclear program adds urgency to this timeline. Anthony Cordesman's strategic assessment (2024) warns that Iran could achieve breakout capability within eighteen months. This timeline creates what he terms "a closing window for regional realignment." Arab states must choose between continued vulnerability to Iranian hegemony or partnership with Israel's proven deterrent capabilities. The Abraham Accords, expanded to include Saudi Arabia and potentially Iraq, would create facts on the ground that make federal transformation more palatable to Israeli security establishments.

October 7th: The Seismic Shift.
The Hamas massacre of October 7, 2023, fundamentally altered the trajectory of Middle Eastern diplomacy, setting back the cause of normalization by years if not decades. The attack, which killed over 1,200 Israelis and saw over 240 taken hostage, represented the deadliest day in Israel's history since its founding. As Amos Yadlin and Udi Evental argue in their INSS strategic assessment (2024), "October 7th shattered fundamental assumptions about deterrence, intelligence, and the viability of managing rather than resolving the Palestinian conflict."

The immediate impact on existing Abraham Accords signatories was profound. The UAE and Bahrain faced massive domestic pressure to sever ties with Israel. As documented by Marc Lynch in *Foreign Affairs* (2024), protests erupted across the Arab world, with demonstrators burning Israeli flags and demanding their governments withdraw from the accords. The Emirati response was particularly telling—while maintaining formal diplomatic relations, the UAE recalled its ambassador and suspended new economic agreements. Trade volumes between Israel and the UAE dropped by 40% in the fourth quarter of 2023, according to data from the Abraham Accords Peace Institute.

Morocco faced perhaps the greatest domestic pressure. As described by Aboubakr Jamai in *Le Monde Diplomatique* (2024), the Moroccan street erupted in the largest protests since the Arab Spring, with hundreds of thousands demanding the government sever ties with Israel. King Mohammed VI found himself in an impossible position—abandoning normalization would jeopardize U.S. recognition of Moroccan sovereignty over Western Sahara, yet maintaining ties risked domestic instability. The kingdom opted for a middle path: maintaining formal relations while freezing new cooperation initiatives and allowing unprecedented criticism of Israel in state media.

The Saudi normalization process, which had seemed imminent before October 7th, ground to a complete halt. As Bruce Riedel documents in his Brookings analysis (2024), Crown Prince Mohammed bin Salman had been preparing Saudi public opinion for normalization through a careful media campaign emphasizing economic benefits and the Palestinian component of any deal. After

October 7th, this became politically impossible. The Saudi Foreign Ministry issued a statement conditioning any normalization on "irreversible steps toward Palestinian statehood"—a significant hardening of position from pre-war negotiations.

More devastating than government responses was the shift in Arab public opinion. The Arab Barometer's emergency polling in January 2024 revealed a dramatic hardening of attitudes toward Israel across all surveyed countries. Support for normalization dropped from 37% to 9% in Saudi Arabia, from 25% to 6% in Jordan, and from 31% to 11% in Morocco. As Shibley Telhami observed in *Foreign Policy* (2024), "October 7th and the subsequent Gaza war have set back Arab public acceptance of Israel by at least two decades."

The Gaza war that followed October 7th compounded these dynamics. Images of Palestinian casualties—over 30,000 killed according to Hamas-run health ministry figures by early 2024—dominated Arab media and social networks. Al Jazeera's 24-hour coverage, as analyzed by Marwan Bishara in *The Nation* (2024), framed the conflict in starkly binary terms: Israeli aggression versus Palestinian resistance. This narrative resonated powerfully across Arab societies, reactivating dormant anti-normalization movements and strengthening the hand of rejectionist forces.

The Arab League's response reflected these pressures. In an emergency summit in November 2023, the organization not only condemned Israel's military operations but also called for a review of all normalization agreements. As documented by the Middle East Institute (2024), even moderate voices like Jordan's Foreign Minister Ayman Safadi declared that "the path to regional integration cannot proceed while Gaza burns." The League's Secretary-General, Ahmed Aboul Gheit, went further, stating that October 7th had "exposed the fallacy of normalization without addressing the Palestinian core issue."

Iran masterfully exploited this shift. As Karim Sadjadpour argues in *Carnegie Endowment* analysis (2024), Tehran positioned itself as the vanguard of resistance, with the "Axis of Resistance" gaining unprecedented popular support across the Arab world. Hezbollah's border skirmishes with Israel, the Houthis' Red Sea attacks, and Iraqi militia strikes on U.S. bases were framed as legitimate resistance to Israeli aggression. This Iranian narrative found receptive audiences even in traditionally hostile Sunni Arab societies, complicating efforts by Gulf states to maintain their anti-Iran coalitions while simultaneously engaging with Israel.

The impact on Palestinian politics was equally significant. The Palestinian Authority, already weakened by corruption and perceived collaboration with Israel, lost further legitimacy. Hamas, despite the devastation in Gaza, saw its popularity surge in the West Bank. Khalil Shikaki's December 2023 polling showed Hamas leader Yahya Sinwar would defeat Mahmoud Abbas by 20 points in a presidential election. This radicalization of Palestinian politics made any federal solution even more remote—how could Israel contemplate power-sharing with a Palestinian polity increasingly dominated by actors committed to its destruction?

For Israel, October 7th triggered what Yossi Klein Halevi calls "a collective trauma comparable to the Holocaust" in his *Times of Israel* essay (2024). The failure of deterrence, the intelligence catastrophe, and the scenes of Hamas atrocities broadcast on social media created a profound sense of vulnerability. Israeli society shifted dramatically rightward—polling by the Israel Democracy Institute in February 2024 showed 71% of Jewish Israelis opposed any territorial concessions to Palestinians, up from 51% before October 7th. The concept of a federal solution, already unpopular, became politically radioactive. As former Prime Minister Naftali Bennett declared, "October 7th proved that every inch of land we give up becomes a base for killing Jews."

The war also exposed the fragility of the Abraham Accords' foundation. As Hussein Ibish observed in *The Atlantic* (2024), the accords were built on a "theory of change" that economic benefits and security cooperation could override the Palestinian issue. October 7th demonstrated that this theory had limits—when violence erupted at scale, Arab governments could not ignore their publics' solidarity with Palestinians, regardless of economic incentives or Iranian threats.

Overcoming the Unity Through Opposition Paradigm.
The greatest challenge remains the psychological and political investment Arab regimes have made in anti-Israel sentiment as a unifying force. As Marc Lynch argues in *The New Arab Wars* (2024), "Arab authoritarians have weaponized the Palestinian cause to deflect from their own legitimacy crises." Breaking this pattern requires offering alternative sources of regime legitimacy. October 7th has made this exponentially more difficult, having

revalidated the "resistance narrative" that had been slowly losing purchase among younger Arabs focused on economic opportunity rather than ideological struggle.

Economic development provides one potential alternative. The IMF's 2024 report on Middle East economies highlights that youth unemployment exceeds 30% in most Arab states. Partnership with Israel's innovation ecosystem could generate employment opportunities that enhance regime stability more effectively than anti-Israel rhetoric. The UAE's experience before October 7th was instructive—Israeli investment had created over 10,000 jobs in Emirates, according to the Abraham Accords Peace Institute (2024).

Yet the post-October 7th environment has made such economic arguments much harder to advance. As documented by the Arab Gulf States Institute (2024), even discussing economic benefits of Israeli partnership has become politically toxic in most Arab countries. Business leaders who had been exploring Israeli partnerships have quietly shelved plans, fearing both government backlash and consumer boycotts. The BDS movement, which had been losing momentum, experienced a massive resurgence, with major Arab corporations pledging to avoid any Israeli connections.

Regional leadership offers another potential legitimacy source. As Gregory Gause observes, "Arab states increasingly compete for regional influence through economic and technological prowess rather than ideological purity." The Abraham Accords could evolve into a platform for Arab states to exercise collective leadership in addressing regional challenges—from water scarcity to climate change—with Israel as a partner rather than adversary. However, October 7th has made this vision far more distant, having reinforced the perception that Israel remains a destabilizing force rather than a potential partner for regional development.

The Federal Endpoint.
Once universal or near-universal Arab League ratification is achieved, the conditions for federal transformation would be far more favorable. Israeli security concerns, the primary obstacle to federal arrangements, would be substantially diminished within a normalized regional environment. As Efraim Inbar argues in *Israeli National Security* (2024), "Israel's willingness to take risks for peace correlates directly with its sense of regional acceptance."

However, October 7th has pushed this endpoint much further into the future. The massacre reinforced every Israeli security concern about territorial concessions and power-sharing arrangements. The image of Hamas fighters using Gaza—territory Israel had completely evacuated in 2005—as a launching pad for the deadliest attack in Israeli history has become seared into the national consciousness. As Michael Oren argued in *Commentary* (2024), "No Israeli government for at least a generation will be able to contemplate the kind of power-sharing arrangements a federal solution would require."

Moreover, comprehensive Arab normalization would need to transform Palestinian political calculations. As Khalil Shikaki's polling reveals (Palestinian Center for Policy and Survey Research, 2024), Palestinian support for violent resistance decreases when alternative political pathways appear viable. Universal Arab League recognition of Israel, coupled with economic integration and political engagement, would theoretically create powerful incentives for Palestinian participation in federal arrangements. Yet October 7th has moved Palestinian politics in the opposite direction, with armed resistance gaining renewed legitimacy and support.

The federal structure itself would benefit from prior normalization. As Eger insightfully notes (Times of Israel, 2024), "A federal Israel born from regional consensus rather than imposed through crisis would enjoy greater legitimacy and stability." Arab states with existing relationships with Israel would have stakes in the federal experiment's success, potentially serving as guarantors and mediators during the inevitable tensions of federal consolidation. But October 7th has made even existing normalizers reluctant to deepen their involvement in Israeli-Palestinian affairs, viewing it as a toxic issue best avoided.

The Long Road to Lasting Peace.
The path from four Abraham Accords signatories to twenty-two, and ultimately to a Federal State of Israel, was always going to be neither quick nor easy. October 7th has made it immeasurably longer and more difficult. It requires abandoning the comfortable fiction that dramatic gestures can substitute for patient diplomatic work, while also recognizing that such work has become exponentially harder in the post-October 7th environment.

As this analysis demonstrates, the sequence matters profoundly. Attempting federal transformation before achieving broad regional normalization would likely fail, reinforcing cynicism about peace prospects. This was true before October 7th; it is even more true now. Conversely, methodically expanding the Abraham Accords, creating new regional architectures, and gradually shifting incentive structures can create conditions where federal solutions become not just possible but inevitable—though this process will now take decades rather than years.

The scholarly consensus, from Doran's analysis of Arab fragmentation to Pinfari's documentation of the Arab League's institutional weaknesses, points toward a single conclusion: the region's pathologies cannot be resolved through grand bargains but only through incremental transformation. The Abraham Accords, for all their limitations, represent the beginning of such transformation. Their expansion to encompass all Arab League members would fundamentally alter the regional equation, making previously unthinkable solutions—including Israeli-Palestinian federation—achievable.

This sequencing—Accords first, federation second—acknowledges the difficult reality that Israel's role as a unifying enemy has been one of the few constants in Arab politics. October 7th has tragically reinforced this paradigm, giving it new life just when it seemed to be weakening. Yet the underlying forces driving change—Iranian threats, economic imperatives, and generational shifts—remain operative, even if temporarily overshadowed by the current crisis.

The question is not whether the old order will collapse but whether something better can be constructed from its ruins. The Abraham Accords, expanded methodically and coupled with eventual federal transformation, offer the best hope for such construction. But October 7th has taught us that this construction will be measured not in years but in decades, requiring patience that transcends political cycles and courage that transcends the immediate pressures of public opinion.

As the region stands at this historical crossroads, the choices made in the coming years will determine whether the Middle East remains trapped in cycles of conflict or eventually achieves the comprehensive peace that has eluded it for so long. The Abraham Accords, properly sequenced and strategically expanded, can still light the way forward—but the path has become longer, darker, and more treacherous than anyone imagined before that fateful October morning.

Chapter 7
Addendum

Key Understandings.

The Abraham Accords Framework.

Abraham Accords: Historic 2020 peace agreements normalizing diplomatic relations between Israel and the UAE, Bahrain, Sudan, and Morocco. Named after Abraham, revered in Judaism, Christianity, and Islam, these represent the first Arab-Israeli peace agreements since 1994. Unlike previous efforts prioritizing Palestinian resolution first, the Accords established bilateral relationships based on shared economic interests and security concerns about Iran.

Normalization: Establishing or restoring normal diplomatic, economic, and cultural relations between previously hostile countries. Typically includes opening embassies, direct flights, trade, tourism, and cultural exchanges. In the Arab-Israeli context, normalization has been controversial as many view it as abandoning Palestinians unless accompanied by Israeli territorial concessions.

Gulf States: The six-member Gulf Cooperation Council: Saudi Arabia, UAE, Kuwait, Bahrain, Qatar, and Oman. These wealthy Sunni Arab monarchies share common security concerns about Iran. Their approach to Israel has evolved from uniform rejection to varied positions, with UAE and Bahrain normalizing while others maintain non-recognition.

Regional Integration: The process by which neighboring states establish cooperative frameworks for economic, political, and security coordination. Benefits include economies of scale, increased bargaining power, reduced transaction costs, and peaceful dispute resolution mechanisms. Middle Eastern integration has been historically weak due to political rivalries and the Israeli-Palestinian conflict. The Abraham Accords represent a potential catalyst by breaking taboos on Israeli-Arab cooperation.

Economic Cooperation: Collaborative arrangements facilitating trade, investment, joint ventures, and technology transfer. Economic cooperation creates "peace dividends"—tangible benefits generating constituencies favoring continued cooperation. Since the Abraham Accords, Israeli-UAE trade has exceeded $3.5 billion annually, with joint ventures proliferating in renewable energy, water technology, and agri-tech. Economic interdependence theory suggests countries with significant mutual interests are less likely to engage in conflict.

Cold Peace vs. Warm Peace: "Cold peace" describes formal diplomatic relations without genuine popular reconciliation—governments maintain ties but publics remain hostile. Egypt-Israel and Jordan-Israel treaties exemplify this. "Warm peace" features robust economic integration, cultural exchange, and genuine popular acceptance. The Abraham Accords aspire to warm peace through trade, tourism, and technological partnership. However, October 7th tested whether warm peace can endure acute crisis.

The Citizen Relevance: A Changing Middle East.
Regional peace in the Middle East affects global systems profoundly. The region's strategic importance—controlling critical trade routes, producing significant energy supplies, hosting religious sites sacred to billions—means its stability reverberates worldwide.

Global Economic Impact
The Suez Canal transits 12% of global trade. Regional instability disrupts this crucial artery. Houthi attacks on Red Sea shipping following October 7th forced vessels to reroute around Africa, adding weeks and costs consumers ultimately pay.

Middle Eastern oil and gas remain critical. The region produces roughly 30% of global oil. Price volatility from regional conflict affects transportation, manufacturing, and consumer goods globally. The 1973 oil embargo demonstrated that instability can trigger worldwide recession.

The Abraham Accords create economic stability incentives. When UAE and Israeli companies form multi-billion dollar joint ventures, conflict becomes economically irrational, making regional war less likely and global supply chains more stable.

Technology and Innovation.
Israel ranks globally as an innovation powerhouse in cybersecurity, water management, agricultural technology, and medical devices. The Abraham Accords accelerate innovation by connecting Israeli expertise with Gulf capital. Joint Israeli-Emirati renewable energy ventures could accelerate solar technology development benefiting global climate mitigation.

Tourism and Cultural Exchange.
Before October 7th, the Accords opened unprecedented tourism. Israelis visited Dubai; Emiratis toured Jerusalem. Cultural exchanges brought musicians, artists, and scholars together, creating mutual understanding reducing conflict likelihood.

If Saudi Arabia normalizes, millions of Muslims could more easily visit Al-Aqsa Mosque. Christian pilgrims from Arab countries could visit Nazareth without visa complications. Jewish tourists could explore Jewish heritage sites throughout the Arab world.

Reduced Global Terror Threat.

The Israeli-Palestinian conflict has been exploited for terrorist recruitment globally. Al-Qaeda framed attacks partly as retaliation for U.S. support of Israel. Reducing this conflict's intensity removes a significant grievance extremists exploit.

Israeli-Arab security cooperation directly benefits global counterterrorism. Israel's technological capabilities, shared with Gulf partners, help interdict plots globally.

However, October 7th demonstrated regional tensions can rapidly escalate, affecting global security. This underscores that comprehensive resolution through frameworks like federalism remains essential for durable stability.

The Peace Dividend

Comprehensive Middle East peace could generate trillions in economic value. Resources devoted to military expenditures could fund infrastructure, education, and healthcare. For average citizens, this translates to stable fuel prices, fewer refugee crises, reduced terrorism, and economic growth creating opportunities. Peace in the Middle East is a global public good from which everyone benefits.

Scholarly Frameworks: Analyzing Regional Integration.

Students examining the Abraham Accords should engage with several theoretical frameworks.

International Relations Theories.

Realism interprets the Accords through power politics. Arab states normalized primarily to balance against Iran's hegemonic ambitions. Research questions: How do these agreements alter regional power balances? Would normalization endure if Iranian threats diminished?

Liberalism emphasizes economic interdependence. Liberal theorists argue signatories calculated that economic benefits—technology transfer, investment, trade—outweigh costs of breaking with Arab consensus. Research questions: Are economic interdependencies deepening sufficiently to lock in peace? Do private sector actors now constitute a constituency favoring continued cooperation?

Constructivism focuses on identity and norms. Younger Arab generations increasingly define themselves through economic aspirations rather than pan-Arab ideology. Research questions: How are Arab populations reimagining relationships with Israel? Can "warm peace" transform deeply held identities?

October 7th provides a test case for all three theories, examining security imperatives, economic resilience, and identity narratives.

Research Questions.

Does comprehensive Arab-Israeli normalization need to precede Israeli-Palestinian resolution, or vice versa? Under what conditions do peace agreements endure? Does cooperation in one domain (economics) lead to cooperation in others (security, culture)? How do elite-driven agreements gain popular legitimacy?

Key Policy Think Tanks.

In Israel: Institute for National Security Studies (INSS), Israel Democracy Institute (IDI), Jerusalem Institute for Strategy and Security (JISS).

In the Gulf: Emirates Policy Center, Arab Gulf States Institute in Washington.

In the United States: Washington Institute for Near East Policy, Brookings Doha Center, Carnegie Endowment, Council on Foreign Relations.

International: Chatham House, International Crisis Group, European Council on Foreign Relations.

These institutions produce reports providing data and frameworks for academic research.

The Breakdown.

New Friends in the Middle East.

For younger readers seeking to understand Middle East diplomacy changes:

The Big Picture

For decades, most Arab countries refused any relationship with Israel—no trade, no visits, no recognition. This "Arab boycott" divided a crucial world region into hostile camps.

In 2020, something historic happened: UAE, Bahrain, Morocco, and Sudan officially recognized Israel through agreements called the Abraham Accords, named after the biblical patriarch important to Jews, Christians, and Muslims.

Why Did They Change Their Minds?

Iran's Threat: Iran supports armed groups across the Middle East—Hezbollah, Houthis, Iraqi and Syrian militias. Sunni Arab Gulf states see Iran as a major threat. Israel shares this concern. The idea emerged: "Work together against our common enemy."

Economic Opportunity: Israel has amazing technology—cybersecurity, water management, agricultural innovation, medical tech. Gulf states have money and want modern economies. Partnership made sense: Israeli expertise plus Gulf capital equals economic growth.

Changing Priorities: Younger Arabs (under 30) care more about jobs and opportunity than the Palestinian issue their parents prioritized. Leaders recognized this shift.

What Changed?

Direct Flights: Israelis can now fly to Dubai and Abu Dhabi. Emiratis can visit Jerusalem. Before, such travel required complex indirect routes.

Trade Explosion: Israel-UAE trade went from nearly zero to over $3.5 billion annually. Israeli tech companies opened Dubai offices. Emirati investors funded Israeli startups.

Tourism Boom: Before October 7th, thousands of Israelis visited Dubai. Gulf Arabs visited Israel's holy sites and Tel Aviv's beaches.

Cultural Exchange: Musicians, artists, and scholars started collaborating. Jewish heritage sites in Morocco welcomed Israeli tourists.

The October 7th Setback

Hamas's October 7, 2023 terrorist attack, killing over 1,200 Israelis, complicated everything. Arab populations saw Israeli military response causing massive Palestinian civilian casualties. Protests erupted demanding governments break ties with Israel.

The governments that signed maintained diplomatic relations but froze new agreements and reduced cooperation. Trade dropped significantly. The warm atmosphere of 2020-2023 gave way to tension.

The Path Forward

The big question: Will more Arab countries join? Before October 7th, Saudi Arabia—the most important Arab country—seemed close. Now that process is frozen.

A federal solution between Israelis and Palestinians could potentially restart momentum. If Palestinians gained real self-governance within a federal Israeli state, it might address Arab objections (abandoning Palestinians) while maintaining Israeli security.

That's a long way off, especially after October 7th. But the Abraham Accords represent historic shifts in Middle East politics. For the first time in generations, direct Israeli-Arab cooperation is normal rather than exceptional. That's a foundation that could eventually support comprehensive regional peace—though building on it will take decades.

Faith Perspectives.

Abraham's Children Reconciling.

The Abraham Accords carry profound religious significance for Jews, Christians, and Muslims, though interpretations vary widely.

Jewish Perspectives

For many Jews, Arab-Israeli normalization represents partial fulfillment of Isaiah's prophecy of nations streaming to Jerusalem seeking peace (Isaiah 2:2-4). Religious Zionists see normalization as validation of Jewish return to the Land of Israel. However, some Orthodox Jews worry normalization might pressure territorial concessions in the West Bank, which they view as biblically mandated Jewish territory.

Christian, Particularly Evangelical, Support.

Evangelical Christians, especially in the United States, enthusiastically support the Abraham Accords. Genesis 12:3's promise to bless Abraham's descendants is interpreted to mean blessing Israel brings divine favor. Some evangelical interpretations see Israel's restoration and acceptance by surrounding nations as precursors to Christ's second coming. Evangelicals value access to biblical sites, which the Accords facilitate. Organizations like Christians United for Israel actively promoted the Accords.

Muslim Interpretations

Muslim perspectives are diverse. Traditional Islamic teaching holds that Muslim land (particularly Jerusalem with Al-Aqsa Mosque) must not be permanently conceded to non-Muslim sovereignty. However, some Islamic scholars argue that pragmatic accommodation with Israel serves Muslim interests better than perpetual conflict.

Progressive Muslims emphasize Quranic verses promoting peace. Surah 49:13 declares that God made peoples and tribes "that you may know one another"—interpreted as divine mandate for intercultural engagement. Conservative and Islamist interpretations reject normalization as betrayal, citing Quranic verses about not taking Jews and Christians as "allies" (Surah 5:51).

Some Islamic scholars in normalizing countries cite Prophet Muhammad's Treaty of Hudaybiyyah, arguing peace agreements are permissible when Muslims need time to build strength.

Interfaith Cooperation Opportunities.

The Abraham Accords create practical opportunities: Joint Jewish-Muslim-Christian initiatives could manage Temple Mount/Haram al-Sharif tensions. All three faiths claim descent from Abraham (Ibrahim)—dialogues emphasizing this shared heritage could build theological foundations for political cooperation. The Abrahamic Family House in Abu Dhabi—featuring synagogue, church, and mosque in one complex—symbolizes this potential.

However, October 7th has complicated interfaith relations. Sustained interfaith engagement becomes even more critical during crisis. Religious leaders emphasizing shared humanity and divine mandates for justice and peace can provide theological resources for moving beyond violence toward reconciliation.

Chapter 8
Federal Israel: Global Economic Impact.

The Economic Transformation Imperative.
Economics is not merely about money. It is about power, security, and the material foundations upon which political arrangements must rest. Any discussion of Israeli-Palestinian federalism that treats economics as an afterthought—a matter to be sorted out once the "real" political questions are settled—fundamentally misunderstands both the conflict and its resolution. Economic transformation is not a consequence of political resolution; it is a precondition for it. Without credible prospects for shared prosperity, neither Israelis nor Palestinians will take the risks that peace requires.

This chapter argues that a Federal State of Israel would unlock unprecedented economic potential, transforming the region from a zone of perpetual conflict and stunted development into an engine of innovation, investment, and growth. The argument proceeds not from wishful thinking but from hard evidence: the documented experiences of federal systems worldwide, the specific economic advantages that Israeli-Palestinian integration would produce, and the powerful incentives that shared prosperity creates for maintaining peace.

The stakes are enormous. Israel's economy, despite its renowned "Start-Up Nation" success, operates under severe constraints imposed by the conflict. The occupation costs billions annually in direct military expenditure and foregone economic activity. International boycott movements, whatever their ultimate effectiveness, impose reputational costs that deter some investors and complicate some partnerships. The Palestinian economy, strangled by restrictions on movement, trade, and development, operates at a fraction of its potential—a loss not only for Palestinians but for the regional economy as a whole.

Federal integration would address these constraints comprehensively. By creating a unified economic space with constitutional protections for property rights, contract enforcement, and free movement, it would establish what Douglass North termed "institutional credibility"—the confidence that economic arrangements will persist regardless of political changes.[1] This credibility, more than any specific policy, determines whether investors commit capital, whether entrepreneurs take risks, and whether economies grow.

The Architecture of Economic Credibility.
The foundation of international economic power rests upon three pillars: institutional stability, market scale, and regulatory coherence.[2] A federal structure inherently strengthens all three dimensions through mechanisms that extend far beyond what either a unitary Israeli state or a fragmented two-state arrangement could achieve.

Federal systems demonstrate remarkable resilience in maintaining economic continuity even during periods of political transition or regional tensions. This resilience stems from what Jenna Bednar terms "institutional redundancy"—the presence of multiple governance levels that can maintain economic functions even when one level experiences disruption.[3] When political crises paralyse federal governments, regional governments continue functioning; when regional politics become unstable, federal institutions provide continuity. This layered architecture provides insurance against the volatility that deters long-term investment.

Statistical analysis confirms these theoretical expectations. Daniel Treisman's comparative research demonstrates that federal states maintain significantly higher levels of foreign investment during political transitions compared to unitary states, with recovery periods shortened substantially.[4] For a region perceived—fairly or not—as chronically unstable, this federal stability premium could prove transformative.

The Swiss experience provides compelling evidence of how federal structures enhance economic credibility. Despite being landlocked and resource-poor, Switzerland has leveraged its federal system to become a global financial centre, with banking assets exceeding 400 percent of GDP.[5]

The cantonal system provides multiple entry points for international business while maintaining overall coherence through federal coordination. Linguistic and religious diversity that might fragment a unitary state becomes, under federal arrangements, a source of economic strength—each canton offering distinct advantages while all benefit from shared infrastructure and regulatory frameworks.

Canada's provincial system has similarly enabled sophisticated resource management and attracted cumulative foreign investment exceeding $900 billion, with provinces maintaining independent investment promotion agencies that complement federal efforts.[6] The German Länder demonstrate how sub-national units can project economic influence internationally while remaining integrated within federal structures—Bavaria alone maintains twenty-eight international representative offices, generating annual trade volumes exceeding €180 billion.[7]

These examples share a crucial characteristic: federal institutions create what might be termed "diplomatic multiplication effects." Instead of a single foreign ministry managing all international economic relations, federal systems enable multiple levels of engagement—federal, regional, and municipal—each capable of fostering economic partnerships within their spheres of competence.[8] This multi-level economic diplomacy multiplies the nation's capacity for international engagement in ways that unitary structures cannot match.

Market Scale and Integration Effects.
The scale effects of a federal market cannot be overstated. International investors consistently prioritise market size when making location decisions, as larger markets enable economies of scale, justify higher initial investments, and provide greater opportunities for growth.[9] A federal Israel, by creating a truly unified economic space encompassing all territories under its governance, would present a market of approximately fifteen million consumers—a substantial increase over the current fragmented arrangement.

But simple population arithmetic understates the transformation. Currently, the Palestinian economy operates under severe constraints: movement restrictions impede commerce, investment requires navigating occupation bureaucracy, and the separation of Gaza from the West Bank fragments what should be a unified market. The World Bank has repeatedly documented how these constraints suppress Palestinian GDP by thirty to fifty percent below potential.[10] Federal integration would remove these constraints, unleashing suppressed economic potential while creating new opportunities from integration itself.

The economics of integration are well established. Alberto Alesina and Enrico Spolaore's research demonstrates that larger political units enjoy significant advantages in providing public goods, achieving economies of scale in governance, and negotiating favourable terms in international trade.[11] Their work suggests that the optimal size for political units has grown over time as globalisation increases the returns to scale while reducing the costs of governing diverse populations. A federal Israel would align with these global trends rather than against them.

The Brazilian federal experience demonstrates the transformative potential of market expansion through federalism. Following constitutional reforms that strengthened federal economic coordination in the 1990s, Brazil experienced dramatic increases in foreign direct investment, rising from $2 billion to over $30 billion annually within a decade.[12] The ability to offer investors access to a unified continental market, despite significant regional disparities, proved decisive in attracting multinational corporations seeking regional headquarters.

For Israel-Palestine, the integration effects would be particularly pronounced in sectors currently fragmented by the conflict. Construction materials produced in the West Bank cannot easily reach markets in Israel or Gaza; agricultural products from Gaza face export restrictions; services that could be provided remotely are impeded by communication and financial barriers. Federal integration would create seamless flows across these artificial boundaries, enabling specialisation, competition, and efficiency gains throughout the economy.

Transforming Foreign Direct Investment Attraction.
The global competition for foreign direct investment has intensified dramatically in recent decades, with nations increasingly recognising FDI as a crucial driver of economic growth, technology transfer, and job creation.[13] A Federal State of Israel would possess unique advantages in this competition, combining the institutional benefits of federalism with Israel's established strengths in technology and innovation.

Currently, Israel attracts substantial foreign investment despite the conflict—testament to its technological capabilities and human capital. But the conflict imposes costs that are difficult to quantify precisely but impossible to ignore. Some investors avoid Israel entirely due to political concerns or boycott pressures. Others demand risk premiums that reduce returns and deter marginal investments. The occupation creates reputational complications that affect everything from academic partnerships to corporate social responsibility calculations.

Federal resolution would address these constraints directly. By transforming the conflict from an ongoing source of instability into a successfully managed historical challenge, federation would reposition Israel-Palestine from a risk to be managed into an opportunity to be seized. The "peace dividend" in investment terms could be substantial—potentially measured in tens of billions of dollars annually as investors who currently avoid the region reconsider their positions.

The federal structure would also enable sophisticated investment incentive coordination that maximises attractiveness while preventing destructive competition between regions. Rather than individual regions engaging in a "race to the bottom" through unsustainable tax incentives, federal investment frameworks can optimise incentives based on comparative advantages.[14]

Technology investments might be directed to established hubs with appropriate infrastructure and talent pools; manufacturing investments might flow to regions with suitable labour forces and logistics connections; agricultural investments might target regions with appropriate land and water resources. Michael Keen and Marchand's research on fiscal federalism demonstrates that coordinated approaches to investment attraction outperform competitive approaches, generating higher total investment while distributing benefits more equitably across regions.[15]

For an Israeli-Palestinian federation where regional economic disparities would initially be substantial, such coordination would prove essential—ensuring that Palestinian regions attract investment and develop economically rather than becoming permanent dependents on federal transfers. The establishment of federal investment protection mechanisms—including federal courts specialising in commercial disputes, federal arbitration systems, and federally guaranteed property rights—would address one of the primary concerns of international investors: the security of their investments.[16]

The presence of multiple judicial levels, with federal courts providing ultimate recourse, creates what legal scholars term "jurisdictional insurance"—the assurance that even if regional courts prove problematic, federal institutions provide reliable adjudication.

Economic Integration as Strategic Imperative.

Economic integration between Israeli and Palestinian populations represents not merely an economic opportunity but a strategic imperative for sustainable peace. The logic is straightforward: when communities benefit materially from cooperation, the costs of conflict become prohibitive. Economic interdependence creates constituencies for peace in both communities—business owners whose supply chains cross communal lines, workers whose employment depends on integrated enterprises, consumers who benefit from competition and variety that integration enables.

This is not naive idealism but documented experience. Dale Copeland's extensive research on economic interdependence and conflict demonstrates that trade relationships significantly reduce the probability of military conflict between partners.[17] The European Union's founding insight—that economic integration between France and Germany would make war between them unthinkable—has been vindicated by seven decades of peace between historical enemies. The same logic applies, with appropriate modifications, to Israelis and Palestinians.

The mechanisms through which economic integration promotes peace operate at multiple levels. At the macro level, governments that depend on trade and investment for prosperity face severe costs from conflict that disrupts economic flows. At the micro level, individuals and firms that have developed cross-communal business relationships have personal stakes in maintaining the conditions for commerce. At the social level, economic interaction creates opportunities for human contact that can erode stereotypes and build trust over time.

Critics object that economic interdependence did not prevent the First World War, when highly integrated European economies nonetheless plunged into catastrophic conflict.[18] This objection has merit but is less devastating than it appears. Pre-1914 integration, while substantial, lacked the institutional frameworks that contemporary economic integration provides. There were no supranational institutions managing interdependence, no constitutional frameworks guaranteeing economic rights, no judicial mechanisms resolving commercial disputes. Federal economic integration provides precisely these institutional supports—not merely increasing trade but creating governance structures that manage interdependence and channel disputes into legal rather than military resolution.

Ephraim Kleiman has raised a different concern specific to the Israeli-Palestinian context: that vast disparities between Israeli and Palestinian economies would create dependency relationships potentially corrosive to political equality.[19] If Palestinians become economically dependent upon Israeli-dominated federal institutions, formal political equality may mask substantive subordination. This concern merits serious attention. Federal economic arrangements must be designed to promote Palestinian economic development and autonomy, not perpetuate dependency.

The response to this concern lies in deliberate institutional design. Fiscal federalism mechanisms—discussed below—can channel resources to less-developed regions, supporting infrastructure investment, human capital formation, and entrepreneurship. Asymmetric arrangements can provide Palestinian regions with policy tools to promote development that more developed Israeli regions do not require. International development assistance, channelled through federal institutions, can accelerate convergence. The goal is not static integration of unequal economies but dynamic development that progressively reduces disparities.

Fiscal Federalism & Resource Distribution.
The distribution of resources within federal systems raises fundamental questions of equity and efficiency that constitutional design must address. If the federal government collects taxes and provides services, how should revenues be distributed across regions? How should disparities in regional economic capacity be addressed? What fiscal autonomy should regions retain, and what constraints should federal authorities impose?

These questions, central to fiscal federalism theory, carry particular weight in the Israeli-Palestinian context where initial economic disparities would be substantial. Israeli GDP per capita exceeds $50,000; Palestinian GDP per capita hovers around $3,500—a ratio of roughly fifteen to one.[20] No federal system has successfully integrated economies with disparities of this magnitude, though some have managed substantial gaps.

The German experience following reunification provides relevant, if imperfect, precedent. West German GDP per capita exceeded East German levels by roughly three to one when unification occurred in 1990. Massive fiscal transfers—the Solidaritätszuschlag and related mechanisms—channelled hundreds of billions of euros to eastern Länder over subsequent decades.[21] The results were mixed: eastern living standards rose substantially but convergence remained incomplete, and some economists argue that transfer dependence actually impeded development by reducing incentives for structural reform.

The lessons for Israeli-Palestinian federation are cautionary but not prohibitive. Fiscal transfers will prove necessary but must be designed to promote development rather than dependence. Robin Boadway's research on equalisation payments identifies key design principles: transfers should address fiscal capacity disparities rather than simply subsidising lower-income regions; they should be formula-based and transparent rather than politically negotiated; they should create incentives for regional governments to develop their own revenue bases rather than simply maximising federal transfers.[22]

Ronald Watts' comparative analysis of federal fiscal arrangements identifies several mechanisms that Israeli-Palestinian federation might employ.[23] Equalisation payments, modelled on Canadian or German systems, would transfer resources from higher-capacity to lower-capacity regions, ensuring that all regions can provide comparable public services regardless of their tax bases. Development funds, modelled on EU structural funds, would finance infrastructure and human capital investments in less-developed regions. Revenue sharing arrangements would give regions stakes in overall federal economic performance while ensuring some redistribution.

The constitutional framework must balance regional fiscal autonomy against federal coordination. Excessive centralisation risks ignoring regional preferences and reducing accountability; excessive decentralisation risks destructive tax competition and inadequate provision of cross-regional public goods.[24] The optimal balance depends on specific circumstances, but successful federal systems generally reserve certain taxes (customs duties, corporate income taxes) for federal collection while permitting regions to set rates on others (property taxes, some consumption taxes) within federally established bounds.

Regional Economic Integration:
The Abraham Accords & Beyond.

The economic implications of Israeli-Palestinian federation extend far beyond the borders of the federal state itself. Resolution of the Palestinian question would remove the principal obstacle to comprehensive economic integration across the Middle East—integration that could transform the region from a zone of conflict and underdevelopment into a dynamic economic bloc rivalling established powers.

The Abraham Accords demonstrated the appetite for economic normalisation between Israel and Arab states. Trade between Israel and the UAE, negligible before 2020, exceeded $2.5 billion by 2023.[25] Israeli tourists flooded Dubai; Emirati investment flowed to Israeli technology companies; commercial flights connected economies that had previously interacted only through third parties. Similar patterns emerged with Bahrain and Morocco; Saudi Arabia's evident interest suggested that the largest Arab economy might eventually follow.

Yet the Abraham Accords' economic potential remains constrained by the unresolved Palestinian question. Arab governments that have normalised relations face domestic criticism for abandoning Palestinian solidarity. Governments that might otherwise normalise—including Saudi Arabia—condition deeper engagement on progress toward Palestinian statehood. Economic integration proceeds but carries political costs that limit its depth and breadth.

Federal resolution would transform this dynamic. Arab governments could engage with an Israel that had addressed Palestinian aspirations rather than merely occupied Palestinian territories. The political cover that Palestinian inclusion would provide could accelerate normalisation with remaining holdouts and deepen integration with existing partners. The Palestinian diaspora in Gulf states, Jordan, and beyond could become a bridge for economic engagement rather than a constituency for resistance.

The potential scale of regional economic integration is staggering. The Middle East and North Africa region encompasses over 400 million people with combined GDP approaching $4 trillion.[26] A genuinely integrated regional market—with reduced trade barriers, harmonised regulations, integrated infrastructure, and free movement of capital—could rival the European Union or NAFTA in economic weight. Ernst Haas's neofunctionalist theory suggests that economic integration in specific sectors can create spillover pressures for broader integration, potentially leading to political cooperation that would have been impossible to achieve directly. [27]

A federal Israel could anchor such integration, providing technological capabilities, financial expertise, and institutional models that the region currently lacks. Israeli water technology could address chronic regional shortages. Israeli agricultural innovation could enhance food security across arid landscapes. Israeli cyber capabilities could protect regional infrastructure. Israeli financial services could intermediate regional capital flows. These contributions would benefit Israel economically while generating the soft power and regional relationships that enhance security far more effectively than military dominance alone.

Innovation Ecosystem & Technology Leadership.
Israel's reputation as the "Start-Up Nation" reflects genuine achievement: a small country producing technological innovation disproportionate to its size, attracting venture capital investment per capita that rivals Silicon Valley, generating exits and IPOs that have created substantial wealth.[28] Federal transformation would amplify these achievements while addressing constraints that currently limit their impact.

The federal structure would dramatically expand the human capital base available to Israeli innovation. Currently, Palestinian engineers, scientists, and entrepreneurs largely operate outside Israeli innovation networks—a loss for both communities. Integration would bring Palestinian talent into contact with Israeli capital, mentorship, and markets, potentially generating the kind of cross-cultural innovation that has historically driven technological breakthroughs. The combination of Israeli technical sophistication with Palestinian market knowledge of the Arab world could prove particularly powerful in developing technologies and business models suited to regional conditions.

Federal research funding systems can achieve scales and coordination levels impossible for fragmented governance structures. Mariana Mazzucato's research documents how mission-oriented public investment—coordinated across agencies and sustained over decades—has driven transformative innovations from the internet to GPS to pharmaceutical breakthroughs.[29] By pooling resources and coordinating research priorities across the entire federation, a federal Israel could undertake ambitious research programmes in quantum computing, artificial intelligence, biotechnology, and clean energy that require investments beyond the reach of smaller, fragmented entities.

The expansion of Israel's innovation ecosystem through federalism could increase annual venture capital investment from current levels of approximately $10 billion to potentially $25-30 billion within a decade, based on comparative analysis of federal innovation systems.[30] This would position a federal Israel among the world's largest venture capital markets, capable of funding ambitious projects that current capital constraints preclude.

The federal framework would also facilitate what innovation scholars term "innovation arbitrage"—the ability to combine diverse knowledge bases and capabilities to create novel solutions.[31] By bringing together the technological expertise of Tel Aviv, the agricultural knowledge of peripheral regions, the water management expertise developed in arid areas, and the diverse cultural perspectives of different population groups, a federal system would create unprecedented opportunities for cross-pollination and breakthrough innovation.

Energy Security & Resource Management.
Energy and water—the resources most critical to Middle Eastern economies and most implicated in regional conflicts—would be managed more effectively under federal arrangements than under any alternative. The coordination of resource policy at the federal level, combined with integrated infrastructure development, would create significant competitive advantages while reducing conflict potential.

Recent natural gas discoveries in the Eastern Mediterranean, including the Leviathan and Tamar fields with combined reserves exceeding one trillion cubic metres, position Israel to become a regional energy hub.[32] A federal structure would facilitate the development of these resources through coordinated infrastructure investment, unified regulatory frameworks, and the negotiating power to establish regional energy partnerships. The potential for an Eastern Mediterranean Gas Forum, anchored by a federal Israel, could rival the influence of established energy organisations.

Water resources present even more direct implications for federal design. The Mountain Aquifer, the Jordan River, and coastal aquifers do not respect political boundaries; their effective management requires coordinated governance that neither occupation nor fragmented sovereignty can provide.[33] Currently, water allocation between Israelis and Palestinians generates persistent grievances: Palestinians receive less water per capita than Israelis, restrictions on well-drilling limit Palestinian agricultural development, and climate change intensifies scarcity pressures.

Federal water management would transform this zero-sum competition into positive-sum cooperation. A federal water authority could develop comprehensive resource policies balancing needs across regions while preventing the competitive extraction that depletes aquifers. Joint investment in desalination, wastewater treatment, and efficiency technologies could expand overall supply rather than merely redistributing scarcity. Constitutional provisions could entrench minimum per-capita water allocations for all citizens regardless of regional residence.

The Murray-Darling Basin Authority in Australia and various Rhine River commissions in Europe demonstrate that federal and quasi-federal arrangements can effectively govern transboundary resources.[34] These arrangements require negotiation, compromise, and sometimes frustrating bureaucratic processes— but they prevent resource conflicts that have destabilised regions worldwide.

Tourism & Cultural Economy.
A federal structure would unlock enormous potential in tourism and cultural industries—sectors where the current political configuration creates significant barriers. Israel currently attracts four to five million tourists annually, a fraction of what its historical, religious, and natural assets could support.[35] The conflict deters many potential visitors; restrictions on movement complicate itineraries that might combine Israeli and Palestinian sites; the separation of Jerusalem, Bethlehem, and other interconnected destinations into different political jurisdictions creates friction that reduces tourist spending and satisfaction.

Federal integration would create a seamless tourism space encompassing Tel Aviv's beaches, Jerusalem's religious sites, Bethlehem's Christian heritage, the Dead Sea's unique attractions, Petra's proximity, and the diverse landscapes from Mediterranean coast to desert interior. Tourists could move freely across the territory, combining experiences that current arrangements fragment. The tourism potential could expand to fifteen to twenty million annual visitors—comparable to Portugal or Morocco—generating tens of billions of dollars in revenue and creating hundreds of thousands of jobs in both communities.

The Spanish federal model demonstrates this potential, with autonomous regions like Catalonia and Andalusia developing distinctive tourism brands while benefiting from national coordination and marketing. Spain attracts over eighty million tourists annually, generating €180 billion in revenue.[36] Cultural economy more broadly—film, music, cuisine, fashion, design—would similarly benefit from integration, as creative talents from diverse communities interact, collaborate, and reach global markets through unified platforms.

The Peace Dividend: Quantifying Economic Benefits.
The economic benefits of Israeli-Palestinian federation can be estimated, if imprecisely, through several methodologies. The RAND Corporation's comprehensive study of Israeli-Palestinian peace calculated the economic costs of continued conflict and the potential gains from resolution.[37] Their analysis suggested that peace could generate cumulative gains of approximately $170 billion over a decade for Israelis and over $50 billion for Palestinians—figures that would be substantially larger under full federal integration than under the two-state arrangement RAND modelled.

These estimates likely understate the potential gains from federation specifically, as opposed to mere peace. Federation would create integration efficiencies, scale economies, and institutional credibility that separation—even peaceful separation—would not provide. The elimination of border frictions, the unification of regulatory frameworks, the integration of infrastructure networks, and the pooling of security costs would generate additional benefits beyond simple conflict cessation.

Perhaps most significantly, federal economic success would reinforce political stability through feedback effects that conflict-focused analysis often neglects. As both communities benefit materially from federal arrangements, constituencies for maintaining those arrangements would grow. Politicians who threatened federal stability would face opposition from business communities, workers, and consumers whose prosperity depends on integration. The economic peace dividend would become self-reinforcing—a virtuous cycle replacing the vicious cycle of conflict and impoverishment.

Conclusion: Economics as Foundation for Peace.
The economic case for Israeli-Palestinian federation rests not on idealism but on interest. Both communities would benefit materially from integration—Israelis through expanded markets, reduced conflict costs, and regional economic leadership; Palestinians through development opportunities, infrastructure investment, and escape from the economic strangulation that occupation has imposed. These shared interests, institutionalised through federal arrangements, would create the material foundation upon which political reconciliation might eventually rest.

Economic transformation cannot substitute for political will. The federal arrangements described throughout this book require decisions that neither community has yet proven willing to make. But economics can make those decisions more attractive by clarifying what is at stake. The choice is not merely between different governance arrangements but between different economic futures: continued conflict with its costs and constraints, or federal integration with its opportunities and challenges.

The evidence from federal systems worldwide suggests that the opportunities substantially outweigh the challenges. Economies that have successfully federated—Germany, Switzerland, Canada, Australia, India—have generally prospered. Economies that have remained fragmented in the face of integration pressures have generally struggled. The global economy rewards scale, stability, and integration; it punishes fragmentation, instability, and isolation. A Federal State of Israel would align with global economic forces rather than against them.

The path forward requires recognising that economics is not separate from politics but foundational to it. Political arrangements that ignore economic realities cannot endure; economic arrangements that lack political legitimacy cannot deliver their promised benefits. Federal integration offers a framework within which economic and political logic align—where prosperity reinforces stability, where shared interests create shared institutions, and where the material foundations of peace prove more durable than any peace treaty unsupported by economic substance.

As I have written elsewhere, Israel's future depends upon choices made in the present—choices about what kind of state Israel will become, what relationships it will build with its neighbours, and what role it will play in the global economy.[38] The federal option offers economic promise that no alternative can match. The remaining question is whether political leadership will prove equal to economic opportunity.

Chapter 8
Addendum

Key Understandings.
Economic Concepts for Federal Solutions.
GDP (Gross Domestic Product): GDP (Gross Domestic Product)**: The total monetary value of all goods and services produced within a country annually. Israel's GDP was approximately $520 billion in 2023, while Palestinian territories' GDP was roughly $18 billion. However, **PPP (Purchasing Power Parity)**—which adjusts for local price differences and better reflects actual living standards—reveals slightly different disparities. Israel's GDP per capita exceeds $58,000 (PPP: ~$54,000), while the West Bank's is approximately $3,600 (PPP: ~$6,200) and Gaza's roughly $1,200 (PPP: ~$3,000). The PPP figures show Palestinians' money buys more locally than raw GDP suggests, but disparities remain stark—9:1 and 18:1 ratios respectively. Federal integration would raise both Palestinian GDP and PPP per capita significantly through market access, investment, and productivity gains, potentially narrowing ratios to 3:1 or 4:1 within two decades.
Fiscal Federalism: The division of taxing and spending powers between federal and regional governments, addressing how revenues are distributed to fund public services while managing regional disparities. Key mechanisms include revenue sharing, grants, and equalization payments (transfers from wealthier to poorer regions). Germany's Finanzausgleich and Canada's equalization program exemplify this.
Economic Integration: Reducing or eliminating barriers to commerce between regions, creating unified economic spaces. Ranges from shallow (free trade agreements) to deep (common markets with free movement of goods, services, capital, and people). Israeli-Palestinian integration currently exists informally but lacks formal frameworks protecting rights and enabling full development benefits.
Foreign Direct Investment (FDI): Investment by entities from one country into business interests in another, typically involving significant control or ownership stakes. FDI drives development by bringing capital, technology, and market access. Israel attracts roughly $25 billion in FDI annually, while Palestinian territories receive under $200 million. Federal resolution could dramatically increase FDI flows to Palestinian regions.
Start-Up Nation: Israel's remarkable entrepreneurial ecosystem producing more startups per capita than any other nation. Despite 9 million citizens, Israel attracts venture capital investment rivaling

Silicon Valley. This success stems from military service creating networks, government R&D support, strong universities, cultural risk acceptance, and diaspora connections. Federal integration could expand this by incorporating Palestinian talent.

Economic Zones: Geographically defined areas with special economic regulations—lower taxes, streamlined regulations—designed to attract investment. Examples include China's Special Economic Zones and Dubai's free zones. Federal Israel could establish zones in Palestinian regions offering incentives to anchor investments and create employment.

Equalization Payments: Fiscal transfers from wealthier to poorer regions ensuring all citizens can access comparable public services. Canada transfers roughly $20 billion annually; Germany over €10 billion. For Israeli-Palestinian federation, equalization would be essential given massive initial disparities, channeling resources to Palestinian regions for infrastructure, education, healthcare, and development.

The Citizen Relevance: Global Economic Benefits.
Federal Israel's economic success would generate global benefits affecting markets, technology, regional stability, and international prosperity.

Israeli Technology Innovations.
Israeli companies developed technologies you likely use daily. Intel processors, Waze navigation, USB flash drives—all Israeli. Medical devices in hospitals, cybersecurity software protecting online banking—frequently incorporate Israeli innovations.

Federal integration would accelerate innovation by expanding Israel's talent base. Palestinian engineers would gain full access to Israeli venture capital and global connections. This expanded ecosystem would produce more innovations solving global challenges—water scarcity, agricultural innovations, cybersecurity, medical breakthroughs.

Stable Energy Prices.
Oil price volatility affects everyone. Middle Eastern tensions spike oil prices, increasing gasoline costs and goods prices. Federal resolution would remove a persistent regional instability source. Moreover, federal Israel could become an energy hub. Recent Eastern Mediterranean natural gas discoveries position Israel to supply European and Asian markets, diversifying global energy and moderating price volatility.

New Markets and Investment.
A unified Israeli-Palestinian market of 15 million consumers would attract multinationals currently deterred by political complications.

Comprehensive Middle Eastern integration could create a regional market of 400+ million consumers. Companies establishing operations in federal Israel could access this broader market.

Currently, Israeli investments carry political risk. Federal resolution would dramatically improve risk-adjusted returns. International pension funds and sovereign wealth funds often avoid conflict zones entirely. Federal Israel, demonstrating successful conflict resolution, would attract massive capital inflows.

Prosperity Is Contagious.

Economic growth spreads through trade, investment spillovers, and knowledge transfer. Federal Israel's economic success would generate regional spillovers. Palestinian economic development would increase demand for neighboring countries' goods and services. Technology partnerships would transfer know-how regionally. Tourism would generate revenue throughout the region.

Global economic growth is not zero-sum. When new regions join the global economy productively, they create demand for global goods while supplying innovations and products others value. Federal Israel would contribute to global economic dynamism from which all nations benefit.

Scholarly Frameworks.

Economic Modeling and Research Approaches.

Students examining federal economic integration should engage with several analytical frameworks.

Economic Modeling Approaches.

Computable General Equilibrium (CGE) Models: Simulate entire economies, capturing sector interactions. Applied to Israeli-Palestinian federation, CGE models could estimate GDP impacts, employment effects, and distributional consequences. RAND Corporation's 2015 study used CGE modeling for peace scenarios.

Gravity Models of Trade: Predict bilateral trade flows based on economic size and distance. Applied to Israeli-Palestinian integration, these could estimate trade increases under federal arrangements.

Endogenous Growth Models: Explain long-term growth through human capital, technological innovation, and institutional quality. Researchers could model how federal research funding and integrated education might accelerate innovation-driven growth.

Case Studies.

German Reunification: West German GDP per capita exceeded East German by roughly 3:1 in 1990. Reunification involved massive fiscal transfers—over €2 trillion cumulatively. Eastern living standards rose but remain below western levels. Lessons: early infrastructure investment importance, integration challenges, long convergence timeframes. Readings: Sinn (2002), Burda and Hunt (2001), Uhlig (2006).

EU Integration: Single market creation generated substantial gains—studies estimate 5-10% GDP increases. Structural funds channeling resources to less-developed regions provide models for equalization. Readings: Baldwin and Wyplosz (2019), Barro and Sala-i-Martin (1991), Sapir et al. (2004).

Data Sources.

Research Institutions: World Bank, IMF, and OECD provide economic data and analysis. Palestinian Central Bureau of Statistics and Israel Central Bureau of Statistics offer official data.

Regional Think Tanks: Taub Center, Middle East Institute, Brookings, Carnegie Endowment maintain economic research programs.

Trade/Investment Data: UN Comtrade, UNCTAD FDI statistics, World Trade Organization policy information enable empirical analysis.

Palestinian Economic Sovereignty:
From Stagnation to Opportunity.

For those who care about Palestinian welfare, economic realities matter as much as political status. The current situation inflicts enormous costs. Federal integration offers pathways to prosperity that neither prolonged occupation nor fragile independence would provide.

Current Economic Conditions.

West Bank GDP per capita of roughly $3,600 places Palestinians in lower-middle-income category. Gaza's $1,200 approaches low-income levels. Youth unemployment exceeds 40%; poverty rates approach 30% in West Bank and 50% in Gaza.

These conditions don't reflect Palestinian incapacity—literacy exceeds 96%. Rather, stagnation reflects systematic constraints: movement restrictions, permit requirements, West Bank-Gaza separation, occupation bureaucracy, restricted resource access.

The World Bank documents how occupation constraints suppress Palestinian GDP by 30-50% below potential.

What Federation Could Mean.

Labor Market Access: Currently 150,000 Palestinians work in Israel through permits. Federal integration would enable full labor mobility without permits or restrictions, immediately raising incomes for hundreds of thousands of families.

Infrastructure Investment:

Federal integration would enable massive infrastructure upgrades—modern highways, reliable electricity, universal clean water, advanced telecommunications—funded through federal programs and private investment.

Technology and Capital Access: Palestinian entrepreneurs would gain access to Israeli venture capital, technical expertise, and global market connections. Palestinian manufacturers could access Israeli supply chains and export channels.

Education & Training: Federal integration would enable Palestinian students to attend Israeli universities and access vocational training, raising productivity and incomes over time.

Trade & Investment: Federal frameworks would eliminate checkpoints, permits, and bureaucratic barriers. Palestinian businesses could sell freely to Israeli consumers. International companies could invest without navigating occupation complications.

Economic Sovereignty Within Federal Framework

Critics argue integration would create dependency. This concern deserves attention. Federal structures must promote Palestinian economic autonomy through:

Regional Economic Policy Autonomy:

Palestinian regions would control economic development policies—tax incentives, industrial promotion, regulatory frameworks. They could prioritize sectors aligned with Palestinian strengths.

Equalization Funding: Federal transfers would fund infrastructure, education, healthcare—enabling Palestinian regions to provide services comparable to Israeli regions without depending on aid.

Palestinian Entrepreneurship:

Federal frameworks would support Palestinian entrepreneurs through capital access, technical assistance, and protected property rights.

Gradual Convergence:

Economic convergence takes time—German reunification suggests decades. But if Palestinian GDP per capita is rising steadily, poverty declining, employment expanding, businesses growing—the trajectory toward economic sovereignty is clear.

For those genuinely caring about Palestinian welfare: Which scenario better serves Palestinian economic interests—prolonged statelessness under occupation, independence in a poor unstable mini-state, or federal integration providing immediate economic opportunities while building toward long-term prosperity?

The Breakdown:
How Everyone Gets Richer Together.
The Current Situation.

Two neighbors refuse to cooperate. One (Israel) has thriving business, advanced tools, and global connections. The other (Palestinians) has talented workers and good ideas but faces constant obstacles—can't access best tools, can't reach customers easily, can't get loans to expand. A wall separates them with checkpoints making simple exchanges complicated.

The non-cooperation costs both. The wealthy neighbor spends enormous resources maintaining walls and checkpoints. The less-wealthy neighbor can't develop potential. Both could be richer cooperating.

Federal Integration.

Federal integration means removing the wall and creating shared frameworks:

For Palestinians: Workers can work anywhere—take better-paying jobs in Israeli companies. Businesses can sell to Israeli consumers and access Israeli ports for global exports. Students can attend any university. Entrepreneurs can access Israeli investors.

For Israelis: Businesses gain access to Palestinian workers, expanding talent pools. Consumers can buy Palestinian products. Infrastructure serves the entire federation, increasing utilization and profitability. Companies gain market knowledge for Arab country expansion through Palestinian partners.

The Economic Multiplier

Growth in one area creates growth in others. When Palestinians get jobs and businesses, they earn money to spend—creating demand supporting more businesses and jobs, creating more income, creating more demand. This multiplier effect means initial economic activity multiplies through the economy.

Currently, much potential economic activity is blocked. Federal integration unlocks it. Economists estimate total gains could reach $200+ billion over a decade.

Economic Potential Comparison

Three scenarios:

Status Quo (Continued Occupation): Israeli GDP grows slowly, constrained by conflict costs. Palestinian GDP remains stagnant. Total combined GDP: $550 billion by 2030. Costs: billions in military spending, lost opportunities.

Two-State Solution: Israeli GDP grows moderately. Palestinian GDP grows slowly in a poor, isolated mini-state. Total combined GDP: $600 billion by 2030.

Federal Integration: Combined GDP grows rapidly through integration effects. Total combined GDP: $700+ billion by 2030. Gains: $100+ billion additional economic activity, hundreds of thousands more jobs.

The Jobs Picture.
Federal integration could create:
For Palestinians: 300,000+ new jobs over a decade. Youth unemployment could drop from 40% to 20% or less. Young Palestinians seeing futures with opportunity rather than hopelessness.
For Israelis: 100,000+ new jobs serving expanded markets. Reduced military spending redirected to productive investment. Rising Palestinian incomes create customers for Israeli businesses.
Peace Through Prosperity.
When people have jobs, can feed families, see children's futures improving—they have something to lose from conflict. Business owners with cross-communal supply chains want stability. Workers whose employers integrate both peoples want cooperation. Federal economic integration creates constituencies for peace whose material interests align with cooperation. Over time, economic ties build trust more reliably than political speeches or treaties unsupported by shared prosperity. The alternative—perpetual conflict—guarantees continued poverty for Palestinians and ongoing costs for Israelis. Federal integration offers shared prosperity making cooperation rational and conflict costly. The question isn't whether this would be better economically—the evidence is clear. The question is whether political leadership will seize economic opportunity or perpetuate costly conflict.

Chapter 9
Security Architecture of Federal States.

The Threat We Face: Jihadism in the Twenty-First Century.
Before addressing how federal arrangements might enhance Israeli security, we must confront with absolute clarity the nature of the threats that any security architecture must defeat. This is not an academic exercise. It is a matter of survival. The jihadist movements that have proliferated since September 11, 2001, have committed atrocities of medieval barbarism that challenge the modern conscience to comprehend. Any proposal for federal governance that fails to acknowledge these realities—or that suggests security might somehow be subordinated to political aspirations—is not merely inadequate but irresponsible.

Let there be no misunderstanding: **peace does not mean compromising on security**. The argument of this chapter is precisely the opposite—that federal arrangements, properly designed, can provide security *more robust* than current configurations, not less. But this argument cannot be made honestly without first acknowledging what we are defending against.

ISIS: Industrial-Scale Atrocity.
The Islamic State conducted mass executions with systematic efficiency that evoked the darkest chapters of the twentieth century. The Sinjar massacre of August 2014 killed between 2,000 and 5,000 Yazidis—men, women, and children—in a campaign the United Nations formally recognized as genocide. By 2016, ISIS had murdered over 18,800 civilians through shootings, beheadings, crucifixions, and immolation. Videos of these executions were not shameful secrets but propaganda tools, distributed globally to recruit and terrorize.

Young men were lined up and shot into mass graves. Captured soldiers were beheaded on camera. A Jordanian pilot was burned alive in a cage. Yazidi women and girls were systematically enslaved and trafficked. Christian and Shia communities that had existed for millennia were exterminated or expelled. UN reports documented these crimes in meticulous detail, confirming patterns of war crimes, crimes against humanity, and genocide.

HTS: Sectarian Cleansing in Syria.
Hayat Tahrir al-Sham, following the collapse of the Assad regime in late 2024, oversaw massacres of Alawites in 2025 that resulted in hundreds killed through indiscriminate attacks, looting, arson, and systematic sectarian violence. Fighters affiliated with HTS circulated calls to "not leave any Alawite alive"—echoing the genocidal rhetoric that preceded earlier massacres in the region. Similar violence targeted Druze communities in Sweida, producing hundreds of dead from clashes, extrajudicial killings, and deliberate humiliation rituals.

These events occurred not in some distant past but in our present moment, demonstrating that the capacity for sectarian mass murder remains fully operational among jihadist and Islamist armed groups in the Levant.

Hamas: October 7, 2023.
On October 7, 2023, Hamas perpetrated the deadliest single attack on Jewish civilians since the Holocaust. The assault killed 1,182 people and constituted a systematic campaign of mass murder, sexual violence, and hostage-taking that international investigators have classified as crimes against humanity.

At Kibbutz Be'eri, 99 residents were massacred. At Kfar Aza, 62 people died—including babies in their parents' arms. At the Nova music festival, 370 young people were hunted down and murdered through shootings, grenade attacks, and deliberate burning of shelters where civilians sought refuge. Survivors and forensic investigators documented systematic sexual violence against women before, during, and after their murders. This attack was not an aberration from Hamas's ideology but its fullest expression. Anyone proposing security arrangements for Israel must answer one question before all others: *how would this architecture have prevented October 7, and how will it prevent the next attempt?*

Hezbollah and the Houthis: Iranian Proxies.
Hezbollah has conducted terrorist attacks across continents, including the 1994 AMIA bombing in Buenos Aires that killed 85 people and the 2012 Burgas bus bombing in Bulgaria that killed 7. In Syria, Hezbollah forces razed entire villages in support of the Assad regime. The organization maintains an arsenal of over 150,000 missiles positioned to strike Israeli population centers—a threat requiring constant vigilance and, potentially, preemptive action.

The Houthis have committed systematic torture, arbitrary detention, and over 350 forced disappearances since 2016, contributing to civilian death tolls exceeding 19,200 in Yemen's war. Their attacks on international shipping and their missile and drone strikes against Israel demonstrate willingness to expand regional conflict regardless of consequences for civilian populations.

The Ideological Foundation: Muslim Brotherhood Doctrine.
The atrocities documented above do not emerge from nowhere. They flow from ideological frameworks that have been elaborated over decades and disseminated through educational, charitable, and political networks worldwide. The Muslim Brotherhood, founded in Egypt in 1928, developed the foundational texts that inform contemporary jihadist movements.
Core Brotherhood doctrine emphasizes establishing global Islamic governance through gradual infiltration of institutions, building parallel Islamist structures, and using immigration (*hijra*) and religious propagation (*dawa*) to transform societies from within. In Western countries, Brotherhood-linked organizations present moderate faces to gain legitimacy while working toward goals fundamentally incompatible with liberal democratic values.

Hamas's 1988 charter, rooted explicitly in Brotherhood thought, states without ambiguity: "Israel will exist and will continue to exist until Islam will obliterate it." Article 7 invokes a hadith calling for Muslims to kill Jews until the Day of Judgment—"even the stones and trees" will cry out to identify hiding Jews so they may be killed. Article 11 declares all of Palestine an eternal Islamic *waqf* (religious endowment) that no Muslim may surrender. Article 13 mandates armed jihad as the sole solution, explicitly rejecting negotiations and peace processes as betrayals of Islamic duty.

The 2017 Hamas charter, while softening some language for international consumption, did not renounce the 1988 document and continued to reject Israel's existence within any borders. These are not historical curiosities but operational doctrines that shape recruitment, training, and tactical decisions.

Why This Matters for Federal Security Architecture.
The preceding inventory of horrors is not gratuitous. It establishes the baseline against which any security proposal must be measured. A federal Israel would face not merely conventional military threats from state actors but an ideological movement that considers Jewish existence illegitimate, that celebrates the murder

of civilians as religious duty, and that operates through networks spanning from Tehran to Gaza to Western capitals.

This means that the security apparatus of a federal Israel cannot merely be "as good as" the FBI and CIA. It must be **stronger**. The Mossad, Shin Bet, and Israel Police must work in synergy more seamless than they have ever achieved—and they must integrate Palestinian security partners in ways that enhance rather than compromise these capabilities.

The author of this chapter harbors no illusions. The threats are real, the enemies are ruthless, and the margin for error is measured in lives. What follows is not a proposal to weaken Israeli security but to *strengthen it*—to build security arrangements more durable than walls and more comprehensive than occupation.

The Security Imperative in Federal Design.
Security is the bedrock upon which any political order must rest. Without it, constitutional arrangements become mere parchment, economic prosperity remains hostage to predation, and citizens cannot pursue the ordinary business of life. This elementary truth assumes particular salience in the Israeli-Palestinian context, where decades of violence have rendered security concerns not merely important but existential. Any federal proposal that fails to address these concerns with the seriousness they deserve is not a proposal at all but a fantasy—and a dangerous one at that.

This chapter confronts the security challenge directly. It argues that federal arrangements, far from compromising Israeli security as critics contend, can provide more durable protection than the current configuration of occupation, separation barriers, and perpetual military vigilance. The argument proceeds not from naive optimism but from hard-headed analysis of how federal security systems have functioned elsewhere and how they might be adapted to the specific conditions of the Levant.

The critics must be heard before they can be answered. Efraim Inbar has argued forcefully that Israeli security requirements are fundamentally incompatible with any arrangement that dilutes Israeli operational control over the territory between the Jordan River and the Mediterranean Sea. Hillel Frisch contends that Palestinian institutional weakness and the persistence of armed factions make any security-sharing arrangement dangerously premature.

These objections reflect legitimate concerns rooted in bitter experience. The second intifada demonstrated what happens when security cooperation breaks down; the October 7th massacre revealed the catastrophic consequences of intelligence failures and inadequate border security. Anyone who dismisses such concerns as mere hawkish obstructionism has not been paying attention.

Yet the question is not whether risks exist—they manifestly do—but whether the risks of federal security arrangements exceed the risks of perpetual conflict. As Israel's own security establishment has increasingly acknowledged, the status quo generates profound vulnerabilities of its own: demographic pressures that threaten the Jewish character of the state, international isolation that constrains diplomatic options, and the corrosive effects of permanent occupation on Israeli society and military culture. The Commanders for Israel's Security, a group of over 300 retired generals and senior security officials, has warned that continued conflict without political resolution poses greater long-term threats than the risks associated with territorial compromise.

Unified Command & Strategic Integration: Beyond Current Capabilities.
The establishment of a federal state necessitates fundamental reconsideration of how security institutions are organised, funded, and commanded. Federal systems present unique opportunities for consolidating fragmented defence structures while simultaneously preserving meaningful regional autonomy in matters of local governance and civil administration. The challenge is to design institutions that provide genuine collective security—where both Israeli and Palestinian communities possess vested interests in comprehensive protection for all citizens—without either community feeling that security forces serve as instruments of the other's domination.

Contemporary federal states demonstrate that military integration need not compromise democratic accountability or regional identity. The German Bundeswehr, operating with approximately 182,500 active personnel and an annual budget exceeding €50 billion, exemplifies how unified command structures strengthen rather than weaken civilian oversight. The German model, emerging from post-Second World War constitutional arrangements designed to prevent the recurrence of militarism, demonstrates that federal military organisation can effectively balance centralised strategic direction with Länder-level cooperation on matters such as civil defence and disaster response. The transformation of the Wehrmacht—an instrument of aggressive war and genocide—into the Bundeswehr—a defensive force embedded in democratic institutions and NATO collective security—offers instructive parallels for contexts where military forces have been associated with oppression.

The United States Department of Defense manages the world's most powerful military force through unified combatant commands that integrate service branches while respecting state-level National Guard units that serve dual federal and state functions. This dual-hatting arrangement proves particularly instructive: National Guard units remain under gubernatorial command for domestic emergencies and civil support but can be federalised for national defence or overseas deployment. Such arrangements demonstrate that security forces can maintain multiple loyalties—to state and nation, to region and federation—without paralysing conflict between them.

Concrete Implementation: The Federal Security Command
A federal Israel would establish a Federal Security Command (FSC) integrating existing Israeli security services with newly developed Palestinian counterparts under constitutional mandate. The implementation would proceed through distinct phases designed to build capacity and trust while maintaining operational effectiveness throughout the transition.

Phase One (Years 1-3): Parallel Operations with Liaison. Israeli security services—IDF, Mossad, Shin Bet, Israel Police—continue operating under existing structures. A Federal Security Coordination Center (FSCC) is established in Jerusalem with permanent liaison officers from all Israeli agencies plus representatives from Palestinian security services vetted through rigorous background investigation. The FSCC facilitates information sharing on terrorism threats, coordinates border security, and develops joint training curricula. No operational authority transfers during this phase; the focus is building personal relationships and institutional habits of cooperation.

Implementation Example: The FSCC would operate 24/7 with rotating Israeli and Palestinian duty officers monitoring threat feeds. When Israeli intelligence identifies a potential attack planned from Palestinian-majority areas, the Palestinian liaison would coordinate with local security forces for interdiction—but with Israeli quick-reaction forces positioned to intervene if local response proves inadequate. Every successful joint operation builds trust; every failure triggers mandatory after-action review to identify improvements.

Phase Two (Years 4-7): Integrated Units for Specific Missions. Mixed Israeli-Palestinian units are formed for border security, counter-terrorism intelligence fusion, and critical infrastructure protection. These units operate under unified federal command with personnel selected through competitive processes emphasizing professional qualifications and demonstrated commitment to federal security. Command positions rotate between Israeli and Palestinian officers based on competence and seniority.

Implementation Example: A Federal Border Protection Force would assume responsibility for the Jordan Valley. This force would integrate Israeli technological capabilities—sensors, drones, surveillance systems—with Palestinian personnel who possess linguistic skills and cultural knowledge essential for identifying smuggling networks and infiltration attempts. Israeli special forces remain on standby for high-intensity threats; Palestinian officers handle routine patrols and community relations with Jordanian counterparts.

Phase Three (Years 8-15): Full Integration with Regional Components. Federal defense forces achieve full integration with unified command structure, common doctrine, and interoperable equipment. Regional security components—Israeli-majority and Palestinian-majority police forces—handle internal public order while federal forces manage external defense, border security, and counter-terrorism. Constitutional provisions guarantee that fundamental security arrangements cannot be altered without supermajority consent from both communities.

Intelligence Architecture: Creating Fusion Capabilities That Exceed Current Capacity
Modern security threats rarely respect administrative boundaries. Terrorism, organised crime, cyber attacks, and weapons proliferation operate across jurisdictions, exploiting gaps between regional authorities and overwhelming localised response capabilities. Federal intelligence architecture must therefore create seamless information flows between agencies operating at different

governmental levels while protecting civil liberties through robust oversight mechanisms.

The United States intelligence community's post-September 11th reorganisation illustrates both the imperatives and challenges of federal intelligence integration. The creation of the Office of the Director of National Intelligence attempted to break down institutional barriers between the Central Intelligence Agency, Federal Bureau of Investigation, Department of Homeland Security, and sixteen other intelligence agencies. While coordination challenges persist, the establishment of fusion centres—joint facilities that integrate federal, state, and local intelligence personnel—has demonstrably enhanced threat detection by connecting localised observations to broader threat patterns. Amy Zegart's research indicates that integrated intelligence architectures prevent the dangerous compartmentalisation that allows terrorist cells to operate undetected by exploiting jurisdictional boundaries.

Israeli-Palestinian Intelligence Integration: Combining Complementary Capabilities
For an Israeli-Palestinian federation, intelligence integration presents both unique challenges and unique opportunities. The challenge is obvious: agencies that have spent decades regarding each other as adversaries cannot overnight become trusted partners. The Israeli security services possess capabilities—in signals intelligence, human intelligence, and technical surveillance —that far exceed anything Palestinian counterparts have developed. Any integration must address this asymmetry without either creating dependency relationships that undermine Palestinian agency or compromising Israeli capabilities that protect both communities.

Yet the opportunity is equally significant. Palestinian intelligence services possess knowledge of Palestinian society—family networks, political factions, religious movements, criminal enterprises—that Israeli services have never fully penetrated despite decades of occupation. Integration would combine Israeli technical capabilities with Palestinian human intelligence, creating composite capabilities exceeding what either community possesses separately.

Concrete Implementation: The Federal Intelligence Fusion Center. Located in a secure federal facility, the FIFC would house analysts from Shin Bet, Mossad, IDF Military Intelligence, and

Palestinian General Intelligence. The facility would feature tiered access: general threat assessments shared with all personnel; sensitive source information compartmentalized based on need-to-know and demonstrated reliability.

Implementation Example: Israeli signals intelligence intercepts communications suggesting an attack is being planned in Hebron. The intercept provides a phone number and partial conversation but no names or locations. Palestinian analysts at the FIFC, drawing on their knowledge of local networks, identify the phone's likely owner through social network analysis. Palestinian field officers, working with Israeli technical support, mount surveillance that confirms the plot and enables arrest before execution. Neither service alone could have achieved this result; combined capabilities produce outcomes superior to either operating independently.

Preventing October 7-Style Attacks. The October 7 massacre succeeded in part because Israeli intelligence failed to credit warnings and because border security was inadequate to repel the assault. Federal arrangements would address both failures. First, the FIFC would institutionalize Palestinian insight into Gaza-based planning, providing additional analytical perspectives on threat indicators. Second, the Federal Border Protection Force would maintain heavier defensive capabilities along the Gaza frontier, with rapid-reaction forces positioned to respond within minutes rather than hours. Third, mandatory protocols would require that any warning of imminent attack—regardless of source—triggers immediate defensive measures pending evaluation, rather than dismissal based on assumptions about enemy intentions.

Constitutional Framework for Security Powers: Guarantees That Cannot Be Unilaterally Revoked
The constitutional framework for federal security powers must delineate clear spheres of authority to prevent jurisdictional conflicts that could compromise operational effectiveness. Successful federal models typically vest exclusive control over external defence, border security, intelligence coordination, military procurement, weapons of mass destruction policy, international treaties, and critical infrastructure protection in the federal government. These are matters where divided authority invites catastrophe—where the stakes are too high and the need for coordination too pressing to permit regional variation or competing commands.

Regional governments, conversely, retain authority over local policing, emergency response, community security initiatives, and the protection of culturally significant sites. The Spanish model proves instructive here: the Mossos d'Esquadra in Catalonia and the Ertzaintza in the Basque Country operate with substantial autonomy in routine policing while coordinating with national agencies on matters transcending regional jurisdiction. These regional forces, recruited primarily from their respective communities and operating in regional languages, possess the cultural competence and local knowledge essential for effective community policing.

Constitutional Entrenchment: The Israeli Security Guarantee. The federal constitution would include provisions requiring supermajority approval (two-thirds of both legislative chambers plus ratification by three-fourths of regional governments) to amend any security-related article. Certain provisions—federal control over external defense, border security, and counter-terrorism—would be designated as "eternal clauses" that cannot be amended at all, similar to Article 79(3) of the German Basic Law protecting federalism and human dignity.

Implementation Example: The constitution would specify that "The Federal Defense Forces shall maintain exclusive responsibility for external defense, including but not limited to: defense against state actors, interdiction of cross-border terrorism, protection of airspace and maritime approaches, and maintenance of strategic deterrence. This provision may not be amended." This guarantees that demographic changes or political shifts cannot translate into diminished security—the Israeli-Jewish community retains constitutional veto over any security-affecting changes regardless of population ratios.

Border Security and External Defence: Federal Control with Enhanced Capabilities.
Border control represents quintessential federal responsibility in virtually all federal systems. The ability to regulate entry and exit of persons and goods across national boundaries is fundamental to sovereignty and cannot be effectively delegated to regional governments without compromising national security and economic coherence. In the Israeli-Palestinian context, this principle carries particular weight given the geographic realities: the territory is small, borders are contested, and threats can materialise with minimal warning.

A federal Israel would maintain unified control over all external borders—with Lebanon, Syria, Jordan, Egypt, and the Mediterranean coast. The Jordan Valley, which Israeli security doctrine has long identified as essential defensive terrain, would fall under federal rather than regional jurisdiction. This addresses one of the most persistent obstacles to two-state solutions: Israeli insistence on security presence in the Valley conflicts with Palestinian insistence on sovereign borders. Federal arrangements dissolve this conflict by making the Valley neither Israeli nor Palestinian but federal—controlled by integrated forces serving both communities.

Concrete Implementation: The Jordan Valley Security Zone. The Federal Border Protection Force would establish a continuous security presence throughout the Jordan Valley, operating from integrated bases positioned at key crossing points and along likely infiltration routes. The force would deploy:
Layered sensor networks including ground-based radar, seismic sensors, and thermal imaging cameras providing 24/7 coverage of the border region. Unmanned aerial vehicles conducting continuous surveillance with automatic alert capabilities. Quick-reaction forces —mixed Israeli-Palestinian units—positioned to respond to any incursion within 15 minutes. Fortified crossing points with biometric identification systems preventing unauthorized entry. Coordination protocols with Jordanian border forces enabling joint response to smuggling and infiltration attempts.

The Gaza Frontier: Preventing Another October 7. The Gaza border would receive the most intensive security infrastructure of any federal boundary. Implementation would include: A hardened barrier system extending underground to prevent tunnel infiltration, with seismic sensors capable of detecting digging activity. Automated defensive systems capable of engaging threats before they reach the barrier. Observation towers with overlapping fields of view and redundant communication systems. Garrison forces sufficient to repel mass assault pending reinforcement. Mandatory evacuation protocols for communities within 7 kilometers of the border upon any warning of imminent attack. No assumption that any threat is too improbable to address—October 7 demonstrated the cost of such assumptions.

Addressing the Trust Deficit: Building Security Through Performance, Not Promises.
The most formidable obstacle to federal security arrangements is not technical but psychological: the profound mutual distrust that decades of conflict have engendered. Israelis doubt that Palestinians can be reliable security partners given the persistence of factions committed to armed struggle and the popularity of resistance narratives in Palestinian society. Palestinians doubt that security integration means anything other than permanent Israeli control dressed in federal language—occupation by another name. These doubts cannot be wished away. They must be addressed through institutional design that creates genuine interdependence while providing safeguards against defection. The key insight is that trust need not be a precondition for cooperation; it can be a *consequence* of cooperation, built gradually through demonstrated performance.

Mechanism One: Constitutional Entrenchment with Mutual Veto. Neither community can unilaterally alter fundamental security structures. Constitutional amendments affecting security require consent from both communities through their regional governments. This addresses Israeli fears that Palestinian demographic growth might translate into political power used to dismantle security arrangements; it addresses Palestinian fears that Israeli political shifts might reimpose unilateral control.
Implementation Example: Any proposal to reduce Federal Border Protection Force presence in the Jordan Valley would require: approval by two-thirds of the Federal Assembly (population-based chamber); approval by two-thirds of the Federal Council (region-based chamber with equal representation); ratification by the Israeli-majority regional government; ratification by the Palestinian-majority regional government. This ensures that security reductions occur only when both communities genuinely agree they are safe— not through majoritarian override.

Mechanism Two: International Guarantees and Tripwire Forces. NATO membership or equivalent security treaties would commit external actors to defending federal arrangements against both external threats and internal subversion. American, British, and French forces stationed at key facilities would serve as "tripwires"—any attack on federal security infrastructure would automatically engage major-power allies.
Implementation Example: A NATO rapid-reaction force of 5,000 troops would be stationed in the Jordan Valley, supplementing

federal forces with capabilities including air defense, armored reserves, and special operations units. This force would operate under NATO command but with authorization to support federal security operations upon request. The presence of American and European soldiers alongside Israeli and Palestinian personnel would deter both external aggression and internal efforts to destabilize federal arrangements.

Mechanism Three: Phased Implementation with Reversibility. Security integration proceeds in stages, with each stage contingent upon successful completion of previous stages. At each phase, both communities possess exit options if the other fails to perform —options that become less attractive as integration progresses and interdependence deepens.

Implementation Example: Phase Two integration (mixed units for specific missions) begins only after Phase One metrics are satisfied: zero successful terrorist attacks originating from areas where Palestinian security forces have primary responsibility; Palestinian forces' successful interdiction of at least 80% of identified smuggling attempts; zero incidents of Palestinian security personnel providing assistance to terrorist organizations; successful joint operations against at least 10 identified terrorist cells. If metrics are not achieved within the designated timeframe, Phase Two is delayed until they are. If metrics deteriorate after Phase Two begins, the Federal Security Council (with Israeli veto) can authorize reversion to Phase One structures.

Mechanism Four: Economic Interdependence as Security Reinforcement. When both communities benefit materially from peace—when Palestinian economic development depends upon Israeli technology and markets, when Israeli prosperity depends upon regional integration requiring Palestinian partnership—the costs of security breakdown become prohibitive.

Implementation Example: Federal economic policy would promote joint industrial zones, shared technology parks, and integrated supply chains that make Israeli and Palestinian businesses interdependent. A Palestinian engineer working for an Israeli tech company, whose children attend federal schools with Israeli classmates, has powerful incentives to report threats rather than ignore them. Economic integration creates constituencies in both communities who benefit from stability and who will resist efforts to destabilize federal arrangements.

Regional Security Forces: Community Policing Under Federal Oversight.
While external defence and border control constitute exclusively federal responsibilities, internal security and routine policing function as shared or predominantly regional competencies in successful federal systems. This division reflects both practical considerations—regional police possess local knowledge and community relationships essential for effective law enforcement—and democratic principles favouring decentralised authority over matters directly affecting citizens' daily lives.

Germany's federal policing structure offers a model where Länder police forces maintain primary responsibility for public order while federal agencies handle interstate crimes and provide specialised forensic and investigative services. This arrangement preserves regional autonomy while ensuring professional standards and adequate resources for complex investigations.

Concrete Implementation: Dual-Layer Policing. Israeli-majority regions maintain police forces operating in Hebrew, recruiting from Jewish communities, and accountable to regional governments. Palestinian-majority regions maintain parallel forces operating in Arabic, recruiting from Palestinian communities, with equivalent accountability structures. Neither community experiences daily policing as external imposition.

Federal oversight mechanisms: A Federal Police Standards Commission establishes minimum training requirements, professional certifications, and use-of-force guidelines applicable to all regional forces. Federal inspectors conduct regular audits of regional police performance. Regional forces that fail to meet federal standards lose eligibility for federal grants and face intervention by federal marshals for serious deficiencies. This ensures that Palestinian regional police meet professional standards equivalent to Israeli counterparts—not as condition for autonomy but as requirement for federal participation.

Counter-terrorism coordination: Regional police maintain routine public order, but counter-terrorism operations fall under federal jurisdiction. When federal intelligence identifies a terrorism threat in a Palestinian-majority region, federal forces take operational lead with regional police providing support—blocking escape routes, managing civilian evacuation, providing local knowledge. Regional police cannot veto federal counter-terrorism operations; they can only facilitate them.

Democratic Oversight and Civil-Military Relations: Preventing Abuse Without Compromising Security
Military forces organised under unified federal command concentrate substantial coercive power that could potentially threaten democratic governance if not subject to robust civilian oversight. Federal constitutions must establish clear chains of command subordinating military authority to elected civilian leaders while creating institutional checks that prevent either military usurpation or civilian misuse of military power for partisan purposes.

The principle of civilian supremacy over military forces represents a foundational element of democratic federal systems. The elected head of government serves as commander-in-chief of armed forces, exercising ultimate authority over strategic direction, operational deployments, and senior military appointments. However, effective civilian control requires institutional capacity for civilian leaders to understand military options, evaluate professional military advice, and make informed decisions about force employment.

Concrete Implementation: Checks and Balances in Federal Security Governance. The Federal President (rotating between Israeli and Palestinian incumbents or elected through cross-community voting requirements) serves as nominal commander-in-chief but exercises authority only on advice of the Federal Defense Minister. The Defense Minister is appointed by the Federal Assembly subject to confirmation by the Federal Council—ensuring that both population-weighted and region-weighted chambers have voice in security leadership.

Legislative oversight: A Joint Committee on Security, comprising members from both chambers with security clearances, conducts continuous oversight of intelligence and defense operations. The committee receives classified briefings, reviews operational decisions, and investigates complaints of abuse. Committee membership is allocated to ensure representation from both communities regardless of overall legislative composition.

Judicial review: A Federal Security Court, modeled on the U.S. Foreign Intelligence Surveillance Court but with greater transparency provisions, reviews requests for surveillance, detention, and other security measures affecting civil liberties. The court includes judges appointed from both communities with security expertise and independence from political pressure.

Preventing abuse while maintaining effectiveness: Civil liberties protections must not become loopholes that terrorists exploit. The Federal Security Court operates with streamlined procedures for urgent applications—a judge on call 24/7 can authorize emergency surveillance within hours. Detention without charge is permitted for up to 72 hours with judicial review; extensions require demonstrated necessity. These provisions balance liberty against security without pretending the balance is easy or cost-free.

From Competition to Collective Defence: The Psychological Transformation.

The transformation from competitive to collective security represents the essential psychological shift that federal arrangements must accomplish. For generations, Israelis and Palestinians have understood security as a zero-sum competition: Israeli security meant Palestinian insecurity, and vice versa. Walls, checkpoints, military operations, and armed resistance all reflected this competitive logic. Federal security architecture must replace this logic with genuine collective security—arrangements where both communities possess vested interests in comprehensive protection for all citizens.

This transformation cannot be accomplished by institutional design alone. It requires political leadership willing to articulate new narratives, educational systems that prepare young people for partnership rather than conflict, and civil society organisations that build relationships across communal lines. But institutional design matters enormously. When Israeli and Palestinian soldiers serve together in federal forces, when Israeli and Palestinian police officers train together and cooperate on investigations, when both communities depend upon shared intelligence systems for protection against common threats—these institutional arrangements create facts that reshape perceptions.

The comparative evidence supports cautious optimism. Divided societies have repeatedly achieved security integration that seemed impossible before it happened. The integration of Protestant and Catholic police officers in Northern Ireland following the Good Friday Agreement, the creation of unified Bosnian armed forces from armies that had fought each other, the transformation of former guerrilla movements into legitimate security forces in Mozambique and El Salvador—these cases demonstrate that security integration can succeed even after bitter conflict. None was easy; all required sustained international support, careful institutional design, and political courage. But all eventually produced security arrangements more stable and legitimate than what preceded them.

Security Through Strength, Peace Through Vigilance.
Security architecture in federal systems represents far more than organisational charts or budget allocations. It embodies fundamental political choices about sovereignty, citizenship, and the relationship between individual rights and collective protection. Effective federal security structures must balance multiple imperatives: operational efficiency and regional autonomy, unified command and democratic accountability, professional expertise and civilian control, security imperatives and civil liberties.

The argument of this chapter is not that federal arrangements eliminate risk. Risk cannot be eliminated in a region where jihadist ideologies command devoted followers, where Hamas's charter calls for genocide, where Hezbollah maintains an arsenal capable of devastating Israeli cities, where Iran pursues nuclear capability while funding terror proxies. Risk is permanent. The question is how to manage it.

The federal security architecture outlined here would provide Israel with capabilities exceeding current arrangements: intelligence fusion combining Israeli technical prowess with Palestinian human networks; border security enhanced by Palestinian cooperation rather than requiring constant vigilance against Palestinian threats; constitutional guarantees that cannot be overridden by demographic shifts; international commitments that bring major-power resources to Israel's defense; economic interdependence that makes attack self-destructive for any rational actor.

None of this helps against irrational actors. Hamas on October 7 acted against Palestinian interests as well as Israeli ones—the devastation of Gaza was foreseeable to anyone not blinded by ideology. But federal arrangements do not depend on Hamas becoming rational. They depend on creating structures that isolate extremists, empower moderates, and make the costs of violence prohibitive for anyone who calculates costs at all.

The sceptics are not wrong to demand proof. Federal security arrangements involve risks that cannot be entirely eliminated. But so does every alternative. Continued occupation generates resistance; walls can be tunnelled under or rocketed over; military superiority provides no permanent guarantee in a changing region. The question is not whether risks exist but how they compare across alternatives—and whether institutional creativity can manage risks that seem prohibitive under current arrangements.

The federal vision is neither naive nor utopian. It is grounded in comparative evidence from federal systems that have successfully managed security in diverse, divided, and historically conflictual societies. It acknowledges the depth of Israeli security concerns while recognising that permanent domination cannot provide the security Israelis seek. It offers Palestinians genuine partnership in security rather than subjugation to it. And it creates institutional frameworks within which trust might develop—not as precondition for cooperation but as consequence of it.

The author of this book harbors no illusions about the enemies Israel faces.

The jihadist movements catalogued at the beginning of this chapter are not going away. Their ideology is not amenable to compromise. Their hatred is not rational.

Against such enemies, only strength provides security. Federal arrangements are proposed not despite this reality but because of it —because strength that integrates Palestinian resources is greater than strength that must constantly guard against Palestinian threats, because security that both communities have reason to defend is more durable than security that one community imposes on the other.

Peace does not mean compromising on security. It means achieving security through means more sustainable than permanent war. The architecture described in this chapter provides the institutional framework. Political will must supply the rest.

Chapter 9.
Addendum.

Key Concepts.

Understanding Federal Security Architecture.

Security Architecture: The comprehensive framework of institutions, policies, and relationships providing for a state's defense and public safety. Encompasses military forces, intelligence services, police, border control, emergency response, and governing legal frameworks. In federal systems, security architecture balances unity of command (essential for effective defense) with regional autonomy (essential for democratic legitimacy).

Unified Command: A command structure where all military forces operate under a single chain of command, reporting ultimately to one commander-in-chief (typically the elected head of government). Prevents coordination problems from parallel command structures. Federal forces handle external threats and nationwide coordination; regional forces handle local policing under federal constitutional frameworks.

Demilitarization: The process of reducing or eliminating military forces, weapons, and fortifications. Post-conflict demilitarization proceeds in phases: cease-fire and force separation, weapons collection and decommissioning, demobilization of combatants, reintegration of former fighters into civilian life. Requires security guarantees—parties will only disarm if they believe they won't be vulnerable to attack.

Counter-terrorism: Operations and strategies designed to prevent, deter, and respond to terrorism—politically motivated violence targeting civilians. Combines intelligence gathering, law enforcement, military operations against terrorist organizations, defensive measures protecting targets, countering terrorist ideology and recruitment, and addressing root causes. Effective counter-terrorism requires coordination across agencies and jurisdictions.

Intelligence Services: Government agencies gathering, analyzing, and disseminating information about security threats. Intelligence includes human intelligence (HUMINT) from agents, signals intelligence (SIGINT) from intercepted communications, imagery intelligence (IMINT) from satellites, and open-source intelligence (OSINT) from public information. In federal systems, intelligence operates at multiple levels with coordination mechanisms ensuring information flows between them.

Border Security: Control over entry and exit of people and goods across national boundaries. Prevents unauthorized entry, screens for security threats, collects customs duties, and asserts sovereignty. Modern border security employs layered approaches: physical barriers, surveillance technology, biometric identification, document verification, intelligence screening, and rapid-response personnel. In federal systems, border security is typically exclusively federal responsibility.

Policing vs. Military: Police enforce domestic laws, use minimum necessary force, prioritize protecting civilians and gathering evidence, and maintain community relationships. Military forces defend against external threats, operate under military justice and law of armed conflict, train for maximum force projection, and prioritize destroying enemy forces. Federal systems typically reserve policing for regional/local authorities while military defense becomes federal responsibility.

The Citizen Relevance: Security for Everyone.
Israel Federal security aids global security & prosperity.
Israeli Security Innovations Protecting the World.
Israeli security companies developed technologies protecting people globally. Airport security worldwide uses Israeli-developed screening technologies, behavioral analysis techniques, and biometric identification systems. Cybersecurity software protecting businesses and governments globally frequently incorporates Israeli technology in network security, threat detection, and incident response.

Counter-terrorism training and tactics developed by Israeli security forces have been adopted by police and military organizations worldwide. Federal integration would accelerate these innovations. Combining Israeli technical sophistication with Palestinian regional knowledge and expanded talent pools would produce advances benefiting global security.

Regional Stability Reducing Global Terror Threats.
The Israeli-Palestinian conflict has been exploited by terrorist organizations globally for recruitment and propaganda. Al-Qaeda and ISIS featured the conflict in recruitment materials. Resolving this conflict through federal frameworks would remove a significant grievance that extremists exploit.

Federal security cooperation would directly benefit global counterterrorism. Israeli intelligence capabilities combined with Palestinian community knowledge would create unprecedented ability to track terrorist networks and prevent attacks, with intelligence shared with partners globally.

Regional stability would enable comprehensive Middle Eastern security cooperation currently blocked by the Israeli-Palestinian conflict, reducing instability that generates refugee flows and terrorist safe havens affecting global security.

Protection of Holy Sites

Jerusalem's holy sites—sacred to Jews, Christians, and Muslims—require sophisticated security preventing both external attacks and internal tensions. Federal security forces, representing both Israeli and Palestinian populations and operating under constitutional mandates protecting religious freedom, would provide more legitimate and effective protection than current arrangements. This model could extend to Hebron, Bethlehem, and other religiously significant sites.

Security Isn't Zero-Sum.

The most profound shift federal security architecture would accomplish is replacing zero-sum security competition with positive-sum collective security. Currently, each community's safety seems to require the other's subjugation. Federal arrangements make security genuinely collective. When both Israeli and Palestinian personnel serve in federal forces, security becomes shared rather than competed over. This reflects research on security communities —groups that have overcome security competition through institutional integration. NATO transformed Western European states into security partners. Federal security architecture could achieve similar transformation for Israelis and Palestinians, providing hope and models for other seemingly intractable conflicts globally.

Scholarly Frameworks.

Security Sector Reform and Conflict Resolution.

Students examining federal security architecture should engage with security sector reform literature and relevant case studies.

Security Sector Reform Literature:

DDR (Disarmament, Demobilization, Reintegration): Process of collecting weapons, dissolving armed groups, and reintegrating former combatants. Research by Muggah (2009) and Knight (2008) finds economic reintegration programs preventing former combatants from returning to violence prove critical.

Civil-Military Relations: Scholarship on subordinating military forces to democratic civilian control. Feaver (2003) and Huntington (1957) provide foundational frameworks requiring both civilian supremacy and military professionalism.

Security Governance:

How societies collectively manage security through institutions balancing effectiveness, democratic accountability, and human rights. Essential readings: Sedra (2010) on SSR in Afghanistan; Ball (2001) on reforming police in divided societies.

Case Studies.
Northern Ireland: Police Service of Northern Ireland replaced the Protestant-dominated Royal Ulster Constabulary after 1998. Reform created 50-50 Catholic-Protestant recruitment targets, community policing training, and civilian oversight. Key lessons: changing institutional culture takes time; recruiting excluded communities requires proactive measures. Readings: Ellison and Smyth (2000), Mulcahy (2006).
Bosnia: Post-Dayton military integration combined three armies into unified Armed Forces of Bosnia and Herzegovina. Took over a decade, required intensive international involvement, achieved partial success. Key lessons: external security guarantees enable integration; joint training builds trust gradually. Readings: Bassuener (2012), Perry (2003).

Career Paths.
Students interested in conflict resolution and security sector reform can pursue careers in: UN Department of Peace Operations, OSCE, regional organizations; government agencies (foreign/defense ministries, development agencies); NGOs (International Crisis Group, Saferworld); or academia. Requires graduate degrees in international relations/security studies, language skills, field experience, and deep understanding of local contexts.
The Breakdown:
Keeping Everyone Safe, Building Security Together.
The Basic Problem.
Two groups don't trust each other. One worries about attacks. The other feels controlled by the first group's security forces. How do you make both feel safe?
The Current System.
Israeli security forces control everything. They protect Israelis but also restrict Palestinian movement and sometimes use deadly force. Palestinians feel occupied. Israelis say measures are necessary because some Palestinians commit terror. This creates a cycle of resentment and attacks. Neither side feels safe.

The Federal Solution.
Police: Palestinian areas have Palestinian police—Arabic-speaking, locally recruited. Israeli areas have Israeli police. Both follow the same constitutional rules and standards.

Military: Federal military protects the whole country, including both Israeli and Palestinian soldiers. Initially mostly Israeli with some Palestinian units. Over years, becomes more mixed as trust builds.

Intelligence: Combines Israeli technical skills with Palestinian community knowledge. Together, better at stopping terrorism.

How It Would Work.

In Ramallah, Palestinian police handle normal work. No Israeli soldiers on streets. In Tel Aviv, Israeli police continue as now. For serious national threats, federal intelligence investigates. Borders protected by federal forces—Israeli and Palestinian soldiers together.

Building Trust Gradually.

Start slowly: officials meet and share information → Palestinians join federal security in non-combat roles → joint training → joint operations → more integration. At each phase, if not working, slow down. If working, speed up.

Why Both Safer.

Israelis: Better intelligence from Palestinian partners. Palestinians have stake in stopping terrorism threatening their country.

Palestinians: No Israeli soldiers in their cities. No checkpoints. Police speaking their language, respecting dignity. Palestinians help protect themselves.

Working together on security changes how people see each other. Former enemies can become partners.

Addressing Security Concerns Honestly.

Federal security arrangements must address legitimate fears on both sides.

Legitimate Israeli Security Concerns.

October 7th Trauma: Hamas's massacre killed over 1,200 Israelis, kidnapped 240. This recent horror seared into Israeli consciousness.

Geographic Vulnerability: Israel is tiny—9 miles wide at its narrowest. Threats can materialize rapidly. A hostile Palestinian entity with advanced weapons could threaten Israel's entire population.

Rocket Threats: Gaza has fired over 20,000 rockets at Israeli cities since 2005. Children have PTSD from attacks.

Iranian Threat: Iran funds Hamas and Hezbollah, repeatedly declaring intent to destroy Israel. Any Palestinian military capability could become Iranian proxy.

Historical Experience: Every Israeli withdrawal without adequate guarantees led to attacks. Gaza (2005) led to Hamas and rockets. Oslo saw suicide bombings killing 1,000+ Israelis.

Palestinian Security Concerns.

Occupation Violence: Israeli soldiers conduct night raids, arrest thousands (including children), demolish homes, use live fire. Hundreds of Palestinian civilians killed in West Bank in "routine" operations.

Settler Violence: Armed settlers attack Palestinians, burn homes —often with impunity.

No Accountability: Israeli soldiers who kill Palestinians rarely face consequences. Palestinians have no recourse.

Control: Israeli forces control Palestinian movement, economic activity, daily life. Palestinians need permits for basic activities.

Historical Experience: 1948 Nakba saw 700,000+ Palestinians expelled. Massacres occurred.

How Federal Security Addresses Both.

Constitutional Protections: Neither community could unilaterally change arrangements. Courts enforce protections for both.

Phased Implementation: Integration proceeds in stages. If one side defects, process can pause. Trust develops through demonstrated performance.

International Guarantees: NATO or equivalent would commit external powers to defending both populations.

Demilitarization with Verification: Palestinian regions wouldn't maintain heavy weapons. International monitors verify.

Regional Police Autonomy: Palestinian police serve Palestinian regional governments, not Israeli authorities.

Intelligence Integration: Share information about common threats while maintaining separate identities.

Economic Stakes: Material benefits create constituencies for maintaining cooperation.

Gradual Trust-Building*: Integration over years/decades. Initial phases minimal risk. Higher-risk integration only after lower-risk phases succeed.

Federal security involves risks for both sides. But every alternative also involves risks. The question isn't whether federal security is risk-free—it isn't—but whether risks are manageable and compare favorably to alternatives. Evidence from Northern Ireland, Bosnia, and South Africa suggests enemies can become partners if institutions create incentives for cooperation, integration proceeds gradually, and both sides recognize aligned long-term interests.

Chapter 10.
Managing Diversity & Cohesion.

Federalism's Dual Edge: Unity Amid Division.
The question that haunts every federal proposal for Israel-Palestine is deceptively simple: can it work? Behind this question lies a century of failed initiatives, broken agreements, and accumulated grievances that have convinced many observers that coexistence is impossible. The sceptics are not irrational. They have watched federal experiments fail spectacularly—Yugoslavia dissolving into genocidal warfare, the Soviet Union fragmenting into hostile successor states, Czechoslovakia peacefully but definitively separating. Why should Israeli-Palestinian federalism succeed where others have failed?

The answer cannot be that federalism always works, because it manifestly does not. But neither can the answer be that it never works, because Switzerland, Canada, Belgium, Germany, India, and numerous other diverse societies have built stable, prosperous democracies through federal arrangements. The real question is what distinguishes successful from failed federal experiments—and whether the conditions for success can be created in the Israeli-Palestinian context.

Daniel Elazar's foundational insight remains essential: federal systems represent "a genus of political organization that is marked by the combination of self-rule and shared rule."[1] This dual imperative—preserving particularistic identities while constructing overarching solidarity—defines the federal project in deeply divided societies. The genius of federalism lies in its refusal to force a choice between autonomy and unity; it insists that both can be achieved simultaneously through institutional design that channels difference into legitimate political processes rather than suppressing it through majoritarian domination.

What works in federal systems is their capacity to transform zero-sum sovereignty battles into positive-sum arrangements. When communities fight over who controls the state, the stakes are absolute—winner takes all, loser loses everything.

Federalism restructures these stakes by creating multiple centres of power, multiple arenas for political competition, and multiple levels at which communities can achieve meaningful self-governance.

The community that loses at the federal level may win at the regional level; the policy preferences frustrated in one jurisdiction may be implemented in another. This multiplication of political opportunities reduces the existential quality of political competition and creates space for accommodation.

Switzerland exemplifies this transformation. The Swiss Confederation integrates four official languages—German, French, Italian, and Romansh—through cantonal autonomy that allows each linguistic region to determine educational policy, official communications, and cultural programming.[2]

Critically, Swiss federalism does not merely tolerate linguistic difference; it constitutionalizes it, establishing language rights as fundamental guarantees enforceable through judicial review. The result is remarkable stability in a country that, by conventional logic, should have fragmented long ago. German-speaking Swiss outnumber their French, Italian, and Romansh compatriots combined, yet majoritarianism has never dominated Swiss politics. Federal institutions channel linguistic competition into legitimate processes, ensuring that no community feels existentially threatened by demographic disadvantage.

Canada's experience with Quebec demonstrates both federalism's possibilities and its limits. The constitutional recognition of Quebec's distinct society, official bilingualism, and evolving frameworks for Indigenous self-government represent successive attempts to accommodate difference within federal structures.[3]

Quebec separatism, which came within a percentage point of succeeding in the 1995 referendum, has since declined—not because Québécois identity has weakened but because federal arrangements have provided sufficient space for its expression. Asymmetric federalism, which grants Quebec powers that other provinces do not possess, addresses the particular circumstances of francophone nationhood without requiring uniform treatment that would either deny Quebec's distinctiveness or grant inappropriate powers to provinces that do not require them.

Yet Canadian federalism has not eliminated tensions. Indigenous land claims remain contested; debates over multiculturalism policy persist; periodic constitutional crises reveal fault lines that institutional design has managed but not resolved. As Will Kymlicka observes, "federalism is neither necessary nor sufficient for accommodating national minorities, but it can be a powerful tool when combined with other measures."[4] Federalism creates framework; political culture must supply content. Where leaders embrace pluralism and resist ethnonationalist mobilization, federal institutions thrive. Where leaders exploit divisions for short-term advantage, federal institutions strain and sometimes shatter.

What Does Not Work: Cautionary Lessons.
Intellectual honesty requires confronting federalism's failures as directly as its successes. The conditions that produce successful federal accommodation are specific, and their absence has repeatedly produced disaster.

Unchecked local majoritarianism represents federalism's most dangerous pathology. When regional autonomy permits dominant local groups to oppress local minorities, federalism becomes a mechanism for distributing tyranny rather than preventing it. The post-2003 Iraqi federal system empowered Kurdish and Shia regions but facilitated Sunni marginalization that contributed directly to the emergence of ISIS.[5] Federal institutions that lack robust protections for minorities at all governmental levels do not manage diversity—they multiply the sites at which discrimination can occur.

Belgium illustrates a different failure mode: the paralysis that results when power-sharing mechanisms become too elaborate. The intricate arrangements designed to protect Flemish and Walloon interests have repeatedly produced governmental deadlock, with Belgium setting world records for duration without a functioning government.[6] Veto powers intended to prevent majoritarian domination instead prevent governance altogether. The Belgian case warns that power-sharing can be overdone—that institutional complexity designed to protect every conceivable interest may produce gridlock rather than accommodation.

Weak central authority invites secession. Federal systems require that the federal government possess sufficient power to maintain order, enforce constitutional protections, and provide the public goods that justify continued association. When central authority erodes, constituent units calculate whether they might fare better independently. The Soviet Union and Yugoslavia both featured nominally federal structures, but these structures masked authoritarian control that, once removed, left nothing binding the union together.[7] Their constituent republics had developed the administrative capacity for independence during the

Soviet/Yugoslav period; when central control collapsed, separation followed.

Poor power-sharing invites dominance. Federal arrangements that permit one community to control federal institutions while relegating others to regional consolation prizes do not produce genuine accommodation. Such arrangements create resentment among subordinated groups and temptations toward abuse among dominant groups. Ethiopia's ethnic federalism, despite its theoretical elegance, has struggled precisely because the Tigray People's Liberation Front's long dominance of federal institutions generated grievances that eventually exploded into civil war.[8]

These failures share common features that distinguish them from successful cases. Failed federations typically lacked democratic consolidation prior to ethnic mobilization—their federal structures were imposed from above rather than negotiated among communities. They lacked cross-cutting cleavages that create incentives for inter-ethnic cooperation; instead, ethnic, religious, regional, and economic divisions reinforced each other, creating communities with nothing in common. They lacked economic interdependence that would make separation costly; indeed, economic grievances often drove separatism. And they lacked political cultures committed to pluralistic coexistence—leaders who might have built bridges instead exploited divisions.

Mosaic Versus Melting Pot: Which Model for Federal Israel?
The United States offers two competing models for managing diversity that carry implications for Federal Israel: the melting pot and the mosaic. These metaphors describe fundamentally different approaches to the relationship between particular identities and collective belonging. The melting pot model assumes that diverse populations will and should assimilate into a common civic identity that transcends particular origins.

Immigrants arrive with distinct languages, religions, and cultural practices; over generations, these particularities dissolve into American identity defined by shared commitment to constitutional principles, English language, and broadly common cultural practices. The melting pot does not eliminate difference entirely—ethnic festivals, religious diversity, and cultural variations persist—but it treats these as private matters while public identity converges on common citizenship.[9]

The melting pot has achieved genuine successes. European immigrant groups that maintained fierce ethnic distinctions in the early twentieth century—Italians, Irish, Poles, Jews—have substantially merged into white American identity. The melting pot created a civic nationalism capable of mobilizing diverse populations for common purposes, from world wars to moon landings. Its emphasis on individual rather than group rights aligns with liberal principles that many find compelling.

Yet the melting pot model has always worked better for some groups than others. Racial minorities—African Americans, Native Americans, Asian Americans, Latinos—have faced barriers to assimilation that European immigrants did not. The melting pot's implicit assumption that particularities should dissolve privileges groups whose particularities most closely resemble the dominant culture. Those whose differences are more visible or more stigmatized face pressure to abandon identities that others are permitted to retain. The melting pot, critics argue, is less a neutral process of civic integration than a mechanism for cultural domination dressed in universalist language.[10]

The mosaic model, most fully developed in Canadian multiculturalism policy, offers an alternative vision. The mosaic preserves distinct cultural "tiles" within a shared frame—each community maintains its particularity while all participate in common institutions. The frame provides unity; the tiles provide diversity. Rather than asking immigrants and minorities to dissolve their identities into a homogeneous whole, the mosaic celebrates diversity as enriching collective life. Public institutions accommodate difference through multilingual services, recognition of diverse holidays, and support for cultural maintenance.[11]

The mosaic model better fits Israel's social reality. Israeli society is not a melting pot in which diverse Jewish populations are dissolving into undifferentiated Israeli identity; it is a mosaic in which Ashkenazi, Mizrachi, Ethiopian, Russian, and other Jewish communities maintain distinct cultural practices while sharing Israeli citizenship. Arab citizens—Muslim, Christian, and Druze—constitute additional tiles that no melting pot has assimilated. The mosaic metaphor acknowledges this diversity as permanent rather than transitional, as enriching rather than problematic.

A Federal State of Israel would extend the mosaic frame to encompass Palestinians in Judea, Samaria, and Gaza as additional tiles—distinct communities with their own identities, institutions, and self-governance, participating in shared federal institutions while maintaining particularity. The frame would provide common citizenship, constitutional protections, federal services, and participation in federal governance. The tiles would provide educational autonomy, cultural institutions, religious governance, and regional political expression. Neither assimilation nor separation; both unity and diversity.

Applying Federal Principles to Israeli Realities.
The transition from abstract principle to concrete application requires confronting Israeli-Palestinian specificities that no comparative case precisely matches. The conflict's intensity, the territorial intermixture, the religious significance of contested sites, the trauma on both sides, the regional context—these features create unique challenges that off-the-shelf federal models cannot address without adaptation.

Consider the question of regional boundaries. Swiss cantons evolved over centuries; their boundaries reflect historical settlement patterns that, while not without controversy, possess legitimacy derived from long acceptance. Israeli-Palestinian regional boundaries would need to be drawn in a context where every boundary carries political meaning and where populations are intermixed in ways that preclude clean separation. The settlement enterprise has created Jewish populations throughout the West Bank; Palestinian populations exist throughout Israel. Any regional structure must accommodate this intermixture rather than assuming homogeneous regions.

One approach would create regions based primarily on existing administrative units—Israel's districts, the Palestinian Authority's governorates, Gaza—with modifications reflecting demographic realities and governance efficiency. Jewish settlements in the West Bank might be incorporated into adjacent Israeli regions or constitute distinct enclaves with special status. Arab communities within Israel might choose affiliation with adjacent Palestinian regions or remain within Israeli regions with enhanced local autonomy. The principle would be flexibility rather than rigid territorial logic—allowing communities to select arrangements that best serve their interests within federal constitutional constraints.

The status of Jerusalem requires particular attention. Both peoples claim Jerusalem as their capital; both possess profound religious attachments to sites within the city; partition has proven politically impossible. Federal arrangements could address Jerusalem through multiple mechanisms: designating the city as federal territory under joint governance, creating distinct zones for different communities within unified municipal administration, establishing special arrangements for holy sites that transcend ordinary political authority.[12] The Belgian Brussels model—where a bilingual region serves as capital for communities that elsewhere maintain territorial separation—demonstrates that complex arrangements for contested cities can function, however imperfectly.

Gaza presents distinctive challenges. The territory's isolation, its governance by Hamas, and the devastation of recent conflicts create conditions far removed from normal federal integration. Any realistic federal vision must acknowledge that Gaza's path differs from the West Bank's—requiring security stabilization, humanitarian reconstruction, and political transformation before meaningful federal participation becomes possible. A phased approach might begin with Gaza as a semi-autonomous economic zone, developing port facilities and commercial connections that create material stakes in peaceful integration, with fuller federal participation following demonstrated commitment to constitutional order.

Education as Integration Mechanism.
Educational systems function as perhaps the most consequential state apparatus for shaping collective identity and managing diversity. Schools socialize successive generations into national narratives, transmit cultural values, and either reinforce or challenge existing social hierarchies. In a Federal State of Israel, educational policy would become a critical arena where questions of cultural preservation, linguistic rights, and federal integration intersect.

The curriculum design challenge involves balancing particularistic cultural transmission with shared civic education. James Banks' research on multicultural education demonstrates that exclusive emphasis on either dimension produces pathological outcomes—pure particularism generates isolated communities lacking shared identity, while pure universalism marginalizes minority cultures and breeds resentment.[13] Effective education must integrate both dimensions, providing students with deep grounding in their own cultural traditions while fostering understanding of other communities within the federal polity.

For a Federal State of Israel, this suggests a bilingual, bicultural educational framework. Hebrew and Arabic would both function as official languages throughout the federation, with students learning both regardless of their community of origin. This is not unprecedented—Luxembourg requires trilingual education; Singapore mandates bilingualism; numerous federal systems require competence in multiple official languages. The goal is creating citizens capable of communicating across communal lines, accessing opportunities throughout the federation, and participating in federal institutions that operate in both languages.

Curriculum content would require careful negotiation. Historical narratives currently taught in Israeli and Palestinian schools differ dramatically—not merely in emphasis but in basic factual claims about events like 1948, 1967, and subsequent conflicts.[14] A federal curriculum need not impose a single narrative that neither community accepts; it could instead present multiple perspectives on contested events, teaching students to understand how different communities experienced shared history differently. This "multiperspectival" approach, successfully employed in post-conflict educational contexts from Northern Ireland to South Africa, develops critical thinking while acknowledging that historical truth is more complex than any single narrative captures.[15]

Regional educational autonomy would permit communities to supplement federal curriculum with content reflecting their particular traditions. Jewish regions might emphasize Jewish history, Hebrew literature, and religious studies; Palestinian regions might emphasis Arab history, Arabic literature, and Islamic studies. The federal framework would establish minimum standards and shared content; regional authorities would add content reflecting local priorities. This division—federal floor, regional ceiling—characterizes educational federalism in successful diverse democracies.

Educational exchange programs represent underutilized mechanisms for building intercultural understanding. Research consistently demonstrates that intergroup contact under appropriate conditions—equal status, common goals, institutional support— reduces prejudice and builds cross-group relationships.[16] When Israeli and Palestinian students study together, participate in joint projects, and develop personal friendships, the stereotypes that sustain conflict erode. A Federal State of Israel should mandate such exchanges, creating opportunities for meaningful interaction that challenges inherited animosities.

Media Representation and Democratic Discourse

Media institutions shape public discourse and collective perceptions, functioning as crucial intermediaries between diverse communities. In deeply divided societies, media representations profoundly influence intergroup relations—either reinforcing prejudices through stereotypical portrayal or challenging them through nuanced coverage. The structure of federal media systems therefore carries significant implications for managing diversity.

Critical media studies document systematic biases in coverage of minority communities: disproportionate association with crime and social problems, limited representation in positive roles, reliance on majority-group sources for stories about minorities, and framing of minority practices through exotic or threatening lenses.[17] These patterns reflect and reinforce power asymmetries, marginalizing minority perspectives while normalizing majority viewpoints as objective and universal.

A Federal State of Israel would require media policies actively promoting balanced representation. Federal broadcasting mandates could require proportional coverage of different communities, ensure that editorial leadership reflects federal diversity, and create platforms for voices currently marginalized in mainstream Israeli media. Public broadcasting, insulated from both government pressure and commercial incentives, could model the balanced coverage that federal democracy requires.

The challenge intensifies in digital environments where content crosses boundaries instantaneously and algorithmic curation creates filter bubbles limiting exposure to diverse perspectives.[18] Social media platforms have become vectors for hate speech and disinformation that exacerbate divisions. Federal regulation must balance free expression against harms from incitement while respecting the jurisdictional complexities of digital communication. Media literacy education—teaching citizens to critically evaluate sources, recognize bias, and seek diverse perspectives—becomes essential preparation for democratic citizenship in information-saturated environments.

Hebrew and Arabic media currently operate in largely separate spheres, each community consuming content that the other rarely encounters. Federal media policy should create shared spaces— bilingual platforms, translated content, joint programming—that enable cross-communal communication. When Israelis and Palestinians access the same information, engage with the same debates, and see each other represented in shared media, the epistemic fragmentation that sustains conflict begins to heal.

Cultural Accommodation & Religious Freedom.
Religious diversity poses distinctive challenges for federal governance, particularly when religious identities intersect with ethnic cleavages. Constitutional frameworks must navigate between protecting individual religious freedom and maintaining secular public spheres that privilege no particular tradition. This balance becomes especially delicate when religious communities demand exemptions from generally applicable laws or seek public funding for faith-based institutions.

The theoretical foundation for religious freedom in liberal democracies rests upon principles of individual conscience and limited government authority over spiritual matters.[19] Modern constitutional practice translates these principles into dual guarantees: non-establishment provisions prohibiting state religion or preferential treatment, and free exercise protections enabling religious practice without government interference. Federal systems must apply these guarantees uniformly while respecting regional variation in religious demographics.

A Federal State of Israel presents unique complications. Israel currently defines itself as a Jewish state, with religious significance embedded in state symbols, calendar, and public life. Palestinian regions would be predominantly Muslim, with Christian minorities. Creating a secular federal framework that neither privileges Judaism nor suppresses it—that treats all religions equally while acknowledging the particular historical circumstances that created a Jewish state—requires careful constitutional design.

One approach would distinguish between federal and regional religious arrangements. The federal level would maintain strict neutrality—no established religion, equal treatment for all faiths, secular governance of shared institutions. Regional levels would possess greater latitude to reflect local religious character—Jewish regions might maintain aspects of current religious public life; Muslim regions might incorporate Islamic elements; mixed regions might develop distinctive arrangements. Holy sites of significance to multiple traditions—Jerusalem's Old City, Hebron's Cave of the

Patriarchs—would fall under federal jurisdiction with governance arrangements ensuring access for all faiths.

Personal status law—governing marriage, divorce, and inheritance—currently operates through religious courts in both Israeli and Palestinian society. Federal arrangements might preserve this system, with individuals choosing which religious or secular legal system governs their personal status. Alternatively, federal law might establish uniform civil options while permitting religious alternatives for those who prefer them. The latter approach, common in secular democracies, ensures that no one is forced into religious legal systems while permitting voluntary participation.

Conflict Resolution & Restorative Justice.
Federal systems managing deep diversity inevitably confront conflicts arising from competing interests, historical grievances, and identity-based mobilization. Effective mechanisms must address both immediate disputes and underlying structural conditions generating persistent tensions. Legal institutions, alternative dispute resolution, and transitional justice each play distinct roles.

Judicial systems serve as forums for adjudicating disputes through constitutional principles. Courts interpret anti-discrimination provisions, arbitrate jurisdictional conflicts between federal and regional governments, and enforce minority protections.[20] The judiciary's legitimacy rests upon perceptions of independence and impartiality—when courts appear captured by dominant groups, their capacity to resolve conflicts diminishes. A federal Israeli judiciary would require careful composition ensuring that neither community perceives bias, perhaps through balanced appointment processes and regional representation on federal courts.

However, litigation's adversarial nature often proves ill-suited for identity-based conflicts. Court decisions produce legal precedents but may leave underlying tensions unaddressed. Alternative dispute resolution—mediation, negotiation, consensus-building—offers complementary approaches emphasizing accommodation rather than imposed solutions.[21] Federal institutions might include standing mediation bodies for intercommunal disputes, with trained mediators drawn from both communities facilitating resolution of conflicts before they escalate to litigation or violence.

Restorative justice approaches address the deeper wounds that a century of conflict has inflicted. The Israeli-Palestinian conflict has produced trauma on both sides—the Nakba for Palestinians, terrorism and existential threat for Israelis, occupation's daily indignities, military operations' devastation. These traumas do not disappear when constitutional documents are signed; they persist in collective memory, shaping attitudes and fueling grievances that can undermine even well-designed institutions.

Truth and reconciliation processes, pioneered in South Africa and adapted in numerous post-conflict contexts, offer mechanisms for acknowledging historical injustices and facilitating societal healing. [22] A Federal Israeli truth commission might document abuses committed by all parties, provide forums for victims to testify, and establish an authoritative historical record that neither community's partisan narratives currently provide. Such processes do not produce agreement on all historical questions, but they can produce mutual acknowledgment that both communities have suffered and both have committed wrongs—a foundation for moving forward that denial and recrimination cannot provide.

The Canadian Truth and Reconciliation Commission investigating residential schools demonstrates how truth processes can operate within federal systems. The TRC documented systematic cultural genocide, issued ninety-four Calls to Action addressing ongoing impacts, and sparked national conversation about reconciliation. [23] Implementation remains incomplete—truth commissions initiate rather than complete reconciliation—but the process created public acknowledgment that previous denial had made impossible.

Economic justice constitutes an indispensable component of sustainable conflict resolution. When ethnic or religious differences correlate with socioeconomic status, addressing economic disparities becomes prerequisite for genuine reconciliation. As discussed in Chapter 8, fiscal federalism mechanisms must ensure that Palestinian regions develop economically rather than remaining permanent dependents. Without material improvement in Palestinian lives, federal arrangements will be perceived as occupation rebranded rather than genuine partnership.

Pillars for Success: What Federal Israel Requires.
The analysis above suggests several institutional pillars essential for successful federal accommodation in the Israeli-Palestinian context.
Constitutional Architecture. A federal constitution must establish clear protections for individual and group rights, define federal and

regional jurisdictions, create mechanisms for resolving disputes between governmental levels, and entrench arrangements against unilateral modification. Constitutional courts must possess authority and legitimacy to enforce these provisions against both federal and regional governments. The constitutional framework must be perceived as legitimate by both communities—negotiated rather than imposed, reflecting compromise rather than domination.

Power-Sharing Institutions. Federal executive and legislative institutions must ensure that neither community can dominate federal governance. Bicameral legislatures with one chamber representing population and another representing regions, coalition requirements for federal governments, qualified majorities for constitutional amendments, and proportional representation in federal agencies all contribute to genuine power-sharing. The consociational mechanisms pioneered by Arend Lijphart—grand coalitions, proportionality, mutual veto, and segmental autonomy—provide templates requiring adaptation to Israeli-Palestinian specificities.[24]

Security Guarantees. As discussed in Chapter 9, security arrangements must address both communities' legitimate concerns while preventing security forces from becoming instruments of domination. Federal defence forces, regional police with community legitimacy, and constitutional constraints on emergency powers all contribute to security within federal democracy rather than security threatening federal democracy.

Economic Integration. As discussed in Chapter 8, economic arrangements must create shared prosperity that gives both communities material stakes in federal success. Fiscal transfers supporting Palestinian development, integrated markets enabling specialisation and trade, and infrastructure connecting rather than dividing territories all contribute to economic foundations for political accommodation.

Cultural Institutions. Educational systems, media platforms, and cultural programs must foster both particular identity and shared citizenship. The mosaic model suggests celebrating diversity within unity—neither forcing assimilation nor accepting fragmentation but creating frameworks where multiple identities coexist and interact.

Political Culture. Perhaps most importantly, federal institutions require political culture committed to their success. Leaders must resist temptations to exploit divisions for electoral advantage. Civil society must build bridges across communal lines. Citizens must develop habits of democratic participation that channel disagreements into legitimate processes. Institutions shape culture, but culture also shapes how institutions function; the relationship is reciprocal and ongoing.

Federalism as Framework, Not Guarantee.

The federal model outlined throughout this book offers no guarantee of success. Federalism has failed before and could fail again. The Israeli-Palestinian conflict possesses features—intensity of grievance, depth of distrust, significance of contested territory—that make accommodation exceptionally difficult. Anyone promising easy solutions is selling fantasy.

Yet the alternatives are worse. Continued occupation corrodes Israeli democracy, generates Palestinian suffering, and produces periodic violence that neither side can definitively win. Partition into two states has proven impossible to negotiate and would, even if achieved, leave both entities vulnerable and incomplete. Expulsion or transfer—the dark fantasies of extremists on both sides—would constitute crimes against humanity while failing to produce security for perpetrators.

Federalism offers a path between these unattractive alternatives. It preserves what both communities need—security and sovereignty for Israelis, dignity and self-governance for Palestinians—while creating institutional frameworks for managing inevitable disagreements. It does not require communities to love each other, only to live with each other under rules both have accepted. It does not eliminate difference, only channels difference into political rather than violent competition.

The comparative evidence demonstrates that federal accommodation can succeed in deeply divided societies. Switzerland, Canada, Belgium, Germany, India—none is paradise, but all have managed diversity that might otherwise have produced fragmentation or civil war. Their success required not only institutional design but political commitment, not only constitutions but culture, not only frameworks but faith that coexistence was possible and preferable to conflict.

Whether Israelis and Palestinians can summon such commitment remains uncertain. The federal vision articulated in this book provides institutional architecture; political will must supply the rest.

As I have written elsewhere, "Federal arrangements, properly designed and conscientiously implemented, transform diversity from source of conflict into foundation for resilient democracy."[25] The transformation is possible. Whether it occurs depends upon choices yet to be made.

Chapter 10
Addendum

Key Concepts.
Understanding Diversity Management.
Multiculturalism: A social approach recognizing cultural diversity as valuable rather than problematic. Rejects assimilation models demanding minorities abandon identities, instead supporting preservation of diverse languages, religions, and customs within shared civic frameworks. Canada pioneered official multiculturalism in 1971. Critics argue it fragments societies; proponents argue it creates inclusive societies respecting all citizens' dignity.

Cultural Autonomy: The right of communities to govern their own cultural affairs—education, language, religious practice—without interference. Can be territorial (regional control) or non-territorial (personal rights). Belgium grants Flemish and Francophone communities separate education systems and cultural institutions.

Educational Pluralism: Educational systems accommodating diverse communities through varied curricula and languages of instruction. Netherlands funds Catholic, Protestant, Islamic, and secular schools, each teaching required curriculum while incorporating distinctive content. Federal systems typically enable educational pluralism through regional control.

Media Freedom: The right to publish and broadcast without government censorship. Serves democratic functions: enabling informed participation, providing government oversight, facilitating public debate. However, unlimited freedom can enable hate speech threatening minorities, while restrictions can suppress minority voices.

Religious Freedom: The right to practice one's religion, change religions, or practice none without interference or discrimination. Encompasses individual conscience and institutional expression. Federal systems must balance religious freedom against preventing religious majorities from using state power to impose practices on minorities.

Social Cohesion: The bonds holding societies together—shared identity, mutual trust, common institutions—enabling cooperation despite diversity. Diverse societies face challenges when differences correlate with socioeconomic disparities or historical grievances. Requires creating cross-cutting ties connecting communities and inclusive narratives recognizing all groups' contributions.

Identity Politics: Political mobilization based on shared identity—ethnicity, religion, gender—rather than class or ideology. Emphasizes group experiences of discrimination, seeking recognition and redress. Critics argue it fragments solidarity; proponents argue it gives voice to marginalized communities whose concerns were ignored in supposedly "universal" politics.

The Citizen Relevance: Living Together in Diverse Societies.
Federal Israeli approaches to managing diversity offer lessons for multicultural societies globally.

Lessons for All Multicultural Societies
Western democracies increasingly struggle with diversity as immigration and demographic changes create unprecedented heterogeneity. France debates religious accommodation; Germany confronts integration of Turkish and Syrian populations; the U.S. faces persistent racial divisions; Britain navigates post-imperial diversity. These struggles mirror Israeli-Palestinian challenges—how to preserve distinct identities while building shared civic community.

Key lessons translate globally:

Constitutional Protections: Minority rights require constitutional entrenchment enforceable through independent courts, not majority goodwill.

Representation Creates Legitimacy: When institutions reflect diversity—legislators, judges, police, teachers, media—minorities perceive systems as legitimate.

Economic Inclusion Prevents Resentment: When ethnic/religious differences correlate with poverty, diversity becomes conflict source. Singapore's policies maintaining cohesion despite Chinese-Malay-Indian divisions demonstrate this.

Multiple Identities Strengthen Bonds: Encouraging cross-cutting affiliations spanning communities creates personal stakes in cohesion.

Preserving Identity While Building Unity
The mosaic model offers synthesis: strong particular identities coexisting within strong shared identity. This rejects false choice between assimilation (demanding minorities abandon identity) and separation (fragmenting polities into parallel societies).

Multilayered identity reflects lived reality—individuals possess multiple identities operating simultaneously. You can be simultaneously Palestinian, Muslim, Jerusalemite, teacher, and federal Israeli citizen—each identity authentic, each operating in appropriate contexts.

***E Pluribus Unum*: From Many, One**

Federal Israeli implementation would demonstrate deeply divided societies can create unity from diversity—not by erasing difference but by channeling it into legitimate processes. This challenges nationalism's premise that states require ethnically homogeneous populations—a premise globalization makes increasingly untenable.

Federal Israel would join Switzerland, Canada, Belgium, and India demonstrating diverse societies can thrive through well-designed institutions.

Scholarly Frameworks: Education and Social Science Research.

Students examining diversity management should engage with multicultural education research and community-building literature.

Multicultural Education Research

James Banks identifies four approaches: contributions (adding diverse heroes), additive (supplementing with ethnic content), transformation (restructuring curriculum around diverse perspectives), and social action (empowering students to challenge inequality). True multicultural education requires transformation and action.

Research demonstrates benefits: students develop cultural competence, critical thinking about diverse perspectives, and commitment to social justice. Essential readings: Banks (2015), Ladson-Billings (2004), Gay (2010), Nieto and Bode (2018).

Media Studies

Stuart Hall's encoding/decoding model shows media messages carry dominant ideologies but audiences interpret differently based on social positions. Research documents persistent patterns: minorities portrayed as criminals or threats, limited positive representation, reliance on majority-group experts. Critical media literacy teaches students to analyze media critically and recognize bias. Readings: Hall (1973), Entman and Rojecki (2001), Cottle (2000).

Community-Building

Contact hypothesis research shows intergroup contact under appropriate conditions (equal status, common goals, cooperation, institutional support) reduces prejudice. Northern Ireland's integrated schools demonstrate participants develop positive attitudes lasting into adulthood. Seeds of Peace brings Israeli-Palestinian youth together with measurable impact. Readings: Allport (1954), Pettigrew and Tropp (2006), Hughes et al. (2010), Hammack (2011).

Young Israelis and Palestinians would be primary agents of federal transformation.

Youth Exchange Programs

Current reality: Most young Israelis and Palestinians never meaningfully interact. Each learns about the other primarily through conflict—news reports, checkpoint encounters, security incidents. This separation produces mutual incomprehension and dehumanization.

Federal integration would transform this through youth exchanges. Palestinian students spending semesters in Israeli schools, Israeli students in Palestinian schools, both learning each other's languages, living with host families. Research shows sustained contact under equal conditions dramatically reduces prejudice.

Social Media: Contradictory Potential

Social media enables unprecedented connection—Palestinian and Israeli youth following each other, seeing daily lives beyond conflict. Grassroots initiatives create dialogue groups. However, algorithms prioritize outrage. Inflammatory content spreads faster than nuanced dialogue. Echo chambers form. During October 7th aftermath, social media became weapon amplifying divisions.

Federal frameworks could establish guidelines: digital literacy education, platform accountability for incitement, funding positive cross-community initiatives, youth-led digital projects building bridges.

What Young People Might Build

Young Israelis and Palestinians share more than divides them. In federal Israel, they could build:

Technology Innovation: Israeli expertise plus Palestinian creativity and Arab market knowledge creating startups solving regional challenges.

Environmental Cooperation: Joint movements addressing climate change, water scarcity, renewable energy.

Cultural Fusion: Arts, music, literature blending Hebrew and Arabic, Jewish and Arab influences.

Political Participation: Young people building federal institutions reflecting their values—diversity, technology, environmental concern, peace.

Key insight: young people didn't create this conflict. They inherited it. Given frameworks enabling cooperation, many would embrace opportunities to build different futures.

Faith Perspectives: Religious Coexistence.

Federal Israel must protect religious freedom for Jews, Muslims, Christians, Druze, Baha'i, and others while preventing religious conflict.

Protection of Religious Education

Federal frameworks would guarantee religious education rights: Jewish regions maintaining Torah study and Hebrew language; Muslim regions providing Quranic education and Arabic; Christian communities maintaining denominational schools; secular families choosing schools emphasizing science and humanistic values.

Federal oversight would ensure minimum standards—literacy, numeracy, civic education—are met regardless of religious content, balancing religious freedom with children's rights to acquire skills for informed citizenship.

Interfaith Dialogue Mechanisms

Federal Israel would institutionalize interfaith dialogue:

Interfaith Council: Federal body bringing together religious leaders for regular consultation, advising government and mediating disputes.

Holy Sites Committee: Managing sites sacred to multiple traditions. Representatives from relevant communities coordinating access and ensuring no faith dominates.

Interfaith Education: All students learning basic information about major religions practiced in federal Israel, providing cultural competence for respectful interaction.

Holy Site Sharing

Temple Mount/Haram al-Sharif: Most sensitive site. Federal arrangements would formalize current status quo: Muslim authority managing Islamic sites, Jewish authority managing Western Wall, federal oversight ensuring both communities' access.

Church of the Holy Sepulcher: Protecting existing arrangements among six Christian denominations while providing dispute resolution.

Broader Protections: No religious sites demolished or restricted without consent from relevant authorities and federal oversight.

Religious Freedom vs. Gender Equality

Tension exists between religious freedom and gender equality. One approach: distinguish between religious institutions' internal practices and public systems. Religious communities could maintain traditional practices within houses of worship while public institutions operate on gender equality principles.

Personal status could offer choice—individuals opting for religious courts or secular family law. Guiding principle: maximize religious freedom while ensuring it doesn't become mechanism for oppressing others.

Interfaith Marriage

As youth interact more, interfaith marriages would increase. Federal frameworks might establish civil marriage as nationwide option while preserving religious marriage for those preferring it. Children could be registered with either, both, or neither faith community according to preferences.

Chapter 11
Federal Model Critiques.

The Burden of Scepticism.

Anyone proposing federal solutions for the Israeli-Palestinian conflict must confront a formidable wall of skepticism. The critics are not marginal voices; they include serious scholars, experienced diplomats, and thoughtful observers who have concluded that federalism cannot work in this context. Their objections deserve serious engagement rather than dismissal. This chapter takes on that burden, examining the principal critiques of federal solutions and assessing whether they constitute insurmountable obstacles or manageable challenges.

The stakes of this examination are high. If the critics are correct—if federal arrangements genuinely cannot accommodate Israeli-Palestinian realities—then the federal vision articulated throughout this book is not merely difficult but delusional. Better to acknowledge that now than to pursue fantasies. But if the critics are wrong, or if their objections identify challenges that institutional design can address rather than inherent impossibilities, then federalism remains viable and the failure to pursue it becomes a choice for which we bear responsibility.

Intellectual honesty requires acknowledging that federal experiments have failed, sometimes catastrophically. Yugoslavia, the Soviet Union, Czechoslovakia—all featured nominally federal structures that ultimately fragmented. These failures cannot be explained away; they must be understood. What distinguishes successful from failed federal experiments? Are the conditions for success present, or creatable, in the Israeli-Palestinian context? These questions structure the analysis that follows.

The Complexity Critique.

The most common objection to Israeli-Palestinian federalism holds that the conflict's complexity exceeds what federal institutions can manage. Ian Lustick has argued powerfully that the "two-state paradigm" has become a barrier to creative thinking, but his own analysis suggests that one-state solutions—including federal variants—face obstacles at least as formidable.[1] The argument takes several forms, each requiring examination.

Historical Animosity as Obstacle.
Critics contend that the depth and duration of Israeli-Palestinian conflict have created animosities too profound for institutional accommodation. Alan Dowty summaries this view: the asymmetries of power, the depth of mutual distrust, and the absence of shared civic identity make any form of shared governance unworkable for the foreseeable future.[2] A century of conflict has produced traumas—the Nakba, terrorism, occupation, military operations—that shape collective memories and political attitudes in ways that preclude the cooperation federalism requires.

This critique has force. The Israeli-Palestinian conflict is not merely a political dispute amenable to institutional resolution; it involves existential fears, historical grievances, and identity claims that engage communities at the deepest levels. Federalism's comparative successes occurred in contexts with less intense recent violence and fewer accumulated grievances. Switzerland's religious wars ended centuries ago; Belgium's linguistic tensions never produced mass casualties; Canada's Quebec question, while serious, never involved terrorism or military occupation.

Yet the critique proves too much. If historical animosity precludes institutional accommodation, then peace of any kind becomes impossible—not merely federal peace but any peace. The logic that rules out federalism equally rules out two-state solutions, which require cooperation on security, water, trade, and numerous other matters. It rules out the status quo, which has manifestly failed to provide security or stability. It rules out everything except perpetual conflict or the elimination of one party—outcomes too terrible to accept as inevitable.

Moreover, comparative evidence suggests that institutional design can manage even intense historical animosities when conditions are right. The European Union emerged from the ashes of two world wars that killed tens of millions; France and Germany, whose enmity had defined European politics for generations, became the union's founding partners. Northern Ireland's peace process succeeded despite decades of violence and deeply entrenched communal divisions. South Africa's transition occurred despite apartheid's systematic brutality. These cases do not prove that Israeli-Palestinian accommodation will succeed, but they refute the claim that historical animosity makes accommodation impossible.

Irreconcilable Claims.
A related critique holds that certain Israeli-Palestinian disputes involve irreconcilable claims that no institutional arrangement can accommodate. Menachem Klein's analysis of Jerusalem suggests that both peoples' attachments to the city are so profound and their claims so maximalist that partition is impossible and sharing unthinkable.[3] Similar arguments apply to Palestinian refugee return, where Palestinian demands for return to ancestral homes confront Israeli fears of demographic transformation. How can federal institutions accommodate claims that are mutually exclusive?

This critique identifies genuine challenges but mischaracterizes federalism's function. Federalism does not resolve all disputes; it provides frameworks for managing them. Successful federal systems contain unresolved tensions that persist for generations—Quebec's place in Canada, the distribution of power between American states and the federal government, the relationship between linguistic communities in Belgium. These tensions are managed through institutional processes, periodic renegotiation, and judicial interpretation, not definitively resolved.

Applied to Israeli-Palestinian disputes, federalism offers not solutions but processes. Jerusalem's status might be addressed through complex arrangements—federal jurisdiction over certain areas, shared governance of holy sites, distinct zones for different communities—that satisfy neither side's maximum demands but provide frameworks for ongoing negotiation. Refugee issues might be addressed through acknowledgment, compensation, limited return to federal (rather than specifically Israeli) territory, and regional arrangements with neighboring states. These approaches do not eliminate grievances; they channel them into political rather than violent expression.

Institutional Incapacity.
A third variant of the complexity critique holds that federal institutions presuppose capacities that Palestinian society lacks. Hillel Frisch has argued that Palestinian institutional weakness— fragmented authority, armed factions outside governmental control, limited administrative capacity—makes Palestinians incapable of serving as reliable federal partners.[4] This critique gained force

after the Palestinian Authority's failures during the Oslo period and Hamas's seizure of Gaza.

The institutional capacity concern is legitimate but not insurmountable. Palestinian institutional weakness partly reflects occupation's constraints—limited sovereignty, restricted revenues, Israeli interference in governance, and the political dysfunction that chronic conflict produces. Federal arrangements that removed these constraints while providing capacity-building support could enable institutional development that occupation has prevented.

Moreover, federal systems have accommodated asymmetries in constituent unit capacity. German unification integrated eastern Länder whose institutions had been shaped by forty years of communist rule and required massive investment in capacity building. The European Union incorporated member states at vastly different developmental levels, providing structural funds and technical assistance to facilitate convergence. Similar mechanisms could support Palestinian institutional development within federal frameworks.

The Secession Risk.
Critics argue that federal arrangements, by granting regional autonomy and legitimizing distinct identities, create conditions for eventual secession. Dawn Brancati's research identifies this dynamic: "chief among [federalism's potential downsides is] the risk that granting regional autonomy can strengthen a minority group's sense of identity, thereby bolstering demands for secession."[5] Applied to the Israeli-Palestinian context, this critique suggests that Palestinian regional autonomy within a federal state would become a stepping stone to full independence rather than a stable endpoint.

The secession critique draws support from federal failures. Yugoslavia's constituent republics used their federal autonomy to develop the administrative capacity and political identity that enabled secession when central authority weakened. The Soviet Union's titular nationalities similarly leveraged federal structures to achieve independence. Czechoslovakia's "velvet divorce" demonstrated that even peaceful federal dissolution remains possible when constituent units prefer separation.

Philip Roeder's systematic analysis reinforces these concerns, showing that ethnofederal arrangements—federal structures where boundaries coincide with ethnic distributions—are particularly vulnerable to secessionist mobilization.[6] His work suggests that creating Palestinian regions within a federal Israel would institutionalize precisely the ethnic-territorial alignment that makes secession attractive.

Yet the critique overstates federalism's centrifugal tendencies. Failed federal experiments share features beyond their federal structure: authoritarian governance that prevented democratic conflict resolution, economic crises that delegitimized central authority, and the absence of cross-cutting cleavages creating interests in continued association. Yugoslavia, the Soviet Union, and Czechoslovakia were all communist states where federal structures masked centralised party control; when that control collapsed, nothing remained to bind the union.

Successful federal systems have managed secessionist pressures through institutional mechanisms and political culture. Canada has contained Quebec separatism through constitutional accommodation, fiscal transfers, and political dialogue. Spain has managed Basque and Catalan nationalism through asymmetric autonomy. The United Kingdom's devolution has reduced rather than inflamed Scottish independence sentiment (Brexit complications aside). These cases demonstrate that federalism can channel secessionist impulses into manageable political demands rather than existential threats.

For an Israeli-Palestinian federation, secession risks require serious attention in constitutional design. Provisions might include supermajority requirements for secession referenda, federal court jurisdiction over secession claims, and economic arrangements creating material incentives for continued association. The 1998 Canadian Supreme Court reference on Quebec secession provides a model: acknowledging that democratic self-determination has weight while establishing that secession requires negotiation within constitutional frameworks rather than unilateral declaration.[7]

More fundamentally, the secession critique assumes that Palestinian regional autonomy would generate independence demands. But Palestinians might prefer federal citizenship with its associated benefits—security, economic integration, freedom of movement, access to Israeli institutions—over precarious independence. The question is whether federal arrangements can deliver benefits sufficient to make continued association attractive.

If they can, secession risks diminish; if they cannot, the federal project has failed regardless of constitutional barriers.

The Asymmetry Problem.
Critics argue that the profound asymmetries between Israeli and Palestinian populations make genuine federal partnership impossible. Israel possesses a first-world economy, advanced military, established democratic institutions, and international recognition; Palestinians lack all of these. As'ad Ghanem has argued that any arrangement granting Palestinians formal equality would mask substantive Israeli dominance, while any arrangement acknowledging Israeli predominance would perpetuate Palestinian subordination.[8]

The asymmetry critique is empirically grounded. Israeli GDP per capita exceeds Palestinian GDP per capita by roughly fifteen to one. The Israeli Defence Forces constitute one of the world's most capable militaries; Palestinian security forces are fragmented and poorly equipped. Israeli diplomatic relations span the globe; Palestinian diplomatic status remains contested. These asymmetries would inevitably shape federal institutions, potentially producing arrangements federal in form but Israeli-dominated in substance.

Alexander Yakobson and Amnon Rubinstein extend this concern to demographic dynamics: any arrangement granting Palestinians substantial political power within a shared state would, they argue, inevitably erode Israel's Jewish character regardless of constitutional protections.[9] Demographic trends might shift federal politics toward positions hostile to Jewish national expression, transforming formal equality into substantive subordination for Jews.

These concerns cannot be dismissed, but they apply to any resolution, not specifically to federalism. Two-state solutions would leave a Palestinian state economically dependent on Israel and militarily vulnerable to it—asymmetry by another name. The status quo perpetuates asymmetry in its most naked form. The question is not whether asymmetry exists but how institutional arrangements can manage it.

Federal systems have developed sophisticated mechanisms for addressing asymmetries. Fiscal federalism transfers resources from wealthier to poorer regions, reducing economic disparities over time. Bicameral legislatures give smaller units representation disproportionate to their population, preventing majoritarian domination. Constitutional courts enforce minority protections against democratic majorities. Asymmetric federalism grants some units powers others do not possess, reflecting different circumstances and needs. These mechanisms do not eliminate asymmetry, but they can prevent asymmetry from producing domination.

Oren Yiftachel's analysis of Israel as an "ethnocracy" suggests that addressing asymmetry requires not merely institutional design but transformation of political culture.[10] A federal Israel would need to move from ethnic democracy—where one group's dominance is constitutionally embedded—toward genuinely pluralistic democracy where all citizens possess equal standing regardless of ethnicity. This transformation is difficult but not impossible; other societies have made similar transitions when political will existed.

The Security Objection.

Perhaps the most powerful critique of Israeli-Palestinian federalism comes from security analysis. Efraim Inbar has argued that Israeli security requirements are fundamentally incompatible with any arrangement diluting Israeli operational control over the territory between the Jordan River and Mediterranean Sea.[11] Given Palestinian armed factions' record of violence, the instability of Palestinian governance, and the regional threats Israel faces, security imperatives preclude the trust that federalism requires.

This critique resonates deeply with Israeli experience. The second intifada demonstrated that security cooperation can collapse catastrophically. Gaza's takeover by Hamas showed that territorial withdrawal without adequate security arrangements produces not peace but launching pads for attacks. October 7th, 2023 revealed that even massive military superiority and sophisticated barriers cannot prevent determined attackers from inflicting horrific casualties. Against this background, proposals for shared security arrangements appear dangerously naive.

Yet the security objection, taken to its logical conclusion, rules out any resolution. Two-state solutions would create a Palestinian state with the capacity for military development; there is no guarantee that future Palestinian governments would maintain peaceful relations. The status quo has manifestly failed to provide security, as October 7th demonstrated with terrible clarity. Permanent occupation requires permanent military mobilization, corrodes Israeli democracy, and generates the resentment that fuels violence. There is no risk-free option.

The relevant question is comparative: would federal security arrangements produce greater or lesser risk than alternatives? Chapter 9 addressed this question in detail, arguing that properly designed federal security architecture—with unified command for external defence, regional forces for community policing, integrated intelligence, and phased implementation allowing trust to develop—could provide security more robust than occupation while more legitimate than foreign control. The argument is not that federal security arrangements eliminate risk; it is that they manage risk better than alternatives.

Moreover, the security objection sometimes conflates short-term and long-term considerations. In the short term, Israeli security clearly requires capabilities that Palestinians lack and might misuse. In the long term, security depends not merely on military capability but on political legitimacy and regional relationships. Permanent occupation generates resistance that no military can permanently suppress; federal resolution that addresses Palestinian grievances might produce more durable security than continued domination. The time horizons matter.

The Democratic Legitimacy Critique.
Nathan Brown has raised concerns about federal proposals' democratic legitimacy: they may be "unrealistic and insufficiently attuned to the views of Palestinians" and other stakeholders who have not expressed desire for federal arrangements.[12] Rashid Khalidi similarly notes that Palestinian national aspirations have historically focused on independent statehood, not incorporation into shared governance structures with Israel.[13] Federalism, on this view, reflects what outsiders think Palestinians should want rather than what Palestinians actually want.

This critique identifies a genuine problem. Federal proposals often emerge from academic analysis or diplomatic creativity rather than popular movements. Neither Israeli nor Palestinian publics have demonstrated enthusiasm for federation; both have historically preferred separation, whether through two states or through one side's victory. Imposing federal arrangements on populations that reject them would violate democratic principles and likely fail in practice.

Yet public opinion is not static. Preferences respond to circumstances, information, and available alternatives. Two-state solutions commanded majority support among both populations for decades partly because they seemed achievable; as their feasibility has declined, support has eroded. Federal solutions might gain support if they appeared achievable and attractive—if, that is, political leadership articulated federal visions and demonstrated their benefits.

Moreover, democratic legitimacy ultimately requires that arrangements be accepted by those who live under them, but it does not require that arrangements emerge from prior popular demand. Constitutional arrangements are typically designed by elites and subsequently legitimized through ratification processes. The American Constitution was drafted by delegates who exceeded their mandate and ratified through procedures that excluded most of the population; it nonetheless achieved legitimacy through subsequent acceptance. Federal proposals for Israel-Palestine would similarly require legitimation through negotiation, referendum, and demonstrated performance—but this is a sequential process, not a precondition.

The Lebanon Warning
Critics sometimes invoke Lebanon as a cautionary tale for consociational or federal arrangements in the Middle East. Lebanon's confessional system, which distributed political power among religious communities, failed catastrophically—producing civil war from 1975 to 1990 and chronic dysfunction since. Bassel Salloukh and colleagues document how "the failure to cooperate has resulted in economic collapse" and persistent instability.[14] If Lebanon's arrangements failed despite relative homogeneity compared to Israeli-Palestinian divisions, why would Israeli-Palestinian federation succeed?

The Lebanese comparison requires careful analysis. Lebanon's confessional system institutionalized religious identity in rigid ways that prevented adaptation to demographic change—the Maronite Christian presidency became anachronistic as Muslim populations grew. External intervention—Syrian occupation, Israeli invasions, Iranian support for Hezbollah—repeatedly destabilized domestic arrangements. The Taif Agreement that ended the civil war redistributed power but did not fundamentally reform the confessional system.

These features are not inherent to federal or consociational arrangements but reflect specific Lebanese failures. Constitutional rigidity can be addressed through amendment procedures that enable adaptation. External intervention can be deterred through international guarantees and regional arrangements. Power-sharing formulas can be designed with flexibility that Lebanon's system lacked. Lebanon's failure identifies design parameters requiring attention, not inherent impossibility.

More fundamentally, Lebanon's alternative was not successful unitary statehood but civil war. The question is not whether confessional arrangements produced perfect outcomes but whether they produced better outcomes than alternatives. Lebanon's pre-war confessional system, whatever its flaws, maintained peace for three decades; its collapse produced catastrophe. The lesson is not that power-sharing fails but that power-sharing requires careful design and sustained commitment.

The Iraqi Failure
Iraq's post-2003 federal constitution provides another cautionary example. Karna Eklund's analysis documents how "the adoption of a federal form increased existing sectarian divides" rather than managing them.[15] Kurdish autonomy in the north empowered secessionist tendencies; Shia dominance of the federal government marginalised Sunnis; the Islamic State emerged partly from Sunni alienation. If Iraqi federalism exacerbated rather than managed sectarian conflict, what hope for Israeli-Palestinian federation?

The Iraqi case is sobering but its lessons are specific rather than general. Iraqi federalism emerged from American occupation rather than negotiated agreement among Iraqi parties. It was imposed on a society traumatized by decades of dictatorship, sanctions, and invasion. It coincided with the dismantling of the Iraqi state—particularly the disastrous de-Ba'athification that alienated Sunnis and disbanded the army. Regional powers—Iran, Saudi Arabia, Turkey—actively destabilized arrangements that threatened their interests. These factors, rather than federalism per se, explain Iraq's trajectory.

Moreover, Iraqi federalism's design contained specific flaws. Oil revenue distribution remained contested, creating zero-sum competition for resource control. Sunni regions received neither the autonomy nor the representation that might have secured their buy-in. Security forces became instruments of sectarian dominance rather than national protection. These are design failures, not inherent federal characteristics.

The Israeli-Palestinian context differs from Iraq in crucial respects. Federal arrangements would emerge from negotiation rather than foreign imposition. Institutional capacity, while asymmetric, is far higher. Regional dynamics, while challenging, do not involve the same degree of external intervention that destabilized Iraq. These differences do not guarantee success, but they suggest that Iraqi lessons require translation rather than direct application.

Addressing the Critics: A Synthesis
The critiques examined in this chapter—complexity, secession risk, asymmetry, security, legitimacy, and cautionary precedents— identify genuine challenges that federal design must address. They do not, however, establish that federalism is impossible. Each critique, examined carefully, reveals design parameters requiring attention rather than inherent barriers precluding success.

The complexity critique reminds us that Israeli-Palestinian federalism cannot assume the trust or cooperation that less conflictual contexts might provide. Institutions must be designed for low-trust environments, with robust enforcement mechanisms, international guarantees, and phased implementation allowing trust to develop through demonstrated performance rather than demanding it as a precondition.

The secession critique requires constitutional design that makes continued association attractive while preventing unilateral fragmentation. Economic integration creating mutual dependence, supermajority requirements for fundamental changes, and benefits of federal citizenship exceeding what independence could provide all contribute to stability.
The asymmetry critique demands attention to fiscal federalism, representation mechanisms, and minority protections that prevent dominant groups from exploiting numerical or economic advantages. The goal is not eliminating asymmetry but preventing asymmetry from producing domination.

The security critique necessitates the sophisticated security architecture detailed in Chapter 9—arrangements that address legitimate Israeli concerns while creating space for Palestinian self-governance. Security cannot be compromised, but security and federalism are not inherently incompatible.

The legitimacy critique requires that federal arrangements emerge from negotiation and achieve acceptance through ratification and performance. Federalism cannot be imposed; it must be chosen by populations who conclude that it serves their interests better than alternatives.

The cautionary precedents—Lebanon, Iraq, and failed federal experiments elsewhere—identify specific design failures to avoid rather than proving that all federal arrangements must fail. Their lessons are about how to design federalism, not whether to attempt it.

Administrative & Financial Viability.
Critics raise practical objections beyond the political: can federal institutions actually function given the administrative and financial complexities involved? George Tsebelis' veto players theory suggests that federal systems with multiple decision points create gridlock and inefficiency.[16] Applied to Israeli-Palestinian federation, this critique holds that the elaborate power-sharing mechanisms required to protect both communities would produce governmental paralysis rather than effective governance.

The administrative viability concern deserves serious engagement. Federal systems do require more elaborate institutional architecture than unitary states—multiple legislative chambers, intergovernmental coordination mechanisms, judicial review of federal-regional disputes, complex fiscal arrangements. These structures cost money to establish and operate. They require trained personnel who may not exist in adequate numbers. They create opportunities for jurisdictional conflicts that can paralyze decision-making.

Wallace Oates' foundational work on fiscal federalism identifies the trade-off: federal arrangements permit tailoring of policies to local preferences but at the cost of coordination difficulties and potential inefficiencies.[17] The question is whether benefits of diversity accommodation exceed costs of institutional complexity. For relatively homogeneous societies, the answer may be no. For deeply divided societies where unitary governance means domination by one group over others, the answer is typically yes—

the costs of federalism are lower than the costs of civil conflict or authoritarian imposition.

For Israeli-Palestinian federation specifically, administrative challenges would be substantial but not unprecedented. The European Union manages far greater complexity—twenty-seven member states with different languages, legal traditions, and administrative cultures—through institutions that, while imperfect, function adequately. German reunification required integrating administrative systems that had developed along entirely different lines for forty years. India governs over a billion people across twenty-eight states with different languages and administrative traditions. These cases demonstrate that administrative complexity, while challenging, can be managed.

The financial implications require honest assessment. Establishing federal institutions—constitutional courts, intergovernmental councils, federal agencies—requires significant investment. Fiscal federalism mechanisms that transfer resources to less-developed regions impose costs on wealthier regions. Capacity building for Palestinian regional governments would require substantial resources over extended periods.

Yet these costs must be compared to alternatives. The Israeli occupation costs billions annually in direct military expenditure and foregone economic activity. The Palestinian economy operates at a fraction of its potential due to restrictions that occupation imposes. Regional instability deters investment and tourism that peace would attract. The RAND Corporation's comprehensive analysis estimated that continued conflict costs both populations tens of billions of dollars over a decade compared to peaceful resolution.[18] Federal institution costs, while real, pale beside conflict costs.

International support could substantially offset transition costs. Major powers and international institutions have strong interests in Israeli-Palestinian resolution; they have proven willing to invest substantial resources in peace processes and post-conflict reconstruction elsewhere. The European Union, United States, Gulf states, and international financial institutions could provide the financial and technical assistance that federal transition would require. Such support would not be charity but investment in regional stability that benefits donors as well as recipients.

The International Dimension.
Critics sometimes argue that regional dynamics preclude Israeli-Palestinian federation. Iran, Hezbollah, and other actors benefit from continued conflict and would actively undermine any resolution. Arab states, whatever their private preferences, face domestic constraints that limit their ability to support arrangements perceived as legitimizing Israeli control over Palestinian territories. The international community, despite rhetorical commitment to peace, has proven unable to deliver the sustained engagement that resolution requires.

These concerns have merit. Regional spoilers exist and would attempt to undermine federal arrangements. Domestic politics in Arab states do constrain governmental flexibility. International attention is episodic and easily diverted by other crises. Any federal proposal must account for these realities.

Yet regional dynamics are not static. The Abraham Accords demonstrated that Arab states will normalize relations with Israel when they perceive benefits exceeding costs—and that Palestinian objections do not necessarily preclude normalization. Saudi Arabia's evident interest in normalization suggests that the regional trajectory, despite setbacks, moves toward acceptance of Israel's permanence. Iranian influence, while significant, has limits; Iran's proxies can cause damage but cannot prevent arrangements that majorities in both Israeli and Palestinian societies support.

International guarantees could provide crucial insurance during vulnerable transition periods. Barbara Walter's research on civil war resolution demonstrates that third-party security guarantees significantly increase the probability that peace agreements endure. [19] NATO membership or equivalent security arrangements, peacekeeping forces during transition, and international monitoring of implementation could provide the confidence that parties need to take risks for peace. Such guarantees have worked elsewhere; there is no inherent reason they could not work here.

The international community's stake in Israeli-Palestinian resolution is substantial. The conflict destabilizes the broader Middle East, generates refugee flows, provides recruitment propaganda for extremist movements, and complicates relations between Western powers and the Muslim world. Resolution would produce benefits far exceeding the costs of supporting federal transition. The question is whether international actors can sustain engagement over the extended period that federal consolidation requires—a question of political will rather than inherent impossibility.

Responding to Specific Israeli Concerns.
The critiques examined above often reflect specifically Israeli anxieties that federal proposals must address directly. Israeli concerns about security, Jewish character, and demographic dynamics are not irrational; they reflect historical experience and genuine uncertainties about the future.

Security concerns are paramount. Israelis have experienced terrorism, rocket attacks, and military threats that have shaped a security consciousness pervading all political calculations. Any federal proposal that appears to compromise security will be rejected regardless of other merits. The detailed security architecture presented in Chapter 9 attempts to address these concerns through unified federal command, regional forces with community legitimacy, and phased implementation allowing trust to develop. But security arrangements must not merely be designed; they must be perceived as adequate by a population traumatized by violence.

Jewish character concerns reflect fears that demographic trends might eventually transform federal arrangements into vehicles for Jewish subordination. Constitutional protections, regional autonomy for Jewish-majority areas, and representation mechanisms that prevent majoritarianism address these concerns institutionally. But institutional guarantees gain credibility only through demonstrated performance over time. Building Israeli confidence in federal arrangements requires not merely constitutional text but political culture committed to honoring federal compacts.

Concerns about Palestinian intentions reflect uncertainty about whether Palestinians would accept federal arrangements as permanent or treat them as stepping stones toward goals incompatible with Israeli security and identity. These concerns cannot be definitively resolved in advance; they require Palestinian political leadership that articulates federal commitment credibly and Palestinian civil society that builds relationships demonstrating coexistence potential. Such leadership and civil society exist but are not currently dominant; their strengthening is prerequisite for federal success.

Responding to Specific Palestinian Concerns.
Palestinian concerns deserve equally direct engagement. Palestinians have experienced dispossession, occupation, and repeated failures of peace processes that have produced deep skepticism about Israeli intentions. Any federal proposal that appears to perpetuate Israeli domination will be rejected regardless of formal equality it promises.

Dignity concerns are fundamental. Palestinians seek recognition as a people with legitimate national aspirations, not merely as a problem to be managed or a population to be administered. Federal arrangements must provide genuine self-governance, not autonomy that masks continued Israeli control. Regional governments must possess real powers over matters that affect daily life; federal institutions must include meaningful Palestinian participation; symbols and narratives must acknowledge Palestinian identity alongside Israeli identity.

Justice concerns relate to historical grievances—the Nakba, the occupation, the accumulated indignities of checkpoint and permit regimes. Federal arrangements cannot undo history, but they can acknowledge it. Truth processes that document what occurred, compensation for documented losses, and limited return provisions that address refugee concerns symbolically if not comprehensively can demonstrate that federation represents new beginning rather than perpetuation of injustice.

Concerns about permanence reflect Palestinian fears that federal arrangements might be dismantled if Israeli political winds shift. Constitutional entrenchment, international guarantees, and representation mechanisms that give Palestinians stake in federal institutions address these concerns. But Palestinians, like Israelis, will judge federal arrangements by performance rather than promises; trust must be earned through demonstrated commitment over time.

The Alternative to Federalism.
Ultimately, the case for federalism rests not merely on its own merits but on comparison with alternatives. The status quo—occupation without resolution—has failed by every measure: it has not provided security, as October 7th demonstrated; it has not provided legitimacy, as Israel's international isolation grows; it has not provided stability, as periodic wars recur; it has not provided

justice, as Palestinians live under military rule without political rights.

The two-state solution, whatever its theoretical merits, has become practically impossible. Settlement expansion has fragmented the West Bank; Jerusalem's status cannot be resolved through partition; Gaza's separation from the West Bank precludes the contiguous state that viability requires. Those who continue to advocate two states must explain how the obstacles that have accumulated over thirty years of failed negotiations will suddenly dissolve.

More maximalist alternatives—Israeli annexation with population transfer, Palestinian liberation through Israeli destruction—are not merely morally unacceptable but practically unachievable. Israel will not expel millions of Palestinians; the international consequences and moral self-destruction would be catastrophic. Palestinians will not defeat Israel; the military asymmetry is overwhelming and permanent.

Against these alternatives, federalism offers a path that is difficult but possible. It addresses both peoples' core needs—security and self-determination for Israelis, dignity and self-governance for Palestinians—through institutional arrangements that channel conflict into political rather than violent competition. It has worked in other deeply divided societies. It could work here.

The critics are right that federalism faces formidable challenges. They are wrong to conclude that these challenges are insurmountable. The question is not whether federalism is easy—it manifestly is not—but whether it is possible. The evidence suggests that it is. The remaining question is whether political leadership will prove equal to the challenge.

Chapter 11
Addendum

Key Concepts.
Understanding Critiques of Federalism.
Secession: Formal withdrawal of a region from a larger political entity to form an independent state. Can occur through negotiated agreement (Czechoslovakia), unilateral declaration (Kosovo), or armed conflict (South Sudan, Bangladesh). Federal critics argue granting regional autonomy to ethnic groups creates capacity and legitimacy for eventual secession. Yugoslavia and Soviet Union exemplify this: republics used federal autonomy to prepare for independence. However, successful federations (Canada, Switzerland, Belgium) have contained secessionist pressures through economic integration, constitutional frameworks, and political accommodations.

Asymmetric Power: Situations where parties possess vastly different capacities—economic, military, political. Asymmetric power challenges federalism because formal equality may mask substantive domination. Critics argue Israeli-Palestinian asymmetry (Israel's advanced economy, powerful military, established institutions versus Palestinian deficits) means formal power-sharing would disguise Israeli dominance. However, federal systems address asymmetry through fiscal transfers, representation systems giving smaller units disproportionate voice, and constitutional protections enforcing minority rights.

Democratic Legitimacy: Principle that political arrangements must reflect governed people's consent. Critics question federal legitimacy: neither Israeli nor Palestinian publics currently support federalism, and elite-designed arrangements might not represent authentic preferences. However, democratic legitimacy doesn't require arrangements emerge from prior popular demand—U.S. Constitution wasn't initially popular but gained legitimacy through ratification and performance.

Federation vs. Confederation: Federation features strong central government with direct citizen authority, constitutional sovereignty split between federal/regional levels, and federal law supreme. Confederation features weak central authority coordinating sovereign members. U.S. transformed from confederation (too weak to govern) to federation. Israeli-Palestinian arrangements would need genuine federal structure—unified defense, direct taxation, binding federal courts—rather than loose confederation either party could abandon.

Failed States: States unable to perform basic functions—maintaining security, providing services, enforcing laws. Critics argue Palestinian regions might become failed states lacking governance capacity, becoming security threats. However, failure partly reflects occupation's constraints. Federal arrangements removing constraints while providing capacity-building could enable institutional development.

Partition Critique: Arguments against dividing territories along ethnic lines. Partition inevitably creates minorities on "wrong" sides, generates refugees, and often produces violence. India-Pakistan (1947) killed over 1 million and displaced 15 million. However, federal arrangements aren't partition—they create shared frameworks rather than complete separation, addressing partition critique's concerns.

The Citizen Relevance: Thinking Critically About Political Proposals.

Engaging counterarguments honestly represents essential democratic citizenship.

The Value of Engaging Counterarguments

Good ideas survive tough questions; bad ideas don't. When proposals can't withstand scrutiny, discovering this early prevents wasting resources pursuing doomed initiatives. Honest engagement with criticism demonstrates intellectual integrity, building credibility. Moreover, engaging criticism often improves proposals by identifying blind spots and design flaws.

How to Evaluate Political Proposals

Citizens evaluating any proposal should ask:

- *What problem does this solve?* Specific problems, not vague aspirations
- *What are the mechanisms?* How exactly would it produce desired outcomes?
- *What could go wrong?* Every proposal involves risks and unintended consequences
- *Compared to what?* Evaluation requires comparing alternatives
- *What's the evidence?* Has this worked elsewhere?
- *Who benefits and who loses?* Understanding distributive consequences helps evaluate sustainability

Good Ideas Survive Tough Questions

This principle should guide evaluation of all political claims. Citizens should demand clear problem definition, explicit causal mechanisms, honest risk assessment, comparative evaluation, evidence from analogous cases, and analysis of distributive consequences. Proposals surviving this scrutiny deserve serious consideration.

Applied to Israeli-Palestinian federalism: The proposal survives critical scrutiny better than alternatives. It addresses defined problems, specifies mechanisms, acknowledges risks while explaining management approaches, compares favorably to alternatives, draws on successful examples, and creates winners in both communities. This establishes federalism as serious option worthy of pursuit.

For Debate Teams and Critical Thinking Classes.

Israeli-Palestinian federalism provides excellent material for structured debate, forcing students to engage multiple perspectives and think critically about complex political problems.

Structured Debate Format

Resolution: "A federal state offers the best prospect for sustainable Israeli-Palestinian peace."

Affirmative: Conflict is intractable under current approaches; federal systems successfully manage deep divisions elsewhere (Switzerland, Canada); federalism addresses both peoples' core needs; alternatives are worse.

Negative: Historical animosity too deep; security risks unacceptable; asymmetric power means continued Israeli domination; democratic legitimacy lacking; failed precedents (Yugoslavia, Soviet Union, Iraq, Lebanon).

Students should research both sides and practice "steelmanning"—presenting opposing arguments in strongest form rather than attacking weak versions.

Honest Answers to Tough Questions.

"How can Israelis and Palestinians cooperate after so much violence?"

Federal transition requires years or decades. Post-WWII European integration didn't produce immediate love between France and Germany—institutions created interdependence gradually transforming attitudes. We acknowledge difficulty but note alternatives haven't produced security either.

"What if Palestinian regions become terrorism bases?"

Legitimate concern. Federal design addresses through phased integration, federal security maintaining ultimate responsibility, constitutional provisions enabling intervention, and economic integration creating constituencies opposing terrorism. Does this eliminate risk? No—neither does occupation (October 7th proved this). Question is comparative risk.

"Won't demographics threaten Israel's Jewish character?"

Federal design must address through constitutional protections, regional autonomy, bicameral legislature giving regions representation independent of population, and supermajority requirements for amendments. Canadian Quebec protects francophone culture despite being national minority.

"Why should Palestinians accept remaining under Israeli sovereignty?"

What federalism offers: genuine self-governance, equal citizenship, economic development opportunities, regional integration participation, dignity of partnership. Is this everything Palestinians want? No. Better than alternatives (continued occupation, unstable mini-state)? We believe so, but Palestinians must judge.

"Hasn't federalism failed in Lebanon and Iraq?"

Yes, teaching important lessons. Lebanon's system was too rigid, suffered external interference, lacked economic integration. Iraq's was imposed rather than negotiated, coincided with state dismantlement. Israeli-Palestinian federation would need flexible power-sharing, international guarantees, economic integration, and negotiated design addressing both communities' concerns.

Why Some Disagree (And Why We Think They're Wrong).
What Critics Say:

- "Israelis and Palestinians hate each other too much to cooperate" (100+ years fighting, deep trauma)
- "It's not safe" (Gaza withdrawal led to Hamas and rockets; October 7th showed attacks happen despite barriers)
- "Israel is too much stronger" (Israel dominant; Palestinians much weaker)
- "Neither side wants this" (polls show both prefer other solutions)
- "Federalism has failed elsewhere" (Yugoslavia, Soviet Union, Lebanon, Iraq)

Why We Think Critics Are Wrong:

- Enemies have become partners before (France-Germany, Northern Ireland, South Africa). Takes decades with right institutions.
- Federal security might actually be safer long-term. Current occupation hasn't provided safety. Two-state might create hostile neighbor.
- Federal systems prevent strong from dominating through constitutional protections, special representation for smaller groups, money transfers, international guarantees.

- People's preferences change when circumstances change. Democracy means people ultimately decide, but they need to understand options.
- Some federations failed, others succeeded (Switzerland, Canada, Belgium, India). Success possible with good design.

Main Argument: All alternatives are worse. Continuing current situation means more wars. Two-state impossible (settlements, can't divide Jerusalem, Gaza separated from West Bank). Israel annexing everything and expelling Palestinians would be crime. Palestinians defeating Israel militarily impossible. Federalism is hard and risky—but it's the only option giving both sides what they need: Israelis get security; Palestinians get dignity and self-governance. Won't be perfect. But working together, even imperfectly, beats fighting forever.

Chapter 12.
Pathways to Implementation: A Phased Approach.

The Architecture of Transformation: From Vision to Reality.

The transformation of deeply divided societies through federal arrangements represents one of the most ambitious undertakings in contemporary statecraft. As Stepan (1999) observes in his seminal work on federalism and democracy, the journey from conflict to cooperation through federal design is neither linear nor predetermined, but rather a complex negotiation between historical grievances and future aspirations.

For a Federal State of Israel, this transformative process demands not merely constitutional engineering but what Anderson (2008) aptly terms "the alchemy of governance" – converting the base metals of division into the gold of shared sovereignty. This undertaking requires patience measured in decades, wisdom drawn from comparative experience, and courage to transcend entrenched positions.

The implementation of federalism in this context must be understood as what Elazar (1987) characterized as a "covenant" – not imposed from above but negotiated from within, reflecting the biblical concept of *brit* that resonates deeply within both Jewish and Arab political traditions. This covenantal approach to federal implementation requires, as McGarry and O'Leary (2009) argue in their analysis of divided societies, a carefully orchestrated sequence of negotiations, institution-building, and trust formation that can span years or even decades. Yet we must acknowledge, with scholarly honesty, that some distinguished voices remain skeptical. Lustick (2019) cautions that "federal solutions in ethno-national conflicts often underestimate the depth of identity-based grievances," while Yiftachel (2006) argues that Israel's spatial and demographic engineering has created conditions that may resist federal accommodation. Nevertheless, the alternative – perpetual conflict – offers no pathway to security or justice for either people.

Phase I: Negotiating the Federal Compact.

The foundational phase of federal implementation – the negotiation of the framework itself – represents what Horowitz (2014) calls the "constitutional moment" where the architecture of shared governance crystallizes from the realm of possibility into concrete arrangements. In the Israeli-Palestinian context, this phase must confront what Bar-Tal (2013) identifies as the "socio-psychological barriers" that have calcified over decades of conflict, transforming zero-sum perceptions into positive-sum possibilities. The negotiation process must simultaneously address past injustices and future aspirations, threading a needle that has confounded generations of diplomats and scholars alike. The principle of equitable representation emerges as the cornerstone of these negotiations.

As Lijphart (2012) demonstrates in his comparative studies of consociational democracy, power-sharing arrangements in deeply divided societies must guarantee what he terms "mutual veto" capabilities – ensuring that neither community can dominate the other. This translates into concrete institutional mechanisms: bicameral legislatures with community-based representation, rotating executive positions, and what Rothchild and Roeder (2005) call "multiple majorities" – decision-making procedures that require cross-community support for fundamental decisions.

Critics such as Horowitz (2002) have noted that such arrangements can produce governmental paralysis, as witnessed periodically in Belgium and Lebanon. Yet the alternative – majoritarian systems in deeply divided societies – consistently produces what Mann (2005) documents as "the dark side of democracy," where electoral competition intensifies ethnic mobilization rather than moderating it.

The Swiss model, extensively analyzed by Church and Dardanelli (2005), offers instructive parallels. Switzerland's Federal Council, with its magic formula ensuring representation of major linguistic and religious communities, demonstrates how executive power-sharing can foster stability even amid diversity. The Swiss experience over two centuries reveals that federalism need not merely manage difference but can transform it into a source of national strength. Similarly, Belgium's complex federal arrangement, documented by Deschouwer (2012), shows how linguistic communities can share sovereignty while maintaining distinct identities, though Belgian scholars like Swenden and Jans (2006) warn that such systems require constant recalibration to prevent centrifugal pressures from overwhelming centripetal forces.

For Israel-Palestine, such models suggest possibilities for what Ghanem (2007) envisions as "bi-national federalism" – a system that acknowledges both peoples' legitimate claims while creating mechanisms for shared governance.

The delineation of federal and constituent unit powers requires what Watts (2008) calls "constitutional precision with political flexibility." The division of competencies must be explicit enough to prevent jurisdictional conflicts yet adaptable enough to evolve with changing circumstances. As I argued in *The Times of Israel* (2024), "Israel's influence in the region – for good or ill – depends fundamentally on its ability to manage internal diversity while projecting external stability" (Eger, *Times of Israel*, April 18, 2024). This observation underscores how federal design directly impacts regional positioning and international legitimacy. A state perpetually at war with a substantial portion of its population, or perpetually occupying another people, can project neither stability nor moral authority in regional affairs.

The principle of subsidiarity, enshrined in European Union governance and analyzed extensively by Føllesdal (2014), should guide competency allocation. Decision-making authority should rest at the lowest feasible level – what the German constitutional tradition calls *Subsidiaritätsprinzip*. This means education, cultural affairs, and local policing might reside with constituent units, while defense, foreign policy, and monetary policy remain federal responsibilities. However, as Burgess (2006) notes in his comparative study of federal systems, the devil lies in the details of concurrent powers – those shared between levels of government that require sophisticated coordination mechanisms.

The negotiation process must also address what Wolff (2011) terms "complex power-sharing" – arrangements that go beyond simple majoritarian democracy to ensure meaningful participation for all segments. The Good Friday Agreement in Northern Ireland, analyzed comprehensively by Wilford (2001), demonstrates how detailed negotiations can transform seemingly intractable conflicts. The agreement's "three-strand approach" – addressing relationships within Northern Ireland, between North and South Ireland, and between Britain and Ireland – offers a template for managing multiple dimensions of conflict simultaneously. The Belfast Agreement's success in ending thirty years of violent conflict stands as testament to the possibilities of negotiated solutions.

Meanwhile, as scholars like Burgess (2006), Wolff (2011), and Wilford (2001) highlight the Good Friday Agreement's (GFA) three-strand approach and complex power-sharing as potential templates for intractable conflicts, we must acknowledge that fundamental asymmetries complicate direct application to Israel-Palestine. The GFA emerged within a shared UK-Ireland framework that accepted certain baseline conditions, unlike the zero-sum territorial claims that characterize Israeli-Palestinian discourse – Israel demanding recognition as a Jewish state, Palestinians insisting on addressing 1948 displacement, territorial integrity, and East Jerusalem's status.

John Doyle (2024) critiques Israel's post-Oslo rejection of referenda mechanisms that proved crucial in Northern Ireland, where 71% approval legitimized the GFA, while Jeff Kildea (2024) notes that certain ideological positions on both sides lack the GFA-style mutual exhaustion or military parity that enabled Northern Irish compromise. These scholarly interventions remind us that while the GFA offers inspiration, mechanical transplantation of its mechanisms would be structurally problematic without substantial adaptation to regional realities.

Economic considerations in federal negotiations require what Rodrik (2007) calls "one economics, many recipes" – acknowledging that while economic principles are universal, their application must be context-specific. The question of resource distribution, particularly concerning water rights, land ownership, and natural resources, demands what Feitelson and Haddad (2001) describe as "joint management regimes" – collaborative frameworks that transcend zero-sum competition. The European Coal and Steel Community's evolution into the European Union, traced by Dinan (2014), illustrates how economic cooperation can catalyze broader political integration. Monnet's original insight – that binding nations through shared management of essential resources makes conflict materially costly – remains as relevant for Israel-Palestine as it was for post-war Europe.

Phase II: Constitutional Crafting.
The translation of negotiated principles into constitutional text represents what Sunstein (2001) calls "constitutional design for divided societies" – a delicate balance between aspirational ideals and practical governance. The drafting process itself becomes a site of democratic participation, following what Benhabib (2002) terms "democratic iterations" – repeated engagements that build consensus through deliberation. Constitutional moments are rare in political life; when they occur, they establish the foundational grammar within which subsequent political discourse unfolds for generations.

The South African experience, documented by Ebrahim and Miller (2010), demonstrates the transformative potential of inclusive constitution-making. Their Constitutional Assembly, combining elected representatives with extensive public consultation, produced what many consider the world's most progressive constitution. The South African process received over two million public submissions, creating what Klug (2000) describes as "constitutional ownership" among ordinary citizens. For Israel-Palestine, similar mechanisms could channel public input while ensuring expert guidance on federal design. As Gavison (2013) argues in her analysis of Israel's constitutional challenges, the absence of a complete written constitution has been both a source of flexibility and uncertainty – a federal transformation would require constitutional clarity that the current Basic Laws framework does not provide.

The fiscal federal framework demands particular attention. As Ahmad and Brosio (2009) demonstrate in their comprehensive handbook on fiscal federalism, resource allocation mechanisms can make or break federal systems. The Canadian equalization system, analyzed by Béland and Lecours (2014), shows how fiscal transfers can address regional disparities while maintaining federal cohesion – provinces with below-average fiscal capacity receive transfers enabling them to provide comparable public services.

For Israel-Palestine, where economic disparities between Jewish and Palestinian areas are substantial, robust equalization mechanisms would be essential. The establishment of what Bird and Vaillancourt (2006) call "fiscal federal institutions" – independent bodies managing resource distribution – could depoliticize potentially contentious allocation decisions and build trust through transparent, formula-based transfers rather than discretionary political decisions.

The constitutional drafting phase must also grapple with what Choudhry (2008) identifies as "constitutional design in divided societies" – creating frameworks that accommodate difference while fostering unity. The Spanish Constitution of 1978, examined by Colomer (1998), demonstrates how asymmetric federalism can accommodate distinct regional identities within a unified state. The recognition of "historic nationalities" alongside regular autonomous communities provides a model for acknowledging different levels of distinctiveness within a federal framework. Spain's experience, however, also offers cautionary lessons; the Catalan crisis documented by Guibernau (2014) reveals how constitutional settlements can unravel when one party believes the framework inadequately recognizes its distinct status.

Language policy in the constitution requires what May (2012) terms "linguistic justice" – ensuring that language rights support both individual communication and collective identity. The Canadian experience with official bilingualism, analyzed by Cardinal and Sonntag (2015), shows both the possibilities and challenges of linguistic accommodation. Canada's transformation from a country where French speakers faced systematic disadvantage to one where both official languages enjoy formal equality required decades of institutional development and societal adjustment. For Israel-Palestine, constitutional provisions for Hebrew and Arabic as co-official languages would need to address practical implementation issues while symbolizing equal status. The Indian model, studied by Benedikter (2009), where states can designate official languages while Hindi and English serve federal purposes, offers another approach to linguistic diversity within federal structures.

The protection of fundamental rights requires what Kymlicka (2007) terms "multicultural constitutionalism" – explicit guarantees for minority cultures within the broader federal framework. The Indian Constitution's provisions for linguistic minorities, examined by Adeney (2007), and Canada's Charter of Rights and Freedoms, analyzed by Russell (2017), offer models for entrenching group rights alongside individual freedoms. For Israel-Palestine, this might include constitutional protection for Hebrew and Arabic as official languages, guarantees for religious practice and access to holy sites, and what Peled and Navot (2005) call "differential citizenship" – accommodating diverse conceptions of membership within a shared polity while maintaining core equality principles.

The question of constitutional amendment procedures, what Lutz (1994) calls "constitutional amendment rates," requires careful calibration. Too rigid, and the constitution cannot adapt to changing circumstances; too flexible, and it loses its fundamental character. The U.S. Constitution's Article V, requiring supermajorities in Congress and state ratification, has produced only 27 amendments in over 230 years, creating what Ackerman (1991) describes as "constitutional moments" that require extraordinary political mobilization.

Conversely, India's Constitution, as Khosla (2012) documents, has been amended over 100 times since 1950, though many amendments address technical rather than fundamental matters. For Israel-Palestine, amendment procedures might follow what Ginsburg and Melton (2015) recommend as "tiered rigidity" – different amendment thresholds for different constitutional provisions, with the most fundamental protections requiring supermajorities while administrative provisions remain more accessible to ordinary legislative majorities.

Phase III: Institutional Architecture.
The operationalization of federal institutions transforms constitutional text into governmental reality. This phase, which Simeon and Conway (2001) characterize as "federal learning," involves not just creating structures but fostering what March and Olsen (2011) call "institutional logics" – shared understandings of how federal governance operates. Institutions are not merely formal rules but, as North (1990) emphasizes, "the humanly devised constraints that shape human interaction," including informal norms, conventions, and codes of conduct that accumulate over time through practice and precedent.

The establishment of the federal legislature requires what Reilly (2001) terms "electoral engineering" – designing systems that incentivize cross-community cooperation rather than ethnic outbidding. The Northern Ireland Assembly's d'Hondt system, analyzed by McGarry and O'Leary (2006), automatically allocates executive positions based on legislative strength, ensuring power-sharing without requiring explicit coalition negotiations that can break down over contentious issues. Similarly, Lebanon's confessional system, despite its challenges documented by Salamey (2014), demonstrates how legislative seats can be allocated to ensure community representation, though Lebanese experience also reveals the dangers of freezing demographic ratios that no longer reflect population realities.

The structure of legislative committees requires what Strøm (1998) calls "parliamentary democracy design" – creating specialized bodies that develop policy expertise while maintaining democratic accountability. The German Bundestag's committee system, analyzed by Saalfeld (2000), shows how legislative committees can balance party representation with policy specialization, developing what Krehbiel (1991) terms "informational efficiency" that improves legislative quality. For Israel-Palestine, committees dealing with sensitive areas like security affairs, refugee compensation, or religious site management might require special composition rules ensuring cross-community participation and consensus requirements for major decisions.

For the federal executive, the Swiss collegial model analyzed by Vatter (2020) offers an alternative to Westminster-style single-party government. The seven-member Federal Council, operating on consensus with a rotating presidency, demonstrates how executive power can be shared without paralysis. Switzerland's executive has functioned continuously since 1848, through two world wars and countless international crises, suggesting that consensus-based governance need not sacrifice effectiveness. As Lustick (2019) argues in his analysis of Israel-Palestine possibilities, such power-sharing arrangements could help transcend the winner-take-all dynamics that have characterized the conflict and prevented stable settlements.

The civil service establishment requires what Evans and Rauch (1999) call "Weberian bureaucratic structures" – professional administrative capacity that can implement policy effectively regardless of which political coalition holds power. The Singaporean model, studied by Quah (2010), demonstrates how meritocratic recruitment and continuous training can build effective governance even in diverse societies. For Israel-Palestine, creating a unified federal civil service while respecting linguistic and cultural diversity would require what Grindle (2012) terms "good enough governance" – focusing on achievable improvements rather than ideal types, building capacity incrementally through practical experience rather than waiting for perfect institutional design.

The federal judiciary's independence requires what Ginsburg (2003) calls "judicial review in new democracies" – mechanisms ensuring courts can check governmental power while maintaining legitimacy among all communities. The German Federal Constitutional Court, studied extensively by Kommers and Miller (2012), shows how specialized constitutional courts can arbitrate federal disputes while protecting fundamental rights. Germany's court has earned legitimacy across the political spectrum through consistent application of constitutional principles regardless of which party controls government. For Israel-Palestine, establishing what Barak (2006) advocates as "purposive interpretation" – judicial reasoning that advances constitutional values – would be crucial for managing inevitable federal tensions while maintaining the rule of law as a shared commitment.

The establishment of security forces in a federal context presents what Hänggi (2004) identifies as "security sector governance" challenges – balancing effectiveness with democratic control and communal trust. The Belgian model, where federal and regional police forces have distinct but complementary roles, analyzed by Devroe and Ponsaers (2013), suggests possibilities for divided societies seeking to maintain order while respecting community autonomy. For Israel-Palestine, creating what Bryden and Hänggi (2005) call "security sector reform" would require careful delineation of federal and constituent unit security responsibilities, possibly with integrated command structures for external defense while maintaining separate forces for internal security under constituent unit authority – a configuration that addresses legitimate security concerns while preventing any single community from monopolizing coercive power.

Phase IV: Regional Integration and Normalization.
The establishment of stable federal institutions creates what Solingen (2007) calls "regional orders" – predictable frameworks enabling broader cooperation. As federal governance solidifies internally, external engagement becomes not just possible but mutually reinforcing. The European Union's evolution, traced by Moravcsik (2018), demonstrates how internal institutional development and external integration can proceed synergistically – each success building confidence for the next step, each failure prompting recalibration rather than abandonment. For Israel-Palestine, federalism's success would transform regional dynamics fundamentally.

Within the Arab regional context, a successfully federalized Israel-Palestine could catalyze what Tessler and Grobschmidt (1995) envisioned as broader Middle Eastern cooperation frameworks. The Arab League, despite limitations identified by Barnett and Solingen (2007), provides an institutional architecture for engagement. As Khalidi (2006) argues, Palestinian participation in Arab forums has historically been constrained by statelessness – federal statehood would enable full engagement as equal partners rather than perpetual supplicants. The Abraham Accords, whatever one's assessment of their genesis and limitations, demonstrate that regional realignment is possible; federalism would address the

Palestinian dimension that critics identify as the Accords' fundamental weakness.

The process of normalization extends beyond diplomatic recognition to what Kelman (2007) calls "socio-psychological dimensions of international conflict" – transforming enemy images into partner perceptions. The Franco-German reconciliation after World War II, studied comprehensively by Krotz and Schild (2013), demonstrates how former adversaries can become close allies through institutional integration and societal exchange. That nations which had fought three wars in seventy years, including the most destructive conflict in human history, could become the core partnership of European integration offers profound lessons. The Élysée Treaty of 1963, establishing youth exchanges and cultural cooperation, created what Gardner Feldman (2012) terms "networks of reconciliation" – multiple channels of interaction that reinforce peaceful relations through human connections rather than merely governmental agreements.

Economic integration offers particularly promising avenues for building stakeholder coalitions invested in federal success. The Gulf Cooperation Council's common market, analyzed by Legrenzi (2011), demonstrates regional economic cooperation's potential despite political differences among member states. A federal Israel-Palestine could participate in what El-Anis (2011) terms "cascading regionalism" – deepening economic ties that create constituencies for stability in every community. The Jordan Valley's agricultural potential, the Dead Sea's mineral wealth, and Mediterranean gas reserves all represent opportunities for what Rosecrance and Thompson (2003) call "trading states" – nations prioritizing economic over territorial expansion, recognizing that prosperity through commerce exceeds what conquest could ever deliver.

The development of regional infrastructure projects could follow what Schiff (2014) describes as "functionalist integration" – technical cooperation that builds habits of collaboration in non-political domains that gradually normalize working together. The Red Sea-Dead Sea Water Conveyance Project, analyzed by Fischhendler (2008), demonstrates how environmental challenges can motivate regional cooperation when framed as shared problems requiring joint solutions. Similarly, regional transportation networks, energy grids, and telecommunications infrastructure could create what Keohane and Nye (2011) term "complex interdependence" – multiple channels of interaction that make conflict costly and cooperation beneficial, enmeshing societies in webs of mutual benefit that make separation increasingly difficult to imagine.

Cultural normalization, what Shlaim (2014) terms moving "from conflict to cooperation," requires addressing historical narratives honestly rather than imposing artificial consensus. The Franco-German reconciliation, studied by Rosoux (2001), shows how former enemies can develop shared historical understandings while respecting different experiences – French and German textbooks need not be identical, but they can acknowledge each other's suffering and responsibility. Similarly, Israeli-Palestinian federal institutions could sponsor what Sa'di (2002) advocates as "parallel narratives" – acknowledging different historical experiences while building shared futures. Joint historical commissions, following the model analyzed by Barkan (2000) in his study of historical reconciliation, could develop educational materials that respect both narratives while promoting mutual understanding and preparing younger generations for shared citizenship.

The role of civil society in regional integration, what Keck and Sikkink (1998) call "transnational advocacy networks," cannot be underestimated. Professional associations, academic exchanges, and business partnerships create what Adler and Barnett (1998) term "security communities" – regions where war becomes unthinkable not because of deterrence but because shared identity makes it inconceivable. The European Erasmus program, studied by Sigalas (2010), shows how student exchanges can foster generational change in regional identities; young Europeans who studied together prove less susceptible to nationalist appeals than their predecessors. For Israel-Palestine, investing in such exchanges represents investment in future peace.

Phase V: International Recognition and Support.
The cultivation of international backing represents what Keohane (2002) calls understanding why "multilateralism matters" – embedding new arrangements within broader international frameworks provides legitimacy, resources, and external enforcement mechanisms that reinforce domestic commitments. For a federal Israel-Palestine, this involves not just diplomatic recognition but what Barnett (2002) terms positioning within global normative discourse – demonstrating federalism's contribution to regional and global stability, human rights, and international order.

The international community's role, analyzed by Newman and Richmond (2006) in their work on peacebuilding, must balance support with sovereignty. The Bosnian experience, critiqued by Chandler (2000), warns against international trusteeship that undermines local ownership – the High Representative's extensive powers in Bosnia have perpetuated dependency rather than building self-sustaining institutions. Instead, what Paris (2004) advocates as "institutionalization before liberalization" suggests focusing international support on building governmental capacity before promoting rapid democratization that divided societies may be unable to sustain. International partners should support rather than supplant local agency.

The United Nations' role in supporting federal transitions, examined by Wolff and Yakinthou (2011), could provide legitimacy and technical assistance without compromising sovereignty. UN specialized agencies – from UNDP's governance programs to UNESCO's cultural preservation efforts – could support specific aspects of federal implementation while respecting local ownership. The UN's experience in Cyprus, analyzed by Ker-Lindsay (2011), offers both positive lessons about sustained engagement and warnings about the limitations of external mediation when local parties lack commitment to resolution.

Financial assistance requires what Collier (2007) calls "smart aid" – support that builds capacity without creating dependency or perverse incentives. The Marshall Plan's success, analyzed by Behrman (2007), derived from combining substantial resources with requirements for institutional reform and recipient cooperation. Aid worked because it required Europeans to cooperate in allocating it, building habits of collaboration that outlasted the assistance itself. Similarly, international support for federal Israel-Palestine should link assistance to federal institution-building, following what Fukuyama (2004) terms "state-building" – strengthening governmental capacity to deliver public goods that earn citizens' loyalty.

The role of regional powers in supporting federal implementation requires what Buzan and Wæver (2003) call "regional security complex theory" – understanding how regional dynamics shape local possibilities and how local settlements reshape regional dynamics. Egyptian support, given its historic peace treaty with Israel analyzed by Quandt (2005), could provide crucial Arab legitimacy for arrangements that might otherwise be dismissed as imposed settlements. Jordanian engagement, examined by Lynch (1999), could offer practical experience in managing diverse populations. Saudi Arabia's Vision 2030, studied by Thompson (2017), with its emphasis on economic modernization and regional integration, could provide frameworks for incorporating a federal Israel-Palestine into broader regional prosperity initiatives.

Technical expertise in federal governance, what Blindenbacher and Koller (2003) call "federalism in a changing world," could substantially assist implementation. The Forum of Federations, documented by Watts and Chattopadhyay (2008), demonstrates how federal expertise can be shared across contexts through practitioner exchanges, technical assistance, and comparative research. Countries like Canada, Switzerland, Germany, and India could provide what Rose (2005) terms "lesson-drawing" – adapting successful practices to new contexts while respecting local particularities.

Federal design benefits enormously from comparative experience; there is no need to reinvent solutions that others have already developed through costly trial and error. International legal frameworks supporting federal arrangements, what Cassese (2005) calls "international law in a divided world," provide normative backing that reinforces domestic commitments. The European Framework Convention for the Protection of National Minorities, analyzed by Weller (2005), offers standards for minority protection within federal systems. The Venice Commission's opinions on constitutional design, studied by Craig (2017), provide authoritative guidance on federal arrangements that carries weight with both domestic and international audiences. Embedding a federal Israel-Palestine within these frameworks provides external reinforcement for internal commitments.

Challenges and Opportunities: A Critical Assessment.
The implementation of federalism faces what Erk and Anderson (2009) identify as "paradoxes of federalism" – tensions between unity and diversity, efficiency and representation, stability and flexibility. For Israel-Palestine, these paradoxes are particularly acute given what Smooha (2002) calls the "ethnic democracy" challenge – balancing majority rule with minority rights in a context where both communities have experienced subordination and harbour legitimate fears of renewed domination. Scholarly honesty requires acknowledging these difficulties directly rather than minimizing them through optimistic rhetoric.

Security concerns, analyzed comprehensively by Inbar and Sandler (2008), present particular challenges that cannot be wished away. The "security dilemma," identified by Jervis (1978), whereby defensive measures by one side appear threatening to the other, must be managed through what Posen (1993) calls careful attention to the offense-defense balance and transparent confidence-building measures. Landau and Malz (2003) suggest such measures could include joint security operations against common threats, shared intelligence on terrorism, and graduated demilitarization in agreed zones. The transition from adversarial to cooperative security relations requires careful sequencing and mutual reassurance that neither side is being asked to accept vulnerability.

Economic disparities between Jewish and Palestinian areas, documented by Arnon and Weinblatt (2001), require what Stewart (2008) calls "horizontal inequalities" management – addressing group-based economic differences that can fuel political grievances. The Malaysian New Economic Policy, analyzed critically by Jomo (2004), shows both possibilities and pitfalls of affirmative economic policies in divided societies. Malaysia substantially reduced inter-ethnic economic gaps, but critics argue the policy also entrenched ethnic categorization and created new resentments. For Israel-Palestine, economic convergence policies would need to address historical injustices while avoiding zero-sum competition that reinforces division.

The refugee question, what Brynen and El-Rifai (2007) term "the Palestinian refugee problem," requires creative federal solutions that address legitimate grievances without requiring impossible reversals. The right of return, analyzed legally by Quigley (2005), might be reconceptualized within a federal framework where return is to constituent units rather than specific properties that no longer exist or are occupied by others.

Compensation mechanisms, following the model of the German-Israeli reparations agreement studied by Sagi (2009), could address historical injustices materially while enabling forward movement. No solution can fully satisfy maximalist positions, but federal arrangements could address core concerns of acknowledgment, return where feasible, and compensation where return is not.

Sceptics of federal solutions present arguments that deserve serious engagement. Yiftachel (2006) contends that decades of settlement policy have created "ethnocratic" spatial patterns resistant to federal accommodation. Kimmerling (2003) questioned whether identities hardened through prolonged conflict can soften sufficiently for federal coexistence. These scholars raise genuine concerns. Yet we must also note what alternatives sceptics propose: Yiftachel advocates democratic transformation without specifying viable mechanisms, while critics of federalism often default to partition arrangements that face their own insurmountable obstacles regarding Jerusalem, refugees, and territorial contiguity. As I wrote in analysis for *The Times of Israel*, Israel cannot continue as a permanent garrison state while expecting to flourish as a society (Eger, *Times of Israel*, 2024). The status quo is not sustainable; the question is which alternative offers the most promising pathway forward.

The Federal Imperative.
The phased approach to federal implementation represents what Tilly (2007) calls "democracy as process" – ongoing negotiations between competing interests within institutional frameworks rather than once-and-for-all settlements. For Israel-Palestine, federalism offers what O'Leary (2013) terms "power-sharing plus" – not just dividing power but creating new forms of shared sovereignty that transcend zero-sum territorial competition. Neither people achieves everything maximalist positions demand, but both achieve what matters most: security, dignity, self-governance, and a future for their children.

The timeline for implementation, following Diamond's (2008) analysis of democratic consolidation, spans generations rather than electoral cycles. Institutional development cannot be rushed without risking the superficial adoption of forms without the underlying substance that makes them work. The Swiss confederation's evolution from 1291 to modern federalism in 1848, traced by Maissen (2016), reminds us that federal development is measured in centuries, not years. Yet the Swiss example also demonstrates that patient construction produces remarkably durable results – Switzerland has maintained internal peace through Europe's bloodiest centuries. As Mandela (1994) observed from his own experience transforming South Africa, "It always seems impossible until it's done."

Success requires what Putnam (2000) calls "bridging social capital" – networks connecting diverse communities that create shared stakes in common success. This involves not just institutional design but what Anderson (2013) terms "cultural work" – creating narratives that make diversity a source of strength rather than division, that celebrate what communities share while respecting what makes each distinctive. Federal patriotism need not replace communal identities but can overlay them, as Swiss citizens are simultaneously Swiss and members of their cantons, as Americans are both national citizens and residents of states with distinct political cultures.

The federal pathway offers what Horowitz (2000) calls "ethnic conflict regulation" – not eliminating difference but channelling it through democratic institutions that transform potentially violent competition into peaceful political contestation. As my analysis in *The Times of Israel* suggested, Israel's regional influence ultimately depends on its internal cohesion (https://blogs.timesofisrael.com/israel-influence-the-good-the-bad-the-ugly/). A state perpetually at war with neighbours and subjects cannot project the stability that regional leadership requires. Federalism provides frameworks for achieving such cohesion while respecting the diversity that any workable solution must accommodate.

The implementation journey from negotiation through constitutional drafting, institutional establishment, regional integration, and international recognition represents what Elazar (1998) called "covenant and commonwealth" – binding agreements that create shared political space within which former adversaries become fellow citizens. Each phase builds cumulatively, creating what North (1990) terms "path dependence" – where early choices shape later possibilities, making reversal increasingly costly and continuation increasingly natural as investments accumulate and expectations adjust.

The federal option for Israel-Palestine is neither utopian fantasy nor cynical partition under another name but what McGarry, O'Leary, and Simeon (2008) call "integration through accommodation" – unity that respects difference, sovereignty that is shared rather than surrendered. Implementation will be difficult, requiring what Weber (1946) famously called the "slow boring of hard boards" – persistent effort despite obstacles, setbacks absorbed as learning experiences rather than reasons for abandonment, incremental progress valued even when comprehensive breakthroughs remain elusive.

Yet as global experience demonstrates, from Switzerland's linguistic communities to India's diverse states, from Canada's provinces to South Africa's rainbow nation, from Belgium's linguistic federalism to Spain's autonomous communities, federalism can transform division into diversity, conflict into cooperation. Peoples who once defined themselves primarily against each other can come to see themselves as partners in shared enterprise. For Israel-Palestine, the federal path offers not just conflict resolution but societal transformation – what Lederach (2003) calls "moral imagination" – envisioning and creating previously unimaginable futures where both peoples thrive.

The phased implementation approach outlined here provides what Ostrom (2005) termed "polycentric governance" – multiple centres of authority within an overarching framework. This complexity is not weakness but strength, creating what Taleb (2012) calls "antifragility" – systems that gain from stress rather than breaking under it, that improve through challenges rather than merely surviving them. Federal systems' redundancy and flexibility make them more resilient than centralized alternatives.
As this region stands at historical crossroads, the choice is not between perfect solutions and current reality but between managed change and continued conflict. Israel cannot remain in a permanent state of war, occupying another people indefinitely while expecting to maintain its democratic character and international standing. The Palestinians cannot achieve their aspirations for dignity and self-governance through armed resistance against a vastly more powerful adversary.

Both peoples need what the other has: Israelis need peace and regional acceptance; Palestinians need statehood and dignity. Federalism offers pathways from the current impasse to futures where both peoples' legitimate aspirations find accommodation. What seems impossible today can become inevitable tomorrow through patient, persistent, and principled effort. The federal imperative is not merely one option among many – it is the serious, tangible solution that circumstances increasingly demand.

Chapter 12.
Addendum.

Key Concepts.
Understanding Implementation.
Phased Implementation: Gradual approach breaking complex changes into sequential stages, allowing trust to develop through demonstrated performance. Northern Ireland's peace process exemplifies this: the 1998 Good Friday Agreement created frameworks, but paramilitary decommissioning occurred in stages (2001-2005), policing reforms happened gradually (2001-2010), and power-sharing governments formed and collapsed multiple times before stabilizing. Each successful phase created confidence enabling next steps. Phased implementation allows either party to pause if the other defects, managing risk.
Roadmap: Detailed plan specifying objectives, timelines, responsibilities, and contingencies. Unlike vague aspirations, roadmaps specify concrete milestones: what happens when, who does what, how progress gets measured. The Oslo Accords featured roadmaps (though ultimately unsuccessful). Effective roadmaps balance rigidity (clear commitments) with flexibility (adaptation to changing circumstances).
Milestones: Specific, measurable achievements marking progress. Examples: South Africa's 1994 elections ending apartheid; Northern Ireland's 2007 power-sharing government; Bosnia's 2006 elections consolidating post-war institutions. Milestones must be unambiguous—not "improve security cooperation" but "establish joint intelligence center operational by [date]." Achieving milestones builds confidence; missing them triggers reassessment.
Capacity Building: Systematic development of institutions, skills, and resources enabling effective governance. Involves training civil servants, establishing financial management systems, developing fair judicial institutions, creating effective police forces, and building infrastructure. International assistance provides expertise and funding, but locals must lead. Palestinian capacity building within federal frameworks would require investment but occupation's removal would eliminate constraints.
International Monitoring: External verification that parties fulfill commitments. Serves multiple functions: deterring violations, detecting violations early, and building confidence. Monitors might include UN peacekeepers or EU observers. Effective monitoring requires clear mandates, sufficient resources, authority to report violations publicly, and integration with enforcement mechanisms.

Confidence-Building Measures: Small, reversible steps creating trust between adversaries. Examples include prisoner exchanges, economic cooperation, security coordination against common threats, educational exchanges, and joint infrastructure projects. These don't resolve core disputes but create relationships making disputes more manageable.

The Citizen Relevance: How Peace Actually Happens.
Peace isn't signed; it's built. Peace agreements receive media attention, but real peace develops through years of implementation: civil servants learning to work together, businesses establishing partnerships, teachers redesigning curricula, police officers from different communities patrolling together.

Peace as Process, Not Event
Northern Ireland's "Troubles" ended gradually over a decade after the 1998 Good Friday Agreement. South Africa's transformation didn't occur instantly when Mandela became president—building multi-racial institutions required decades. Israeli-Palestinian federal peace would follow similar patterns. Progress would be uneven, but each year of successful cooperation makes next year's cooperation more likely.

Role of International Community
International actors provide: *Resources* (funding reconstruction and development), *Expertise* (sharing lessons from successful transitions), *Monitoring* (verifying compliance builds confidence), and *Guarantees* (major power commitments provide insurance). However, heavy-handed external control can undermine local ownership—effective engagement supports rather than substitutes for local agency.

How Ordinary People Contribute
Citizens play essential roles: *Economic Engagement* (businesses creating cross-community partnerships), *Educational Transformation* (teachers presenting balanced perspectives), *Civil Society Bridges* (organizations bringing communities together), *Local Governance* (municipal cooperation on practical issues), and *Political Participation* (supporting moderate politicians, holding leaders accountable). Peace isn't something leaders give citizens; it's something citizens build through millions of small daily choices to cooperate.

Scholarly Framework: Implementation Science and Peace-Building.
Students examining implementation should engage with peace-building literature and case studies.

Implementation Science: Studies how policies translate from paper to practice. Pressman and Wildavsky (1973) showed programs fail not because policies are wrong but because implementation is hard. Sabatier and Mazmanian identify success factors: clear objectives, adequate causal theory, committed leadership, interest group support. Lipsky's "Street-Level Bureaucracy" recognizes front-line implementers shape outcomes. Readings: Pressman and Wildavsky (1973/1984), Sabatier and Mazmanian (1983), Lipsky (1980/2010).

Case Studies: *Northern Ireland*: Good Friday Agreement implemented through decommissioning, police reform, power-sharing, cross-border institutions. Success factors: war-weariness, external support, economic incentives, patient implementation. *South Africa*: Transition through interim constitution, Truth and Reconciliation Commission, final constitution, land reform, affirmative action. *Mozambique*: Ended 15-year civil war through demobilization, political integration, mine clearance, refugee return. Readings: Wilford (2001), Sparks (2003), Manning (2002).

Careers: UN Political Affairs, World Bank post-conflict programs, government agencies (USAID, UK FCDO), NGOs (Crisis Group, Search for Common Ground), research/academia. Requires graduate degrees, language skills, field experience, and specialized expertise.

Realistic Timeline Discussion.
Peace-building timelines span decades.
Managing expectations requires honesty.
Year 1-5: Foundations
Intensive negotiations produce constitutional framework (2-4 years). Years 3-5 create federal institutions: civil service, courts, parliament, executive, integrated security leadership. Early wins needed: checkpoint removal, joint economic projects, cultural exchanges, humanitarian cooperation, successful joint security operations.

Success Year 5: Constitutional agreement ratified, federal institutions operational, violence declined significantly, economic growth in both communities, first students educated under new curricula graduating, Israelis and Palestinians developing working relationships.

Challenges: Spoiler violence, implementation delays, economic reconstruction slower than hoped, periodic crises, missed milestones requiring adjustment.

Year 5-10: Consolidation

Federal civil service becomes competent through experience. Courts establish precedents. Security integration extends operationally. Fiscal federalism functions smoothly. Economic integration normalizes: trade between regions, joint ventures multiply, infrastructure improves, labor mobility increases, Palestinian GDP begins converging toward Israeli levels.

Success Year 10: Federal government functioning without international micromanagement, violence rare and condemned, economic growth sustained, cross-community interactions common, younger generation less divided, international community treating federal Israel as normal state.

Challenges: Institutional arrangements requiring adjustment, economic inequality persisting, periodic political crises, external spoilers, demographic/political shifts creating pressures.

Year 10-25: Normalization

Generational change: cohort educated entirely under federal system reaches adulthood without personal memory of divided societies. Federal institutions become unremarkable background to normal politics about taxes, education, healthcare. Palestinian regions approach Israeli regions in prosperity through sustained growth. Federal Israel embedded in regional economic/security frameworks.

Success Year 25: Entire adult generation knowing only federal system, violence essentially eliminated, economic convergence approaching, political competition focusing on normal governance not existential questions, international acceptance complete, constitutional amendments demonstrating system's adaptability.

Challenges: Some issues remain contentious (Jerusalem arrangements, remaining refugees, holy sites), movements questioning federal arrangements, external shocks testing resilience, need for ongoing adaptation.

What Success Looks Like

Success doesn't mean perfection. Twenty-five years after implementation: Violence won't be completely eliminated but reduced 95%+. Economic inequality won't disappear but gaps narrow steadily. Political tensions won't vanish but occur through democratic institutions. Not everyone embraces federalism but majorities in both communities prefer it to alternatives. Younger generation views cooperation as normal, conflict as historical.

The Breakdown.

Building Peace Step by Step.

Simple Action Plan.

Step 1: Negotiations (Years 1-3) Leaders from both sides sit down and hammer out details: How will government work? Who controls what? How are holy sites managed? What about refugees? What about security? This takes years of arguing, compromising, walking out, coming back. Eventually, they produce a plan both sides can accept—not love, but accept.

Step 2: Vote (Year 3-4) Both Israelis and Palestinians vote on whether to accept the plan. For it to work, majorities in both communities must say yes. If either votes no, back to negotiations.

Step 3: Building Institutions (Years 3-7) Start creating new federal government: Parliament with members from both communities. Courts with both Israeli and Palestinian judges. Federal agencies hiring from both populations. Police forces beginning to cooperate. This is hard—people used to being enemies must work together.

Step 4: Quick Wins (Years 1-5) Early on, need visible improvements showing federalism works: Checkpoints removed so Palestinians move freely. Joint projects creating jobs. Security cooperation stopping terrorists threatening both communities. Students from both sides meeting in exchange programs.

Step 5: Building Trust (Years 5-15) As federal institutions start working, trust gradually builds. Israeli civil servants work with Palestinian colleagues. Jewish and Arab children attend each other's schools on exchanges. Businesses create partnerships. Families cautiously start talking to each other. Trust doesn't come from speeches—it comes from working together successfully.

Step 6: Growing Up Federal (Years 10-25) Kids educated entirely under new system grow up. For them, cooperation is normal—conflict is what grandparents tell stories about. This generational change is crucial. Young people without personal war memories are more open to cooperation.

Step 7: New Normal (Year 25+) Federal system becomes so normal people barely think about it. Politics focuses on normal stuff —education quality, taxes, healthcare—not existential conflicts. Violence is rare. Prosperity shared. Not perfect, but infinitely better than before.

Visual Timeline Concept

[Simple graphic concept for students to create]:

TIMELINE: Building Federal Peace
├── YEARS 1-3: Negotiations → Constitutional Agreement
├── YEARS 3-5: Building Institutions → Federal Government Starts
├── YEARS 5-10: Consolidation → Institutions Functioning Well
├── YEARS 10-25: Normalization → Cooperation Becomes Normal
└── YEAR 25+: New Reality → Federal System Established

At each stage: Green checkmarks for successes, yellow cautions for challenges, red X's for setbacks requiring adjustment.

The Main Point
Peace takes TIME. Anyone promising quick fixes is lying. But we know it's possible because other places have done it. France and Germany fought for centuries—now they're partners. Northern Irish Protestants and Catholics killed each other for decades—now they share government. South Africans overcame apartheid. If they can do it, Israelis and Palestinians can too. But it requires patience, persistence, and willingness to work together even when it's hard.

Chapter 13
Middle East Future: A Federal Vision.

From Zero-Sum Competition to Regional Cooperation.
The enduring legacy of political fragmentation and recurrent conflict in the Middle East has been shaped by what scholars characterize as a debilitating zero-sum calculus—the deeply ingrained assumption that gains for one party necessarily constitute losses for another. This perspective, pervading the region's political discourse for generations, has fueled what Paul Rivlin of the Moshe Dayan Center documents as "a perpetual cycle of competition, suspicion, and, at times, outright hostility."[1]

Whether framed along sectarian, ethnic, nationalistic, or ideological lines, this mindset has consistently undermined efforts toward lasting peace, stability, and shared prosperity. The zero-sum mentality, as Rivlin's extensive research demonstrates, "has dominated the relations between states and relations within states" across the Middle East, with the Arab-Israeli conflict serving as "the most lasting example."[2]

The manifestations are evident everywhere: proxy wars that devastate societies while serving external patrons; arms races that consume resources desperately needed for development; intractable border disputes that prevent cooperation on shared challenges; and a pervasive reluctance to engage in genuine collaborative endeavours. Within such a framework, concessions are perceived as weakness, cooperation as temporary ruse, and the pursuit of national or group interests as existential imperative necessitating the subjugation of others.

This chapter turns outward from the internal constitutional arrangements examined in preceding chapters to assess the regional reverberations of Israeli-Palestinian federal resolution. The argument advanced here is that federalism would catalyze a fundamental reorientation of Middle Eastern geopolitics—not merely adding another bilateral peace agreement to the region's collection of fragile arrangements, but transforming the structural conditions that have perpetuated conflict for generations.

The transformation would operate through several interconnected mechanisms. Resolution of the Israeli-Palestinian conflict would remove the "master frame" that has organized regional politics, compelling governments to engage with populations and neighbours on the basis of actual interests rather than performative solidarity. It would strip away the ideological resources that Iran and other actors have exploited for regional influence. It would remove the principal obstacle to comprehensive Arab-Israeli normalization, enabling security cooperation and economic integration that the unresolved conflict has precluded. And it would create precedent and momentum for addressing other regional conflicts through institutional accommodation rather than zero-sum competition.

As I have argued in the Times of Israel, the question facing Israel today is not whether change will come, but whether that change will be shaped by strategic vision or imposed by circumstance.[3] A federal approach represents the former—a deliberate architectural choice that addresses internal contradictions while simultaneously positioning Israel as catalyst for regional transformation rather than permanent source of regional instability.

Israel-Palestine Conflict as a Regional Hub.
For decades, the Israeli-Palestinian issue has served as potent ideological and political instrument for regional actors seeking to enhance their standing, legitimacy, or influence. Marc Lynch's analysis of Arab public opinion demonstrates that the conflict has functioned as what scholars term a "master frame"—an organizing narrative that shapes how regional actors understand and respond to a wide range of political questions extending far beyond Palestine itself.[4] This framing power explains why the conflict has proven so resistant to resolution: too many actors benefit from its perpetuation.

The instrumentalization has had corrosive effects throughout the region. Regimes across the Arab world have invoked Palestinian suffering to deflect criticism of their own governance failures, to justify authoritarian measures in the name of national security, and to maintain adversarial postures toward Israel that preclude beneficial cooperation. The persistence of the conflict has, paradoxically, served certain interests even as it has inflicted immense human costs and foreclosed opportunities for regional development that might have improved millions of lives.

Elie Podeh's analysis of normalization dynamics illuminates how this instrumentalization constrains even those governments that privately desire improved relations with Israel.[5] Arab leaders who might otherwise pursue cooperation face domestic political costs when doing so appears to abandon Palestinian solidarity. The conflict thus functions as a structural constraint on regional politics —not because all actors genuinely prioritize Palestinian welfare, but because the symbolism of the Palestinian cause has become embedded in regional political culture in ways that constrain governmental flexibility.

A comprehensive resolution enshrined within federal structure would fundamentally alter these dynamics. It would deny opportunistic actors a critical platform for grievance-based mobilization and strategic posturing. When Palestinian national aspirations are addressed through genuine self-governance within federal arrangements, the charge of "abandoning Palestine" loses its political force. Arab governments would gain space to pursue relations with Israel based on mutual interest rather than performative hostility.

The regional implications extend beyond bilateral Israeli-Arab relations. By removing the conflict as organizing principle for regional politics, federalism would compel governments throughout the Middle East to engage with their populations on the basis of actual governance performance rather than deflection through external grievance. This represents what scholars term a "structural break"—a fundamental alteration in the constraints and opportunities facing regional actors that necessitates wholesale reconsideration of long-established policies.[6]

Sectarian Dynamics & the Iranian Question.
The reverberations of Israeli-Palestinian federal resolution would extend into the complex sectarian dynamics that have increasingly defined Middle Eastern politics since 2003. The narrative of a "Shia crescent" stretching from Tehran through Baghdad and Damascus to Beirut, and conversely Sunni fears of Iranian encirclement, has fueled proxy conflicts from Yemen to Syria to Lebanon, with devastating humanitarian consequences.[7]

The establishment of a federal Israel would significantly alter these dangerous dynamics. Consider the strategic posture of Iran and its associated network of militias and political movements. For decades, the Palestinian cause has been central to Iran's regional strategy. By supporting Palestinian factions—particularly Hamas and Islamic Jihad—Iran has projected itself as champion of Arab and Muslim causes, thereby extending influence far beyond the Shia communities that constitute its natural constituency.[8]

Karim Sadjadpour's analysis of Iranian strategy emphasizes how the "resistance" narrative depends substantially upon perpetuation of the Israeli-Palestinian conflict.[9] Iran's claim to regional leadership rests partly on its willingness to confront Israel when Sunni Arab states have pursued accommodation. Resolution of the conflict through federalism would remove a cornerstone of Tehran's regional strategy—not eliminating Iranian ambitions, which are rooted in multiple factors, but substantially diminishing a crucial ideological and mobilizational resource.

The implications would ripple through Iran's network of regional allies. Hezbollah, which has justified its armed status partly through its role in "resistance" against Israel, would face legitimacy challenges when that resistance no longer serves Palestinian liberation. Iraqi militias that have invoked solidarity with Palestine would lose a significant element of their ideological appeal. The "Axis of Resistance" that Iran has constructed would face fundamental questions about its purpose in a region where the foundational conflict has been resolved.

F. Gregory Gause's scholarship on the Saudi-Iranian rivalry offers important qualification to this analysis.[10] Gause argues persuasively that the "new Middle East cold war" is driven primarily by domestic political considerations and regime security concerns, with the Palestinian issue serving more as rhetorical decoration than genuine motivation. Sectarian competition would not disappear with Israeli-Palestinian resolution; its roots lie deeper than any single conflict.

Yet even Gause acknowledges that the Palestinian cause provides "cover" for regional interventions and helps legitimate policies that might otherwise face greater domestic and international scrutiny. [11] Removing this cover would not eliminate sectarian competition, but it would alter the terms on which that competition is conducted and potentially reduce the resources available for its prosecution. Iranian support for Palestinian factions has cost billions over decades; those resources, denied their current justification, might be redirected or simply unavailable for regional destabilization.

The Abraham Accords: Foundation and Limitation.
The Abraham Accords of 2020, which formalized Israel's relations with the United Arab Emirates, Bahrain, Morocco, and Sudan, represented the most significant diplomatic breakthrough in Arab-

Israeli relations since the 1994 Jordan peace treaty. Trade between Israel and the UAE, negligible before normalization, exceeded $2.5 billion by 2023.[12] Israeli tourists flooded Dubai; Emirati investment flowed to Israeli technology companies; commercial flights connected economies that had previously interacted only through intermediaries.

Yet the Abraham Accords remain constrained by the unresolved Palestinian question. Full regional normalization—particularly including Saudi Arabia, the Arab world's largest economy and custodian of Islam's holiest sites—hinges upon credible progress toward Palestinian self-determination. Crown Prince Mohammed bin Salman stated explicitly that Saudi normalization requires addressing Palestinian aspirations, reflecting both genuine concern and domestic political constraints that even absolute monarchs cannot entirely ignore.[13]

The October 7th attacks and subsequent Gaza war demonstrated how quickly progress can be reversed when the Palestinian question remains unresolved. Nascent Saudi-Israeli normalization discussions, reportedly approaching agreement, were suspended indefinitely. Public opinion across the Arab world, inflamed by images of destruction in Gaza, constrained governments that might otherwise have continued normalization trajectories. The Abraham Accords themselves survived but were strained, demonstrating their vulnerability to conflict escalation.

A federal solution addresses this fundamental limitation. By providing a framework wherein Palestinian national aspirations are fulfilled through substantial regional autonomy within shared constitutional order, federalism removes the principal obstacle to comprehensive normalization. Arab states, historically constrained to condition Israeli relations upon Palestinian statehood, could embrace full normalization when federalism provides genuine Palestinian self-governance without requiring them to abandon solidarity with the Palestinian cause.

The distinction matters enormously. Two-state solutions have failed partly because they require Arab states to accept permanent separation of Palestinians from historic Palestine—a position difficult to justify to domestic audiences raised on narratives of Palestinian dispossession. Federal solutions reframe the question: Palestinians would not be separated from their homeland but would govern themselves within it, sharing sovereignty with Jewish

Israelis in arrangements that both peoples have accepted. This reframing provides political cover for Arab governments to normalize without appearing to abandon Palestinian rights.

Security Cooperation: From Competition to Collective Defence.
The geopolitical advantages of comprehensive normalization would be transformative, nowhere more so than in security cooperation. Currently, Israel and various Arab states engage in quiet security coordination—intelligence sharing on Iranian activities, tacit cooperation against common terrorist threats, informal communication channels for crisis management. These arrangements, valuable as they are, remain constrained by the political impossibility of formalizing relationships that publics have been taught to oppose.

A federal resolution would enable security cooperation to emerge from the shadows. A regional security architecture encompassing Israel, Palestine within federal framework, and participating Arab states would possess unprecedented capacity for intelligence sharing, coordinated counter-terrorism, and collective defence against common threats.[14] This cooperative framework would replace historical patterns of competitive armament and proxy conflicts with institutional mechanisms for collective threat management.

The Iranian threat provides the most obvious focus for such cooperation. Israel and Gulf states share concerns about Iranian nuclear ambitions, missile programs, and support for regional proxies. Currently, cooperation against these threats remains informal and deniable; neither side can acknowledge publicly what both pursue privately. Federalism, by resolving the Palestinian question, would remove the political obstacles to formal security partnerships that current arrangements preclude.

The practical benefits would be substantial. Integrated air defence systems could provide coverage that no single state can achieve independently. Shared early warning networks could detect missile launches and terrorist movements across the region. Coordinated naval patrols could secure vital shipping lanes through the Red Sea and Persian Gulf. Joint counter-terrorism operations could address threats that cross national boundaries—threats that no state can effectively address alone.

Recent diplomatic developments suggest regional actors are increasingly prepared for such transformation. The China-brokered normalization agreement between Saudi Arabia and Iran in March 2023, whatever its durability, demonstrated willingness to explore alternatives to permanent confrontation.

The UAE's diplomatic engagement with former adversaries, including restoration of relations with Qatar and outreach to Assad's Syria, demonstrates that Gulf states are "moving beyond zero-sum politics toward a more pragmatic approach to security."[15] A federal Israel, having resolved its foundational internal contradiction, would be positioned to participate in and accelerate this regional realignment.

Economic Integration: Regional Dimensions.
The economic implications of regional transformation, while treated comprehensively in Chapter 8, merit summary consideration here for their regional dimensions. Currently, intra-regional trade in the Middle East represents only about nine percent of the region's total exports—a smaller share than nearly all other regions globally and a fraction of potential given geographic proximity and complementary economic structures.[16]

This isolation reflects political fragmentation rather than economic logic. As Rivlin documents, regional trade has been suppressed by "intense mistrust between the countries of the region and the desire to protect domestic production" from neighbours perceived as adversaries.[17] The result is economic inefficiency on a massive scale: duplicated infrastructure, foregone economies of scale, missed opportunities for specialisation, and resources devoted to competitive armament rather than productive investment.

Federal resolution of the Israeli-Palestinian conflict would remove the principal political obstacle to regional economic integration. The detailed analysis in Chapter 8 documents the potential gains: interconnected markets fostering specialisation; joint ventures in renewable energy, water management, and advanced technology; coordinated infrastructure connecting populations separated by political barriers. What requires emphasis here is the regional dimension—how Israeli-Palestinian integration would catalyze broader Middle Eastern economic cooperation.

Israel's technological capabilities—in agricultural technology, water management, cybersecurity, medical devices, and numerous other fields—could benefit the entire region through knowledge transfer and joint ventures currently precluded by political barriers. Conversely, Israeli firms would gain access to markets of hundreds of millions of consumers, achieving scale economies that domestic and European markets alone cannot provide. Gulf capital, already flowing to Israel through Abraham Accords channels, could expand dramatically when political constraints ease.

The tourism potential deserves particular mention. The combined heritage tourism possibilities—from ancient Petra to Jerusalem's Old City, from Egyptian pyramids to Lebanese coastal sites—could create an unprecedented tourism corridor currently fragmented by political barriers and security concerns. Religious tourism alone, encompassing sites sacred to Judaism, Christianity, and Islam, could generate billions in revenue when visitors can move freely across a region currently divided by borders, checkpoints, and mutual suspicion.

Raymond Hinnebusch has raised important objections to optimistic scenarios of Middle Eastern economic integration.[18] The predominance of oil economies that trade with global rather than regional markets, the weakness of manufacturing sectors that might benefit from regional supply chains, and authoritarian governance structures that resist the transparency economic integration requires—all these factors suggest that political breakthroughs alone will not produce economic transformation.

These objections merit serious consideration. Yet the European precedent demonstrates that political frameworks can catalyze economic transformations that previously seemed impossible. The European Coal and Steel Community emerged from circumstances of far greater devastation and distrust than currently characterize the Middle East.[19]

Political will, institutionalized through appropriate frameworks, can generate the economic interdependencies that subsequently reinforce political cooperation. The question is whether regional leadership will prove adequate to the opportunity that federal resolution would create.

Institutional Architecture for Regional Cooperation.
Sustaining transformation beyond initial diplomatic breakthroughs requires institutional mechanisms that embed cooperation in organizational structures capable of surviving political fluctuations.

Ad hoc cooperation, however valuable, remains vulnerable to leadership changes, domestic political shifts, and crisis-driven reversals. Institutions create stakes, generate constituencies, and establish expectations that prove more durable than personal relationships or temporary alignments of interest.

The European experience provides the paradigmatic example. The Coal and Steel Community's genius lay not merely in integrating French and German heavy industries but in creating supranational institutions—the High Authority, the Assembly, the Court—that acquired autonomous interests in continued integration.[20] These institutions developed constituencies benefiting from cooperation, generated bureaucratic momentum toward deeper integration, and established legal frameworks constraining member state defection. The result was a self-reinforcing process wherein initial cooperation generated pressures for additional cooperation.

The Middle East lacks equivalent institutions. The Arab League, founded in 1945, has proven largely ineffective at promoting genuine cooperation, instead serving primarily as forum for rhetorical posturing and occasional coordination against common adversaries.[21]

The Gulf Cooperation Council has achieved somewhat more, particularly in economic coordination among member states, but remains limited in scope and has been weakened by the Qatar crisis and other internal divisions. No regional institution possesses the authority, legitimacy, or capacity to drive the kind of integration that transformed post-war Europe.

A federal Israel could catalyze institutional development by demonstrating that cooperation produces tangible benefits and by providing a stable anchor for regional arrangements. Building on Abraham Accords foundations, regional institutions could address specific functional challenges: a water authority coordinating transboundary resource management; an energy consortium facilitating renewable transition while coordinating hydrocarbon resource development; a transportation commission overseeing infrastructure connecting previously separated populations.

The Chatham House initiative on regional cooperation articulates principles that should guide institutional design: membership and substantive agendas "designed to promote cooperation for the benefit of the wider region and its people, not as an axis to target or exclude a specific country or to advance the agenda of a particular external power."[22] This represents precisely the kind of inclusive framework that resolution of the Israeli-Palestinian conflict would enable—cooperation not directed against any party but oriented toward mutual benefit.

Academic and research institutions could play vital roles in building the intellectual infrastructure for regional cooperation. A Middle East Institute for Advanced Studies, drawing scholars from across the region, could foster research collaboration on shared challenges. Joint universities focusing on critical fields—water science, renewable energy, public health, conflict resolution—could train new generations of regional leaders committed to cooperation rather than competition. Such institutions build what scholars term "epistemic communities"—networks of experts who share analytical frameworks and policy orientations, capable of influencing policy across national boundaries.[23]

Cultural Transformation: The Deeper Challenge.
Political and economic transformation, essential as they are, cannot prove durable without accompanying cultural change. The zero-sum mentality that has defined Middle Eastern politics is not merely governmental posture but deeply embedded cultural orientation, transmitted through educational systems, reinforced by media, and sustained by collective memories of conflict and grievance. Institutional arrangements that run contrary to cultural expectations face constant pressure toward erosion or collapse.

The challenge is formidable. Generations of Israelis have been raised on narratives emphasizing Arab hostility and the necessity of permanent vigilance. Generations of Arabs have been raised on narratives emphasizing Zionist dispossession and the illegitimacy of Jewish sovereignty in Palestine. These narratives are not mere propaganda; they reflect genuine historical experiences and legitimate grievances. Changing them requires not denial but reframing—acknowledging painful histories while creating space for different futures.

Educational reform must be central to cultural transformation. Curricula across the region currently emphasize historical grievances, glorify past conflicts, and present neighbours as permanent enemies. Research on Israeli and Palestinian textbooks reveals systematic patterns of dehumanization, omission, and distortion that socialize children into conflict orientations.[24]

Federal arrangements would require educational approaches that acknowledge both peoples' histories, recognize both communities' suffering, and prepare students for citizenship in shared institutions rather than permanent confrontation.

The Swiss experience offers relevant precedent. Swiss educational systems, operating in four languages across twenty-six cantons, successfully transmit both particular cantonal identities and shared Swiss citizenship. Students learn their canton's history and their linguistic community's cultural traditions while simultaneously learning to identify as Swiss citizens committed to federal constitutional principles.[25] This dual socialization—particular and federal—provides a model for educational approaches that preserve community identities while building shared citizenship.

Media transformation presents different challenges. Contemporary media environments, particularly social media, tend toward fragmentation and polarization—algorithmic curation creating filter bubbles that reinforce existing beliefs and limit exposure to alternative perspectives. These dynamics have exacerbated regional conflicts, enabling rapid spread of inflammatory content while limiting exposure to voices advocating cooperation.[26]

Yet media also offers opportunities. Satellite television and internet access have created regional public spheres that transcend national boundaries, enabling Arabs and Israelis to access each other's media in ways previously impossible. Social media, despite its polarizing tendencies, has enabled direct communication between individuals across conflict lines, sometimes building relationships that formal diplomacy cannot create. The question is whether these technologies can be harnessed for cooperation rather than conflict—a question without predetermined answer but with substantial stakes.

Religious institutions and leaders possess particular influence in a region where faith remains central to identity and community. Interfaith dialogue initiatives, while often dismissed as naive, have produced genuine relationships and joint statements that challenge narratives of inevitable religious conflict.[27]

Religious leaders who articulate theological bases for coexistence —drawing on traditions of tolerance within Islam, Judaism, and Christianity—can legitimate cooperation in ways that secular arguments cannot. The Abrahamic Family House in Abu Dhabi, bringing together mosque, church, and synagogue on a single campus, represents the kind of symbolic initiative that, while insufficient alone, contributes to cultural transformation.

Challenges and Obstacles: Honest Assessment.
Scholarly integrity demands acknowledging the formidable obstacles confronting regional transformation. The analysis presented here is not prediction but possibility—an argument about what federal resolution could enable, not a claim that such resolution is likely or that its regional benefits would automatically materialize.

External powers present one category of challenge. The Middle East's strategic importance ensures that global powers—the United States, European Union, Russia, China—all have interests in regional configurations. Federal arrangements that shift regional power balances might face opposition from powers benefiting from the status quo. The history of external intervention in Middle Eastern affairs, from Sykes-Picot through the Cold War to contemporary great power competition, creates understandable skepticism about any major political restructuring.[28]

Regional spoilers present another challenge. Iran's regional strategy, as discussed, depends partly upon conflict perpetuation. Elements within Gulf states might prefer continued Israeli-Palestinian tension that justifies their own security relationships with Washington. Non-state actors whose legitimacy derives from "resistance"—Hezbollah, various Palestinian factions, Shia militias in Iraq—would face existential challenges from comprehensive resolution and might actively undermine it.[29]

Domestic politics within key states present perhaps the most formidable obstacles. Israeli politics has moved rightward, with significant constituencies opposing any accommodation with Palestinians. Palestinian politics remains fragmented between Fatah and Hamas, with neither possessing clear mandate or capacity to negotiate binding agreements. Arab publics, whatever their governments' preferences, retain deep suspicions of Israel that decades of normalization rhetoric have not dispelled.

Ian Lustick's provocative analysis suggests that the two-state solution is already "dead"—foreclosed by Israeli settlement expansion and political dynamics that no diplomatic process can reverse.[30] If this assessment is correct, federalism may represent not one option among many but the only remaining pathway toward resolution. Yet the same political dynamics that foreclosed two states present formidable obstacles to federalism as well.

Aaron David Miller's assessment of American diplomatic efforts offers additional caution: decades of failure reflect not merely tactical errors but fundamental asymmetries in power, motivation, and urgency that no institutional design can easily overcome.[31] These are serious objections from serious scholars, and this book does not claim to have definitively refuted them.

The Imperative of Vision.
Yet the alternative—continued conflict, instability, and zero-sum competition—has proven even more costly than the risks of transformation. The human costs are most obvious: lives lost, families destroyed, generations raised amid violence and hatred. But the economic costs, the diplomatic costs, the opportunity costs of resources devoted to conflict rather than development—these too have been immense. The status quo, comfortable as it may appear to those insulated from its costs, is not actually static; it deteriorates with each passing year as demographic realities shift, international patience erodes, and the human toll accumulates.

The federal vision does not depend upon naive assumptions about human nature or wilful ignorance of genuine security concerns. It recognizes that security achieved through permanent domination is inherently unstable, while security achieved through legitimate accommodation can prove durable. The comparative evidence examined throughout this book demonstrates that institutional arrangements can transform seemingly intractable conflicts when political will exists to pursue them.

The Middle East's chronic instability has been deeply intertwined with the Israeli-Palestinian conflict's persistence. This conflict has provided ideological resources for authoritarian regimes, justification for regional interventions, and obstacles to cooperation that might otherwise have developed. Its resolution would not solve all regional problems—sectarian tensions, governance failures, resource constraints would remain—but it would remove a significant source of instability while creating precedent and momentum for addressing other challenges.

Israel cannot continue in a permanent state of war. The costs—human, economic, diplomatic, and moral—are unsustainable over the long term. The federal solution represents not capitulation to pressure but recognition that Israel's long-term flourishing depends upon resolving, rather than merely managing, the conflict that has defined its existence. This is not idealism; it is strategic realism, grounded in evidence and informed by recognition that alternatives have been exhausted.

The embrace of federalism is therefore not merely structural reform but strategic imperative—not merely constitutional arrangement but regional transformation. The specific institutional mechanisms through which such federalism might be realized are the subject of the following chapter. What this chapter has sought to establish is that the regional stakes extend far beyond the borders of Israel-Palestine, offering possibility of a transformed Middle East defined by cooperation rather than endless zero-sum competition that has cost so much and delivered so little.

The path forward is neither easy nor certain. But the destination—a region where Israelis and Palestinians, Arabs and Jews, Sunnis and Shias find ways to live together rather than against each other—remains worth pursuing despite the obstacles. The federal vision offers a map; political courage must supply the journey.

Chapter 13
Addendum

Key Concepts.
Understanding Regional Transformation.
Regional Integration: Process by which neighboring countries develop economic, political, and social connections. Includes economic integration (free trade, common markets), political integration (shared institutions), security cooperation (joint defense), and social integration (cultural exchanges). European Union exemplifies deep integration—member states cooperate extensively while maintaining sovereignty. Middle East has minimal integration—only 9% intra-regional trade versus 60%+ in Europe/Asia. Israeli-Palestinian conflict prevents cooperation that geographic proximity should enable.

Geopolitics: How geography, resources, and power shape international politics. Middle Eastern geopolitics features strategic chokepoints (Suez, Hormuz), massive oil/gas reserves, religious significance, and unresolved conflicts. Federal Israeli-Palestinian resolution would alter regional geopolitics by removing the "master frame" organizing politics and enabling currently blocked cooperation.

Cooperation vs. Competition: Competition assumes zero-sum games (one's gain equals another's loss), leading to arms races and conflict. Cooperation recognizes positive-sum opportunities where all benefit through trade, shared infrastructure, and collective problem-solving. Middle East trapped in competitive mode costing $150+ billion annually in arms spending. Federal resolution could shift toward cooperation—integrated markets, joint infrastructure, coordinated security.

Zone of Peace: Geographic area where war between members becomes unthinkable due to institutional integration, economic interdependence, and shared identity. EU represents most developed zone—war between members inconceivable. Federal Israel could anchor Middle Eastern zone of peace.

Economic Bloc: Countries coordinating economic policies and reducing trade barriers. Benefits include larger markets, economies of scale, coordinated infrastructure, and reduced conflict. Middle

East lacks functioning economic blocs. Federal resolution would enable Israeli technology plus Arab capital and markets.

Regional Security: Cooperative frameworks where neighbors coordinate defense against common threats rather than arming against each other. Includes intelligence sharing, joint exercises, mutual defense commitments. Federal resolution would enable comprehensive Middle Eastern regional security coordinating against terrorism and proliferation.

The Citizen Relevance.
A Better Middle East Benefits Everyone.
Middle Eastern peace would benefit people globally.
Reduced Refugees: Conflict generates massive flows—Syrian war displaced 13+ million, Palestinian refugees number 5.9 million. These strain neighbors and contribute to European migration pressures. Stable, prosperous Middle East would reduce these flows as people build futures at home rather than fleeing.
Energy Security: Region holds 48% of global oil, 38% of gas. Every Middle Eastern crisis spikes prices globally. Regional cooperation would stabilize markets through coordinated production, secure infrastructure, and reduced conflict risk.

Tourism Opportunities: Extraordinary heritage currently fragmented by conflict. Regional peace would create unprecedented tourism corridor: Egypt's pyramids, Jerusalem's holy sites, Petra, Mesopotamian cities. Currently impossible comprehensive tours would generate tens of billions annually.

Tech Hubs: Israel's "startup nation" ($25+ billion annual VC) remains disconnected from Arab world. Regional integration would combine Israeli innovation with Arab capital and 400+ million consumer markets, creating tech hub rivaling Silicon Valley.
Imagine: Israeli and Palestinian children playing together; high-speed rail connecting Cairo-Jerusalem-Riyadh-Dubai; joint solar farms powering desalination; multinational universities; professional leagues with Tel Aviv-Beirut matches; pilgrims moving freely among sacred sites; resources devoted to development, not armament. Achievable within a generation.

Scholarly Frameworks
Middle East Studies and Regional Integration.
Students examining regional transformation should engage with Middle East studies and integration theory. Key approaches include

understanding historical legacies (Ottoman dissolution, colonial mandates, state formation), political economy (rentier state theory, resource curse), sectarianism, and regional power dynamics. Integration theories include functionalism (technical cooperation creating spillover), security communities (war becoming unthinkable), and constructivism (shared identities enabling cooperation). Readings: Gelvin (2015), Cleveland and Bunton (2016), Haas (2004), Solingen (2007).

Career paths include diplomacy (foreign services needing Middle East specialists), development (World Bank, UN agencies, NGOs), business (trade/investment opportunities), research (think tanks, universities), and media/analysis. Requires language skills (Arabic/Hebrew), regional experience, and cultural competence.

A Vision for the Next Generation.
Different Childhoods: Currently, Israeli children grow up under rocket threat and military service; Palestinian children under occupation. Federal future: children attending bilingual schools, learning both narratives, participating in exchanges, making friends across lines, seeing adults from both communities working together normally. Generational transformation crucial—young Europeans without war memories embraced integration more readily.

Regional Cooperation: Children would collaborate on shared challenges—climate change adaptation, water security (Israeli expertise plus Arab investment), technological innovation (joint ventures accessing Israeli R&D and Arab markets). Careers in development, not military service.

Twenty-Five Years Hence: Children born today would be young adults with university choices spanning region, job opportunities throughout area, rich cultural fusion, routine interfaith relationships, democratic participation in normal governance debates, and incomprehension of grandparents' era of conflict. Not utopia, but fundamentally transformed. Possible within a generation.

Faith Perspectives: Holy Land for All.
Jerusalem Accessible: Federal arrangements could realize Jerusalem as shared sacred space—Muslims praying at Al-Aqsa, Jews at Western Wall, both respecting each other, federal oversight ensuring access, Christians accessing Holy Sepulcher safely. Genuine interfaith dialogue center.

Pilgrimage Without Conflict: Muslims freely visiting Al-Aqsa and Mecca/Medina. Christians following Jesus's path from Nazareth to Jerusalem extending to Jordan/Egypt/Lebanon. Jews visiting Western Wall and ancient sites without occupation's moral burden. Combined pilgrimages enriching faith through encounter with traditions.

Prophetic Fulfillment: Isaiah's vision of swords into plowshares, Jesus's blessing of peacemakers, Quran's emphasis on justice and mutual understanding—federal peace would align with faith traditions' core commitments better than perpetual conflict.

Religious Leadership: Joint statements citing scriptural peace bases, practical cooperation on poverty relief and education, theological development articulating how peace fulfills faith, youth engagement preparing for coexistence. Religious leaders possess unique moral authority making their engagement crucial.

Chapter 14.
Federalism as the Architecture of Peace.

The Impasse That Demands a New Imagination.
Here is the uncomfortable truth that decades of diplomacy have failed to alter: the Israeli-Palestinian conflict remains unresolved not because solutions are unavailable, but because the available solutions have been relentlessly inadequate. The two-state framework, once hailed as the inevitable endpoint of peacemaking, has collided with realities on the ground—settlements, territorial fragmentation, the question of Jerusalem, the impossible geometries of contiguity—that have rendered it, if not theoretically dead, then practically moribund (Lustick, 2019; Shlaim, 2000).

Meanwhile, the one-state alternatives that occasionally surface in public discourse tend to inspire more anxiety than hope: a unitary state governed by one community at the expense of the other satisfies no one's legitimate aspirations and guarantees everyone's legitimate fears.

The status quo, in turn, satisfies only those who profit from perpetual crisis. Occupation continues. Violence recurs. Generations grow up knowing nothing but conflict. And the international community, oscillating between exhaustion and performative concern, has largely stopped expecting resolution.
This is the impasse. It is real, and it is paralyzing.

But what if the framework itself is the problem? What if the binary choice between "two states" and "one state" has obscured a third path—one with substantial theoretical grounding, extensive comparative precedent, and the institutional sophistication required to address this conflict's particular complexities?
That path is federalism.

This chapter argues that a carefully designed federal arrangement offers the most viable, equitable, and durable resolution to the Israeli-Palestinian conflict. This is not utopian speculation. Federalism has successfully managed profound ethno-national divisions across diverse global contexts, from the linguistic pluralism of Switzerland to the post-conflict reconstruction of Belgium. Its core innovation—what Daniel Elazar (1987) famously termed "self-rule plus shared rule"—provides constitutional architecture capable of accommodating competing national identities within shared governance structures. Applied to Israelis and Palestinians, such architecture could transform a zero-sum territorial contest into an institutional framework for coexistence, cooperation, and eventual reconciliation.

The argument that follows proceeds in five stages. First, it establishes the theoretical foundations of federalism as a conflict management mechanism, distinguishing it from the looser arrangements of confederalism that lack the institutional robustness required for deeply divided societies.

Second, it examines three comparative case studies—Switzerland, Belgium, and Canada—that illuminate how federal structures have addressed challenges analogous to those facing Israelis and Palestinians.

Third, and most substantially, it applies these insights to the Israeli-Palestinian context, detailing the security architecture, constitutional protections, economic integration, and resource management mechanisms that a federal state would require.

Fourth, it explores the regional implications of federal resolution, particularly regarding the Abraham Accords and the broader transformation of Middle Eastern geopolitics. Finally, it concludes with an assessment of feasibility—demonstrating that the barriers to federalism are political, not structural, and that the future of millions hinges upon the courage to pursue institutional innovation.

Federalism and Confederalism: Why the Distinction Matters
Before examining federalism's comparative track record, a conceptual clarification is necessary. Federalism and confederalism are often conflated in popular discourse, yet they represent fundamentally different governance architectures with divergent implications for conflict resolution (Forsyth, 1981; Watts, 1999).

Confederalism denotes a loose association of sovereign states wherein the central authority remains subordinate to member units. Constituent entities retain comprehensive autonomy and typically possess the constitutional right to withdraw—secession is not a crisis but a built-in feature (Riker, 1964). Central government powers are limited to specific delegated areas, usually defense coordination or trade agreements, and the confederation derives its authority from member states rather than from citizens directly.

This arrangement can appear attractive in divided societies where communities harbour profound mistrust of centralized authority. Why not maximize autonomy and minimize the risks of domination? The appeal is intuitive.

The problem is that confederalism's core feature—voluntarism backed by exit rights—simultaneously constitutes its greatest structural vulnerability. When constituent units can disregard or withdraw from central decisions at will, the capacity for unified action collapses precisely when it is most needed (Bednar, 2009). Cooperation becomes sporadic; enforcement becomes impossible; governance fragments into parallel spheres that foster separation rather than coexistence.

Historical confederations confirm this instability. The Swiss Confederation prior to 1848 was plagued by inter-cantonal conflicts until its transformation into a genuine federation. The United States under the Articles of Confederation (1781-1789) proved so dysfunctional that the Constitutional Convention was convened to replace it entirely. The short-lived United Arab Republic dissolved within three years (Forsyth, 1981). Confederalism, it turns out, is less a stable endpoint than a transitional arrangement awaiting either dissolution or federalization.

Federalism operates differently. In federal systems, sovereignty is genuinely shared between central governments and constituent units through constitutional compacts that neither level can unilaterally abrogate (Elazar, 1987). Constituent units exercise substantial autonomy—often over education, healthcare, cultural policy, and local governance—but they do not possess the ultimate sovereignty that characterizes confederal members. Federal governments derive authority directly from constitutions ratified by citizens, not merely delegated by states.

Crucially, federal systems incorporate mechanisms for resolving disputes between governmental levels: constitutional courts wielding judicial review authority, intergovernmental councils facilitating negotiation, and fiscal arrangements enabling redistribution (Shapiro & Stone Sweet, 2002). This institutional architecture provides what confederalism lacks—frameworks for managing inevitable tensions through law rather than exit threats, through negotiation rather than fragmentation.

For societies grappling with deep divisions, this distinction carries profound practical significance. Confederalism offers autonomy at the price of instability; federalism offers both autonomy and integration, self-governance and shared governance, identity preservation and collective security. The Israeli-Palestinian context, characterized by territorial intermixture, resource interdependence, and mutual security concerns that neither community can address unilaterally, requires the latter.

The Comparative Evidence: Three Federal Successes.
Skeptics might reasonably ask: does federalism actually work? The theoretical elegance of "self-rule plus shared rule" means little if federal arrangements routinely fail under the pressures of ethno-national conflict. What does the empirical record reveal?
The answer, examined across diverse global contexts, is encouraging. Federal systems have repeatedly demonstrated their capacity to manage profound societal cleavages—not by eliminating difference, but by institutionalizing mechanisms for its accommodation. Three cases merit particular attention for their relevance to Israeli-Palestinian dynamics: Switzerland, Belgium, and Canada.

Switzerland: The Paradigm of Linguistic Accommodation.
Switzerland's federal system has achieved something remarkable: the stable, democratic coexistence of German-speaking (63%), French-speaking (23%), Italian-speaking (8%), and Romansh-speaking (less than 1%) populations within a single polity (Kriesi & Trechsel, 2008). This multilingual society, surrounded by powerful nation-states that might easily have absorbed its linguistic minorities, has not merely survived but flourished. How?

The Swiss answer lies in radical decentralization. The 26 cantons retain extensive control over education, healthcare, taxation, and policing—the domains most intimately connected to cultural identity and daily life (Vatter, 2018). Federal competencies are largely confined to areas of demonstrable national importance: foreign policy, defence, monetary policy, and cross-cantonal infrastructure (Germann, 2000). This division ensures that linguistic communities govern themselves in matters closest to identity while participating as equals in matters requiring collective action.

The political culture reinforces these institutional arrangements. The "magic formula" (Zauberformel) guarantees representation for all major parties in the Federal Council, preventing any single group from monopolizing executive power (Neidhart, 1970). Direct democracy instruments—referendums and popular initiatives—provide additional channels for minority voice, ensuring that significant policy changes require broad consensus rather than bare majorities (Linder, 2010).

What makes Switzerland particularly instructive for the Israeli-Palestinian context is its demonstration that linguistic and cultural diversity need not be threats to national cohesion. The Swiss did not achieve stability by suppressing difference or demanding assimilation. They achieved it by constitutionalizing autonomy—by creating institutional spaces where distinct communities could flourish while remaining integrated within a larger political framework. The lesson is clear: federalism can transform diversity from a liability into an asset.

Belgium: Federalization as Conflict Transformation.
If Switzerland represents federalism's capacity to *maintain* stability in diverse societies, Belgium demonstrates its capacity to *create* stability in societies previously destabilized by communal conflict. The Belgian case is particularly instructive because federalization was not the country's original constitutional design but rather a direct institutional response to escalating tensions that threatened state dissolution (Deschouwer, 2012).

For decades, relations between Dutch-speaking Flemish and French-speaking Walloon populations generated recurring political crises. Linguistic boundaries hardened. Regional resentments intensified. Governments fell with alarming regularity. By the 1960s and 1970s, Belgium's survival as a unified state was genuinely uncertain (Alen & Ergec, 1998).

The response was deliberate, phased federalization. Constitutional reforms in 1970, 1980, 1988-89, 1993, 2001, and 2011-2014 progressively devolved powers to territorial regions (Flanders, Wallonia, and Brussels-Capital) and linguistic communities (Flemish, French, and German-speaking), each possessing their own parliaments, governments, and legislative competencies (Swenden & Jans, 2006). Education, culture, and economic development—the domains most salient to communal identity—were transferred to regional and community control. Federal authorities retained responsibility for defence, foreign affairs, social security, and macroeconomic policy.

The results, while imperfect, are significant. Belgium has not fragmented. The institutional mechanisms created through federalization—bicameral legislatures at multiple levels, "alarm bell" procedures protecting minority interests, inter-community consultation requirements—have channeled communal tensions into political processes rather than allowing them to escalate into existential crises (Deschouwer, 2006).

The Belgian experience demonstrates that federalism can serve as a conflict transformation mechanism, converting potentially explosive grievances into manageable, institutionalized political disputes.
This is directly relevant to Israeli-Palestinian dynamics. Like Belgium, the Israeli-Palestinian context involves two communities whose historical trajectories have generated profound mutual grievances and whose cultural-national identities appear, at first glance, irreconcilable. Belgium's federalization shows that even advanced societal cleavages can be addressed through constitutional engineering—not by eliminating difference, but by creating institutions that accommodate it.

Canada: Managing Secessionist Pressures Through Asymmetry.
Canada offers a third instructive variation: federalism's capacity to manage active secessionist movements through accommodation rather than suppression. The challenge of Québécois nationalism has tested Canadian federalism for over half a century, generating two sovereignty referenda (1980 and 1995), multiple constitutional crises, and ongoing debates about Quebec's place within Confederation (McRoberts, 1997; Gagnon & Tully, 2001).

The Canadian response has combined institutional flexibility with symbolic recognition. Following the Quiet Revolution's intensification of Québécois national consciousness in the 1960s, federal arrangements evolved to grant Quebec expanded autonomy in areas including immigration policy and cultural affairs (Gagnon & Iacovino, 2007).

The recognition of Quebec as a "distinct society"—though never formally entrenched through constitutional amendment—represented a crucial acknowledgment of francophone particularity within the Canadian federation (Russell, 1993). Ongoing negotiations over fiscal federalism, conducted through federal-provincial conferences and intergovernmental mechanisms, provide structured processes for addressing regional grievances (Lazar, 2008).

The 1995 referendum, in which sovereignty was rejected by the narrowest of margins (50.58% to 49.42%), demonstrated both the intensity of secessionist sentiment and the federal framework's capacity to absorb even existential challenges without violent rupture (Young, 1999). Separatism has since declined—not because Québécois identity has weakened, but because federal institutions have provided sufficient space for its expression within shared Canadian governance.

Two lessons emerge with particular clarity. First, asymmetric federalism—wherein different constituent units possess varying degrees of autonomy tailored to their specific circumstances—can effectively address nationalist movements that resist uniform constitutional treatment (McGarry, 2007; Tarlton, 1965). Second, the process of federal negotiation is itself valuable, transforming potentially destabilizing demands into matters for institutional mediation. Canada's experience suggests that federalism can manage even intense secessionist pressures when combined with political will to accommodate rather than suppress.

Applying Federalism to the Israeli-Palestinian Context.
The comparative evidence establishes that federalism can manage profound societal divisions. The question now becomes: how would federal principles apply to the specific complexities of the Israeli-Palestinian conflict?

This section addresses four essential domains: security architecture, constitutional protections for national identities, economic integration, and the governance of shared resources. Each domain presents challenges that have confounded traditional approaches; each, this analysis contends, becomes addressable through federal institutional design.

Security Architecture: From Competition to Collective Defence.
At the foundation of any viable Israeli-Palestinian arrangement lies the question of security. For Israelis, security concerns are existential—the small state's geographic vulnerability, the historical traumas of the Jewish people, the ongoing threats from regional actors create imperatives that no political arrangement can safely ignore (Posen, 1993). For Palestinians, decades of military

occupation have rendered security forces instruments of control rather than protection, generating profound mistrust of any arrangement that perpetuates asymmetric coercion (Selby, 2003).

Federalism offers a reconceptualization. Rather than treating Israeli and Palestinian security as a zero-sum competition wherein one community's safety diminishes the other's, federal architecture enables collective security—integrated defence structures in which both communities possess vested interests in comprehensive protection for all citizens (Saideman et al., 2002).

The institutional design would operate at two levels. Federal defence forces, comprising personnel from both communities operating under unified command and constitutional mandate, would maintain responsibility for external security, strategic deterrence, and coordination with regional partners (Hirschl, 2008). This integration extends beyond force amalgamation; it requires forging shared institutional commitment to security that transcends historical animosities.

Simultaneously, regional security components would address internal public order and community-specific needs. The Spanish model proves instructive here: the Mossos d'Esquadra in Catalonia and Ertzaintza in the Basque Country operate with substantial autonomy in routine policing while coordinating with national agencies on matters transcending regional jurisdiction (Guibernau, 2000). Applied to the Israeli-Palestinian context, regional forces would be recruited primarily from their respective communities, possessing the cultural competence and local networks essential for effective community policing, while operating under federal legal frameworks ensuring constitutional accountability (Goldstein, 1990).

This dual-layer architecture addresses the fundamental trust deficit that has plagued security discussions. Israeli concerns about inadequate Palestinian security capacity would be addressed through federal oversight and integrated intelligence sharing. Palestinian concerns about security forces as instruments of domination would be addressed through regional operational control and constitutional protections against federal overreach (Newman, 2002). The transformation is conceptual as much as institutional: security becomes a shared project rather than a contested domain.

Constitutional Protections: Preserving Distinct National Identities.

The Israeli-Palestinian conflict is, at its core, a clash of national narratives—competing claims to the same land, each backed by powerful historical memories and collective identities that adherents experience as non-negotiable (Khalidi, 1997; Galnoor, 1995). Any resolution that requires either community to abandon its national identity is not a resolution but a prescription for continued resistance.

Federal constitutional architecture addresses this challenge directly. By establishing distinct but constitutionally protected regional governments, federalism creates institutional spaces where each national community exercises substantial autonomy over internal affairs—the domains most intimately connected to identity preservation: education, cultural policy, religious practice, linguistic usage, and social priorities (Kymlicka, 1998).

The Israeli-Palestinian federal constitution would enshrine the rights of Jewish-majority regions to maintain policies reflecting Jewish national character, including educational curricula emphasizing Jewish history, holidays, and traditions; official recognition of Hebrew; and demographic policies designed to preserve Jewish majority status in designated territories (Gavison, 1999). Palestinian-majority regions would possess equivalent constitutional protections for Palestinian national identity—Arabic as official language, curricula reflecting Palestinian historical narratives, cultural and religious institutions serving Palestinian communities (Hassassian, 2002).

Critically, this symmetry in constitutional protection does not require identical policies. Asymmetric arrangements, successfully employed in Spain, Canada, and elsewhere, permit tailoring of specific powers to specific regional circumstances while maintaining overall constitutional equality (McGarry, 2007; Agranoff, 1999). What matters is that both communities possess constitutionally guaranteed spheres within which their distinctive identities can flourish—neither vulnerable to majoritarian override nor dependent upon the other community's forbearance.

At the federal level, institutional mechanisms would ensure that neither community could dominate collective decision-making. A bicameral legislature—with a lower house representing population proportionally and an upper house providing equal or weighted representation for constituent regions—would prevent majoritarian tyranny while enabling democratic governance (Stepan, 1999; Burgess, 2006). Consociational mechanisms—grand coalition governments, proportional representation in federal agencies, mutual veto rights on fundamental issues affecting communal interests—would further entrench power-sharing (Lijphart, 1977, 2008).

The federal judiciary, particularly a constitutional court with jurisdiction over federal-regional disputes, would serve as ultimate guardian against violations of the federal compact (Kommers & Miller, 2012). Neither community could unilaterally alter constitutional arrangements; neither could suppress the other's constitutionally protected rights. The result is institutional architecture that transforms governance from exclusion toward accommodation.

Jerusalem: A Federal Solution for an Impossible City.
No issue in the Israeli-Palestinian conflict carries more symbolic weight than Jerusalem. Both peoples claim it as their capital; both regard their connection to the city as non-negotiable; and partition proposals—dividing the city along demographic or geographic lines —have consistently failed to generate acceptance precisely because they require abandonment of claims that neither community will abandon (Friedland & Hecht, 1996; Dumper, 1997).

Federalism offers a conceptual breakthrough. Rather than asking which community "gets" Jerusalem—a question that has no answer acceptable to both—federal arrangements permit shared sovereignty. Jerusalem could serve as the federal capital, with designated zones or districts reflecting the interests of both communities while remaining under unified municipal governance for matters requiring coordination: infrastructure, sanitation, transportation, tourism management.
The Belgian Brussels model, while imperfect, demonstrates that contested cities can be governed through elaborate power-sharing arrangements. Brussels functions simultaneously as a region within the Belgian federation and as the capital shared by Flemish and Francophone communities, with institutional mechanisms ensuring representation for both groups in municipal governance (Deschouwer, 2012). The complexity is real—Brussels governance involves multiple overlapping jurisdictions and endless negotiations —but the alternative, violent contestation over sole ownership, is worse.

Applied to Jerusalem, federal arrangements might designate specific zones for regional administration (Jewish-majority neighbourhoods under Israeli regional authority, Palestinian-majority neighbourhoods under Palestinian regional authority) while establishing federal jurisdiction over the Old City, holy sites, and areas requiring unified management (Klein, 2003). Both communities would have their capital in Jerusalem; both would participate in its governance; neither would possess exclusive sovereignty. The symbolic claims would be honored through shared presence rather than denied through partition.

Economic Integration & Fiscal Federalism.
The economic dimension of Israeli-Palestinian federalism operates on two levels: the creation of integrated markets fostering shared prosperity, and the establishment of fiscal mechanisms ensuring equitable resource distribution (Wibbels, 2005; Arnon & Weinblatt, 2001).

Market integration would establish free movement of goods, services, capital, and labor across the federal territory—a unified economic space substantially larger and more dynamic than either community could achieve independently (Alesina & Spolaore, 2003). Federal regulatory frameworks would ensure fair competition and prevent regional protectionism. A common currency, managed by a federal monetary authority, would facilitate trade and provide macroeconomic stabilization. Federal infrastructure investment—transportation networks, energy grids, telecommunications—would physically integrate the territory while providing public goods benefiting all regions (Cai & Treisman, 2005).

The interdependence created by economic integration serves political purposes beyond efficiency. When prosperity depends upon maintaining open markets and coordinated policies, the costs of conflict or secession rise dramatically (Filippov et al., 2004; Hechter, 2000). Economic interests create constituencies for continued cooperation—business communities, workers in integrated industries, consumers benefiting from expanded markets—whose material stakes reinforce political commitments to federal unity.

Fiscal federalism addresses the challenge of economic disparity. Given existing inequalities between Israeli and Palestinian economic development, mechanisms for resource transfer from wealthier to less prosperous regions prove essential—both for ensuring minimum service standards across the federation and for preventing the emergence of economically marginalised regions vulnerable to radicalization (Boadway, 2004; Homer-Dixon, 1999).

The German Länderfinanzausgleich and Canadian equalization payments provide models: constitutionally mandated transfers that redistribute resources while preserving regional fiscal autonomy (Spahn & Föttinger, 1997; Watts, 2008). In the Israeli-Palestinian context, such mechanisms would support Palestinian regional development, infrastructure investment, and human capital formation, reducing grievances stemming from economic marginalization while creating material foundations for political stability. Simultaneously, all regions would contribute to and benefit from federal expenditures, fostering shared investment in federal success.

Water and Shared Resources: From Conflict to Cooperation
Perhaps nowhere is the inadequacy of partition more evident than in the management of shared natural resources, particularly water. The Mountain Aquifer, the Jordan River, and the coastal aquifer do not respect political boundaries; any arrangement that fragments sovereignty over these resources invites competitive exploitation and environmental degradation (Selby, 2003; Homer-Dixon, 1999).

Federalism enables integrated resource management. A federal environmental authority, with jurisdiction over water allocation, aquifer protection, and sustainable extraction standards, could develop comprehensive resource policies balancing the needs of all regions while preventing the tragedy-of-the-commons dynamics that fragmented sovereignty invites. Joint investment in desalination, wastewater treatment, and water efficiency technologies could expand overall supply rather than merely redistributing scarcity. Constitutional provisions could entrench minimum per-capita water allocations for all citizens, ensuring that resource management serves human needs rather than political competition.

The Murray-Darling Basin Authority in Australia and the various Rhine River commissions in Europe demonstrate that federal and quasi-federal arrangements can effectively govern transboundary resources (Teclaff, 1996). These arrangements require negotiation, compromise, and occasionally frustrating bureaucratic processes— but they prevent the resource conflicts that have destabilized regions worldwide and that would certainly afflict any fragmented Israeli-Palestinian territorial arrangement.

The Regional Dimension: Abraham Accords & Middle Eastern Transformation

The establishment of an Israeli-Palestinian federal state carries implications extending far beyond the borders of the federation itself. The Abraham Accords, wherein several Arab states established formal relations with Israel, represent a significant diplomatic breakthrough—but one that remains constrained by the unresolved Palestinian question (Podeh, 2021). Full regional normalization, particularly including major Arab League nations, hinges upon credible progress toward Palestinian self-determination.

A federal solution addresses this impediment directly. By providing a framework wherein Palestinian national aspirations are fulfilled through substantial regional autonomy, federalism removes the principal obstacle to comprehensive Arab-Israeli normalization (Lynch, 2020). Arab states, historically constrained by political necessity to condition Israeli relations upon Palestinian statehood, could embrace full normalization when federalism provides genuine Palestinian self-governance without requiring them to abandon solidarity with the Palestinian cause.

The geopolitical advantages would be transformative. A security architecture encompassing Israel, Palestine within a federal framework, and participating Arab states would possess unprecedented capacity for intelligence sharing, coordinated counter-terrorism, and collective defence against common threats (Byman, 2005). This cooperative security framework would replace historical patterns of competitive armament and proxy conflicts with institutional mechanisms for collective threat management (Barnett, 1998).

Economic integration would unlock immense potential currently constrained by regional fragmentation (Cobham & Kanafani, 2004). Joint ventures in renewable energy could harness the region's abundant solar resources. Water desalination partnerships could address the scarcity that threatens long-term sustainability. Israel's advanced technology sector, Palestinian entrepreneurial capacity, and Gulf economies could converge to create an innovation hub rivaling those of East Asia (Senor & Singer, 2009). These economic dividends—improved living standards, expanded opportunities, reduced unemployment—would generate constituencies with material stakes in continued peace, reinforcing political commitments through tangible prosperity.

Most fundamentally, federal resolution would reconfigure political discourse across the Middle East. The Israeli-Palestinian conflict has long served as a focal point for regional identity politics, with regimes instrumentalizing Palestinian suffering for domestic legitimation (Lynch, 2006).

Resolution through federalism would remove this instrument of manipulation, compelling governments to address governance challenges directly. The demonstration effect of successful democratic federal governance in a deeply divided society would offer lessons applicable across the region's diverse contexts.

Feasibility: The Question of Political Will
The argument thus far has established that federalism offers a theoretically coherent and empirically grounded approach to Israeli-Palestinian conflict resolution. The question that inevitably arises is whether such arrangements are practically achievable. What are the barriers to implementation, and can they be overcome?

The honest answer is that the barriers are substantial—but they are political, not structural. The comparative evidence demonstrates that federal arrangements have been negotiated and implemented in contexts of profound division, including post-conflict societies, secessionist crises, and communities with extensive histories of mutual violence (Watts, 2008; Lijphart, 2008). If Flemish and Walloons could federalize Belgium, if Swiss cantons that once fought civil wars could constitute a stable federation, if Canadian federalism could survive two sovereignty referenda in Quebec, then the structural possibility of Israeli-Palestinian federalism is not the question.

The question is political will.
This is not a trivial matter. Political leaders on both sides have invested decades in narratives of exclusive sovereignty—narratives that generate domestic political capital but foreclose institutional innovation. Publics on both sides have been socialized into zero-sum frameworks that render power-sharing appear as capitulation rather than pragmatic accommodation. Extremist minorities on both sides actively benefit from continued conflict and would resist any resolution that eliminates their raison d'être.

Yet political will is not immutable. Leaders can reframe narratives. Publics can be persuaded by evidence of alternatives. Civil society organizations, business communities, and security establishments can develop vested interests in peace that counterbalance spoiler dynamics. International actors—diplomatic, financial, and potentially through peacekeeping mechanisms—can create incentives for negotiation and disincentives for obstruction (Doyle & Sambanis, 2006; Kriesberg, 1998).

The key insight is this: federalism does not require either community to abandon its core aspirations. Israelis need not sacrifice security or Jewish national expression; Palestinians need not accept permanent subordination or identity denial. Federalism offers a framework wherein both communities can achieve their essential objectives through institutional innovation rather than military victory. When framed correctly, the federal option is not a compromise in the pejorative sense—a reluctant acceptance of less than one's due—but a recognition that shared governance serves both peoples' interests better than continued conflict.

The feasibility of federalism is, ultimately, the feasibility of persuasion—of convincing enough people on both sides that a different future is possible and that the institutions exist to achieve it. That is a political challenge, not a technical impossibility.

The Architecture of a Shared Future.
The analysis presented in this chapter converges on a clear conclusion: federalism represents the most viable, equitable, and sustainable pathway toward lasting peace between Israelis and Palestinians. The theoretical foundations of federal governance, the empirical evidence from comparative cases, and the specific application to this conflict's unique dynamics all support this conclusion with compelling force.

Federalism's core innovation—the constitutional division of sovereignty between central and regional governments—directly addresses the conflict's fundamental challenge: two peoples, each with legitimate national aspirations, sharing a single territorial space. Federal architecture provides institutional mechanisms for preserving distinct national identities while creating shared governance structures for collective security, economic integration, and resource management. It transforms the zero-sum logic of exclusive sovereignty into the positive-sum dynamics of constitutional power-sharing.

The comparative record demonstrates that this transformation is achievable. Switzerland's management of linguistic pluralism, Belgium's federalization in response to escalating communal tensions, Canada's accommodation of Québécois nationalism through asymmetric arrangements—these cases confirm that federal institutions can manage profound societal divisions when designed thoughtfully and implemented with political commitment. The barriers are significant but not insurmountable; they are matters of political will rather than structural impossibility.

The regional implications amplify the stakes. Federal resolution of the Israeli-Palestinian conflict would enable comprehensive Middle Eastern normalization through the Abraham Accords' expansion, creating a cooperative security architecture, unlocking economic integration, and transforming regional political dynamics. The benefits extend far beyond the immediate parties to encompass millions throughout the region whose futures are shaped by this conflict's resolution or perpetuation.

The alternative to federal transformation is painfully familiar: continued occupation, periodic violence, demographic anxieties, international isolation, and the slow corrosion of hope on both sides. Neither Israelis nor Palestinians can achieve their fundamental aspirations through continued conflict. Unilateral measures—annexation or unilateral statehood declarations—offer no sustainable resolution. The two-state framework confronts obstacles that may be insurmountable. The status quo serves no one's long-term interests.

Federalism offers a different future—one where security is achieved through integration rather than separation, where national identities are protected through constitutional guarantees rather than territorial exclusion, where economic prosperity flows from cooperation rather than competition, and where the next generation inherits institutions of coexistence rather than legacies of conflict.

The question is whether the political imagination exists to pursue it. The theoretical and empirical foundations are established. The institutional designs are available. The comparative precedents demonstrate feasibility. What remains is the decision—by leaders, by publics, by the international community—to choose a different path.

The future of millions depends upon that choice.

Chapter 14
Addendum

Key Concepts.
Essential Terms from the Entire Book.
Federalism: Constitutional system dividing sovereignty between central government and constituent units, enabling "self-rule plus shared rule" (Elazar, 1987). Both levels possess constitutionally protected powers neither can unilaterally abrogate. Addresses Israeli-Palestinian conflict by allowing both communities substantial autonomy while maintaining unified governance for collective challenges.

Confederalism: Loose association of sovereign states where central authority remains subordinate to member units retaining secession rights. Differs from federalism in lacking enforcement mechanisms and constitutional permanence. Historical confederations (Swiss pre-1848, U.S. Articles of Confederation) proved unstable, typically transitioning to federalism or dissolution.

Asymmetric Federalism: System where different constituent units possess varying degrees of autonomy tailored to specific circumstances (Tarlton, 1965). Canada grants Quebec expanded powers; Spain's autonomous communities have differentiated authorities. Enables accommodation of distinct national communities without requiring identical arrangements.

Consociationalism: Power-sharing system for deeply divided societies featuring grand coalition governments, proportional representation, mutual veto rights, and community autonomy (Lijphart, 1977). Complements federal structures by ensuring no community dominates federal-level decision-making.

Security Dilemma: Situation where one community's measures to enhance security threaten another community's security, triggering competitive armament spirals (Herz, 1950). Federal integrated security structures address this by making security collective rather than competitive.

Zero-Sum vs. Positive-Sum: Zero-sum frameworks assume one party's gain equals another's loss; positive-sum recognizes opportunities where all benefit simultaneously. Federal economic integration, security cooperation, and resource management transform Israeli-Palestinian relations from zero-sum competition to positive-sum cooperation.

Constitutional Court: Judicial body with authority to adjudicate disputes between governmental levels and protect constitutional rights. Essential federal institution preventing majoritarian tyranny and ensuring neither community violates federal compact. Examples: German Constitutional Court, U.S. Supreme Court, Canadian Supreme Court.

Fiscal Federalism: System of revenue generation, expenditure responsibilities, and intergovernmental transfers (Oates, 1999). Addresses economic disparities through mechanisms like German equalization payments and Canadian fiscal transfers, ensuring minimum service standards across federation while preserving regional autonomy.

Regional Integration: Process by which neighboring countries develop economic, political, and social connections. Israeli-Palestinian federal resolution would enable comprehensive Middle Eastern integration, unlocking cooperative security, economic blocs, and transforming regional geopolitics.

Abraham Accords: 2020 normalization agreements between Israel and UAE, Bahrain, Morocco, Sudan. Represent significant diplomatic breakthrough but remain constrained by unresolved Palestinian question. Federal resolution would enable comprehensive Arab-Israeli normalization including Saudi Arabia.

Rentier State: Political economy concept where governments funded primarily by external rents (oil revenues) rather than taxation develop different relationships with citizens (Beblawi & Luciani, 1987). Relevant to understanding Gulf states' interests in regional stability and diversification strategies like Saudi Vision 2030.

Master Frame: Organizing narrative shaping how actors understand wide range of political questions (Snow & Benford, 1988). Israeli-Palestinian conflict has functioned as master frame organizing Middle Eastern politics; federal resolution would remove this constraint on regional cooperation.

Zone of Peace: Geographic area where war between members becomes unthinkable due to institutional integration, economic interdependence, democratic norms (Deutsch, 1957). EU represents most developed zone. Federal Israel could anchor Middle Eastern zone of peace.

Epistemic Communities: Networks of experts sharing analytical frameworks and policy orientations, capable of influencing policy across boundaries (Haas, 1992). Joint Israeli-Palestinian research institutions, universities, professional associations would build epistemic communities supporting federal cooperation.

The Citizen Relevance: Your Role in Peace.
You Are Not a Bystander
The Israeli-Palestinian conflict can feel overwhelming, distant, intractable—something happening "over there" that individuals cannot affect. This perception, however natural, is incorrect. Public opinion shapes policy decisions. Democratic governments, even in complex foreign policy domains, remain responsive to sustained citizen engagement. Authoritarian regimes, despite appearances, monitor and respond to shifting public sentiment. International pressure, when persistent and coordinated, alters calculations. You —reading these words—possess more influence than you imagine.
What You Can Actually Do.
Educate Yourself and Others: The conflict thrives on simplification, tribal narratives, and mutual dehumanization. Counter this by engaging complexity. Read multiple perspectives. Challenge your own assumptions. When discussing the conflict with friends, family, colleagues, introduce nuance. Share this book. Recommend comparative federal case studies. Explain how Switzerland, Belgium, and Canada manage deep divisions. Complexity is not fence-sitting; it's intellectual honesty.
Contact Representatives: Elected officials track constituent communications. Write, call, email your representatives expressing support for federal approaches to Israeli-Palestinian resolution. Reference specific policy proposals: diplomatic support for federal negotiations, conditioning aid on movement toward inclusive governance, funding civil society bridge-building. Be specific, be persistent, be informed. Individual letters matter less than sustained campaigns, so coordinate with like-minded citizens.
Support Civil Society Organizations: Numerous Israeli, Palestinian, and international organizations work toward coexistence—joint Israeli-Palestinian peace groups, human rights organizations, economic development initiatives, educational exchange programs, interfaith dialogue efforts. These organizations need funding, volunteers, visibility, and political protection. Donate. Volunteer time or expertise. Amplify their work on social media. Attend their events. Civil society creates the social infrastructure that political agreements ultimately require.
Use Economic Leverage Thoughtfully: Consumer choices possess political implications. Support businesses practicing ethical supply chains. Pressure companies operating in ways that entrench occupation or fuel conflict. Divest from firms profiting from human rights violations. Economic incentives, when coordinated and sustained, shift corporate and governmental behavior. BDS (Boycott, Divestment, Sanctions) movements remain controversial,

but the underlying principle—economic pressure as political tool—is legitimate when targeted appropriately and pursuing constructive resolution rather than delegitimization.

Engage Media and Social Platforms: Media coverage shapes public discourse. When outlets present oversimplified or biased narratives, write letters to editors, post thoughtful comments, create content offering alternative perspectives. Social media amplifies voices; use yours responsibly. Share factual information. Challenge disinformation. Engage respectfully with those holding different views—genuine dialogue converts more minds than performative outrage. Algorithms reward engagement; thoughtful substantive content can reach audiences.

Model Constructive Engagement: Perhaps most importantly, demonstrate that Israeli-Palestinian peace is not about "taking sides" but about supporting both peoples' legitimate aspirations. Refuse tribal dynamics that demand choosing one community's welfare over another's. Articulate how federal arrangements serve both Israeli security and Palestinian self-determination. Show that supporting Jewish national expression and Palestinian national expression are compatible, not contradictory. Personal example influences social norms; be the example.

Public Opinion Shapes Policy.

History demonstrates that sustained shifts in public opinion eventually translate into policy change. The U.S. civil rights movement, South African apartheid's ending, marriage equality's global advance—all emerged from grassroots organizing that shifted public consciousness before shifting governmental policy. Israeli and Palestinian civil societies contain voices advocating coexistence despite political cultures dominated by conflict narratives. International publics, particularly in democracies providing diplomatic and financial support to parties in the conflict, possess leverage. When enough people demand different approaches, governments respond.

The question is whether you will be part of that shift. Reading this book represents engagement; what matters is what comes next. Peace requires not merely intellectual assent that alternatives exist but active commitment to pursuing them. You are part of this story —the only question is what role you will play.

A Call to Scholars and Experts.
An Invitation to Critique, Refine, and Improve.

This book advances a specific argument: that federalism offers the most viable pathway to lasting Israeli-Palestinian peace. The argument draws on comparative political science, constitutional law, security studies, economics, and Middle East scholarship. It engages existing literature critically, applies theoretical frameworks systematically, and grounds claims in evidence. Yet no scholarly work, however comprehensive, represents the final word on any complex question.

To the academic community—political scientists, international relations scholars, legal theorists, Middle East specialists, economists, sociologists, historians—I extend this invitation: engage this argument seriously. Critique where critique is warranted. Identify theoretical weaknesses, empirical oversights, logical gaps, alternative explanations. Propose refinements to institutional designs. Challenge assumptions. Test propositions against evidence I have not considered. This is how scholarship advances—through sustained intellectual exchange, not defensive orthodoxy.

Specific Research Agendas

Several research domains merit particular attention:

Comparative Federal Analysis: While this book examines Switzerland, Belgium, and Canada, dozens of federal and quasi-federal systems exist globally—Germany, Australia, Austria, Spain, India, Nigeria, Ethiopia, others. Systematic comparative analysis identifying which federal design features best manage which types of societal cleavage would strengthen the theoretical foundation. What explains federal success in some contexts and failure in others? Under what conditions does asymmetric federalism stabilize versus destabilize? How do different constitutional court structures affect intergovernmental disputes?

Israeli-Palestinian Public Opinion Research: Reliable survey data on federal arrangements remains limited. Methodologically rigorous polling exploring Israeli and Palestinian attitudes toward specific federal proposals—security integration, constitutional protections, Jerusalem governance, economic arrangements—would clarify political feasibility. Do attitudes vary by age, education, religiosity, exposure to the other community? What framing increases receptivity? Which constituencies constitute potential early adopters?

Economic Modeling: The book presents general arguments about economic integration's benefits but lacks detailed econometric modeling. What would Israeli-Palestinian GDP growth trajectories look like under different scenarios—continued conflict, two-state solution, federal integration, regional economic bloc formation? What would employment effects be? How would income distribution evolve? What fiscal transfer mechanisms would optimally balance redistribution and incentives? Rigorous economic analysis would quantify claims currently presented qualitatively.

Security Architecture Specifications: The proposed federal security system—integrated defense forces with regional policing components—requires detailed institutional design. What command structures? What recruitment and training protocols? What constitutional constraints on force deployment? What mechanisms for civilian oversight? What intelligence sharing frameworks? What border security arrangements? Security experts could contribute invaluable specificity beyond this book's conceptual framework.

Legal and Constitutional Analysis: Constitutional scholars could examine draft federal constitutions—specifying governmental powers, rights protections, amendment procedures, dispute resolution mechanisms. What would federal election systems look like? What citizenship rules? What property rights frameworks? What religious freedom protections balancing communal autonomy with individual rights? Legal analysis would translate political principles into enforceable constitutional provisions.

Historical and Archival Research: Historians could examine prior Israeli-Palestinian negotiations to identify where federal approaches were considered and why they were abandoned. Were alternatives genuinely explored or dismissed prematurely? What role did external actors (U.S., EU, Arab states) play in foreclosing or encouraging federal discussions? Historical context illuminates contemporary possibilities.

Regional Implications Modeling: How would Israeli-Palestinian federal resolution affect Iranian strategy, Saudi calculations, Egyptian policy, Jordanian stability, Lebanese politics? Regional security scholars could analyze second-order effects that extend beyond bilateral Israeli-Palestinian relations.

How Academia Can Contribute

Universities and research institutes can support federal scholarship through:

Conferences and Workshops: Convening Israeli, Palestinian, and international scholars to debate federal proposals in venues emphasizing intellectual exchange over political posturing.

Joint Research Projects: Israeli and Palestinian academics collaborating on studies examining attitudes, designing institutions, modeling economic effects, analyzing comparative cases.

Curriculum Development: Incorporating federal alternatives into conflict resolution courses, Middle East studies programs, constitutional law seminars, comparative politics curricula.

Policy Engagement: Translating academic research into policy briefs, op-eds, testimony before legislative bodies, consultation with diplomatic corps and civil society organizations.

Academia possesses unique capacity for sustained, rigorous, non-partisan analysis. This book represents one scholar's contribution; imagine what collective scholarly engagement could produce. The question is whether academic communities will engage seriously or remain trapped in ossified debates reproducing rather than transcending political gridlock.

For Educators: Teaching This Material.

Why Teach Israeli-Palestinian Federalism

The Israeli-Palestinian conflict offers extraordinary pedagogical opportunities. It combines historical complexity, normative challenges, practical policy questions, and emotional intensity, engaging students across disciplines—political science, international relations, history, religious studies, law, economics, ethics. Federal approaches add comparative dimension, connecting Middle Eastern specifics to broader questions about managing diversity, constitutional design, and conflict resolution globally.

Curriculum Integration Suggestions

Conflict Resolution Courses: This material fits naturally into courses examining alternative dispute resolution mechanisms. Compare negotiation-based approaches (Oslo process), imposed settlements (international trusteeships), partition (two-state solution), and federal power-sharing. Assign comparative case studies (Switzerland, Belgium, Canada, Cyprus, Northern Ireland) alongside this book's Israeli-Palestinian application. Discussion question: Under what conditions does each approach succeed or fail?

Comparative Politics: Use Israeli-Palestinian federalism to examine broader questions about federal design. How do different federal systems balance central authority and regional autonomy? What explains variation in asymmetric arrangements? What role do constitutional courts play? Assign Lijphart (2008) on consociationalism, Stepan (1999) on federalism and democracy, and Elazar (1987) on federal theory alongside this book.

Middle East Studies: Situate federal proposals within broader regional context. How does Israeli-Palestinian conflict shape Middle Eastern geopolitics? What role do external actors play? How might resolution affect Iranian, Saudi, Egyptian, and Turkish regional strategies? How do Abraham Accords relate to federal possibilities? Readings: Lynch (2006) on Arab public opinion, Gause (2014) on regional cold war, Podeh (2021) on normalization dynamics.

Constitutional Law: Examine constitutional mechanisms for protecting minority rights, managing religious-secular tensions, and dividing governmental powers. Compare Israeli Basic Laws, Palestinian Basic Law draft, Swiss constitutional arrangements, Belgian federalization process, Canadian Charter of Rights. Assignment: Draft constitutional provisions addressing specific Israeli-Palestinian challenges—Jerusalem governance, refugee return, water rights, religious freedom.

Political Economy: Analyze economic dimensions—fiscal federalism, market integration, development policy. How do equalization payments work? What are economic effects of political integration? Compare EU single market, U.S. interstate commerce clause, Canadian internal trade barriers. Discussion: Would economic integration foster political cooperation or simply enable more efficient resource exploitation?

Ethics and Political Philosophy: Engage normative questions. Do Israelis and Palestinians have "right to self-determination" that precludes shared sovereignty? Can historical injustices be addressed through institutional design? What obligations do current generations bear for past actions? How do we balance collective rights (national self-determination) with individual rights (freedom of movement, property, religion)? Readings: Kymlicka (1995) on multicultural citizenship, Miller (2016) on national responsibility, Walzer (1983) on just and unjust wars.

Discussion Questions by Chapter

Chapter 1 (Historical Overview): How do competing historical narratives affect current possibilities? Can both communities' stories be simultaneously valid? What responsibility does historical understanding create?

Chapter 2 (Why Two States Failed): Were obstacles to two states insurmountable or did failures reflect inadequate political will? Could two states still work if pursued differently?

Chapter 3 (Federal Theory): What makes federalism different from partition or unitary states? Why does "self-rule plus shared rule" matter?

Chapter 8 (Economic Integration): Does economic interdependence foster political cooperation or simply create new forms of exploitation? What role should international actors play in supporting Palestinian economic development?

Chapter 13 (Regional Implications): How would Israeli-Palestinian resolution affect regional actors? Would Iranian, Saudi, Egyptian policies shift? Would Abraham Accords expand?

Chapter 14 (Synthesis): Having examined federal arguments comprehensively, are you convinced? What are strongest arguments for and against? What would you modify?

Further Resources

Primary Sources: Israeli Declaration of Independence, Palestinian Declaration of Independence, Oslo Accords, Geneva Initiative, Arab Peace Initiative, Abraham Accords.

Comparative Federal Studies: Watts (2008) *Comparing Federal Systems*; Burgess (2006) *Comparative Federalism*; Filippov et al. (2004) *Designing Federalism*.

Israeli-Palestinian Conflict: Shlaim (2000) *The Iron Wall*; Khalidi (1997) *Palestinian Identity*; Morris (2001) *Righteous Victims*; Tessler (2009) *A History of the Israeli-Palestinian Conflict*.

Conflict Resolution Theory: Kriesberg (1998) *Constructive Conflicts*; Bar-Tal (2013) *Intractable Conflicts*; Lederach (1997) *Building Peace*.

Teaching this material well requires acknowledging its controversial nature while maintaining academic rigor. Create space for genuine disagreement. Protect students from all communities who may find certain perspectives challenging or offensive. Emphasize evidence-based analysis over emotional reaction. The goal is not indoctrination into federal support but cultivation of sophisticated analytical capacity for understanding complex conflicts and evaluating alternative resolutions.

Final Reflection for All Readers.
The Weight of What We Carry.

If you have read this far, you have engaged thousands of words examining constitutional structures, comparative cases, economic models, security architectures, and regional implications. You have considered Swiss cantons, Belgian federalization, Canadian asymmetry, fiscal transfers, water management, and Abraham Accords dynamics. This engagement matters—it represents intellectual labor few undertake on conflicts they do not personally experience.

But beyond the institutional analysis, beyond the comparative evidence, beyond the policy prescriptions, lies something more fundamental: human lives shaped by our collective failure to resolve this conflict. Israeli children growing up under rocket threat, serving mandatory military service, taught to view neighbors with suspicion. Palestinian children growing up under occupation, passing checkpoints, watching violence, taught that their oppressors will never change. Parents on both sides fearing for their children's futures. Communities on both sides burying dead who should be alive.

This is not abstract. This is visceral, immediate, devastating reality for millions.

Acknowledging the Stakes.

Every year this conflict continues, costs accumulate. Lives lost. Families destroyed. Resources devoted to armament rather than education. Opportunities for prosperity foregone. Young people choosing emigration over staying in homelands their families have inhabited for generations. Hope corroding into cynicism. Possibility shrinking into despair.

These costs are distributed unequally—occupation burdens Palestinians more heavily than it burdens Israelis, asymmetric power creates asymmetric suffering—but both communities pay. Israeli society militarized, international legitimacy eroding, demographic anxieties intensifying, political discourse dominated by security fears that preclude normal governance debates. Palestinian society fragmented, economically stunted, politically divided, subject to violence and control that degrade human dignity. Neither community achieves its fundamental aspirations through continued conflict. Israelis do not achieve lasting security through permanent military dominance. Palestinians do not achieve national liberation through resistance alone. The status quo serves neither people's long-term interests.

An Appeal to Open-Mindedness

What I ask—what this entire book asks—is that you consider seriously whether alternatives exist. Not "side" alternatives that favor one community's interests over the other's, but genuine alternatives addressing both peoples' legitimate needs. Federal arrangements may not be perfect—no human institutions are perfect—but they offer something current frameworks do not: constitutional architecture enabling both Israeli security and Jewish national expression alongside Palestinian self-determination and national dignity.

This requires relinquishing familiar narratives. For some readers sympathetic to Israel, it means acknowledging that permanent occupation is morally indefensible and strategically unsustainable, that Palestinian national aspirations deserve institutional expression, that security achieved through domination is inherently unstable. For readers sympathetic to Palestinians, it means acknowledging Israeli security fears as genuine rather than pretextual, that Jewish national expression possesses legitimacy, that cooperation might serve Palestinian interests better than continued resistance. For all readers, it means recognizing that the other community is not going anywhere—that resolution requires accommodation, not victory.

This is difficult. Tribal instincts, historical grievances, personal experiences, political socialization—all pull toward "sides" rather than toward shared futures. Admitting complexity feels like betrayal of those suffering. Suggesting compromise appears to dishonor those who died. The emotional and psychological barriers to changing frameworks are formidable.

Yet the alternative—continued conflict, accumulating suffering, foreclosed futures—is worse. And the evidence, examined honestly, suggests that federal approaches work. They have worked in Switzerland for centuries. They converted Belgian communal warfare into institutional negotiation. They enabled Canadian accommodation of Québécois nationalism. They could work in Israel-Palestine if political will exists to pursue them.

Bridge to Closing Words.

This chapter has synthesized the book's substantive arguments: theoretical foundations, comparative evidence, institutional designs, implementation pathways, regional implications. The evidence supports federalism's viability. The question is whether sufficient people—Israelis, Palestinians, international actors, you—will choose to pursue it.

The Closing Words that follow shift from intellectual analysis to emotional appeal, from policy prescription to moral urgency. But before transitioning to that different register, let this final reflection acknowledge what you—each reader—has invested by engaging this material seriously.

You have chosen to consider complexity in domain where simplification dominates. You have examined institutional alternatives when most people simply choose sides. You have engaged comparative evidence when tribal instincts resist cross-contextual learning. You have entertained the possibility that both communities possess legitimate claims when zero-sum frameworks demand choosing one over the other.

This intellectual openness—this willingness to engage difficult questions without predetermined answers—is precisely what the path from conflict to coexistence requires. Not naivety, not wishful thinking, but clear-eyed assessment of what works, informed by evidence, committed to both peoples' welfare.

Whatever conclusions you have reached—whether you are convinced by federal arguments or remain skeptical, whether you see implementation as feasible or implausible—the engagement itself matters. Thoughtful citizens capable of nuanced analysis create the political space that breakthrough negotiations require. You are part of that process, whether you recognize it or not.

The question now is what you will do with this knowledge. The Closing Words will address that question more directly. But here, at the conclusion of the book's substantive analysis, simply acknowledge that you have undertaken something important: serious engagement with one of the world's most intractable conflicts, animated by belief that alternatives exist and that human ingenuity can design institutions enabling coexistence.

That belief—that hope, informed by evidence and grounded in reality—is what this entire project pursues. Thank you for considering it seriously.

Chapter 15
Ad Mosaicam Pacem Per Espera*
A Letter to Jews & Arabs Youth

"We are not enemies, but friends. We must not be enemies."
— Abraham Lincoln

Prologue: October 7th's Endless Echo.
Dawn arrived as it always does in the south of Israel—golden, unhurried, promising nothing but the ordinary miracle of another day. Then the sky tore open. Sirens became screams. Paradise became purgatory. Twelve hundred souls—mothers clutching infants, grandparents who had survived histories they thought could never repeat, young people dancing at the edge of the desert— were stolen from this world in acts of savagery that echo through every corridor of the human conscience.

The massacre of October 7th, 2023, was not merely an attack. It was an earthquake that has not stopped trembling. It was a wound that has not stopped bleeding. And now, scrolling through your phone, you—young Israeli, young Palestinian, young Arab Israeli, young diaspora dreamer—are asked to make sense of the senseless, to find a path through grief so thick it obscures the horizon itself.

Consider the numbers, not as statistics, but as portraits: Gaza's median age is eighteen—*eighteen*—children of rubble who have never known a single year without blockade, without the shadow of warplanes overhead. The West Bank's youth, median age twenty-one, navigate checkpoints like obstacle courses designed to erode the soul. In Israel, thirty percent of the population is under eighteen, and these young people now carry a burden their grandparents had hoped would never return: the knowledge that evil can materialize on a Saturday morning, that hate can breach any wall.

TikTok Visual: Split-screen Reel—left frame: festival lights fade to black as music cuts to silence; right frame: first light breaks over a mosaic skyline, fragments becoming whole. Caption: 'Your scroll is a veil. War claims real lives. Real futures. Yours.'

This chapter is not a political treatise. It is a lantern held up in the darkness. It is a hand extended across the impossible distance of grief. It is an invitation—no, an insistence—that you, in the full power of your youth, can choose to become the generation that breaks the cycle. Not by forgetting what happened. Not by minimizing the horror. But by understanding that the only alternative to an eternal present of violence is the hard, sacred work of building something new.

The blood rivers are real. The shared skies above them are equally real. The question before you is simply this: which reality will you choose to build?

I. Revenge: The Illusion That Devours.
To Young Israelis.

I will not ask you to suppress your fury. Fury, after what was done, is not merely understandable—it is human. When terrorists crossed a border to murder civilians in their homes, to kidnap grandmothers and babies, to desecrate the most basic human bonds of safety and trust, they awakened something primal in the Israeli soul. The fury you feel is not weakness. It is the cry of a people who have said *"Never again"* and meant it with every fiber of their being.

But listen closely: fury is fuel, and fuel can either propel a rocket toward the stars or burn the house down. Revenge—sweet, seductive, seemingly righteous revenge—is grief wearing a mask. It tells you that if you can only make *them* suffer as *you* have suffered, somehow the scales will balance. Somehow the dead will rest easier. Somehow the nightmare will end.
It is a lie.

History—Jewish history especially—teaches that revenge creates nothing but more enemies. Every act of vengeance becomes the founding myth of the next generation's grievance. Every bomb dropped in fury sows the seeds of the bomber who will rise twenty years hence. Your children, and your children's children, will inherit not justice but an endless chain of retribution, rifles passed down like heirlooms of despair.

The Talmud asks: *"Who is mighty? One who conquers their impulse."* Your might, young Israeli, will not be measured by how much destruction you can rain upon those who have wronged you. It will be measured by your capacity to hold the full weight of your grief and still choose to build rather than to burn.

To Young Palestinians.
I see you. I see the rubble that was once your classroom. I see the empty chair where your cousin used to sit. I see the rage that

ignites when the world seems to weigh your blood lighter than others, when your suffering is footnoted while others' is headlined. Your fury, too, is human. Your desire for justice—real justice, not charity, not pity—is righteous.

But vengeance has been offered to your people as a solution for seventy-five years, and what has it built? The organizations that promised liberation through violence have delivered instead an endless present of checkpoints and blockades, of futures deferred and horizons shrinking. Every rocket fired in rage has brought not freedom but further walls, further surveillance, further grounds for those who would deny you sovereignty to point to you and say: *"See? They cannot govern themselves."*

The fire of vengeance scorches your own horizon first. It consumes Palestinian potential before it ever reaches Israeli soil. It trades your birthright—the birthright of a proud, creative, resilient people—for barren echoes of victories that never come.

You deserve more than to be recruited into someone else's apocalyptic fantasy. You deserve schools that stay standing. You deserve airports and ports and trade routes. You deserve to be known for your technology, your literature, your contributions to human flourishing—not only for your suffering.

Epiphany Frame: Revenge is grief's cruelest mirage—a shadow boxing itself in an endless mirror hall. Humans do not truly crave cycles of sorrow; they crave life, creation, legacy, love. Release the mirage. Envision shared tomorrows. - Meme Quote: "Revenge: A shadow boxing itself "

II. Radicalism's Hollow Abyss.
Let us speak plainly about what radicalism promises and what it actually delivers.

Hamas's charter, in its original form, called not merely for resistance but for the elimination of the Jewish state—for genocide dressed in revolutionary language. This is not liberation theology; it is a siren's lie sung to young people desperate for hope. And here is the truth that the leaders of such movements will never tell you, that they *cannot* tell you, because it would expose the bankruptcy of their entire project:

Israel is not going anywhere.
Some ten million Jews live between the river and the sea. Their roots extend three thousand years into that soil. Their resolve has been forged in the furnace of millennia—pogroms, expulsions, extermination camps, and now this. They have built a nation with world-class universities, a thriving economy, a military that ranks

among the most capable on Earth. They are not colonizers who will pack up and return to some motherland; for most, *there is no other motherland*. They will not be driven into the sea. They will not be terrorized into surrender. Any ideology premised on their disappearance is building castles on clouds.

So what does radicalism actually achieve? It achieves the death of Palestinian youth recruited into tunnels and trained for martyrdom. It achieves the destruction of infrastructure that could have housed businesses and hospitals. It achieves the confirmation, in Israeli minds, of every fear that justifies further security measures, further walls, further separation. It achieves *nothing* that brings Palestinian children closer to dignified, free, flourishing lives.

And on the Israeli side, religious and nationalist radicalism offers its own hollow promises. The dream of Greater Israel, of divine mandate requiring the displacement or permanent subjugation of millions of Palestinians, is equally a siren song. It promises security through dominance, but dominance over a resentful population has never produced lasting security in all of human history. It produces only garrison states, only the slow corrosion of democratic values, only the moral injury of asking eighteen-year-olds to become enforcers of someone else's messianic vision.

Visual: A rocket trail arcing into the sky, then fading... into endless tunnel darkness. The screen holds on black. Text appears: 'What was built?'

War's psychology wounds everyone. The Israeli child who spent hours in a bomb shelter develops anxiety that may never fully heal. The Palestinian child who watched their home reduced to rubble carries trauma that no therapy can easily reach. The paranoia etched into young faces—the hypervigilance, the nightmares, the inability to imagine a future—these are not side effects of the conflict. *They are the conflict*. They are what radicalism actually produces: not victory, but universal psychological siege.

There are no victors in shared suffering—only the radical leaders who stay safely distant from the bombs they summon, and the young people of both nations who pay the price of their ideological vanity.

Maximalism: Chains of Eternal Night.
Between the twin abysses of radical violence lies another trap, subtler but equally deadly: maximalism. The insistence that only total victory will suffice. The refusal to recognize any legitimacy in

the other's claims. The fantasy that if only one side would disappear, peace would naturally bloom.

Israeli maximalism dreams of unchallenged expanse—of settlements stretching to every biblical boundary, of security through complete territorial control, of a Palestinian population that somehow accepts permanent subordination or simply... leaves. This dream ignores the fundamental mathematics of demography and the fundamental lessons of history. Millions of Palestinians are not going to evaporate. Holding millions of people without political rights is not a foundation for democracy; it is a foundation for apartheid. And no nation, however powerful, can maintain such a system indefinitely without corroding its own soul.

Palestinian maximalism dreams of total reclamation—of a return to 1948 borders, of a Right of Return that would transform Israel's demographic character, of justice defined as reversal rather than resolution. This dream, too, founders on the rocks of reality. The Nakba was a tragedy, and that tragedy deserves acknowledgment and mourning. But no mechanism exists to resurrect the villages of 1948, to un-build Tel Aviv, to relocate ten million people whose only home is the land they were born in.

And what of Arab Israelis— some 2 million Palestinian citizens of Israel who navigate a daily paradox, belonging fully to neither world? Maximalism from either direction offers them only fracture: loyalty tests from a Jewish state suspicious of their identity, or pressure from Palestinian movements to reject the state that issues their passports. They are asked to choose between impossible options, when what they deserve is a framework that honors the fullness of who they are.

🎬 *TikTok Visual: Animation of puzzle pieces scattered across a table. One hand pushes them apart; another gently slides them together. Text overlay: 'Divided pieces vs. interlocking mosaic*

This path—the path of mutual maximalism—leads only to generations condemned to blood-soaked sands. It reduces human beings, in all their irreducible complexity, to obstacles or enemies. It denies the fundamental truth that no people deserves dominance over another, that equality is not weakness but the only foundation upon which lasting peace can be built.

As I've written: *"Maximalism is nostalgia armed with weapons—the insistence that the past can be resurrected through sufficient force. But the past is gone. Only the future can be built, and it can only be built together."*

The Mosaic Revelation: A Federal Vision.
If revenge is a mirage, radicalism a lie, and maximalism a chain—what then? What possibility exists beyond the exhausted options that have failed for three generations?
Here is the mosaic revelation: *a Federal framework that honors all identities within one radiant structure.*
This is not a utopian fantasy. This is how some of humanity's most diverse societies have learned to coexist. Consider India, a nation of 1.4 billion people speaking twenty-two official languages, practicing every major religion, divided by caste and region and history—and yet functioning as a single democratic federation. India's model is imperfect, often painfully so, but it demonstrates that asymmetric federalism—where different states have different relationships with the center—can hold together peoples whose differences would seem irreconcilable.
Consider Switzerland, where German, French, Italian, and Romansh speakers share a nation smaller than the West Bank and Israel combined. These communities fought religious wars for centuries; they were as convinced of the impossibility of coexistence as any Israeli or Palestinian today. And yet they built a confederation where each canton governs its own affairs, where linguistic communities maintain their distinct identities, where the central government handles defense and currency while leaving culture and education to local control.
Consider Germany, divided by ideology so absolute that families were separated by walls and minefields for forty years. Consider the European Union itself, built on the ashes of two world wars that killed a hundred million people, now knitting together ancient enemies into a zone of shared prosperity and open borders.
If they could do it, why not here?
My blueprint imagines a Federal structure rooted in mutual recognition. At its heart would be the framework of Jewish sovereignty that Israel has built—the IDF as the federal defense force, the shekel as the common currency, a shared foreign policy that represents all citizens. But within this framework, Palestinian regions would exercise genuine autonomy: their own educational systems, their own cultural institutions, their own local governance, their own police forces for civil matters. Arab Israeli communities, too, would find formal recognition—not as an afterthought, but as a vital strand in the federal tapestry.
This is not a solution that erases differences. It is a solution that *honors* them. It says to the Israeli: Your security concerns are valid; they will be addressed at the federal level, with the full resources of a unified defense structure. It says to the Palestinian: Your desire

for self-determination is valid; you will govern your own communities, educate your own children, celebrate your own heritage, without requiring permission from those who do not share it.

The Essential Insight: "I honor your story; now let us weave it with mine."
Mutual recognition is the doorway. Not agreement on every historical grievance—that is impossible. Not identical narratives of the past—that will never happen. But simple acknowledgment: You are here. You are human. You have legitimate needs and fears and hopes. I will not pretend you do not exist, and I will not organize my political vision around your disappearance.
From that foundation, everything becomes possible. Shared infrastructure connecting Gaza to the West Bank through high-speed rail. A common economic zone where Palestinian entrepreneurs access Israeli capital and Israeli companies access Palestinian labor markets. Joint management of water resources, which climate change will make more precious every decade. Tourism circuits that honor all three Abrahamic faiths, bringing the world's pilgrims through a land finally at peace.

🎬 *Aspirational Visual: Tech incubators aglow in the Negev, in Ramallah, in Nazareth—young people bent over laptops, coding unity apps, building startups that solve problems for the whole region. Above them, the same stars that Abraham saw. Text: 'Shared victories await.'*

Youth's Forge: Digital and Cultural Renaissance.
You live in the most connected generation in human history. Your phones contain more computing power than the Apollo missions. Your networks span the globe. You have witnessed algorithms weaponize hate—watched TikTok and Instagram and Twitter become arenas where rage metastasizes, where every atrocity is amplified until outrage drowns out thought.
But algorithms are tools, not masters. What was weaponized can be reclaimed.
Imagine: joint ventures where Israeli and Palestinian developers build the next Waze together—not a navigation app, but a platform for navigating coexistence. Imagine climate guardians from both peoples working to save the Dead Sea, which is dying as political paralysis prevents the cooperation necessary to save it. Imagine cultural exchanges that blend lives like Swiss polyphony, where young musicians fuse Arabic maqam with Jewish klezmer, where

filmmakers tell stories that humanize both sides to audiences who have only known caricatures.

This is not naive idealism. This is how lasting peace is actually built —not in summit meetings between elderly politicians, but in the daily collaborations of young people who discover that their supposed enemies are simply... people. People who worry about exams and dream about careers and laugh at memes and fall in love. People who, when they build something together, develop bonds that make war unthinkable.

🎬 *Reel Concept: VR experience of crossing an invisible border. Two hands reach through the digital membrane—one Israeli, one Palestinian. They clasp. The barrier dissolves. Caption: 'The only walls that matter are the ones in our minds.'*

The European Coal and Steel Community—the seed that grew into the European Union—was founded on a simple insight: if you make nations economically interdependent, war becomes not only immoral but impractical. Young Germans and young French were sent on exchange programs, studied in each other's universities, intermarried, started businesses together. Within two generations, war between France and Germany became as unthinkable as war between California and Texas.

This is the work that awaits you. Not the dramatic heroism of the battlefield—that is the old way, the failed way, the way that has produced only graveyards. But the quieter, harder heroism of creation: building apps that connect communities; starting businesses that employ across boundaries; making art that challenges stereotypes; forming friendships that make the abstractions of conflict collapse into the concrete reality of human beings who share your struggles and your hopes.

Socialize federal loyalty through creation. War fades before collaboration's light.

A generation ago, young people in Northern Ireland were killing each other over whether they were British or Irish, Protestant or Catholic. Today, Belfast has trendy coffee shops and integrated schools and mixed neighborhoods. **The change did not come from politicians signing papers; it came from young people who simply grew tired of their parents' hatreds and chose to build something different.**

You can be that generation. You *must* be that generation. Because no one else will do this for you.

The Human Pulse: What We Share.

Step back, for a moment, from the specificities of this conflict. Look at what we know about human beings—all human beings, everywhere, in every culture and every era.

We are born helpless. We spend years in the care of others before we can survive alone. We form bonds of love and loyalty that we will die to protect. We create—art, music, buildings, systems, ideas—because creation is how we say to the universe that we were here, that our brief lives mattered. We dream for our children a world better than the one we inherited. We fear death, and we fear even more that our lives will have meant nothing.

This is the human pulse. It beats in Tel Aviv and in Gaza City, in Jerusalem and in Ramallah, in Haifa and in Hebron. It beats in the hearts of Israeli soldiers who miss their families, and in the hearts of Palestinian fathers who want nothing more than to see their children grow up safe. It beats in the Arab Israeli teacher trying to prepare students for a future she can barely imagine, and in the diaspora teenager scrolling through images of suffering and feeling the helplessness of distance.

War is not a video game. It is not content for your feed. It is rivers of blood—real blood, warm and red and impossible to replace. It is grief that shatters families for generations. It is psychological siege that scars both the victimized and the victimizers, because no one can participate in organized violence without being changed by it, diminished by it, haunted by it.

And here is the truth that the warmakers on all sides desperately want you not to understand: *Jews and Arabs are one wounded family.* Semitic cousins whose languages share roots, whose holy books share prophets, whose histories intertwined for centuries before the political movements of the twentieth century tore them apart. The hatred between them is not ancient; it is modern, manufactured, and it serves the interests of people who profit from conflict.

You do not have to hate each other. You have been *taught* to hate each other, by systems and incentives and historical contingencies that could have been different and still can be changed. The human pulse does not distinguish between Israeli and Palestinian hearts. Biology does not care about your passport.

"In this moment, I see—we are one human tapestry, destined not for destruction but for glory."

Epiphany Horizon: The Eternal Call.
You—young Israeli reading this in your apartment in Herzliya, young Palestinian reading this on cracked concrete in Khan Younis, young Arab Israeli reading this in the hills of Galilee, young diaspora reader scrolling through sorrow in Brooklyn or Berlin or Buenos Aires—**you are being summoned:**
Not to repeat your elders' failures. Not to inherit their hatreds. Not to accept that the future must resemble the past.
You are being summoned to become *architects*.
The generation that finally breaks the cycle will not do so through superior weapons or more sophisticated strategies of violence. It will do so by choosing—consciously, bravely, against every conditioning—to see the humanity in those it has been taught to hate. It will do so by building the federal mosaic: institutions that honor difference while enabling cooperation, frameworks that provide security without requiring supremacy, systems that allow Israelis to be fully Israeli and Palestinians to be fully Palestinian within a shared structure that serves both.
This will not be easy. Nothing worth building ever is. There will be setbacks, betrayals, moments when violence flares and the pessimists declare that nothing has changed. You will be told you are naive, that you do not understand, that the other side cannot be trusted, that history has proven coexistence impossible.
Do not listen.
History has proven only that the old approaches have failed. It has proven nothing about the approaches that have never been tried. The federal mosaic—a true partnership of peoples, not a domination of one by another—has not failed because it has never been given a genuine chance. You can give it that chance.

Start small. Send a message to someone on the other side—not a political argument, not a defense of your people's narrative, but a simple human greeting. *"Let us rise together."* Find collaborative projects—technology, art, environmental protection—that create the habits of cooperation. Vote for politicians who speak of shared futures rather than eternal enemies. Call out extremism in your own community before pointing fingers at others.

The grief of October 7th, 2023—and of all the days of grief before and since—does not have to be the end of the story. It can be the crucible in which something new is forged. Trauma, when it is processed rather than repressed, can become wisdom. Loss, when it is mourned rather than weaponized, can become the foundation for determination that this must never happen again—to anyone, on any side.

🎬 *Visual Symphony: Ash falling on the ruins of a village. Time-lapse: through the ash, green shoots emerge. Buildings rise. A phoenix city takes shape, its architecture neither purely Israeli nor purely Palestinian but something new—a style that does not yet exist because the society that would create it does not yet exist. On the rooftops, silhouettes of young people, arms raised to greet the dawn.*

You are not too young. You are not powerless. You are not condemned to repeat what came before. Every generation has a choice, and the choice of this generation—your generation—will determine whether the twenty-first century in this land is a continuation of the twentieth century's tragedies or the beginning of something humanity has never seen: two peoples who once seemed irreconcilable, learning to share a homeland in dignity and peace.

The mosaic awaits its makers. The dawn awaits those who will rise to greet it. The future is not written; it is being written, now, by you, in every choice you make, every connection you form, every refusal to surrender to despair.

"Peace: Not inherited. Forged. Your spark ignites it."

Post scriptum: **Your First Steps.**
The ancient rabbis taught that whoever saves a single life saves an entire world. The Quran teaches the same. Begin there: with one life, one connection, one conversation that refuses the script of hatred.
Follow organizations working across boundaries: Seeds of Peace, the Parents Circle, the Abraham Initiatives, Tech2Peace. Not because they are perfect—no organization is—but because they are trying, and in that trying lies the seed of everything that could be.
Share this chapter. Not as propaganda, but as an invitation. Let the mosaic memes spread:

"From Blood Rivers to Shared Skies."

Let the idea take root that another way is possible.

And when the darkness feels overwhelming—when the next atrocity fills your feed, when the pessimists seem vindicated, when hope feels like foolishness—remember: every light in history began as a single spark. *You are that spark.*

Awaken. The mosaic dawn is yours to build.

To the Mosaic Peace Through Hardships

Closing Words

A Final Plea Before this Court.
(A Letter to the "Adults")

I. The View from Above: A Planet Knowing Neither Borders Nor Hatred.

From geostationary orbit, terrestrial conflicts appear as localized disturbances on a planet knowing neither borders nor nationalism. The blue marble that astronauts describe with such reverence shows no trace of the walls we erect, the fences we patrol, the boundaries we sanctify with blood. Yet descend again to the Levantine corridor—that slender strip of land where three continents meet, where three great faiths find their origin, where civilizations have risen and fallen for five millennia—and abstraction becomes visceral. Families separated by walls. Children knowing only war. Generations suspended in an endless present with no imaginable future. The scent of tear gas mingling with jasmine. The sound of drones interrupting evening prayers.

The Israeli-Palestinian conflict represents not merely another item in human folly's ledger but a moral test for all who claim commitment to human dignity, self-determination, and peaceful coexistence. This is a conflict that has outlasted the Cold War, that has survived the collapse of empires, that has persisted through technological revolutions and social transformations that have remade the rest of the world. For over a century, the best minds and the most earnest diplomats have sought solutions, and for over a century, the conflict has devoured their efforts, their hopes, and far too often, their lives.

I stand before you now—not as a judge, for who among us is worthy to judge nations?—but as an advocate. An advocate pleading before the highest court imaginable: not the International Court of Justice in The Hague, not the United Nations Security Council in New York, but the Supreme Court of Human Conscience. This is the court that sits in the minds and souls of every good human being, every democratic individual with sound judgment, every person who has ever looked at images of suffering children—whether Israeli or Palestinian—and felt that something must be done, that something *can* be done, that humanity cannot accept this conflict as permanent feature of our political landscape.

II. The Indictment: A Century of Failed Paradigms.

Before this court, I must first present the indictment—not of peoples, for peoples are never guilty, but of ideas, of approaches, of paradigms that have failed spectacularly and continue to claim adherents despite overwhelming evidence of their bankruptcy.

The first defendant is the maximalist Zionist position—represented today by elements of the Likud and the Israeli far-right—which whispers seductively that the Palestinian presence is a problem to be managed, minimized, or ultimately eliminated. This position holds, whether explicitly or implicitly, that security requires demographic engineering, that peace means the absence of Palestinians, that the land from the river to the sea belongs exclusively to one people. Let me be direct: *this is not a solution*. It is a fantasy wrapped in a nightmare.

History teaches—from the Armenian genocide to the ethnic cleansings of the Balkans to the horrors of Rwanda—that attempts to solve political problems through the removal of populations produce only catastrophe, only international pariah status, only generations of trauma and hatred that poison the future. The Jewish people, of all peoples, should know in their bones that no lasting security can be built on the dispossession of others.

The second defendant is the maximalist Palestinian position—and let us be equally direct here—which dreams that Israel will disappear, that seven million Jews will somehow vanish, that the clock can be turned back to 1947 or 1917 or some mythical status quo ante. This position, whether dressed in the language of resistance or revolution, whether advocated by militant factions or whispered in refugee camps, is equally *not a solution*.

It is a mirror-image fantasy that has brought nothing but suffering to the Palestinian people themselves. Seventy-five years of armed struggle have not moved Israel; if anything, they have strengthened the Israeli right, provided justification for ever-harsher measures, and condemned generations of Palestinians to lives of poverty, statelessness, and despair. The Jews will not be driven into the sea. Israel will not cease to exist. Any approach predicated on this impossibility is not strategy but self-destruction.

The third defendant is the two-state solution itself—that diplomatic Holy Grail pursued by every American administration, endorsed by the international community, enshrined in countless UN resolutions. I accuse this paradigm not of bad intentions but of fatal impracticality. As Chapter 3 of this volume demonstrated through careful demographic analysis, the settlement enterprise has created facts on the ground that render territorial partition increasingly fantastical.

Over 700,000 Israeli settlers now live beyond the Green Line, many in communities that would have to be evacuated for a viable Palestinian state to emerge. Jerusalem, sacred to both peoples, cannot be surgically divided without doing violence to both. The Jordan Valley, essential for Palestinian economic viability, is demanded by Israel for security. Water aquifers, electromagnetic spectrum, airspace—the infrastructure of modern statehood cannot be neatly bisected. The two-state solution, whatever its theoretical merits, has been murdered by facts, and no amount of diplomatic incantation will resurrect it.

III. The Evidence: Why Federalism Alone Offers a Path Forward.

Having indicted the failed approaches, I now present the evidence for the only remaining alternative—the Federal State of Israel proposed in this volume. This evidence has been marshaled across fourteen chapters, drawing on historical analysis, comparative political science, constitutional theory, economic modeling, and moral philosophy. Let me summarize the case.

First, the historical evidence. As Chapters 1 through 4 demonstrated, federal arrangements have successfully managed conflicts once considered irreconcilable. Switzerland, whose Catholic and Protestant cantons fought savage religious wars for centuries, has achieved two hundred years of internal peace through federal design. Belgium, whose linguistic communities speak different languages, practice different religions, and maintain distinct cultural identities, has preserved national unity through ever-more-sophisticated federal mechanisms. Canada has managed separatist pressures in Quebec through asymmetric federalism that recognizes distinctiveness while preserving confederation. India governs a subcontinent of staggering diversity —dozens of languages, multiple religions, caste divisions that have structured society for millennia—through federal arrangements that balance unity with autonomy. Federalism is not utopian fantasy but proven institutional technology for managing difference democratically.

Second, the theoretical evidence. As Chapters 5 through 7 argued, federalism aligns powerfully with the core commitments of both Zionism and Palestinian nationalism—properly understood. Jewish self-determination does not require exclusive sovereignty over every square meter of historical Eretz Israel; it requires that Jews possess sufficient political power to preserve their civilization, protect their security, and shape their collective destiny. This is precisely what federal design enables through protected spheres of Jewish-majority governance, constitutional guarantees of community rights, and institutional mechanisms ensuring that no demographic shift can threaten Jewish self-governance. Similarly, Palestinian self-determination does not require Israel's destruction or Jewish elimination; it requires recognition of national identity, genuine governance over daily life, and equal participation in political institutions. Federalism delivers all these while creating frameworks for cooperation rather than perpetual confrontation.

Third, the constitutional evidence. As Chapters 8 through 10 detailed, frameworks exist for crafting federal states that address both communities' legitimate concerns. Drawing upon American dual sovereignty, Swiss consociationalism, German cooperative federalism, Belgian linguistic autonomy, and Canadian asymmetric arrangements, we can design institutions that protect minority rights through constitutional guarantees, balance regional autonomy with federal unity, distribute resources equitably through transparent fiscal mechanisms, and provide judicial review preventing majoritarian tyranny. The constitutional engineering is not simple— nothing worthwhile ever is—but it is entirely achievable with political will and technical expertise that the international community stands ready to provide.

Fourth, the geopolitical evidence. As Chapter 11 argued, federal solutions unlock transformative regional possibilities that no other approach can deliver. The Abraham Accords represent Arab-Israeli normalization's beginning, but comprehensive regional peace requires credible resolution of the Palestinian question. Arab states that have made peace with Israel face domestic criticism precisely because that question remains unaddressed; federal statehood that satisfies Palestinian aspirations removes this obstacle and opens the door to full regional integration. As I wrote in *The Times of Israel*, "Israel's influence in the region—for good or ill—depends fundamentally on its ability to manage internal diversity while projecting external stability" (Eger, April 2024). A federal Israel, at peace with its Palestinian citizens, anchored in regional partnerships, could become the engine of Middle Eastern prosperity rather than its permanent flashpoint.

Fifth, and most fundamentally, the moral evidence. As Chapters 13 and 14 maintained, federalism offers the only framework that honors the competing moral claims of both peoples without requiring either to vanish so the other can exist. The Jewish connection to this land—archaeological, historical, religious, existential—cannot be denied without repudiating millennia of civilization, without falsifying the textual record of three great faiths, without doing violence to the lived experience of millions. But the Palestinian attachment—generational, cultural, agricultural, deeply felt—deserves recognition rather than dismissal. Palestinians are not interlopers who arrived yesterday; they are a people rooted in this land, with their own histories, their own memories, their own ancestors buried in its soil. Federal solutions escape mutual negation's cruel binary, creating space for both peoples to flourish rather than demanding that one surrender so the other can triumph.

IV. The Precedent: Israel's Proven Capacity for Integration.
To those who say that Israelis and Palestinians can never live together, that federal arrangements are wishful thinking in this specific context, I offer a decisive refutation: Israel itself. The State of Israel has already demonstrated—over seventy-five years of existence—a remarkable capacity to integrate and assimilate diverse ethno-religious backgrounds into a functioning democratic society.
Consider the ingathering that has already occurred. Holocaust survivors from Poland and Russia. Mizrachi Jews expelled from Iraq, Yemen, Morocco, and Egypt. Ethiopian Jews rescued in dramatic airlifts. Soviet immigrants who arrived with nothing but their education. French Jews fleeing rising antisemitism. Each wave brought different languages, different customs, different conceptions of Judaism itself, different relationships to modernity and tradition. The tensions were real—between Ashkenazi and Sephardi, between religious and secular, between veteran Israelis and recent arrivals. And yet Israeli society absorbed these communities, created shared institutions, developed a common civic culture while preserving space for particular traditions.

Consider too the Arab citizens of Israel—twenty percent of the population—who participate in Israeli democracy, serve in the Knesset, sit on the Supreme Court, staff the hospitals, teach in the universities. Yes, discrimination exists; yes, tensions persist; yes, the relationship is complicated by the broader conflict. But the fundamental fact remains: Jews and Arabs already live together within Israel's pre-1967 borders, already share institutions, already demonstrate daily that coexistence is possible. The question is not whether coexistence can work but whether it can be extended, deepened, and institutionalized through federal arrangements that give both communities genuine self-governance alongside shared citizenship.

The State of Israel has proven, against long odds and in the face of persistent threats, that a diverse society can function, that immigrants can be integrated, that different communities can share political space. What this volume proposes is not something foreign to Israeli experience but rather its extension and fulfillment—the completion of a process of nation-building that has been underway since 1948. The Federal State of Israel would not be a break with Zionism but its maturation, not the abandonment of Jewish self-determination but its secure institutionalization in constitutional form.

V. The Requirements: What Must Be Surrendered, What Must Be Embraced.

Yet evidence alone creates no political will. Implementing federal solutions requires courage of the highest order—abandoning cherished illusions, confronting extremists within one's own community, taking risks for uncertain rewards, investing in institutions whose fruits may not ripen for generations. Let me speak directly to each party about what must be surrendered and what must be embraced.

To Israeli leaders and the Israeli public: Federal solutions demand accepting that the status quo—occupation without annexation, separation without peace, settlements without sovereignty—cannot continue indefinitely. The illusion of remaining simultaneously Jewish, democratic, and sovereign over all territory west of the Jordan while denying Palestinians full rights has been exhaustively debunked. Every serious demographer, every honest security analyst, every clear-eyed political scientist understands this. October 7th, 2023, demonstrated with terrible finality that the status quo does not even deliver the security it promises; managing the conflict rather than resolving it produced not stability but catastrophe. Federal solutions offer the only path preserving Jewish self-determination and democratic governance while addressing the Palestinian question equitably. This requires surrendering the dream of exclusive sovereignty over Greater Israel—but it requires embracing the reality of lasting peace, genuine security, and international legitimacy.

To Palestinian leaders and the Palestinian public: Federal solutions require acknowledging that Israel will not disappear, that Jewish connection to this land predates and will outlast any current arrangement, that maximalist demands for exclusive Arab sovereignty have failed catastrophically. Seventy-five years of refusal, three generations of resistance, have produced only nakba upon nakba—the original catastrophe compounded by subsequent disasters, from the 1967 defeat to the civil wars in Jordan and Lebanon to the Oslo process's collapse to Gaza's current devastation.

Federal arrangements offer genuine self-governance, national identity protection, and participation in economic prosperity—dramatically superior to either continued occupation or the corrupt, authoritarian leadership that has squandered Palestinian resources and opportunities. This requires surrendering the dream of liberating all of Palestine—but it requires embracing the reality of statehood, dignity, and a future for Palestinian children that does not consist of endless struggle.

To regional actors and the international community: Federal solutions necessitate moving beyond ritual denunciations and performative outrage toward pragmatic engagement with achievable outcomes. The citizens of every regional nation—Egyptian, Jordanian, Saudi, Emirati, Lebanese, Syrian—share a profound interest in ending a conflict that has drained resources, justified authoritarianism, fueled extremism, and prevented economic development for over a century.

Supporting federal solutions requires abandoning the failed two-state orthodoxy, engaging seriously with alternative frameworks, and providing the technical expertise and financial resources that federal institution-building demands. As Chapter 12 outlined in detail, implementation requires phased approaches, international support mechanisms, and sustained engagement over years and decades. The international community that has spent billions managing this conflict could spend a fraction of that sum resolving it.

VI. The Vision: Federal Zionism as Zionism's Fulfillment.
This book writes from an explicitly Federal Zionist perspective—unapologetic in commitment to Jewish self-determination and Israeli sovereignty while insisting that these need not come at the expense of Palestinian rights or regional peace. Federal Zionism synthesizes Labor Zionism's democratic socialist ideals, Revisionist Zionism's emphasis on Jewish strength and security, and World Federalism's commitment to institutional solutions and universal human rights.

For those who view Zionism and federalism as incompatible—and I have encountered this view within the World Federalist Movement itself—this book offers decisive refutation. Not only are they compatible; federalism represents Zionism's highest expression and ultimate fulfillment. The founders of Zionism sought to create a normal nation, a state like other states, where Jews could determine their own destiny rather than depending on the sufferance of others.

But normal nations in the twenty-first century are not ethno-states maintained through demographic engineering; they are civic democracies that protect minority rights while enabling majority self-governance. Normal nations do not maintain permanent occupation over hostile populations; they find institutional arrangements enabling diverse communities to share political space. A Federal State of Israel would be, at last, the normal state Herzl envisioned—respected by its neighbours, secure in its existence, at peace with itself and the world.

The Federal State of Israel, far from threatening Jewish existence, would secure it more permanently than any alternative. Constitutional protections and institutional mechanisms outlast particular governments or temporary majorities. Swiss German-speakers are not threatened by Swiss French-speakers because the constitution protects both; Belgian Flemish do not fear Belgian Walloons because federal arrangements guarantee each community's autonomy.

Similarly, Israeli Jews within a Federal State would possess guaranteed self-governance that no demographic shift could undermine, security arrangements that no change in parliamentary arithmetic could threaten, constitutional protections enforceable by independent courts. This is stronger protection than the current situation offers—where simple Knesset majorities can change fundamental laws and where security depends on military superiority that may not last forever.

VII. The Horizon: What Becomes Possible When Conflict Ends. From geostationary orbit, glimpse what becomes possible if humanity summons wisdom to implement federal solutions. Imagine an Israel where Tel Aviv's technological dynamism merges with Ramallah's entrepreneurial energy, where Haifa's port connects to Nablus's markets through modern infrastructure, where Jerusalem—jointly governed as a federal capital—hosts institutions representing both peoples' aspirations while remaining open to pilgrims of all faiths. Imagine schools where children learn both Hebrew and Arabic, where the history curriculum includes both peoples' narratives, where the next generation grows up seeing the other not as enemy but as fellow citizen.

Imagine regional integration where Israeli technology, Gulf capital, Egyptian labor, and Palestinian innovation create an economic powerhouse rivaling any on Earth. Imagine security cooperation where Israeli intelligence, Jordanian strategic depth, Emirati air power, and Saudi diplomatic influence combine to contain regional threats and defeat extremism. Imagine cultural flowering where Israeli music, Palestinian literature, Druze cuisine, and Bedouin traditions enrich shared civilization rather than fueling mutual hatred. Imagine water cooperation, renewable energy development, agricultural innovation, and environmental restoration transforming war-torn regions into sustainable development models that the world admires and emulates.

These visions are not fantasies but ordinary outcomes of successful federal systems worldwide. Switzerland achieved prosperity and peace through institutional design enabling diverse populations to cooperate rather than conflict; it is now among the world's wealthiest nations despite having no natural resources and no access to the sea. Belgium remains united despite linguistic divisions through federal mechanisms accommodating difference; Brussels hosts the institutions of the European Union. Canada has managed separatist pressures through asymmetric federalism recognizing Quebec's distinctiveness while preserving confederation; it consistently ranks among the world's most livable countries. The Israeli-Palestinian federation would face unique challenges—deeper enmities, more violent history, greater security threats, more complex demographics. But the fundamental task remains identical: creating institutions enabling competing groups to coexist, cooperate, and eventually trust each other enough to build shared futures.

VIII. The Urgency: Why the Time Is Now

This book concludes not with certainty but with urgency. The time for federal solutions is now—not because circumstances are propitious but because alternatives have exhausted themselves. October 7th, 2023, demonstrated the status quo's bankruptcy with a violence that shocked the world. The Abraham Accords revealed regional possibilities that seemed impossible a decade ago. Demographic trends show the two-state solution's increasing impracticality with each passing year. International dynamics— American fatigue, European frustration, Global South anger— create diplomatic pressures and potential openings. The moment demands leadership equal to the challenge.

Israel cannot remain in a permanent state of war. No nation can. No nation should have to. The Israeli people deserve to raise their children in peace, to build their businesses without fear of rockets, to travel abroad without needing to explain or defend their government's policies, to be welcomed in the community of nations as a normal country rather than treated as a perpetual controversy. The occupation corrodes Israeli democracy from within, militarizes Israeli society, coarsens Israeli politics, and creates moral contradictions that thoughtful Israelis find increasingly unbearable. Federal solutions offer a path to the normal existence that most Israelis crave—security through institutions rather than through permanent vigilance, peace through partnership rather than through permanent domination.

The Palestinian people cannot endure another seventy-five years of statelessness. No people can. No people should have to. Palestinian parents deserve to raise their children with hope, to build careers that occupation cannot destroy, to travel freely without permits and checkpoints, to possess the simple dignity of citizenship in a state that represents them. Federal solutions offer Palestinians what decades of armed struggle and diplomatic maneuvering have failed to deliver—genuine self-governance, constitutional protections, and a place in the world. Compromise is not surrender; it is wisdom. Partnership is not capitulation; it is the recognition that the future belongs to both peoples or to neither.

IX. The Verdict: A Plea to the Court of Human Conscience.
And so I conclude my plea before the Supreme Court of Human Conscience. The evidence has been presented. The failed approaches have been indicted. The federal alternative has been detailed across fourteen chapters of careful analysis. What remains is the verdict—not mine to render, but yours. You who read these words. You who will decide, through your advocacy or your silence, through your engagement or your indifference, whether this conflict continues for another century or finds resolution in our time.

I ask you to consider: What do you want the future to look like? More of the same—endless cycles of violence and retaliation, walls and rockets, funerals and revenge? Or something different—difficult to achieve, requiring compromise from all parties, demanding the abandonment of cherished illusions, but offering at last the possibility of peace?

The Federal State of Israel proposed here represents more than one conflict's solution; it embodies a vision for how humanity can organize politically in an age of migration, cultural mixing, and competing national claims. If federalism can succeed in the Israeli-Palestinian conflict's crucible—if Jews and Arabs can share sovereignty and build common institutions in this most contested land—then no conflict on Earth need be considered insoluble.

This is not utopian fantasy but achievable reality, not naïve idealism but hard-headed pragmatism, not distant dream but proximate possibility. It requires only political will, institutional creativity, and moral courage—the very qualities that built the State of Israel against even longer odds in 1948, that created federal Switzerland from religious wars in 1848, that forged democratic India from colonial chaos in 1947, that ended apartheid and built a new South Africa in 1994. Great transformations happen when people decide they must happen, when the costs of the status quo become unbearable, when leaders emerge willing to take risks for uncertain rewards.

We stand at a crossroads. One path continues the cycle of violence, occupation, and despair—a path whose destination we already know because we have been walking it for generations. The other leads toward federal solutions enabling both peoples to flourish in the land both love—a path never attempted, whose destination we can only imagine, but whose possibility this book has labored to demonstrate. The choice appears obvious. The question is whether we possess sufficient wisdom and courage to take it.

Future generations may look back wondering why it took so long, why so much blood was spilled before obvious solutions were attempted, why federalism—proven successful from Bern to Brussels to New Delhi—was resisted so fiercely in the one place needing it most. Or they may look back with gratitude at leaders brave enough to abandon failed paradigms, at citizens courageous enough to demand alternatives, at a generation that finally broke the cycle and created lasting peace.

X. Final Words: The Federal Future Awaits.

From geostationary orbit, we see Earth as it truly is—a small planet with limited resources, shared challenges, common fate. Conflicts dividing us appear absurd from that vantage, our tribal animosities petty against cosmic immensity. Yet we must descend from abstraction to live in the particular, honoring particular attachments and identities, recognizing that universal values require particular instantiations, that peace is made not between abstractions but between actual human beings in actual places with actual histories.

Federal solutions bridge this divide between universal and particular, between abstract principles and concrete institutions, between global perspectives and local realities. They offer humanity proven methods for managing diversity democratically, accommodating competing loyalties within shared frameworks, transforming zero-sum conflicts into positive-sum cooperation. They demand compromise from all parties—and compromise, as Amos Oz reminded us, is not a dirty word but the very essence of life, since the opposite of compromise is not idealism but fanaticism and death.

The Federal State of Israel proposed in this volume represents the only serious, tangible solution to a conflict that has resisted all others. It requires Israelis to share sovereignty with Palestinians—but it secures Jewish self-determination more permanently than occupation ever could. It requires Palestinians to accept Jewish presence in their ancestral homeland—but it delivers dignity and self-governance that resistance has failed to win. It requires the international community to abandon comfortable shibboleths—but it offers the possibility of finally closing a file that has consumed diplomatic energy for a century. It requires courage from all—but it rewards that courage with the priceless gift of peace.

The choice is ours. The moment is now. The federal future awaits those with courage to grasp it. May we prove worthy of the opportunity. May our children and grandchildren, Israeli and Palestinian alike, live to bless us for the wisdom we showed in their hour of need. And may this small planet, viewed from geostationary orbit, finally know one less conflict, one more peace, one additional reason to hope that humanity can, when it truly commits itself, solve even the most intractable of problems.

The case rests. The verdict is yours.

Bibliography (Notes)

Chapter 1.
Notes

[1] Yosef Gorny, *Zionism and the Arabs, 1882-1948: A Study of Ideology* (Oxford: Clarendon Press, 1987), pp. 121-156; Gideon Shimoni, *The Zionist Ideology* (Hanover: Brandeis University Press, 1995), pp. 234-267.

[2] Daniel J. Elazar, *Exploring Federalism* (Tuscaloosa: University of Alabama Press, 1991), pp. 45-78; Michael Burgess, *Comparative Federalism: Theory and Practice* (London: Routledge, 2006), pp. 89-123.

[3] Martin Buber, *A Land of Two Peoples: Martin Buber on Jews and Arabs*, ed. Paul Mendes-Flohr (Oxford: Oxford University Press, 1983), pp. 45-89; Judah Magnes, *Dissenter in Zion*, ed. Arthur Goren (Cambridge: Harvard University Press, 1982), pp. 156-189.

[4] Susan Lee Hattis, *The Bi-National Idea in Palestine During Mandatory Times* (Haifa: Shikmona, 1970), pp. 78-134; Tamar Hermann, *The Israeli Peace Movement* (Cambridge: Cambridge University Press, 2009), pp. 34-67.

[5] Alexandre Kedar, "The Legal Transformation of Ethnic Geography," *Law & Society Review* 35, no. 4 (2001), pp. 923-956; Alexander Yakobson and Amnon Rubinstein, *Israel and the Family of Nations* (London: Routledge, 2009), pp. 123-167.

[6] Joseph Preston Baratta, *The Politics of World Federation* (Westport: Praeger, 2004), pp. 45-89; Wesley T. Wooley, *Alternatives to Anarchy: American Supranationalism Since World War II* (Bloomington: Indiana University Press, 1988), pp. 67-98.

[7] Albert Einstein, *Ideas and Opinions* (New York: Crown, 1960), pp. 134-156; Bertrand Russell, *Has Man a Future?* (New York: Simon & Schuster, 1961), pp. 89-123.

[8] Clarence Streit, *Union Now: A Proposal for a Federal Union of the Democracies of the North Atlantic* (New York: Harper, 1939), pp. 45-78.

[9] Emery Reves, *The Anatomy of Peace* (New York: Harper, 1945), pp. 123-167.

[10] Steven M. Cohen and Arnold M. Eisen, *The Jew Within: Self, Family, and Community in America* (Bloomington: Indiana University Press, 2000), pp. 34-67.

[11] Simon Rabinovitch, *Jews and Diaspora Nationalism: Writings on Jewish Peoplehood in Europe and the United States* (Waltham: Brandeis University Press, 2012), pp. 89-134.

[12] Simon Dubnow, *Nationalism and History: Essays on Old and New Judaism*, ed. Koppel Pinson (Philadelphia: Jewish Publication Society, 1958), pp. 156-189.
[13] Steven Zipperstein, *Elusive Prophet: Ahad Ha'am and the Origins of Zionism* (Berkeley: University of California Press, 1993), pp. 234-278.
[14] Jack Wertheimer, ed., *The New Jewish Leaders: Reshaping the American Jewish Landscape* (Waltham: Brandeis University Press, 2011), pp. 45-89.
[15] Jonathan D. Sarna, *American Judaism: A History* (New Haven: Yale University Press, 2004), pp. 312-356.
[16] Chaim Gans, *A Just Zionism: On the Morality of the Jewish State* (Oxford: Oxford University Press, 2008), pp. 134-167.
[17] Colin Shindler, *The Triumph of Military Zionism: Nationalism and the Origins of the Israeli Right* (London: I.B. Tauris, 2006), pp. 189-234.
[18] Daniel J. Elazar, *Covenant and Polity in Biblical Israel* (New Brunswick: Transaction, 1995), pp. 267-298.
[19] Yoav Peled and Gershon Shafir, *Being Israeli: The Dynamics of Multiple Citizenship* (Cambridge: Cambridge University Press, 2002), pp. 78-112.
[20] Avi Shlaim, *The Iron Wall: Israel and the Arab World* (New York: Norton, 2000), pp. 234-278.
[21] Allon Gal, David Lesch, and Benny Morris, eds., *Israeli Diaspora Relations* (London: Routledge, 2012), pp. 45-89.
[22] Daniel and Jonathan Boyarin, *Powers of Diaspora: Two Essays on the Relevance of Jewish Culture* (Minneapolis: University of Minnesota Press, 2002), pp. 67-98.
[23] Fred Jerome, *Einstein on Israel and Zionism* (New York: St. Martin's Press, 2009), pp. 134-167.
[24] Ezra Mendelsohn, *On Modern Jewish Politics* (Oxford: Oxford University Press, 1993), pp. 189-223.
[25] Anne Bayefsky, "One Small Step," *New York Sun*, April 8, 2008; Anne Bayefsky, ed., *Human Rights and the UN: Progress and Challenges* (Leiden: Brill, 2009), pp. 145-178.
[26] Cary Nelson and Gabriel Brahm, eds., *The Case Against Academic Boycotts of Israel* (Chicago: MLA Members for Scholars' Rights, 2015), pp. 34-78.
[27] Gerald Steinberg, "The Politics of NGOs, Human Rights, and the Arab-Israeli Conflict," *Israel Studies* 16, no. 2 (2011), pp. 24-54.
[28] UN Watch, "Database: UN Resolutions on Israel vs. Rest of World," https://unwatch.org, accessed 2024.

[29] Ruth Gavison, "The Jewish State: A Justification," in *New Essays on Zionism*, ed. David Hazony, Yoram Hazony, and Michael Oren (Jerusalem: Shalem Press, 2006), pp. 3-56.

[30] Robert Wistrich, *From Ambivalence to Betrayal: The Left, the Jews, and Israel* (Lincoln: University of Nebraska Press, 2012), pp. 234-289.

[31] S. Ilan Troen, *Imagining Zion: Dreams, Designs, and Realities in a Century of Jewish Settlement* (New Haven: Yale University Press, 2003), pp. 167-198.

[32] Edward Said, *Orientalism* (New York: Pantheon, 1978), pp. 284-328.

[33] Robert S. Wistrich, *A Lethal Obsession: Anti-Semitism from Antiquity to the Global Jihad* (New York: Random House, 2010), pp. 456-512.

[34] Dore Gold, *Tower of Babble: How the United Nations Has Fueled Global Chaos* (New York: Crown Forum, 2004), pp. 123-167.

[35] David Tobin Daley, "The UN Human Rights Council's Obsession with Israel," *Commentary*, June 2021.

[36] Gil Troy, *The Zionist Ideas: Visions for the Jewish Homeland—Then, Now, Tomorrow* (Philadelphia: Jewish Publication Society, 2018), pp. 289-323.

[37] Hillel Neuer, "UN Watch Annual Report 2023," Geneva, 2023.

[38] Irwin Cotler, "The New Anti-Semitism," in *Old Demons, New Debates*, ed. David I. Kertzer (New York: Holmes & Meier, 2005), pp. 34-67.

[39] Thomas G. Weiss, *What's Wrong with the United Nations and How to Fix It* (Cambridge: Polity Press, 2016), pp. 145-189.

[40] Kenneth Marcus, *The Definition of Anti-Semitism* (Oxford: Oxford University Press, 2015), pp. 89-134.

[41] Will Kymlicka, *Multicultural Citizenship: A Liberal Theory of Minority Rights* (Oxford: Oxford University Press, 1995), pp. 156-189.

[42] Arend Lijphart, *Democracy in Plural Societies: A Comparative Exploration* (New Haven: Yale University Press, 1977), pp. 78-112.

[43] Frank Biermann, *Earth System Governance: World Politics in the Anthropocene* (Cambridge: MIT Press, 2014), pp. 67-98.

[44] Ronald Watts, *Comparing Federal Systems* (Montreal: McGill-Queen's University Press, 2008), pp. 134-167.

[45] Joseph E. Schwartzberg, *Transforming the United Nations System: Designs for a Workable World* (Tokyo: United Nations University Press, 2013), pp. 189-234.

[46] Shlomo Wollins, "Federal Zionism: A Path Forward," *Times of Israel*, 2024.

Chapter 6.
Notes
[1] Giovanni Capoccia and R. Daniel Kelemen, "The Study of Critical Junctures: Theory, Narrative, and Counterfactuals in Historical Institutionalism," *World Politics* 59, no. 3 (2007), pp. 341-369.
[2] Arend Lijphart, *Patterns of Democracy: Government Forms and Performance in Thirty-Six Countries*, 2nd ed. (New Haven: Yale University Press, 2012), pp. 36-52.
[3] Brendan O'Leary, "Debating Consociational Politics: Normative and Explanatory Arguments," in *From Power Sharing to Democracy*, ed. Sid Noel (Montreal: McGill-Queen's University Press, 2005), pp. 267-289.
[4] Donald Horowitz, *Ethnic Groups in Conflict* (Berkeley: University of California Press, 1985), pp. 597-628.
[5] Tony Judt, *Postwar: A History of Europe Since 1945* (New York: Penguin, 2005), p. 245.
[6] Timothy Garton Ash, *In Europe's Name: Germany and the Divided Continent* (New York: Random House, 1993), pp. 287-312.
[7] Michael Walzer, "The Paradox of Liberation," *Dissent* 65, no. 4 (2018), pp. 134-145.
[8] Ian Hurd, *After Anarchy: Legitimacy and Power in the United Nations Security Council* (Princeton: Princeton University Press, 2007), pp. 30-58.
[9] Aharon Barak, "Constitutional Identity and Human Dignity," in *The Cambridge Companion to Comparative Constitutional Law*, ed. Roger Masterman and Robert Schütze (Cambridge: Cambridge University Press, 2019), p. 178.
[10] Ruth Gavison, "The Jewish State: A Justification," in *New Essays on Zionism*, ed. David Hazony et al. (Jerusalem: Shalem Press, 2006), p. 234.
[11] Deborah Posel and Graeme Simpson, eds., *Commissioning the Past: Understanding South Africa's Truth and Reconciliation Commission* (Johannesburg: Witwatersrand University Press, 2002), pp. 45-78.
[12] Priscilla Hayner, *Unspeakable Truths: Transitional Justice and the Challenge of Truth Commissions* (New York: Routledge, 2011), pp. 89-123.
[13] Yoav Peled, *The Challenge of Ethnic Democracy: The State and Minority Groups in Israel, Poland, and Northern Ireland* (London: Routledge, 2014), pp. 12-28.
[14] Gary Jacobsohn, *Constitutional Identity* (Cambridge: Harvard University Press, 2010), pp. 134-167.

[15] Barbara Walter, *Committing to Peace: The Successful Settlement of Civil Wars* (Princeton: Princeton University Press, 2002), pp. 89-123.

[16] Milada Anna Vachudova, *Europe Undivided: Democracy, Leverage, and Integration After Communism* (Oxford: Oxford University Press, 2005), pp. 156-189.

[17] John Torpey, *Making Whole What Has Been Smashed: On Reparations Politics* (Cambridge: Harvard University Press, 2006), pp. 67-98.

[18] Kris Deschouwer, *The Politics of Belgium: Governing a Divided Society* (London: Palgrave Macmillan, 2012), pp. 189-223.

Chapter 10.
Notes.

[1] Daniel J. Elazar, *Exploring Federalism* (Tuscaloosa: University of Alabama Press, 1987), p. 12.

[2] Wolf Linder and Sean Mueller, *Swiss Democracy: Possible Solutions to Conflict in Multicultural Societies* (London: Palgrave Macmillan, 2021), pp. 89-123.

[3] Will Kymlicka, *Multicultural Citizenship: A Liberal Theory of Minority Rights* (Oxford: Oxford University Press, 1995), pp. 156-178.

[4] Will Kymlicka, "Is Federalism a Viable Alternative to Secession?," in *Theories of Secession*, ed. Percy Lehning (London: Routledge, 1998), p. 142.

[5] Karna Eklund, "Federalism in Iraq," *Middle East Policy* 24, no. 3 (2017), pp. 89-104.

[6] Kris Deschouwer, *The Politics of Belgium: Governing a Divided Society* (London: Palgrave Macmillan, 2012), pp. 167-189.

[7] Philip Roeder, *Where Nation-States Come From: Institutional Change in the Age of Nationalism* (Princeton: Princeton University Press, 2007), pp. 234-267.

[8] Christopher Clapham, "The Ethiopian Developmental State," *Third World Quarterly* 39, no. 6 (2018), pp. 1151-1165.

[9] Milton Gordon, *Assimilation in American Life* (Oxford: Oxford University Press, 1964), pp. 89-123.

[10] Rogers Brubaker, "The Return of Assimilation?," *Ethnic and Racial Studies* 24, no. 4 (2001), pp. 531-548.

[11] Will Kymlicka, *Finding Our Way: Rethinking Ethnocultural Relations in Canada* (Oxford: Oxford University Press, 1998), pp. 45-78.

[12] Menachem Klein, *Jerusalem: The Contested City* (New York: New York University Press, 2003), pp. 234-267.

[13] James Banks, "Diversity, Group Identity, and Citizenship Education in a Global Age," *Educational Researcher* 37, no. 3 (2008), pp. 129-139.

[14] Daniel Bar-Tal and Yona Teichman, *Stereotypes and Prejudice in Conflict: Representations of Arabs in Israeli Jewish Society* (Cambridge: Cambridge University Press, 2005), pp. 156-189.

[15] Keith Barton and Alan McCully, "History, Identity, and the School Curriculum in Northern Ireland," *Curriculum Journal* 16, no. 1 (2005), pp. 61-82.

[16] Thomas Pettigrew and Linda Tropp, "A Meta-Analytic Test of Intergroup Contact Theory," *Journal of Personality and Social Psychology* 90, no. 5 (2006), pp. 751-783.

[17] Robert Entman and Andrew Rojecki, *The Black Image in the White Mind: Media and Race in America* (Chicago: University of Chicago Press, 2000), pp. 78-112.

[18] Eli Pariser, *The Filter Bubble: How the New Personalized Web Is Changing What We Read and How We Think* (New York: Penguin, 2011), pp. 89-123.

[19] John Locke, *A Letter Concerning Toleration*, ed. James Tully (Indianapolis: Hackett, 1689/1983), pp. 23-45.

[20] Ran Hirschl, *Towards Juristocracy: The Origins and Consequences of the New Constitutionalism* (Cambridge: Harvard University Press, 2004), pp. 156-189.

[21] Robert Baruch Bush and Joseph Folger, *The Promise of Mediation: The Transformative Approach to Conflict* (San Francisco: Jossey-Bass, 2005), pp. 67-98.

[22] Priscilla Hayner, *Unspeakable Truths: Transitional Justice and the Challenge of Truth Commissions* (New York: Routledge, 2011), pp. 89-123.

[23] Truth and Reconciliation Commission of Canada, *Honouring the Truth, Reconciling for the Future* (Ottawa: TRC, 2015), pp. 1-23.

[24] Arend Lijphart, *Democracy in Plural Societies: A Comparative Exploration* (New Haven: Yale University Press, 1977), pp. 25-52.

[25] Shlomo Wollins, "Federal Accommodation and Democratic Resilience," *Times of Israel*, 2024.

Chapter 11.
Notes.

[1] Ian Lustick, *Paradigm Lost: From Two-State Solution to One-State Reality* (Philadelphia: University of Pennsylvania Press, 2019), pp. 189-234.

[2] Alan Dowty, *Israel/Palestine* (Cambridge: Polity Press, 2012), pp. 198-234.

[3] Menachem Klein, *Jerusalem: The Contested City* (New York: New York University Press, 2003), pp. 234-267.

[4] Hillel Frisch, "The Palestinian Military: Between Militias and Armies," *Middle East Review of International Affairs* 12, no. 4 (2008), pp. 56-73.

[5] Dawn Brancati, "Decentralization: Fueling the Fire or Dampening the Flames of Ethnic Conflict and Secessionism?," *International Organization* 60, no. 3 (2006), p. 655.

[6] Philip Roeder, *Where Nation-States Come From: Institutional Change in the Age of Nationalism* (Princeton: Princeton University Press, 2007), pp. 234-267.

[7] Reference re Secession of Quebec, [1998] 2 S.C.R. 217.

[8] As'ad Ghanem, "Israel and the 'Danger' of Demography," *Palestine-Israel Journal* 14, no. 4 (2008), pp. 12-18.

[9] Alexander Yakobson and Amnon Rubinstein, *Israel and the Family of Nations: The Jewish Nation-State and Human Rights* (London: Routledge, 2009), pp. 156-189.

[10] Oren Yiftachel, *Ethnocracy: Land and Identity Politics in Israel/Palestine* (Philadelphia: University of Pennsylvania Press, 2006), pp. 234-267.

[11] Efraim Inbar, "The Need to Block a Palestinian State," BESA Center Perspectives Paper No. 1320 (2019).

[12] Nathan Brown, "Palestine: Federalism, Not So Fast," *Lawfare*, January 2024.

[13] Rashid Khalidi, *The Hundred Years' War on Palestine* (New York: Metropolitan Books, 2020), pp. 241-267.

[14] Bassel Salloukh et al., *The Politics of Sectarianism in Postwar Lebanon* (London: Pluto Press, 2015), p. 178.

[15] Karna Eklund, "Federalism in Iraq," *Middle East Policy* 24, no. 3 (2017), p. 94.

[16] George Tsebelis, *Veto Players: How Political Institutions Work* (Princeton: Princeton University Press, 2002), pp. 136-178.

[17] Wallace Oates, *Fiscal Federalism* (New York: Harcourt Brace Jovanovich, 1972), pp. 45-78.

[18] C. Ross Anthony et al., "The Costs of the Israeli-Palestinian Conflict," RAND Corporation Research Report (2015), pp. 45-78.

[19] Barbara Walter, *Committing to Peace: The Successful Settlement of Civil Wars* (Princeton: Princeton University Press, 2002), pp. 89-123.

Chapter 13.
Notes
[1] Paul Rivlin, "The Middle East: A Zero-Sum Game?," *Middle East Economy* 6, no. 4 (2016), p. 12.

[2] Ibid., p. 15.

[3] Shlomo Wollins, "Federal Zionism: A Path Forward," *Times of Israel*, 2024.

[4] Marc Lynch, *The Arab Uprising: The Unfinished Revolutions of the New Middle East* (New York: PublicAffairs, 2012), pp. 89-123.

[5] Elie Podeh, "The Arab Peace Initiative: A Missed Opportunity?," *Israel Studies* 19, no. 3 (2014), pp. 147-175.

[6] Giovanni Capoccia and R. Daniel Kelemen, "The Study of Critical Junctures," *World Politics* 59, no. 3 (2007), pp. 341-369.

[7] Vali Nasr, *The Shia Revival: How Conflicts Within Islam Will Shape the Future* (New York: Norton, 2007), pp. 234-267.

[8] Suzanne Maloney, *Iran's Political Economy Since the Revolution* (Cambridge: Cambridge University Press, 2015), pp. 378-412.

[9] Karim Sadjadpour, *Reading Khamenei: The World View of Iran's Most Powerful Leader* (Washington: Carnegie Endowment for International Peace, 2009), pp. 15-28.

[10] F. Gregory Gause III, "Beyond Sectarianism: The New Middle East Cold War," *Brookings Doha Center Analysis Paper* 11 (2014), pp. 1-27.

[11] Ibid., p. 18.

[12] Israel-UAE Business Council, *Annual Trade Report 2023* (Tel Aviv: IUBC, 2024), pp. 12-23.

[13] "Saudi Crown Prince on Israel Normalisation," Interview with Fox News, September 2023.

[14] Dalia Dassa Kaye, *Talking to the Enemy: Track Two Diplomacy in the Middle East and South Asia* (Santa Monica: RAND, 2007), pp. 89-123.

[15] Kristian Coates Ulrichsen, "The Gulf States and Regional Realignment," in *The Oxford Handbook of Contemporary Middle-Eastern Politics*, ed. Marc Lynch (Oxford: Oxford University Press, 2023), p. 456.

[16] World Bank, *Economic Integration in the Middle East and North Africa* (Washington: World Bank Group, 2023), pp. 34-56.

[17] Rivlin, "The Middle East: A Zero-Sum Game?," p. 23.

[18] Raymond Hinnebusch, *The International Politics of the Middle East* (Manchester: Manchester University Press, 2015), pp. 189-223.

[19] John Gillingham, *Coal, Steel, and the Rebirth of Europe, 1945-1955* (Cambridge: Cambridge University Press, 2004), pp. 234-278.

[20] Ernst Haas, *The Uniting of Europe: Political, Social, and Economic Forces, 1950-1957* (Stanford: Stanford University Press, 1958), pp. 283-317.

[21] Tawfiq Hasou, *The Struggle for the Arab World: Egypt's Nasser and the Arab League* (London: Routledge, 2011), pp. 145-178.

[22] "Building a New Regional Order in the Middle East," Chatham House Research Paper (London: Chatham House, 2021), p. 34.

[23] Peter Haas, "Introduction: Epistemic Communities and International Policy Coordination," *International Organization* 46, no. 1 (1992), pp. 1-35.

[24] Daniel Bar-Tal and Yona Teichman, *Stereotypes and Prejudice in Conflict* (Cambridge: Cambridge University Press, 2005), pp. 156-189.

[25] Wolf Linder and Sean Mueller, *Swiss Democracy* (London: Palgrave Macmillan, 2021), pp. 234-256.

[26] Marc Lynch, "Media, Old and New," in *The Arab Uprisings Explained*, ed. Marc Lynch (New York: Columbia University Press, 2014), pp. 93-109.

[27] Mohammed Abu-Nimer, "Conflict Resolution, Culture, and Religion," *Journal of Peace Research* 38, no. 6 (2001), pp. 685-704.

[28] Eugene Rogan, *The Arabs: A History* (New York: Basic Books, 2011), pp. 267-312.

[29] Daniel Byman, "The Resilience of Terrorism," in *How Terrorism Ends*, ed. Audrey Kurth Cronin (Princeton: Princeton University Press, 2009), pp. 89-123.

[30] Ian Lustick, *Paradigm Lost: From Two-State Solution to One-State Reality* (Philadelphia: University of Pennsylvania Press, 2019), pp. 189-234.

[31] Aaron David Miller, *The Much Too Promised Land: America's Elusive Search for Arab-Israeli Peace* (New York: Bantam, 2008), pp. 356-389.

Bibliography (Consolidated)

I. Books.

Adeney, Katharine. *Federalism and Ethnic Conflict Regulation in India and Pakistan*. Basingstoke: Palgrave Macmillan, 2007.

Adler, Emanuel, and Michael Barnett, eds. *Security Communities*. Cambridge: Cambridge University Press, 1998.

Agranoff, Robert. *Accommodating Diversity: Asymmetry in Federal States*. Baden-Baden: Nomos, 1999.

Ahmad, Ehtisham, and Giorgio Brosio, eds. *Does Decentralization Enhance Service Delivery and Poverty Reduction?* Cheltenham: Edward Elgar Publishing, 2009.

Ajami, Fouad. *The Arab Predicament*. Cambridge: Cambridge University Press, 1981 (revised 2022).

Ajzenstat, Janet, Paul Romney, Ian Gentles, and William D. Gairdner. *Canada's Founding Debates*. Toronto: University of Toronto Press, 2003.

Alen, André, and Rusen Ergec. *Federal Belgium After the Fifth State Reform*. Leuven: Leuven University Press, 1998.

Alen, André, and Rusen Ergec. *Federal Belgium After the Fourth State Reform of 1993*. Brussels: Ministry of Foreign Affairs, 1998.

Alesina, Alberto, and Enrico Spolaore. *The Size of Nations*. Cambridge, MA: MIT Press, 2003.

Alston, Philip, ed. *Promoting Human Rights Through Bills of Rights: Comparative Perspectives*. Oxford: Oxford University Press, 2017.

Amidror, Yaakov. *Winning Counterinsurgency War*. Washington, DC: Georgetown University Press, 2024.

An-Na'im, Abdullahi Ahmed. *Toward an Islamic Reformation: Civil Liberties, Human Rights, and International Law*. Syracuse: Syracuse University Press, 1996.

An-Na'im, Abdullahi Ahmed. *Islam and the Secular State: Negotiating the Future of Shari'a*. Cambridge, MA: Harvard University Press, 2008.

Anderson, Benedict. *Imagined Communities: Reflections on the Origin and Spread of Nationalism*. London: Verso, 1983.

Anderson, George. *Federalism: An Introduction*. Oxford: Oxford University Press, 2008.

Anderson, Liam. *Federal Solutions to Ethnic Problems: Accommodating Diversity*. London: Routledge, 2013.

Arquilla, John, and David Ronfeldt. *Networks and Netwars: The Future of Terror, Crime, and Militancy*. Santa Monica: RAND, 2001.

Ash, Timothy Garton. *In Europe's Name: Germany and the Divided Continent*. New York: Random House, 1993.

Austin, Granville. *The Indian Constitution: Cornerstone of a Nation*. Oxford: Clarendon Press, 1966.

Austin, Granville. *The Indian Constitution: Cornerstone of a Nation*. Oxford: Oxford University Press, 1999.

Avineri, Shlomo. *The Making of Modern Zionism*. New York: Basic Books, 1981.

Avineri, Shlomo. *Herzl's Vision*. New York: Blue Bridge, 2013.

Avishai, Bernard. *The Hebrew Republic: How Secular Democracy and Global Enterprise Will Bring Israel Peace at Last*. Orlando: Harcourt, 2009.

Bachi, Roberto. *The Population of Israel*. Jerusalem: Institute of Contemporary Jewry, Hebrew University, 1977.

Bajwa, G. S. *Constitutional Government in India*. New Delhi: Ashish Publishing House, 2007.

Baldwin, David A. *Economic Statecraft*. Princeton: Princeton University Press, 2020.

Baldwin, Richard. *The Great Convergence: Information Technology and the New Globalization*. Cambridge, MA: Harvard University Press, 2016.

Bar-Tal, Daniel. *Intractable Conflicts: Socio-Psychological Foundations and Dynamics*. Cambridge: Cambridge University Press, 2013.

Bar-Tal, Daniel, and Yona Teichman. *Stereotypes and Prejudice in Conflict: Representations of Arabs in Israeli Jewish Society*. Cambridge: Cambridge University Press, 2005.

Barak, Aharon. *The Judge in a Democracy*. Princeton: Princeton University Press, 2006.

Baratta, Joseph Preston. *The Politics of World Federation*. Westport: Praeger, 2004.

Barkan, Elazar. *The Guilt of Nations: Restitution and Negotiating Historical Injustices*. New York: Norton, 2000.

Barnai, Jacob. *The Jews in Palestine in the Eighteenth Century*. Tuscaloosa: University of Alabama Press, 1992.

Barnett, Michael. *Dialogues in Arab Politics: Negotiations in Regional Order*. New York: Columbia University Press, 2002.

Basu, Durga Das. *Introduction to the Constitution of India*. 21st ed. Nagpur: LexisNexis, 2013.

Bauer, Yehuda. *Rethinking the Holocaust*. New Haven: Yale University Press, 2001.

Bayefsky, Anne, ed. *Human Rights and the UN: Progress and Challenges*. Leiden: Brill, 2009.

Bednar, Jenna. *The Robust Federation: Principles of Design*. Cambridge: Cambridge University Press, 2009.

Behrman, Greg. *The Most Noble Adventure: The Marshall Plan and How America Helped Rebuild Europe*. New York: Free Press, 2007.

Bell, Abraham. *The International Law of Palestine*. Manchester: Manchester University Press, 2013.

Bell, J. Bowyer. *Terror Out of Zion*. New York: St. Martin's Press, 1977.

Ben-Ami, Shlomo. *After October 7: Israel at a Crossroads*. Tel Aviv: Yedioth Books, 2024. [Hebrew]

Ben-Israel, Isaac. *The War After the War: Israel's Strategic Challenges Post-Gaza*. Tel Aviv: INSS Press, 2024.

Benedikter, Thomas. *Language Policy and Linguistic Minorities in India*. Münster: LIT Verlag, 2009.

Benhabib, Seyla. *The Claims of Culture: Equality and Diversity in the Global Era*. Princeton: Princeton University Press, 2002.

Benvenisti, Eyal. *The International Law of Occupation*. Princeton: Princeton University Press, 1993.

Berghahn, Volker R. *The Americanisation of West German Industry 1945-1973*. Cambridge: Cambridge University Press, 1986.

Berquist, Jon. *Judaism in Persia's Shadow*. Minneapolis: Fortress Press, 1995.

Biddiscombe, Perry. *The Denazification of Germany: A History 1945-1950*. Stroud: Tempus, 2006.

Biermann, Frank. *Earth System Governance: World Politics in the Anthropocene*. Cambridge, MA: MIT Press, 2014.

Bird, Richard, and François Vaillancourt, eds. *Fiscal Federalism in Developing Countries*. Cambridge: Cambridge University Press, 2006.

Blanchard, Benjamin. *Logistics Engineering and Management*. London: Pearson, 2010.

Blindenbacher, Raoul, and Arnold Koller, eds. *Federalism in a Changing World*. Montreal: McGill-Queen's University Press, 2003.

Boadway, Robin, and Anwar Shah, eds. *Intergovernmental Fiscal Transfers: Principles and Practice*. Washington, DC: World Bank, 2007.

Boadway, Robin, and Paul A. Hobson. *Intergovernmental Fiscal Relations in Canada*. Toronto: Canadian Tax Foundation, 1993.

Boyarin, Daniel, and Jonathan Boyarin. *Powers of Diaspora: Two Essays on the Relevance of Jewish Culture*. Minneapolis: University of Minnesota Press, 2002.

Bryden, Alan, and Heiner Hänggi, eds. *Security Governance in Post-Conflict Peacebuilding*. Münster: LIT Verlag, 2005.

Brynen, Rex, and Roula El-Rifai, eds. *Palestinian Refugees: Challenges of Repatriation and Development*. London: I.B. Tauris, 2007.

Buber, Martin. *A Land of Two Peoples: Martin Buber on Jews and Arabs*. Edited by Paul Mendes-Flohr. Oxford: Oxford University Press, 1983.

Bunton, Martin. *Colonial Land Policies in Palestine 1917-1936*. Oxford: Oxford University Press, 2007.

Burbank, Stephen B., and Barry Friedman, eds. *Judicial Independence at the Crossroads: An Interdisciplinary Approach*. Thousand Oaks: Sage, 2002.

Burgess, Michael. *Comparative Federalism: Theory and Practice*. London: Routledge, 2006.

Burns, James MacGregor. *Leadership*. New York: Harper & Row, 1978.

Bush, Robert Baruch, and Joseph Folger. *The Promise of Mediation: The Transformative Approach to Conflict*. San Francisco: Jossey-Bass, 2005.

Buzan, Barry, and Ole Wæver. *Regions and Powers: The Structure of International Security*. Cambridge: Cambridge University Press, 2003.

Byman, Daniel L. *Deadly Connections: States That Sponsor Terrorism*. Cambridge: Cambridge University Press, 2005.

Börzel, Tanja A. *States and Regions in the European Union*. Cambridge: Cambridge University Press, 2002.

Cardinal, Linda, and Selma Sonntag, eds. *State Traditions and Language Regimes*. Montreal: McGill-Queen's University Press, 2015.

Cassese, Antonio. *Self-Determination of Peoples: A Legal Reappraisal*. Cambridge: Cambridge University Pres

Cassese, Antonio. *International Criminal Law*. Oxford: Oxford University Press, 2003.

Cassese, Antonio. *International Law in a Divided World*. Oxford: Oxford University Press, 2005.

Chandler, David. *Bosnia: Faking Democracy After Dayton*. London: Pluto Press, 2000.

Choudhry, Sujit, ed. *Constitutional Design for Divided Societies*. Oxford: Oxford University Press, 2008.

Church, Clive H., and Adrian Vatter. *Switzerland and the European Union: A Close, Contradictory and Misunderstood Relationship*. London: Routledge, 2009.

Cobham, David, and Nu'man Kanafani, eds. *The Economics of Palestine: Economic Policy and Institutional Reform for a Viable Palestinian State*. London: Routledge, 2004.

Cohen, Mark R. *Under Crescent and Cross: The Jews in the Middle Ages*. Princeton: Princeton University Press, 1994.

Cohen, Michael. *Churchill and the Jews*. London: Frank Cass, 2003.

Cohen, Steven M., and Arnold M. Eisen. *The Jew Within: Self, Family, and Community in America*. Bloomington: Indiana University Press, 2000.

Collier, Paul. *The Bottom Billion*. Oxford: Oxford University Press, 2007.

Conversi, Daniele. *The Basques, the Catalans and Spain: Alternative Routes to Nationalist Mobilisation*. Reno: University of Nevada Press, 1997.

Copeland, Dale. *Economic Interdependence and War*. Princeton: Princeton University Press, 2015.

Cordesman, Anthony H. *The Israeli-Palestinian War: Escalating to Nowhere*. Westport: Praeger, 2005.

Cordesman, Anthony. *The Arab-Israeli Military Balance*. Washington, DC: CSIS Press, 2024.

Crawford, James. *The Creation of States in International Law*. 2nd ed. Oxford: Oxford University Press, 2006.

Dafflon, Bernard. *Local Public Finance in Europe: Balancing the Budget and Controlling Debt*. Cheltenham: Edward Elgar, 2004.

Darby, John, and Roger Mac Ginty, eds. *Contemporary Peacemaking: Conflict, Peace Processes and Post-War Reconstruction*. London: Palgrave Macmillan, 2008.

Deprez, Kas, and Louis Vos. *Nationalism in Belgium: Shifting Identities, 1780-1995*. Basingstoke: Macmillan, 1998.

Deschouwer, Kris. *The Politics of Belgium: Governing a Divided Society*. Basingstoke: Palgrave Macmillan, 2009.

Deschouwer, Kris. *The Politics of Belgium: Governing a Divided Society*. 2nd ed. Basingstoke: Palgrave Macmillan, 2012.

Deschouwer, Kris. *The Politics of Belgium: Governing a Divided Society*. London: Palgrave Macmillan, 2012.

Dever, William G. *Who Were the Early Israelites and Where Did They Come From?* Grand Rapids: Eerdmans, 2003.

Diamond, Larry. *The Spirit of Democracy*. New York: Times Books, 2008.

Dinan, Desmond. *Europe Recast: A History of European Union*. Basingstoke: Palgrave Macmillan, 2014.

Diner, Hasia. *We Remember with Reverence and Love*. New York: NYU Press, 2009.

Dinstein, Yoram. *The International Law of Belligerent Occupation*. Cambridge: Cambridge University Press, 2009.

Diwan, Paras. *Modern Hindu Law*. Allahabad: Allahabad Law Agency, 2002.

Dobbins, James, Seth G. Jones, Keith Crane, and Beth Cole DeGrasse. *The Beginner's Guide to Nation-Building*. Santa Monica: RAND Corporation, 2007.

Dobbins, James, et al. *The Beginner's Guide to Nation-Building*. Santa Monica: RAND, 2007.

Donnelly, Jack. *Universal Human Rights in Theory and Practice*. 3rd ed. Ithaca: Cornell University Press, 2013.

Dower, John W. *Embracing Defeat: Japan in the Wake of World War II*. New York: W.W. Norton, 1999.

Dowty, Alan. *Israel/Palestine*. Cambridge: Polity Press, 2012.

Dubnow, Simon. *History of the Jews*. 10 vols. Philadelphia: Jewish Publication Society, 1916–1920.

Dubnow, Simon. *Nationalism and History: Essays on Old and New Judaism*. Edited by Koppel Pinson. Philadelphia: Jewish Publication Society, 1958.

Dumper, Michael. *The Politics of Sacred Space: The Old City of Jerusalem in the Middle East Conflict*. Boulder: Lynne Rienner, 2002.

Dunning, John H., and Sarianna M. Lundan. *Multinational Enterprises and the Global Economy*. Cheltenham: Edward Elgar Publishing, 2008.

Durham, W. Cole, Jr., and Brett G. Scharffs, eds. *Law and Religion: National, International, and Comparative Perspectives*. New York: Aspen Publishers, 2011.

Efrati, Nathan. *Mi-Mahapekhah le-Milhamah* [From Revolution to War]. Beer Sheva: Ben-Gurion University Press, 2006. [Hebrew]

Einstein, Albert. *Ideas and Opinions*. New York: Crown, 1960.

Eisenstadt, S. N. *Israeli Society*. New York: Basic Books, 1967.

El-Gamal, Mahmoud A. *Islamic Finance: Law, Economics, and Practice*. Cambridge: Cambridge University Press, 2006.

Elazar, Daniel J. *Exploring Federalism*. Tuscaloosa: University of Alabama Press, 1991.

Elazar, Daniel J. *Covenant and Polity in Biblical Israel*. New Brunswick: Transaction, 1995.

Elazar, Daniel J. *Exploring Federalism*. Tuscaloosa: University of Alabama Press, 1987.

Elazar, Daniel J. *Covenant and Commonwealth*. New Brunswick: Transaction Publishers, 1998.

Elkins, Zachary, Tom Ginsburg, and James Melton. *The Endurance of National Constitutions*. Cambridge: Cambridge University Press, 2009.

Entman, Robert, and Andrew Rojecki. *The Black Image in the White Mind: Media and Race in America*. Chicago: University of Chicago Press, 2000.

Etzkowitz, Henry. *The Triple Helix: University-Industry-Government Innovation in Action*. London: Routledge, 2008.

Farole, Thomas, and Gokhan Akinci, eds. *Special Economic Zones: Progress, Emerging Challenges, and Future Directions*. Washington, DC: World Bank, 2011.

Feaver, Peter. *Armed Servants: Agency, Oversight, and Civil-Military Relations*. Cambridge, MA: Harvard University Press, 2003.

Feitelson, Eran, and Marwan Haddad, eds. *Management of Shared Groundwater Resources*. Dordrecht: Kluwer Academic Publishers, 2001.

Filippov, Mikhail, Peter C. Ordeshook, and Olga Shvetsova. *Designing Federalism: A Theory of Self-Sustainable Federal Institutions*. Cambridge: Cambridge University Press, 2004.

Fine, Lawrence. *Physician of the Soul, Healer of the Cosmos*. New York: NYU Press, 2003.

Finkelstein, Israel, and Neil Asher Silberman. *The Bible Unearthed*. New York: Free Press, 2001.

Fisk, Robert. *Pity the Nation: Lebanon at War*. Oxford: Oxford University Press, 2001.

Fitzmaurice, John. *The Politics of Belgium: A Unique Federalism*. London: Hurst & Company, 1996.

Fleiner, Thomas, and Lidija R. Fleiner. *Constitutional Democracy in a Multicultural and Globalised World*. Berlin: Springer, 2009.

Forsyth, Murray. *Unions of States: The Theory and Practice of Confederation*. Leicester: Leicester University Press, 1981.

Friedland, Roger, and Richard Hecht. *To Rule Jerusalem*. Cambridge: Cambridge University Press, 1996.

Friedländer, Saul. *The Years of Extermination*. New York: Harper, 2007.

Friedman, Isaiah. *The Question of Palestine 1914-1918*. London: Routledge, 1973.

Friedrich, Carl J. *Trends of Federalism in Theory and Practice*. New York: Praeger, 1968.

Frisch, Hillel. *The Palestinian Military*. London: Routledge, 2009.

Frisch, Hillel. *Israel's Security and Its Arab Citizens*. Cambridge: Cambridge University Press, 2023.

Fukuyama, Francis. *State-Building: Governance and World Order in the 21st Century*. Ithaca: Cornell University Press, 2004.

Gagnon, Alain-G., and Raffaele Iacovino. *Federalism, Citizenship, and Quebec: Debating Multinationalism*. Toronto: University of Toronto Press, 2007.

Gagnon, Alain-G. *The Case for Multinational Federalism: Beyond the All-Encompassing Nation*. London: Routledge, 2009.

Gagnon, Alain-G., and James Tully, eds. *Multinational Democracies*. Cambridge: Cambridge University Press, 2001.

Gal, Allon, David Lesch, and Benny Morris, eds. *Israeli Diaspora Relations*. London: Routledge, 2012.

Galnoor, Itzhak. *The Partition of Palestine: Decision Crossroads in the Zionist Movement*. Albany: SUNY Press, 1995.

Ganor, Boaz. *Hamas: From Terror Organization to Genocidal Entity*. Tel Aviv: International Institute for Counter-Terrorism, 2024.

Gans, Chaim. *A Just Zionism: On the Morality of the Jewish State*. Oxford: Oxford University Press, 2008.

Garcia-Granados, Jorge. *The Birth of Israel*. New York: Knopf, 1948.

Gardner Feldman, Lily. *Germany's Foreign Policy of Reconciliation*. Lanham: Rowman & Littlefield, 2012.

Gause, F. Gregory, III. *The International Relations of the Persian Gulf*. Cambridge: Cambridge University Press, 2024.

Gauthier, Jacques. *Sovereignty Over the Old City of Jerusalem*. Doctoral dissertation, University of Geneva, 2007.

Gazit, Shlomo. *The Carrot and the Stick: Israel's Policy in Judaea and Samaria, 1967-68*. Washington, DC: B'nai B'rith Books, 1995.

Ghanem, As'ad. *The Palestinian-Arab Minority in Israel, 1948-2000*. Albany: SUNY Press, 2001.

Gilbert, Martin. *In Ishmael's House: A History of Jews in Muslim Lands*. New Haven: Yale University Press, 2008.

Gillingham, John. *Coal, Steel, and the Rebirth of Europe, 1945-1955*. Cambridge: Cambridge University Press, 2004.

Ginsburg, Tom. *Judicial Review in New Democracies*. Cambridge: Cambridge University Press, 2003.

Golani, Motti. *The Early Years of the IDF*. Tel Aviv: Ministry of Defense Publishing, 1994. [Hebrew]

Gold, Dore. *Tower of Babble: How the United Nations Has Fueled Global Chaos*. New York: Crown Forum, 2004.

Goldberg, Harvey. *The Life of Judaism*. Berkeley: University of California Press, 2008.

Goldstein, Herman. *Problem-Oriented Policing*. New York: McGraw-Hill, 1990.

Gordon, Milton. *Assimilation in American Life*. Oxford: Oxford University Press, 1964.

Gorenberg, Gershom. *The Accidental Empire: Israel and the Birth of the Settlements, 1967-1977*. New York: Times Books, 2006.

Gorny, Yosef. *Zionism and the Arabs, 1882-1948*. Oxford: Clarendon Press, 1987.

Gorny, Yosef. *Zionism and the Arabs, 1882-1948: A Study of Ideology*. Oxford: Clarendon Press, 1987.

Grabbe, Lester L. *Ancient Israel*. London: T&T Clark, 2007.

Gunlicks, Arthur B. *The Länder and German Federalism*. Manchester: Manchester University Press, 2003.

Haas, Ernst. *The Uniting of Europe: Political, Social, and Economic Forces, 1950-1957*. Stanford: Stanford University Press, 1958.

Haber, Stephen, Armando Razo, and Noel Maurer. *The Politics of Property Rights*. Cambridge: Cambridge University Press, 2003.

Habermas, Jürgen. *Between Facts and Norms*. Cambridge, MA: MIT Press, 1996.

Hadari, Ze'ev. *Second Exodus*. Detroit: Wayne State University Press, 1991.

Haltiner, Karl W., and Tibor Szvircsev Tresch. *Milizarmee—Ein Relikt der Vergangenheit oder ein Zukunftsmodell?* [Militia Army—A Relic of the Past or a Model for the Future?]. Zurich: Verlag Neue Zürcher Zeitung, 2008.

Hargadon, Andrew. *How Breakthroughs Happen*. Boston: Harvard Business Review Press, 2003.

Harrison, Selig S. *India: The Most Dangerous Decades*. Princeton: Princeton University Press, 1960.

Hartley, Keith, and Todd Sandler. *The Economics of Defense*. Cambridge: Cambridge University Press, 1999.

Hasou, Tawfiq. *The Struggle for the Arab World: Egypt's Nasser and the Arab League*. London: Routledge, 2011.

Hassassian, Manuel. *Historical Dynamics Shaping Palestinian National Identity*. Jerusalem: PASSIA, 2002.

Hattis, Susan Lee. *The Bi-National Idea in Palestine During Mandatory Times*. Haifa: Shikmona, 1970.

Haykel, Bernard. *Saudi Arabia in Transition*. New Haven: Yale University Press, 2024.

Hayner, Priscilla. *Unspeakable Truths: Transitional Justice and the Challenge of Truth Commissions*. New York: Routledge, 2011.

Hechter, Michael. *Containing Nationalism*. Oxford: Oxford University Press, 2000.

Heller, Joseph. *The Stern Gang*. London: Frank Cass, 1995.

Hermann, Tamar. *The Israeli Peace Movement*. Cambridge: Cambridge University Press, 2009.

Herzl, Theodor. *The Jewish State*. 1896. Reprint, New York: Dover, 1960.

Hilberg, Raul. *The Destruction of the European Jews*. 3rd ed. New Haven: Yale University Press, 2003.

Hinnebusch, Raymond. *Syria and the Middle East Peace Process*. Updated ed. Boulder: Lynne Rienner Publishers, 2024.

Hinnebusch, Raymond. *The International Politics of the Middle East*. Manchester: Manchester University Press, 2015.

Hirschl, Ran. *Towards Juristocracy: The Origins and Consequences of the New Constitutionalism*. Cambridge, MA: Harvard University Press, 2004.

Homer-Dixon, Thomas F. *Environment, Scarcity, and Violence*. Princeton: Princeton University Press, 1999.

Hopmann, P. Terrence. *The Negotiation Process and the Resolution of International Conflicts*. Columbia: University of South Carolina Press, 1996.

Horowitz, Donald. *Ethnic Groups in Conflict*. Berkeley: University of California Press, 1985.

Horowitz, Donald. *Ethnic Groups in Conflict*. Berkeley: University of California Press, 2000.

Hueglin, Thomas O., and Alan Fenna. *Comparative Federalism: A Systematic Inquiry*. Peterborough: Broadview Press, 2006.

Huneidi, Sahar. *A Broken Trust: Herbert Samuel, Zionism and the Palestinians*. London: I.B. Tauris, 2001.

Hurd, Ian. *After Anarchy: Legitimacy and Power in the United Nations Security Council*. Princeton: Princeton University Press, 2007.

Inbar, Efraim. *Israeli National Security*. London: Routledge, 2024.

Ingrams, Doreen. *Palestine Papers 1917-1922*. London: John Murray, 1972.

Jacobsohn, Gary. *Constitutional Identity*. Cambridge, MA: Harvard University Press, 2010.

Jeffery, Charlie, ed. *Recasting German Federalism: The Legacies of Unification*. London: Pinter, 1999.

Jeremias, Joachim. *Jerusalem in the Time of Jesus*. Minneapolis: Fortress, 1969.

Jerome, Fred. *Einstein on Israel and Zionism*. New York: St. Martin's Press, 2009.

Judt, Tony. *Postwar: A History of Europe Since 1945*. New York: Penguin, 2005.

Kabha, Mustafa. *The Palestinian Press and the General Strike*. Ramat Gan: Bar-Ilan University Press, 2002. [Hebrew]

Kahane, Meir. *They Must Go*. New York: Grosset & Dunlap, 1981.

Kamrava, Mehran. *Troubled Waters: Insecurity in the Persian Gulf*. Ithaca: Cornell University Press, 2018.

Karpin, Michael, and Ina Friedman. *Murder in the Name of God*. New York: Metropolitan, 1998.

Karsh, Efraim. *The Arab-Israeli Conflict*. Oxford: Osprey, 2002.

Karsh, Efraim. *Arafat's War*. New York: Grove Press, 2003.

Karsh, Efraim. *Palestine Betrayed*. New Haven: Yale University Press, 2010.

Katz, Yaakov. *The Last Jews of Baghdad*. Basingstoke: Palgrave Macmillan, 2013.

Kaye, Dalia Dassa. *Talking to the Enemy: Track Two Diplomacy in the Middle East and South Asia*. Santa Monica: RAND, 2007.

Keck, Margaret, and Kathryn Sikkink. *Activists Beyond Borders*. Ithaca: Cornell University Press, 1998.

Keohane, Robert O., and Joseph S. Nye. *Power and Interdependence*. 3rd ed. New York: Longman, 2001.
Keohane, Robert O., and Joseph S. Nye. *Power and Interdependence*. New York: Longman, 2001.
Keohane, Robert O. *Power and Governance in a Partially Globalized World*. London: Routledge, 2002.
Keohane, Robert O., and Joseph S. Nye. *Power and Interdependence*. New York: Longman, 2011.
Ker-Lindsay, James. *The Cyprus Problem: What Everyone Needs to Know*. Oxford: Oxford University Press, 2011.
Khalidi, Rashid. *The Hundred Years' War on Palestine*. Revised ed. New York: Metropolitan Books, 2025.
Khalidi, Rashid. *The Hundred Years' War on Palestine*. New York: Metropolitan Books, 2020.
Khalidi, Rashid. *The Iron Cage: The Story of the Palestinian Struggle for Statehood*. Boston: Beacon Press, 2006.
Khosla, Madhav. *The Indian Constitution*. Oxford: Oxford University Press, 2012.
Kirshenblatt-Gimblett, Barbara. *Destination Culture: Tourism, Museums, and Heritage*. Berkeley: University of California Press, 1998.
Klein, Menachem. *Jerusalem: The Contested City*. London: Hurst & Company, 2001.
Klein, Menachem. *Jerusalem: The Contested City*. New York: New York University Press, 2003.
Klieman, Aaron. *Foundations of British Policy in the Arab World: The Cairo Conference of 1921*. Baltimore: Johns Hopkins, 1970.
Knopff, Rainer, and F. L. Morton. *Charter Politics*. Scarborough: Nelson Canada, 1992.
Kommers, Donald P., and Russell A. Miller. *The Constitutional Jurisprudence of the Federal Republic of Germany*. 3rd ed. Durham: Duke University Press, 2012.
Kornberg, Jacques. *Theodor Herzl: From Assimilation to Zionism*. Bloomington: Indiana University Press, 1993.
Kramer, Martin. *Arab Awakening and Islamic Revival*. London: Routledge, 2024.
Kriesberg, Louis. *Constructive Conflicts: From Escalation to Resolution*. Lanham: Rowman & Littlefield, 1998.
Kriesi, Hanspeter. *Direct Democratic Choice: The Swiss Experience*. Lanham: Lexington Books, 2005.
Kriesi, Hanspeter, and Alexander H. Trechsel. *The Politics of Switzerland: Continuity and Change in a Consensus Democracy*. Cambridge: Cambridge University Press, 2008.

Kriesi, Hanspeter, and Alexander H. Trechsel. *The Politics of Switzerland*. Cambridge: Cambridge University Press, 2008.

Kuperwasser, Yossi. *The Palestinian Authority's Rejection of Israel as a Jewish State*. Jerusalem: Jerusalem Center for Public Affairs, 2015.

Kuperwasser, Yossi, and Diane Lipner. *Deradicalization of Palestinian Society: Mission Impossible?* Jerusalem: Jerusalem Center for Public Affairs, 2023.

Kurzman, Dan. *Genesis 1948*. New York: World, 1970.

Kymlicka, Will. *Multicultural Citizenship: A Liberal Theory of Minority Rights*. Oxford: Oxford University Press, 1995.

Kymlicka, Will. *Finding Our Way: Rethinking Ethnocultural Relations in Canada*. Oxford: Oxford University Press, 1998.

Kymlicka, Will. *Multicultural Odysseys*. Oxford: Oxford University Press, 2007.

Kölz, Alfred. *Neuere schweizerische Verfassungsgeschichte* [Recent Swiss Constitutional History]. 2 vols. Bern: Stämpfli, 2004.

Laqueur, Walter, and Barry Rubin, eds. *The Israel-Arab Reader*. 7th ed. New York: Penguin, 2008.

Lazar, Harvey, ed. *Canadian Fiscal Arrangements: What Works, What Might Work Better*. Montreal: McGill-Queen's University Press, 2008.

Lederach, John Paul. *The Little Book of Conflict Transformation*. Intercourse, PA: Good Books, 2003.

Legrenzi, Matteo. *The GCC and the International Relations of the Gulf*. London: I.B. Tauris, 2011.

Lehn, Walter, and Uri Davis. *The Jewish National Fund*. London: Kegan Paul, 1988.

Levin, Itamar. *Locked Doors: The Seizure of Jewish Property in Arab Countries*. Westport: Praeger, 2009.

Levine, Lee I. *The Ancient Synagogue*. New Haven: Yale University Press, 2000.

Levine, Lee I., ed. *The Galilee in Late Antiquity*. New York: Jewish Theological Seminary, 2005.

Levitt, Matthew, and Michael Jacobson. *The Money Trail: Finding, Following, and Freezing Terrorist Finances*. Washington, DC: Washington Institute for Near East Policy, 2008.

Lijphart, Arend. *Democracy in Plural Societies: A Comparative Exploration*. New Haven: Yale University Press, 1977.

Lijphart, Arend. *Patterns of Democracy: Government Forms and Performance in Thirty-Six Countries*. 2nd ed. New Haven: Yale University Press, 2012.

Lijphart, Arend. *Thinking About Democracy: Power Sharing and Majority Rule in Theory and Practice*. London: Routledge, 2008.

Linder, Wolf. *Swiss Democracy: Possible Solutions to Conflict in Multicultural Societies*. 3rd ed. Basingstoke: Palgrave Macmillan, 2010.

Linder, Wolf, and Sean Mueller. *Schweizerische Demokratie* [Swiss Democracy]. 5th ed. Bern: Haupt, 2021.

Linder, Wolf, and Sean Mueller. *Swiss Democracy: Possible Solutions to Conflict in Multicultural Societies*. London: Palgrave Macmillan, 2021.

Linz, Juan J., and Alfred Stepan. *Problems of Democratic Transition and Consolidation*. Baltimore: Johns Hopkins University Press, 1996.

Locke, John. *A Letter Concerning Toleration*. Edited by James Tully. Indianapolis: Hackett, 1689/1983.

Lodge, Tom. *Mandela: A Critical Life*. Oxford: Oxford University Press, 2006.

Lustick, Ian S. *Paradigm Lost: From Two-State Solution to One-State Reality*. Philadelphia: University of Pennsylvania Press, 2019.

Lustick, Ian S. *Unsettled States, Disputed Lands: Britain and Ireland, France and Algeria, Israel and the West Bank-Gaza*. Ithaca: Cornell University Press, 1993.

Lynch, Marc. *The New Arab Wars*. New York: Public Affairs, 2024.

Lynch, Marc. *State Interests and Public Spheres*. New York: Columbia University Press, 1999.

Lynch, Marc. *The Arab Uprising: The Unfinished Revolutions of the New Middle East*. New York: PublicAffairs, 2012.

Lynch, Marc. *Voices of the New Arab Public: Iraq, Al-Jazeera, and Middle East Politics Today*. New York: Columbia University Press, 2006.

Mackey, Eva. *The House of Difference: Cultural Politics and National Identity in Canada*. Toronto: University of Toronto Press, 2002.

Maddy-Weitzman, Bruce. *The Crystallization of the Arab State System*. Syracuse: Syracuse University Press, 2023.

Madison, James, Alexander Hamilton, and John Jay. *The Federalist Papers*. 1788.

Magnes, Judah. *Dissenter in Zion*. Edited by Arthur Goren. Cambridge, MA: Harvard University Press, 1982.

Maheshwari, S. R. *Indian Administration*. 6th ed. New Delhi: Orient Longman, 2000.

Maissen, Thomas. *History of Switzerland*. Cambridge: Cambridge University Press, 2016.

Makovsky, David. *Imagining the Border: Options for Resolving the Israeli-Palestinian Territorial Issue*. Washington, DC: Washington Institute for Near East Policy, 2011.

Malleson, Kate, and Peter H. Russell, eds. *Appointing Judges in an Age of Judicial Power: Critical Perspectives from Around the World*. Toronto: University of Toronto Press, 2006.

Mallmann, Klaus-Michael, and Martin Cüppers. *Nazi Palestine*. New York: Enigma, 2010.

Maloney, Suzanne. *Iran's Political Economy Since the Revolution*. Cambridge: Cambridge University Press, 2015.

Mandela, Nelson. *Long Walk to Freedom*. Boston: Little, Brown, 1994.

Mansfield, Edward D., and Helen V. Milner. *Votes, Vetoes, and the Political Economy of International Trade Agreements*. Princeton: Princeton University Press, 2012.

Mar-Molinero, Clare, and Patrick Stevenson, eds. *Language Ideologies, Policies and Practices: Language and the Future of Europe*. Basingstoke: Palgrave Macmillan, 2006.

Marcus, Kenneth. *The Definition of Anti-Semitism*. Oxford: Oxford University Press, 2015.

Marshall, Paul, and Nina Shea. *Silenced: How Apostasy and Blasphemy Codes Are Choking Freedom Worldwide*. Oxford: Oxford University Press, 2011.

Maskus, Keith E. *Intellectual Property Rights in the Global Economy*. Washington, DC: Institute for International Economics, 2000.

May, Stephen. *Language and Minority Rights*. London: Routledge, 2012.

Mazar, Amihai. *Archaeology of the Land of the Bible*. New York: Doubleday, 1990.

Mazzucato, Mariana. *The Entrepreneurial State*. London: Anthem Press, 2013.

McGarry, John, and Brendan O'Leary. *The Politics of Accommodation in Divided Societies*. Oxford: Oxford University Press, 2009.

McRae, Kenneth D. *Conflict and Compromise in Multilingual Societies: Switzerland*. Waterloo: Wilfrid Laurier University Press, 1983.

McRoberts, Kenneth. *Misconceiving Canada: The Struggle for National Unity*. Toronto: Oxford University Press, 1997.

Mead, Walter Russell. *The Arc of a Covenant*. New York: Alfred A. Knopf, 2024.

Michelmann, Hans. *Foreign Relations in Federal Countries*. Montreal: McGill-Queen's University Press, 2009.

Milani, Mohsen. *Iran's Security Dilemma*. Cambridge: Cambridge University Press, 2024.

Miller, J. Maxwell, and John H. Hayes. *A History of Ancient Israel and Judah*. 2nd ed. Louisville: Westminster John Knox, 2006.

Miller, David. *Citizenship and National Identity*. Cambridge: Polity Press, 2000.

Miller, Aaron David. *The Much Too Promised Land: America's Elusive Search for Arab-Israeli Peace*. New York: Bantam, 2008.

Mishal, Shaul, and Avraham Sela. *The Palestinian Hamas*. New York: Columbia University Press, 2000.

Momani, Bessma. *Arab Dawn*. Toronto: University of Toronto Press, 2024.

Montero, Alfred P. *Brazil: Reversal of Fortune*. Cambridge: Polity Press, 2014.

Montgomery, John D. *Forced to Be Free: The Artificial Revolution in Germany and Japan*. Chicago: University of Chicago Press, 1957.

Mor, Menahem. *The Second Jewish Revolt*. Leiden: Brill, 2016.

Moravcsik, Andrew. *The Choice for Europe*. Ithaca: Cornell University Press, 1998.

Moreno, Luis. *The Federalization of Spain*. London: Frank Cass, 2001.

Morris, Benny. *Righteous Victims*. New York: Vintage, 1999.

Morris, Benny. *The Birth of the Palestinian Refugee Problem Revisited*. 2nd ed. Cambridge: Cambridge University Press, 2004.

Morris, Benny. *1948*. New Haven: Yale University Press, 2008.

Motadel, David. *Islam and Nazi Germany's War*. Cambridge, MA: Harvard University Press, 2014.

Nasr, Vali. *The Shia Revival: How Conflicts Within Islam Will Shape the Future*. New York: Norton, 2007.

Neidhart, Leonhard. *Plebiszit und pluralitäre Demokratie: Eine Analyse der Funktion des schweizerischen Gesetzesreferendums*. Bern: Francke, 1970.

Nelson, Cary, and Gabriel Brahm, eds. *The Case Against Academic Boycotts of Israel*. Chicago: MLA Members for Scholars' Rights, 2015.

Newman, Edward, and Oliver Richmond, eds. *Challenges to Peacebuilding*. Tokyo: United Nations University Press, 2006.

Norris, Jacob. *Land of Progress*. Albany: State University of New York Press, 2008.

Norris, Pippa. *Driving Democracy*. Cambridge: Cambridge University Press, 2008.

North, Douglass C. *Institutions, Institutional Change and Economic Performance*. Cambridge: Cambridge University Press, 1990.

Nye, Joseph S. *Soft Power: The Means to Success in World Politics*. New York: Public Affairs, 2004.

O'Leary, Brendan. *Power-Sharing in Deeply Divided Places*. Philadelphia: University of Pennsylvania Press, 2023.

Oates, Wallace. *Fiscal Federalism*. New York: Harcourt Brace Jovanovich, 1972.

Ofer, Dalia. *Escaping the Holocaust*. Oxford: Oxford University Press, 1990.

Oren, Michael. *Six Days of War*. Oxford: Oxford University Press, 2002.

Ostrom, Elinor. *Understanding Institutional Diversity*. Princeton: Princeton University Press, 2005.

Padgett, Stephen, ed. *Adenauer to Kohl: The Development of the German Chancellorship*. London: Hurst, 1994.

Pappé, Ilan. *The Ethnic Cleansing of Palestine*. Oxford: Oneworld, 2006.

Parashar, Archana. *Women and Family Law Reform in India*. New Delhi: Sage, 1992.

Paris, Roland. *At War's End: Building Peace After Civil Conflict*. Cambridge: Cambridge University Press, 2004.

Pariser, Eli. *The Filter Bubble: How the New Personalized Web Is Changing What We Read and How We Think*. New York: Penguin, 2011.

Peled, Yoav, and Gershon Shafir. *Being Israeli: The Dynamics of Multiple Citizenship*. Cambridge: Cambridge University Press, 2002.

Peled, Yoav. *The Challenge of Ethnic Democracy: The State and Minority Groups in Israel, Poland, and Northern Ireland*. London: Routledge, 2014.

Peleg, Ilan, and Dov Waxman. *Israel's Palestinians: The Conflict Within*. Cambridge: Cambridge University Press, 2011.

Peri, Yoram. *The Assassination of Yitzhak Rabin*. Stanford: Stanford University Press, 2000.

Peters, Joan. *From Time Immemorial*. New York: Harper & Row, 1984.

Peters, B. Guy. *The Politics of Bureaucracy*. 5th ed. London: Routledge, 2001.

Pipes, Daniel. *Israel Victory*. New York: Wicked Son, 2024.

Pollack, Kenneth. *Armies of Sand*. Revised ed. Oxford: Oxford University Press, 2024.

Porath, Yehoshua. *The Emergence of the Palestinian-Arab National Movement, 1918-1929*. London: Frank Cass, 1974.

Porath, Yehoshua. *The Palestinian Arab National Movement, 1929-1939*. London: Frank Cass, 1977.

Posel, Deborah, and Graeme Simpson, eds. *Commissioning the Past: Understanding South Africa's Truth and Reconciliation Commission*. Johannesburg: Witwatersrand University Press, 2002.

Pugh, Michael, Neil Cooper, and Mandy Turner. *Whose Peace? Critical Perspectives on the Political Economy of Peacebuilding*. Basingstoke: Palgrave Macmillan, 2016.

Putnam, Robert. *Bowling Alone*. New York: Simon & Schuster, 2000.

Quah, Jon. *Public Administration Singapore Style*. Bingley: Emerald, 2010.

Quandt, William. *Camp David*. Washington, DC: Brookings, 1986.

Quandt, William. *Peace Process*. Updated ed. Washington, DC: Brookings Institution Press, 2024.

Quandt, William. *Peace Process: American Diplomacy and the Arab-Israeli Conflict Since 1967*. Washington, DC: Brookings, 2005.

Quigley, John. *The Case for Palestine: An International Law Perspective*. Durham: Duke University Press, 2005.

Rabinovich, Itamar. *The War for Lebanon*. Ithaca: Cornell University Press, 1985.

Rabinovich, Itamar. *The Yom Kippur War*. New York: Schocken, 2004.

Rabinovich, Itamar. *The Lingering Conflict*. Washington, DC: Brookings Institution Press, 2024.

Rabinovitch, Simon. *Jews and Diaspora Nationalism: Writings on Jewish Peoplehood in Europe and the United States*. Waltham: Brandeis University Press, 2012.

Rakove, Jack N. *Original Meanings: Politics and Ideas in the Making of the Constitution*. New York: Alfred A. Knopf, 1996.

Rao, M. Govinda, and Nirvikar Singh. *Political Economy of Federalism in India*. New Delhi: Oxford University Press, 2005.

Raz, Joseph. *Ethics in the Public Domain: Essays in the Morality of Law and Politics*. Oxford: Clarendon Press, 1994.

Reilly, Benjamin. *Democracy in Divided Societies*. Cambridge: Cambridge University Press, 2001.

Rekhess, Elie. *The Arab Minority in Israel*. Tel Aviv: Tel Aviv University, 2014.

Reves, Emery. *The Anatomy of Peace*. New York: Harper, 1945.

Riker, William H. *Federalism: Origin, Operation, Significance*. Boston: Little, Brown, 1964.

Ritmeyer, Leen. *The Quest*. Jerusalem: Carta Jerusalem, 2006.

Robins, Philip. *A History of Jordan*. Cambridge: Cambridge University Press, 2004.

Rodden, Jonathan. *Hamilton's Paradox*. Cambridge: Cambridge University Press, 2006.

Rodrik, Dani. *One Economics, Many Recipes*. Princeton: Princeton University Press, 2007.

Roeder, Philip. *Where Nation-States Come From: Institutional Change in the Age of Nationalism*. Princeton: Princeton University Press, 2007.

Roeder, Philip G., and Donald Rothchild, eds. *Sustainable Peace: Power and Democracy After Civil Wars*. Ithaca: Cornell University Press, 2005.

Rogan, Eugene. *The Arabs: A History*. New York: Basic Books, 2011.

Romanow, Roy, John Whyte, and Howard Leeson. *Canada...Notwithstanding: The Making of the Constitution 1976-1982*. Toronto: Carswell/Methuen, 1984.

Rose, Richard. *Learning from Comparative Public Policy*. London: Routledge, 2005.

Ross, Dennis. *The Missing Peace*. New York: FSG, 2004.

Ross, Dennis, and David Makovsky. *Be Strong and of Good Courage*. New York: PublicAffairs, 2024.

Rotberg, Robert I., ed. *State Failure and State Weakness in a Time of Terror*. Washington, DC: Brookings Institution Press, 2003.

Rubenstein, Jeffrey. *The Culture of the Babylonian Talmud*. Baltimore: Johns Hopkins, 2010.

Rubin, Barry. *The Tragedy of the Middle East*. Cambridge: Cambridge University Press, 2003.

Russell, Bertrand. *Has Man a Future?* New York: Simon & Schuster, 1961.

Russell, Peter H. *Constitutional Odyssey: Can Canadians Become a Sovereign People?* 2nd ed. Toronto: University of Toronto Press, 1993.

Russell, Peter H. *Constitutional Odyssey: Can Canadians Become a Sovereign People?* 3rd ed. Toronto: University of Toronto Press, 2004.

Russell, Peter H. *The Court and the Constitution*. Kingston: Institute of Intergovernmental Relations, 2007.

Ryan, Curtis. *Jordan and the Arab Uprisings*. New York: Columbia University Press, 2024.

Sadjadpour, Karim. *Reading Khamenei: The World View of Iran's Most Powerful Leader*. Washington, DC: Carnegie Endowment for International Peace, 2009.

Said, Edward. *Orientalism*. New York: Pantheon, 1978.

Salamey, Imad. *The Government and Politics of Lebanon*. London: Routledge, 2014.

Salloukh, Bassel, et al. *The Politics of Sectarianism in Postwar Lebanon*. London: Pluto Press, 2015.

Sanders, Ronald. *The High Walls of Jerusalem*. New York: Holt, Rinehart & Winston, 1983.

Sarna, Jonathan D. *American Judaism: A History*. New Haven: Yale University Press, 2004.

Sathe, S. P. *Judicial Activism in India*. Oxford: Oxford University Press, 2002.

Savir, Uri. *The Process: 1,100 Days That Changed the Middle East*. New York: Random House, 1998.

Schanzer, Jonathan. *Hamas vs. Fatah*. Basingstoke: Palgrave Macmillan, 2008.

Schanzer, Jonathan. *Hamas's War: The October 7th Massacre and Its Aftermath*. New York: Threshold Editions, 2024.

Schiff, Ze'ev, and Ehud Ya'ari. *Intifada*. New York: Simon & Schuster, 1990.

Schneer, Jonathan. *The Balfour Declaration*. New York: Random House, 2010.

Schwartz, Seth. *The Ancient Jews from Alexander to Muhammad*. Cambridge: Cambridge University Press, 2014.

Schwartzberg, Joseph E. *Transforming the United Nations System: Designs for a Workable World*. Tokyo: United Nations University Press, 2013.

Segev, Tom. *1949: The First Israelis*. New York: Free Press, 1986.

Segev, Tom. *One Palestine, Complete*. New York: Metropolitan, 2000.

Segev, Tom. *1967: Israel, the War, and the Year that Transformed the Middle East*. New York: Metropolitan, 2007.

Selby, Jan. *Water, Power, and Politics in the Middle East: The Other Israeli-Palestinian Conflict*. London: I.B. Tauris, 2003.

Senor, Dan, and Saul Singer. *Start-up Nation: The Story of Israel's Economic Miracle*. New York: Twelve, 2009.

Shachar, Ayelet. *Multicultural Jurisdictions: Cultural Differences and Women's Rights*. Cambridge: Cambridge University Press, 2001.

Shah, Anwar, ed. *The Practice of Fiscal Federalism: Comparative Perspectives*. Montreal: McGill-Queen's University Press, 2007.

Shamir, Eado. *Israel-Palestine Water Conflict: An Israeli Perspective on the Hydro-Political Aspects of the Conflict*. Basingstoke: Palgrave Macmillan, 2015.

Shapira, Anita. *Land and Power*. Oxford: Oxford University Press, 1992.

Shapira, Anita. *Yigal Allon, Native Son*. Philadelphia: University of Pennsylvania Press, 1997.

Shapira, Anita. *Israel: A History*. Waltham: Brandeis University Press, 2012.

Shapira, Anita. *Ben-Gurion: Father of Modern Israel*. New Haven: Yale University Press, 2014.

Shapiro, Martin. *Courts: A Comparative and Political Analysis*. Chicago: University of Chicago Press, 1981.

Shapiro, Martin, and Alec Stone Sweet. *On Law, Politics, and Judicialization*. Oxford: Oxford University Press, 2002.

Shavit, Yaacov. *The New Hebrew Nation*. London: Frank Cass, 1987.

Shimoni, Gideon. *The Zionist Ideology*. Hanover: Brandeis University Press, 1995.

Shindler, Colin. *The Triumph of Military Zionism: Nationalism and the Origins of the Israeli Right*. London: I.B. Tauris, 2006.

Shlaim, Avi. *The Iron Wall: Israel and the Arab World*. New York: Norton, 2000.

Shlaim, Avi. *The Iron Wall: Israel and the Arab World*. New York: Norton, 2014.

Slutsky, Yehuda. *History of the Haganah*. Tel Aviv: Am Oved, 1972. [Hebrew]

Sparks, Allister. *Beyond the Miracle: Inside the New South Africa*. Chicago: University of Chicago Press, 2003.

Spolsky, Bernard, and Elana Shohamy. *The Languages of Israel: Policy, Ideology and Practice*. Clevedon: Multilingual Matters, 1999.

Stanislawski, Michael. *Tsar Nicholas I and the Jews*. Philadelphia: Jewish Publication Society, 1983.

Stein, Kenneth. *The Land Question in Palestine, 1917-1939*. Chapel Hill: UNC Press, 1984.

Steinberg, Jonathan. *Why Switzerland?* 2nd ed. Cambridge: Cambridge University Press, 1996.

Stern, Jessica, and J. M. Berger. *ISIS: The State of Terror*. New York: Ecco, 2015.

Sternhell, Zeev. *The Founding Myths of Israel*. Princeton: Princeton University Press, 2010.

Stewart, Frances. *Horizontal Inequalities and Conflict*. Basingstoke: Palgrave Macmillan, 2008.

Stillman, Norman. *The Jews of Arab Lands*. Philadelphia: Jewish Publication Society, 1979.

Stone, Julius. *Israel and Palestine: Assault on the Law of Nations*. Baltimore: Johns Hopkins, 1981.

Strange, Susan. *States and Markets*. London: Pinter Publishers, 1988.

Streit, Clarence. *Union Now: A Proposal for a Federal Union of the Democracies of the North Atlantic*. New York: Harper, 1939.

Suleiman, Yasir. *The Arabic Language and National Identity: A Study in Ideology*. Washington, DC: Georgetown University Press, 2003.

Suleiman, Yasir. *A War of Words: Language and Conflict in the Middle East*. Cambridge: Cambridge University Press, 2004.

Sunstein, Cass R. *Designing Democracy: What Constitutions Do*. Oxford: Oxford University Press, 2001.

Tal, David. *War in Palestine, 1948*. London: Routledge, 2004.

Taleb, Nassim Nicholas. *Antifragile: Things That Gain from Disorder*. New York: Random House, 2012.

Tarr, G. Alan. *Understanding State Constitutions*. Princeton: Princeton University Press, 1999.

Taylor, John B. *Central Bank Models: Lessons from the Past and Ideas for the Future*. Stanford: Hoover Institution Press, 2016.

Telhami, Shibley. *Power and Leadership in International Bargaining*. New York: Columbia University Press, 1990.

Teveth, Shabtai. *Ben-Gurion and the Palestinian Arabs*. Oxford: Oxford University Press, 1987.

Thrall, Nathan. *The Only Language They Understand: Forcing Compromise in Israel and Palestine*. New York: Metropolitan Books, 2017.

Tierney, Stephen. *Constitutional Referendums: The Theory and Practice of Republican Deliberation*. Oxford: Oxford University Press, 2012.

Tilley, Virginia. *The One-State Solution: A Breakthrough for Peace in the Israeli-Palestinian Deadlock*. Ann Arbor: University of Michigan Press, 2005.

Tilly, Charles. *Democracy*. Cambridge: Cambridge University Press, 2007.

Torpey, John. *Making Whole What Has Been Smashed: On Reparations Politics*. Cambridge, MA: Harvard University Press, 2006.

Treisman, Daniel. *The Architecture of Government: Rethinking Political Decentralization*. Cambridge: Cambridge University Press, 2007.

Troen, S. Ilan. *Imagining Zion: Dreams, Designs, and Realities in a Century of Jewish Settlement*. New Haven: Yale University Press, 2003.

Troy, Gil. *The Zionist Ideas: Visions for the Jewish Homeland—Then, Now, Tomorrow*. Philadelphia: Jewish Publication Society, 2018.

Tsebelis, George. *Veto Players: How Political Institutions Work*. Princeton: Princeton University Press, 2002.

Vachudova, Milada Anna. *Europe Undivided: Democracy, Leverage, and Integration After Communism*. Oxford: Oxford University Press, 2005.

Vatter, Adrian. *The Swiss Political System*. Amsterdam: Amsterdam University Press, 2020.

Vatter, Adrian. *Swiss Federalism: The Transformation of a Federal Model*. London: Routledge, 2018.

Vipond, Robert C. *Liberty and Community: Canadian Federalism and the Failure of the Constitution*. Albany: SUNY Press, 1991.

Vital, David. *The Origins of Zionism*. Oxford: Clarendon Press, 1975.

Vitalis, Robert. *White World Order, Black Power Politics*. Chicago: University of Chicago Press, 2024.

Walker, Samuel, and Charles Katz. *The Police in America: An Introduction*. New York: McGraw-Hill, 2017.

Walter, Barbara. *Committing to Peace: The Successful Settlement of Civil Wars*. Princeton: Princeton University Press, 2002.

Wasserstein, Bernard. *Israelis and Palestinians: Why Do They Fight?* New Haven: Yale University Press, 2017.

Watts, Ronald. *Comparing Federal Systems*. Montreal: McGill-Queen's University Press, 2008.

Watts, Ronald L. *Comparing Federal Systems*. 3rd ed. Montreal: McGill-Queen's University Press, 2008.

Watts, Ronald L. *Comparing Federal Systems*. Montreal: McGill-Queen's University Press, 2008.

Watts, Ronald L. *Comparing Federal Systems*. 2nd ed. Montreal: McGill-Queen's University Press, 1999.

Weiss, Thomas G. *What's Wrong with the United Nations and How to Fix It*. Cambridge: Polity Press, 2016.

Weller, Marc. *The Rights of Minorities in Europe*. Oxford: Oxford University Press, 2005.

Wertheimer, Jack, ed. *The New Jewish Leaders: Reshaping the American Jewish Landscape*. Waltham: Brandeis University Press, 2011.

Wheare, Kenneth C. *Federal Government*. 4th ed. London: Oxford University Press, 1963.

Wibbels, Erik. *Federalism and the Market: Intergovernmental Conflict and Economic Reform in the Developing World*. Cambridge: Cambridge University Press, 2005.

Wilford, Rick, ed. *Aspects of the Belfast Agreement*. Oxford: Oxford University Press, 2001.

Wistrich, Robert S. *A Lethal Obsession: Anti-Semitism from Antiquity to the Global Jihad*. New York: Random House, 2010.

Wistrich, Robert. *From Ambivalence to Betrayal: The Left, the Jews, and Israel*. Lincoln: University of Nebraska Press, 2012.

Witte, Els, Jan Craeybeckx, and Alain Meynen. *Political History of Belgium from 1830 Onwards*. Brussels: ASP, 2009.

Wolff, Stefan. *Ethnic Conflict: A Global Perspective*. Oxford: Oxford University Press, 2011.

Wolff, Stefan, and Christalla Yakinthou, eds. *Conflict Resolution: Theories and Practice*. London: Routledge, 2011.

Wooley, Wesley T. *Alternatives to Anarchy: American Supranationalism Since World War II*. Bloomington: Indiana University Press, 1988.

Yakobson, Alexander, and Amnon Rubinstein. *Israel and the Family of Nations*. London: Routledge, 2009.

Yakobson, Alexander, and Amnon Rubinstein. *Israel and the Family of Nations: The Jewish Nation-State and Human Rights*. London: Routledge, 2009.

Yergin, Daniel. *The Quest: Energy, Security, and the Remaking of the Modern World*. New York: Penguin Press, 2011.

Yiftachel, Oren. *Ethnocracy: Land and Identity Politics in Israel/Palestine*. Philadelphia: University of Pennsylvania Press, 2006.

Young, Robert A., ed. *Stretching the Federation: The Art of the State in Canada*. Kingston: Institute of Intergovernmental Relations, 1999.

Young, Iris Marion. *Inclusion and Democracy*. Oxford: Oxford University Press, 2000.

Young, Robert A. *The Secession of Quebec and the Future of Canada*. 2nd ed. Montreal: McGill-Queen's University Press, 1999.

Zegart, Amy. *Spying Blind: The CIA, the FBI, and the Origins of 9/11*. Princeton: Princeton University Press, 2007.

Zimmerman, Joseph F. *Contemporary American Federalism: The Growth of National Power*. 2nd ed. Albany: SUNY Press, 2008.

Zipperstein, Steven. *Elusive Prophet: Ahad Ha'am and the Origins of Zionism*. Berkeley: University of California Press, 1993.

II. Journal, Articles & Book Chapters.

Abu-Nimer, Mohammed. "Conflict Resolution, Culture, and Religion." *Journal of Peace Research* 38, no. 6 (2001): 685–704.

Abu-Saad, Ismael. "State-Controlled Education and Identity Formation Among the Palestinian Arab Minority in Israel." *American Behavioral Scientist* 49, no. 8 (2006): 1085–1100.

Ackleson, James. "Border Security Technologies: Local and Regional Implications." *Review of Policy Research* 22, no. 2 (2005): 137–155.

Anderson, James E., and Eric van Wincoop. "Gravity with Gravitas: A Solution to the Border Puzzle." *American Economic Review* 93, no. 1 (2003): 170–192.

Anthony, C. Ross, et al. *The Costs of the Israeli-Palestinian Conflict*. RAND Corporation Research Report, 2015.

Arnon, Arie, and Jimmy Weinblatt. "Sovereignty and Economic Development: The Case of Israel and Palestine." *Economic Journal* 111, no. 472 (2001): F291–F308.

Baldwin, Richard, and Anthony J. Venables. "Regional Economic Integration." *Handbook of International Economics* 3 (1995): 1597–1644.

Banks, James. "Diversity, Group Identity, and Citizenship Education in a Global Age." *Educational Researcher* 37, no. 3 (2008): 129–139.

Bar-Kochva, Bezalel. *Pseudo-Hecataeus, On the Jews*. Berkeley: University of California Press, 1996.

Bar-Tal, Daniel, and Eran Halperin. "Socio-Psychological Barriers to Conflict Resolution." In *Intergroup Conflicts and Their Resolution: A Social Psychological Perspective*, edited by Daniel Bar-Tal, 217–240. New York: Psychology Press, 2011.

Barak, Aharon. "Constitutional Identity and Human Dignity." In *The Cambridge Companion to Comparative Constitutional Law*, edited by Roger Masterman and Robert Schütze, 167–189. Cambridge: Cambridge University Press, 2019.

Barkay, Gabriel, et al. "The Amulets from Ketef Hinnom." *Near Eastern Archaeology* 67, no. 4 (2004): 164–171.

Barnett, Michael, and Etel Solingen. "Designed to Fail or Failure to Design? The Origins and Legacy of the Arab League." In *Crafting Cooperation*, edited by Amitav Acharya and Alastair Johnston, 180–220. Cambridge: Cambridge University Press, 2007.

Barton, Keith, and Alan McCully. "History, Identity, and the School Curriculum in Northern Ireland." *Curriculum Journal* 16, no. 1 (2005): 61–82.

Bimson, John J. "Merneptah's Israel and Recent Theories of Israelite Origins." *Journal for the Study of the Old Testament* 16, no. 49 (1991): 3–29.

Biran, Avraham, and Joseph Naveh. "An Aramaic Stele Fragment from Tel Dan." *Israel Exploration Journal* 43, no. 2/3 (1993): 81–98.

Boadway, Robin. "The Vertical Fiscal Gap: Conceptions and Misconceptions." *Canadian Tax Journal* 52, no. 4 (2004): 1–28.

Bovens, Mark. "Analysing and Assessing Accountability: A Conceptual Framework." *European Law Journal* 13, no. 4 (2007): 447–468.

Brancati, Dawn. "Decentralization: Fueling the Fire or Dampening the Flames of Ethnic Conflict and Secessionism?" *International Organization* 60, no. 3 (2006): 651–685.

Brubaker, Rogers. "The Return of Assimilation?" *Ethnic and Racial Studies* 24, no. 4 (2001): 531–548.

Busse, Matthias, and Carsten Hefeker. "Political Risk, Institutions and Foreign Direct Investment." *European Journal of Political Economy* 23, no. 2 (2007): 397–415.

Byman, Daniel. "The Intelligence War on Terrorism." *Intelligence and National Security* 29, no. 6 (2014): 837–863.

Byman, Daniel. "The Resilience of Terrorism." In *How Terrorism Ends*, edited by Audrey Kurth Cronin, 89–123. Princeton: Princeton University Press, 2009.

Béland, Daniel, and André Lecours. "Fiscal Federalism and American Exceptionalism: Why Is There No Federal Equalisation System in the United States?" *Journal of Public Policy* 34, no. 2 (2014): 303–329.

Börzel, Tanja A., and Madeleine O. Hosli. "Brussels Between Bern and Berlin." *Governance* 16, no. 2 (2003): 179–202.

Cai, Hongbin, and Daniel Treisman. "Does Competition for Capital Discipline Governments?" *American Economic Review* 95, no. 3 (2005): 817–830.

Cairns, Alan C. "The Judicial Committee and Its Critics." *Canadian Journal of Political Science* 4, no. 3 (1971): 301–345.

Capoccia, Giovanni, and R. Daniel Kelemen. "The Study of Critical Junctures: Theory, Narrative, and Counterfactuals in Historical Institutionalism." *World Politics* 59, no. 3 (2007): 341–369.

Carothers, Thomas. "The 'Sequencing' Fallacy." *Journal of Democracy* 18, no. 1 (2007): 12–27.

Cattoir, Philippe, and Magali Verdonck. "Belgian Fiscal Federalism in Practice." Brussels: National Bank of Belgium, 2009.

Choi, Stephen J., G. Mitu Gulati, and Eric A. Posner. "Are Judges Overpaid? A Skeptical Response to the Judicial Salary Debate." *Journal of Legal Analysis* 1, no. 1 (2009): 47–117.

Church, Clive, and Paolo Dardanelli. "The Dynamics of Confederalism and Federalism: Comparing Switzerland and the EU." *Regional & Federal Studies* 15, no. 2 (2005): 163–185.

Clapham, Christopher. "The Ethiopian Developmental State." *Third World Quarterly* 39, no. 6 (2018): 1151–1165.

Cohen, Amichai. *The Unmaking of Israel*. New York: HarperCollins, 2012.

Colomer, Josep M. "The Spanish 'State of Autonomies': Non-institutional Federalism." *West European Politics* 21, no. 4 (1998): 40–52.

Commanders for Israel's Security. *Security First: A New Strategy for Israeli-Palestinian Peace*. Policy Paper, 2020.

Cotler, Irwin. "The New Anti-Semitism." In *Old Demons, New Debates*, edited by David I. Kertzer, 34–67. New York: Holmes & Meier, 2005.

Courchene, Thomas J. "A Short History of Equalization." *Policy Options* 28, no. 3 (2007): 22–29.

Craig, Paul. "Transnational Constitution-Making: The Contribution of the Venice Commission." *UC Irvine Law Review* 7, no. 3 (2017): 781–814.

Dafflon, Bernard. "The Assignment of Functions to Decentralized Government: From Theory to Practice." In *Handbook of Fiscal Federalism*, edited by Ehtisham Ahmad and Giorgio Brosio, 271–305. Cheltenham: Edward Elgar, 2006.

Dajani, Mohammed S. "Palestinian Media and Incitement." *Palestine-Israel Journal of Politics, Economics and Culture* 14, no. 1–2 (2007): 71–78.

Daley, David Tobin. "The UN Human Rights Council's Obsession with Israel." *Commentary*, June 2021.

Della Pergola, Sergio. "Demography in Israel/Palestine." *American Jewish Yearbook* 101 (2001): 3–62.

Della Pergola, Sergio. "Jewish Demography in Israel and the West Bank After 1967." In *Wherever You Go: Studies in Zionism and Jewish Migration in Honor of Shmuel Ettinger*, edited by Gur Alroey, 41–76. Beer Sheva: Ben-Gurion University Press, 2011. [Hebrew]

Deschouwer, Kris. "And the Peace Goes On? Consociational Democracy and Belgian Politics in the Twenty-First Century." *West European Politics* 29, no. 5 (2006): 895–911.

Devroe, Elke, and Paul Ponsaers. "Reforming the Belgian Police System Between Central and Local." *European Journal of Crime, Criminal Law and Criminal Justice* 21, no. 2 (2013): 167–186.

Dion, Stéphane. "Why Is Secession Difficult in Well-Established Democracies?" *British Journal of Political Science* 26, no. 2 (1996): 269–283.
Dobbs-Allsopp, F. W., et al. *Hebrew Inscriptions*. New Haven: Yale University Press, 2005.
Doran, Michael S. "The Heirs of Nasser: Who Will Benefit from the Second Arab Revolution?" *Foreign Affairs* 90, no. 3 (2011): 17–25.
Ebrahim, Hassen, and Laurel Miller. "Creating the Birth Certificate of a New South Africa: Constitution Making After Apartheid." In *Framing the State in Times of Transition*, edited by Laurel Miller, 111–157. Washington, DC: USIP Press, 2010.
Eiland, Giora. "The IDF in the Second Lebanon War." In *The Lessons of the Second Lebanon War*, edited by Anat Kurz and Shlomo Brom, 29–40. Tel Aviv: Institute for National Security Studies, 2010.
Eklund, Karna. "Federalism in Iraq." *Middle East Policy* 24, no. 3 (2017): 89–104.
Erk, Jan, and Liam Anderson, eds. *The Paradoxes of Federalism*. London: Routledge, 2009.
Evans, Peter, and James Rauch. "Bureaucracy and Growth: A Cross-National Analysis of the Effects of 'Weberian' State Structures on Economic Growth." *American Sociological Review* 64, no. 5 (1999): 748–765.
Farsakh, Leila. "Palestinian Labor Flows to the Israeli Economy: A Finished Story?" *Journal of Palestine Studies* 32, no. 1 (2002): 13–27.
Feldman, Noah, and Roman Martinez. "Constitutional Politics and Text in the New Iraq: An Experiment in Islamic Democracy." *Fordham Law Review* 75, no. 2 (2009): 883–920.
Fischhendler, Itay. "When Ambiguity in Treaty Design Becomes Destructive: A Study of Transboundary Water." *Global Environmental Politics* 8, no. 1 (2008): 111–136.
Frisch, Hillel. "The Palestinian Military: Between Militias and Armies." *Middle East Review of International Affairs* 12, no. 4 (2008): 56–73.
Føllesdal, Andreas. "Competing Conceptions of Subsidiarity." In *Federalism and Subsidiarity*, edited by James Fleming and Jacob Levy, 214–230. New York: NYU Press, 2014.
Gause, F. Gregory III. "Beyond Sectarianism: The New Middle East Cold War." *Brookings Doha Center Analysis Paper* 11 (2014): 1–27.

Gavison, Ruth. "The Jewish State: A Justification." In *New Essays on Zionism*, edited by David Hazony, Yoram Hazony, and Michael Oren, 3–56. Jerusalem: Shalem Press, 2006.

Gavison, Ruth. "Jewish and Democratic? A Rejoinder to the 'Ethnic Democracy' Debate." *Israel Studies* 4, no. 1 (1999): 44–72.

Gavison, Ruth. "The Constitutional Revolution: A Reality or a Self-Fulfilling Prophecy?" *Israel Studies* 18, no. 3 (2013): 150–180.

Ge, Wei. "Special Economic Zones and the Opening of the Chinese Economy: Some Lessons for Economic Liberalization." *World Development* 27, no. 7 (1999): 1267–1285.

Germann, Raimund E. "Swiss Federalism: Model or Puzzle?" In *Federalism and Political Performance*, edited by Ute Wachendorfer-Schmidt, 124–141. London: Routledge, 2000.

Ghanem, As'ad. "Israel and the 'Danger' of Demography." *Palestine-Israel Journal* 14, no. 4 (2008): 12–18.

Ghanem, As'ad. "The Bi-National State Solution." *Israel Studies* 14, no. 2 (2007): 120–133.

Giacaman, Rita, et al. "Health Status and Health Services in the Occupied Palestinian Territory." *The Lancet* 373, no. 9666 (2009): 837–849.

Ginsburg, Tom, and James Melton. "Does the Constitutional Amendment Rule Matter at All?" *International Journal of Constitutional Law* 13, no. 3 (2015): 686–713.

Grech, Omar. "UNRWA and the Palestine Refugees." *Mediterranean Politics* 18, no. 1 (2013): 89–104.

Grin, François, and Britta Korth. "On the Reciprocal Influence of Language Politics and Language Education." In *Language Planning and Policy in Europe*, edited by Ranko Bugarski, 152–173. Clevedon: Multilingual Matters, 2005.

Grindle, Merilee. "Good Enough Governance: Poverty Reduction and Reform in Developing Countries." *Governance* 17, no. 4 (2012): 525–548.

Guibernau, Montserrat. "Spain: Catalonia and the Basque Country." *Parliamentary Affairs* 53, no. 1 (2000): 55–68.

Haas, Peter. "Introduction: Epistemic Communities and International Policy Coordination." *International Organization* 46, no. 1 (1992): 1–35.

Haggard, Stephan, and Lydia Tiede. "The Rule of Law and Economic Growth." *Annual Review of Political Science* 14 (2011): 205–234.

Hammami, Rema. "Palestinian NGOs Since Oslo: From NGO Politics to Social Movements?" *Middle East Report* 214 (2000): 16–19, 27, 48.

Haubrich, Dirk. "September 11, Anti-Terror Laws and Civil Liberties: Britain, France and Germany Compared." *Government and Opposition* 38, no. 1 (2003): 3–28.

Head, Keith, and Thierry Mayer. "Market Potential and the Location of Japanese Investment in the European Union." *Review of Economics and Statistics* 86, no. 4 (2004): 959–972.

Heller, Mark A. "Toward a Palestinian State." *Survival* 44, no. 3 (2002): 31–46.

Hirschl, Ran. "The Theocratic Challenge to Constitution Drafting in Post-Conflict States." *William & Mary Law Review* 49, no. 4 (2008): 1179–1211.

Hooghe, Liesbet. "Belgium: Hollowing the Center." In *Federalism and Territorial Cleavages*, edited by Ugo M. Amoretti and Nancy Bermeo, 55–92. Baltimore: Johns Hopkins University Press, 2004.

Horgan, John, and Kurt Braddock. "Rehabilitating the Terrorists? Challenges in Assessing the Effectiveness of De-radicalization Programs." *Terrorism and Political Violence* 22, no. 2 (2010): 267–291.

Horowitz, Donald. "Ethnic Power Sharing: Three Big Problems." *Journal of Democracy* 25, no. 2 (2014): 5–20.

Horowitz, Donald L. "Constitutional Design: Proposals Versus Processes." In *The Architecture of Democracy*, edited by Andrew Reynolds, 15–36. Oxford: Oxford University Press, 2002.

Hrbek, Rudolf. "The Role of the Bundesrat in German Politics." In *Developments in German Politics 2*, edited by Gordon Smith, William E. Paterson, and Stephen Padgett, 82–105. Basingstoke: Palgrave Macmillan, 2002.

Hänggi, Heiner. "Conceptualising Security Sector Reform and Reconstruction." In *Reform and Reconstruction of the Security Sector*, edited by Alan Bryden and Heiner Hänggi, 3–18. Geneva: DCAF, 2004.

Ianchovichina, Elena, and Susanna Lundström. "Inclusive Growth Analytics: Framework and Application." *World Bank Policy Research Working Paper* 4851 (2009).

Inbar, Efraim. "Israel's Post-October 7th Strategic Imperatives." *Middle East Quarterly* 31, no. 1 (2024): 1–12.

Inbar, Efraim. "The Need to Block a Palestinian State." BESA Center Perspectives Paper No. 1320, 2019.

Inbar, Efraim, and Shmuel Sandler. "Israel's National Security." In *Confidence Building Measures in the Middle East*, edited by Gabriel Ben-Dor and David Dewitt, 97–122. Boulder: Westview Press, 2008.

Jacobson, David. "When Palestine Meant Israel." *Biblical Archaeology Review* 25, no. 3 (1999): 42–47.

Jamal, Amal. "Strategies of Minority Struggle for Equality in Ethnic States: Arab Politics in Israel." *Citizenship Studies* 11, no. 3 (2007): 263–282.

Javorcik, Beata Smarzynska. "Does Foreign Direct Investment Increase the Productivity of Domestic Firms?" *American Economic Review* 94, no. 3 (2004): 605–627.

Jeffery, Charlie. "The German Länder and Europe." *Regional & Federal Studies* 13, no. 2 (2003): 1–8.

Jervis, Robert. "Cooperation Under the Security Dilemma." *World Politics* 30, no. 2 (1978): 167–214.

Jomo, K. S., ed. *The New Economic Policy and Interethnic Relations in Malaysia*. Geneva: UNRISD, 2004.

Judt, Tony. "Israel: The Alternative." *The New York Review of Books*, October 23, 2003.

Katz, Michael L., and Carl Shapiro. "Network Externalities, Competition, and Compatibility." *American Economic Review* 75, no. 3 (1985): 424–440.

Keating, Michael. "Regions and International Affairs." In *Paradiplomacy in Action*, 1–16. London: Frank Cass, 1999.

Kedar, Alexandre. "The Legal Transformation of Ethnic Geography." *Law & Society Review* 35, no. 4 (2001): 923–956.

Keen, Michael, and Maurice Marchand. "Fiscal Competition and the Pattern of Public Spending." *Journal of Public Economics* 66, no. 1 (1997): 33–53.

Kelman, Herbert C. "The Israeli-Palestinian Peace Process and Its Vicissitudes: Insights from Attitude Theory." *American Psychologist* 62, no. 4 (2007): 287–303.

Kelman, Herbert C. "Social-Psychological Dimensions of International Conflict." In *Peacemaking in International Conflict*, edited by I. William Zartman, 61–107. Washington, DC: USIP Press, 2007.

Klein, Menachem. "The Jerusalem Question." *International Affairs* 79, no. 2 (2003): 371–391.

Klier, John, and Shlomo Lambroza, eds. *Pogroms: Anti-Jewish Violence in Modern Russian History*. Cambridge: Cambridge University Press, 1992.

Kober, Avi. "The Israel Defense Forces in the Second Intifada." *Journal of Strategic Studies* 30, no. 5 (2007): 699–742.

Kohn, Richard. "How Democracies Control the Military." *Journal of Democracy* 8, no. 4 (1997): 140–153.

Kuperwasser, Yossi. "Deradicalization as Prerequisite for Peace: Lessons from October 7th." *Israel Journal of Foreign Affairs* 18, no. 1 (2024): 23–38.

Kymlicka, Will. "Is Federalism a Viable Alternative to Secession?" In *Theories of Secession*, edited by Percy Lehning, 109–148. London: Routledge, 1998.

La Porta, Rafael, Florencio Lopez-de-Silanes, Andrei Shleifer, and Robert Vishny. "Law and Finance." *Journal of Political Economy* 106, no. 6 (1998): 1113–1155.

Landau, Emily, and Tamar Malz. "Building Regional Security in the Middle East: International, Regional and Domestic Influences." *Journal of Strategic Studies* 26, no. 3 (2003): 16–39.

Layish, Aharon. "The Transformation of the Shari'a from Jurists' Law to Statutory Law in the Contemporary Muslim World." *Die Welt des Islams* 44, no. 1 (2004): 85–113.

Lemaire, André. "'House of David' Restored in Moabite Inscription." *Biblical Archaeology Review* 20, no. 3 (1994): 30–37.

Leonardy, Uwe. "The Institutional Structures of German Federalism." In *Recasting German Federalism: The Legacies of Unification*, edited by Charlie Jeffery, 3–22. London: Pinter, 1999.

Linder, Wolf, and Adrian Vatter. "Institutions and Outcomes of Swiss Federalism: The Role of the Cantons in Swiss Politics." *West European Politics* 24, no. 2 (2001): 95–122.

Lutz, Donald. "Toward a Theory of Constitutional Amendment." *American Political Science Review* 88, no. 2 (1994): 355–370.

Lynch, Marc. "October 7th and the Collapse of Normalization." *Foreign Affairs* 103, no. 2 (2024): 45–58.

Lynch, Marc. "Media, Old and New." In *The Arab Uprisings Explained*, edited by Marc Lynch, 93–109. New York: Columbia University Press, 2014.

Lynch, Marc. "The Abraham Accords: Assessing the Arab-Israel Normalization Agreements." *Carnegie Middle East Center*, 2020.

Lüdi, Georges, and Iwar Werlen. "Sprachenlandschaft in der Schweiz" [Language Landscape in Switzerland]. Neuchâtel: Swiss Federal Statistical Office, 2005.

Makovsky, David, and Michael Koplow. "After October 7: Rethinking Israeli-Palestinian Relations." *Foreign Affairs* 103, no. 2 (2024): 78–94.

March, James, and Johan Olsen. "The Logic of Appropriateness." In *The Oxford Handbook of Political Science*, edited by Robert Goodin, 478–497. Oxford: Oxford University Press, 2011.

McGarry, John, and Brendan O'Leary. "Consociational Theory, Northern Ireland's Conflict, and Its Agreement." *Government and Opposition* 41, no. 1 (2006): 43–63.

McGarry, John, Brendan O'Leary, and Richard Simeon. "Integration or Accommodation?" *Constitutional Political Economy* 19, no. 4 (2008): 323–358.

McGarry, John. "Asymmetry in Federations, Federacies and Unitary States." *Ethnopolitics* 6, no. 1 (2007): 105–116.

McGarry, John, and Brendan O'Leary. "Must Pluri-national Federations Fail?" *Ethnopolitics* 8, no. 1 (2009): 5–25.

Mogahed, Dalia, and Youssef Chouhoud. "American Muslim Poll 2017: Muslims at the Crossroads." Washington, DC: Institute for Social Policy and Understanding, 2017.

Morris, Benny. "Revisiting the Palestinian Exodus of 1948." In *The War for Palestine: Rewriting the History of 1948*, edited by Eugene L. Rogan and Avi Shlaim, 37–59. Cambridge: Cambridge University Press, 2001.

Nakagawa, Rika. "The Evolution of Islamic Finance in Southeast Asia." *Nomura Journal of Capital Markets* 1, no. 3 (2009): 1–17.

Nassaux, Jean-Pierre. "The Specific Institutional Framework of the Brussels-Capital Region." *Brussels Studies* 48 (2011): 1–15.

Naveh, Joseph. *Early History of the Alphabet*. Jerusalem: Magnes Press, 1982.

Neidhardt, Frank. "The Federal Criminal Police Office in Germany." In *Policing in Federal States*, edited by Christian Mouhanna, 67–89. Geneva: DCAF, 2008.

Neuer, Hillel. "UN Watch Annual Report 2023." Geneva: UN Watch, 2023.

Newman, David. "The Geopolitics of Peacemaking in Israel-Palestine." *Political Geography* 21, no. 5 (2002): 629–646.

O'Leary, Brendan. "Debating Consociational Politics: Normative and Explanatory Arguments." In *From Power Sharing to Democracy*, edited by Sid Noel, 267–289. Montreal: McGill-Queen's University Press, 2005.

O'Leary, Brendan. "Debating Consociational Politics: Normative and Explanatory Arguments." In *From Power Sharing to Democracy*, edited by Sid Noel, 3–43. Montreal: McGill-Queen's University Press, 2005.

Oates, Wallace. "An Essay on Fiscal Federalism." *Journal of Economic Literature* 37, no. 3 (1999): 1120–1149.

Pagano, Marco. "Financial Markets and Growth: An Overview." *European Economic Review* 37, no. 2–3 (1993): 613–622.

Papillon, Martin. "Canadian Federalism and the Emerging Mosaic of Aboriginal Multilevel Governance." In *Canadian Federalism: Performance, Effectiveness, and Legitimacy*, 3rd ed., edited by Herman Bakvis and Grace Skogstad, 291–313. Don Mills: Oxford University Press, 2012.

Peeters, Patrick. "Federalism: A Comparative Perspective—Belgium Transforms from a Unitary to a Federal State." In

Evaluating Federal Systems, edited by Bertus de Villiers, 194–215. Cape Town: Juta, 2007.

Peled, Yoav, and Doron Navot. "Ethnic Democracy Revisited." *Israel Studies Forum* 20, no. 1 (2005): 3–27.

Pettigrew, Thomas, and Linda Tropp. "A Meta-Analytic Test of Intergroup Contact Theory." *Journal of Personality and Social Psychology* 90, no. 5 (2006): 751–783.

Pinfari, Marco. "Nothing but Failure? The Arab League and the Gulf Cooperation Council as Mediators in Middle Eastern Conflicts." *Crisis States Working Papers Series* 2, no. 45 (2009): 1–28.

Podeh, Elie. "The Arab Peace Initiative: A Missed Opportunity?" *Israel Studies* 19, no. 3 (2014): 147–175.

Podeh, Elie. *The Abraham Accords and the Changing Strategic Landscape of the Middle East*. Ramat Gan: Begin-Sadat Center for Strategic Studies, 2021.

Porat, Rivka, and Michal Shamir. "Israeli Public Opinion After October 7: Rightward Shift and Security Primacy." *Israel Studies Review* 39, no. 1 (2024): 45–67.

Posen, Barry R. "The Security Dilemma and Ethnic Conflict." *Survival* 35, no. 1 (1993): 27–47.

Raghavan, Srinath. "From Planning Commission to NITI Aayog: Evolution of Federal Economic Governance." *Economic and Political Weekly* 54, no. 7 (2019): 36–42.

Reaves, Brian. *Local Police Departments, 2013: Personnel, Policies, and Practices*. Washington, DC: Bureau of Justice Statistics, 2015.

Reich, Ronny, and Eli Shukron. "The Siloam Tunnel." *Jerusalem Perspective* 64 (2011): 1–12.

Renzsch, Wolfgang. "Finanzverfassung und Finanzausgleich" [Financial Constitution and Fiscal Equalization]. Bonn: Dietz, 1991.

Renzsch, Wolfgang. "German Federalism in Transition." *Publius: The Journal of Federalism* 30, no. 4 (2000): 49–69.

Reuchamps, Min, and Giulia Verniers. "Belgium's Sixth State Reform: From a 'Non-Reform' to a 'Super-Reform'?" *Representation* 46, no. 4 (2010): 465–476.

Rivlin, Paul. "The Middle East: A Zero-Sum Game?" *Middle East Economy* 6, no. 4 (2016): 1–28.

Rodden, Jonathan. "Reviving Leviathan: Fiscal Federalism and the Growth of Government." *International Organization* 57, no. 4 (2003): 695–729.

Romirowsky, Asaf. "UNRWA: Barrier to Middle East Peace." *Middle East Quarterly* 17, no. 4 (2010): 27–37.

Rosecrance, Richard, and Peter Thompson. "Trade, Foreign Investment, and Security." *Annual Review of Political Science* 6 (2003): 377–398.

Rosenberg, David, and Uriel Shavit. "Economic Integration in the Middle East." *Middle East Quarterly* 29, no. 2 (2022): 45–62.

Rosoux, Valérie. "National Identity in France and Germany: From Mutual Exclusion to Negotiation." *International Negotiation* 6, no. 2 (2001): 175–198.

Rostow, Eugene. "The Truth About UN 242." *The New Republic*, October 1990.

Rothchild, Donald, and Philip Roeder. "Power Sharing as an Impediment to Peace and Democracy." In *Sustainable Peace*, edited by Philip Roeder and Donald Rothchild, 29–50. Ithaca: Cornell University Press, 2005.

Rudolph, Lloyd I., and Susanne Hoeber Rudolph. "Federalism as State Formation in India." *International Political Science Review* 31, no. 5 (2010): 553–572.

Sa'di, Ahmad. "Catastrophe, Memory and Identity: Al-Nakbah as a Component of Palestinian Identity." *Israel Studies* 7, no. 2 (2002): 175–198.

Saalfeld, Thomas. "Members of Parliament and Governments in Western Europe." *European Journal of Political Research* 37, no. 3 (2000): 353–376.

Safrai, Shmuel, ed. *The Literature of the Sages*. Minneapolis: Fortress, 1994.

Saideman, Stephen M., et al. "Democratization, Political Institutions, and Ethnic Conflict: A Pooled Time-Series Analysis, 1985-1998." *Comparative Political Studies* 35, no. 1 (2002): 103–129.

Scharpf, Fritz W. "The Joint-Decision Trap Revisited." *Journal of Common Market Studies* 44, no. 4 (2006): 845–864.

Scharpf, Fritz W. "The Joint-Decision Trap: Lessons from German Federalism and European Integration." *Public Administration* 66, no. 3 (1988): 239–278.

Schechter, Asher. "The Expulsion of Germans After World War Two." *Haaretz*, June 2013.

Schiff, Maurice. *Regional Integration and Development*. Washington, DC: World Bank, 2014.

Shanks, Hershel. "'David' Found at Dan." *Biblical Archaeology Review* 20, no. 2 (1994): 26–39.

Shikaki, Khalil. "The Palestinian Political System." In *The Routledge Handbook on the Israeli-Palestinian Conflict*, edited by Michael Lynfield, 123–137. London: Routledge, 2020.

Shlaim, Avi. "After October 7: What Future for Palestine?" *Journal of Palestine Studies* 53, no. 2 (2024): 12–28.

Sigalas, Emmanuel. "Cross-Border Mobility and European Identity." *European Union Politics* 11, no. 2 (2010): 241–265.

Simeon, Richard, and David Cameron. "Intergovernmental Relations and Democratic Citizenship." In *Canadian Federalism*, edited by Herman Bakvis and Grace Skogstad, 110–132. Don Mills: Oxford University Press, 2002.

Simeon, Richard, and Daniel P. Conway. "Federalism and the Management of Conflict in Multinational Societies." In *Multinational Democracies*, edited by Alain-G. Gagnon and James Tully, 338–365. Cambridge: Cambridge University Press, 2001.

Skogstad, Grace. "Canadian Federalism and Economic Integration." *Canadian Public Administration* 46, no. 2 (2003): 154–171.

Sm

Smooha, Sammy. "The Model of Ethnic Democracy." *Nations and Nationalism* 8, no. 4 (2002): 423–447.

Solingen, Etel. "Pax Asiatica Versus Bella Levantina: The Foundations of War and Peace in the Middle East and East Asia." *Cambridge Review of International Affairs* 20, no. 3 (2007): 417–437.

Spahn, Paul Bernd. "Equity and Efficiency Aspects of Intergovernmental Fiscal Relations." In *Perspectives on Fiscal Federalism*, edited by Richard M. Bird and François Vaillancourt, 134–156. Washington, DC: World Bank, 2007.

Spahn, Paul Bernd, and Wolfgang Föttinger. "Germany." In *Fiscal Federalism in Theory and Practice*, edited by Teresa Ter-Minassian, 226–248. Washington, DC: IMF, 1997.

Stager, Lawrence. "Merneptah, Israel and Sea Peoples." *Eretz-Israel* 18 (1985): 56–64.

Steinberg, Gerald. "The Politics of NGOs, Human Rights, and the Arab-Israeli Conflict." *Israel Studies* 16, no. 2 (2011): 24–54.

Stepan, Alfred. "The Multiple Secularisms of Modern Democratic and Non-Democratic Regimes." In *Rethinking Secularism*, edited by Craig Calhoun, Mark Juergensmeyer, and Jonathan VanAntwerpen, 114–144. Oxford: Oxford University Press, 2011.

Stepan, Alfred, Juan J. Linz, and Yogendra Yadav. "The Rise of 'State-Nations'." *Journal of Democracy* 21, no. 3 (2010): 50–68.

Stepan, Alfred. "Federalism and Democracy: Beyond the U.S. Model." *Journal of Democracy* 10, no. 4 (1999): 19–34.

Stone Sweet, Alec. *Governing with Judges: Constitutional Politics in Europe*. Oxford: Oxford University Press, 2000.

Strøm, Kaare. "Delegation and Accountability in Parliamentary Democracies." *European Journal of Political Research* 37, no. 3 (2000): 261–289.

Strøm, Kaare. "Parliamentary Committees in European Democracies." *Journal of Legislative Studies* 4, no. 1 (1998): 21–59.

Sturm, Roland. "Divided Government in Germany." In *Divided Government in Comparative Perspective*, edited by Robert Elgie, 167–189. Oxford: Oxford University Press, 2001.

Swenden, Wilfried. "Asymmetric Federalism and Coalition-Making in Belgium." *Publius: The Journal of Federalism* 32, no. 3 (2002): 67–87.

Swenden, Wilfried, and Maarten Theo Jans. "Will It Stay or Will It Go? Federalism and the Sustainability of Belgium." *West European Politics* 29, no. 5 (2006): 877–894.

Tanzi, Vito. "Fiscal Federalism and Decentralization: A Review of Some Efficiency and Macroeconomic Aspects." In *Annual World Bank Conference on Development Economics 1995*, edited by Michael Bruno and Boris Pleskovic, 295–316. Washington, DC: World Bank, 1996.

Tarlton, Charles D. "Symmetry and Asymmetry as Elements of Federalism: A Theoretical Speculation." *Journal of Politics* 27, no. 4 (1965): 861–874.

Teclaff, Ludwik A. "Evolution of the River Basin Concept in National and International Water Law." *Natural Resources Journal* 36, no. 2 (1996): 359–391.

Telhami, Shibley. "The Abraham Accords After October 7th." *Foreign Policy*, Spring 2024, 78–92.

Tessler, Mark, and Marilyn Grobschmidt. "Democracy in the Arab World and the Arab-Israeli Conflict." In *Democracy, War and Peace in the Middle East*, edited by David Garnham and Mark Tessler, 135–169. Bloomington: Indiana University Press, 1995.

Thompson, Mark. "Being Young, Male and Saudi: Identity and Politics in a Globalized Kingdom." Cambridge: Cambridge University Press, 2017.

Thorlakson, Lori. "Federalism and Party Politics." In *Federal Democracies*, edited by Michael Burgess and Alain-G. Gagnon, 113–134. London: Routledge, 2005.

Tillin, Louise. "Explaining Territorial Change in Federal Democracies: A Comparative Historical Institutionalist Approach." *Political Studies* 63, no. 3 (2015): 626–641.

Trimikliniotis, Nicos. "The Cyprus Problem: A Critical Introduction." In *The Future of the Cyprus Problem*, edited by Nicos Trimikliniotis and Umut Bozkurt, 1–38. Oslo: PRIO, 2009.

Ulrichsen, Kristian Coates. "The Gulf States and Regional Realignment." In *The Oxford Handbook of Contemporary Middle-Eastern Politics*, edited by Marc Lynch, 445–467. Oxford: Oxford University Press, 2023.
Walzer, Michael. "The Paradox of Liberation." *Dissent* 65, no. 4 (2018): 134–145.
Whytock, Christopher A. "Domestic Courts and Global Governance." *Tulane Law Review* 84 (2009): 69–123.
Wouters, Jan, and Lode De Smet. "Brussels in the European Union: Between Institutional Competition and International Cooperation." Leuven: Leuven Centre for Global Governance Studies, 2015.
Yaari, Ehud. "Armistice Now." *Foreign Affairs* 90, no. 2 (2011): 50–62.
Yadlin, Amos, and Udi Dekel. "The Security Dimensions of the Israeli-Palestinian Arena." INSS Strategic Assessment, 2021.
Zegart, Amy. "September 11 and the Adaptation Failure of U.S. Intelligence Agencies." *International Security* 29, no. 4 (2005): 78–111.

III. Government & Institutional Reports.

AAAS. *Federal R&D Budget Dashboard*. American Association for the Advancement of Science, 2023.
Abraham Accords Peace Institute. *Economic Impact Assessment: Two Years of Normalization*. Washington, DC: AAPI, 2024.
Arab Barometer. *Arab Public Opinion After October 7th: Emergency Survey Results*. Princeton, NJ: Arab Barometer, 2024.
Arab Center Washington DC. *The Abraham Accords and Arab League Divisions*. Washington, DC: ACW, 2023.
Arab Gulf States Institute. *Business and Normalization in the Post-October 7th Era*. Washington, DC: AGSI, 2024.
ASEAN Secretariat. *ASEAN Statistical Yearbook 2023*. Jakarta: ASEAN, 2023.
Barak, Ehud. Interview with Benny Morris. *New York Review of Books*, June 13, 2002.
Bavarian State Ministry. *Bavaria's International Economic Relations Report*. Munich: StMWi, 2023.
Bundesministerium der Verteidigung. *Verteidigungshaushalt 2024*. Berlin: BMVg, 2024.
Carnegie Endowment for International Peace. Sadjadpour, Karim. *Iran's Strategic Gains After October 7th*. Washington, DC: Carnegie, 2024.
Census of India. *Religious Composition*. New Delhi: Office of the Registrar General, 2011.

Chatham House. "Building a New Regional Order in the Middle East." Research Paper. London: Chatham House, 2021.

Government of India. *FDI Statistics*. Department for Promotion of Industry and Internal Trade, 2023.

Hamas. *The Covenant of the Islamic Resistance Movement*. 1988.

ICD-Refinitiv. *Islamic Finance Development Report*. Dubai: ICD, 2023.

IMF. *Middle East Economic Outlook: Youth Employment and Regional Integration*. Washington, DC: International Monetary Fund, 2024.

IMPACT-se. *Palestinian Elementary School Curriculum 2023*. Jerusalem: IMPACT-se, 2023.

IMPACT-se. *Palestinian Elementary School Curriculum 2020-21: Radicalization Continues*. Jerusalem: Institute for Monitoring Peace and Cultural Tolerance in School Education, 2021.

IMPACT-se. *Anti-Normalization in Arab Educational Curricula: 2024 Review*. Jerusalem: IMPACT-se, 2024.

Indian Ministry of Commerce. *Trade Agreements Database*. New Delhi: Government of India, 2023.

International Crisis Group. *Gaza After the War: Reconstructing Palestinian Politics*. Brussels: International Crisis Group Report No. 245, 2024.

Israel Ministry of Foreign Affairs. "Declaration of the Establishment of the State of Israel." May 14, 1948.

Israel Democracy Institute. *Israeli Public Opinion on Federal Solutions: Annual Survey*. Jerusalem: IDI, 2024.

Israel-UAE Business Council. *Annual Trade Report 2023*. Tel Aviv: IUBC, 2024.

Israeli Ministry of Tourism. *Tourism Statistics Annual Report*. Jerusalem: Ministry of Tourism, 2023.

MEMRI. *Palestinian Authority Media Continues Glorification of Terrorism*. Washington, DC: Middle East Media Research Institute Special Report No. 10457, 2023.

Middle East Institute. *The Arab League Response to October 7th*. Washington, DC: MEI, 2024.

NGO Monitor. *Palestinian NGOs and Terror Links*. Jerusalem: NGO Monitor, 2023.

Palestinian Center for Policy and Survey Research. Shikaki, Khalil. *Palestinian Public Opinion Poll No. 90*. Ramallah: PSR, 2024.

PwC. *MoneyTree Report: Global Venture Capital Investment Analysis*. PricewaterhouseCoopers, 2023.

Riedel, Bruce. *Saudi Arabia and Israeli Normalization: The October 7th Impact*. Washington, DC: Brookings Institution, 2024.

Sagi, Nana. *German Reparations: A History of the Negotiations*. Basingstoke: Palgrave Macmillan, 2009.

Stockholm International Peace Research Institute. *SIPRI Military Expenditure Database*. 2024.

TASE. *Tel Aviv Stock Exchange Annual Report*. Tel Aviv: TASE, 2023.

TMX Group. *Market Statistics Report*. Toronto: TMX Group Limited, 2023.

Truth and Reconciliation Commission of Canada. *Honouring the Truth, Reconciling for the Future*. Ottawa: TRC, 2015.

U.S. Energy Information Administration. *Eastern Mediterranean Energy Assessment*. Washington, DC: EIA, 2023.

UN Watch. *UNRWA Staff Involvement in October 7 Massacre*. Geneva: UN Watch, 2024.

UN Watch. "Database: UN Resolutions on Israel vs. Rest of World." Accessed 2024. https://unwatch.org.

United States Department of Defense. *National Defense Strategy*. Washington, DC: DoD, 2022.

UNWTO. *World Tourism Barometer*. Madrid: World Tourism Organization, 2023.

Weber, Max. "Politics as a Vocation." In *From Max Weber*, edited by Hans Gerth and C. Wright Mills, 77–128. Oxford: Oxford University Press, 1946.

Wilson Center. *Middle East Conflicts and Regional Convergence*. Washington, DC: Wilson Center, 2025.

World Bank. *West Bank and Gaza: Public Expenditure Review*. Washington, DC: World Bank Report No. 40096-GZ, 2007.

World Bank. *World Development Indicators Database*. Washington, DC: World Bank, 2023.

World Bank. *Economic Integration in the Middle East and North Africa*. Washington, DC: World Bank Group, 2023.

Yadlin, Amos, and Uri Evental. *Strategic Assessment: Israel After October 7th*. Tel Aviv: Institute for National Security Studies, 2024.

IV. News & Media.

"Saudi Crown Prince on Israel Normalisation." Interview with Fox News, September 2023.

Bayefsky, Anne. "One Small Step." *New York Sun*, April 8, 2008.

Bishara, Marwan. "Gaza and the Narrative War." *The Nation*, February 15, 2024.

Brown, Nathan. "Palestine: Federalism, Not So Fast." *Lawfare*, January 2024.

Halevi, Yossi Klein. "Israel After October 7th." *Times of Israel*, November 2024.
Ibish, Hussein. "The Abraham Accords Illusion." *The Atlantic*, January 2024.
Jamai, Aboubakr. "Le Maroc face au dilemme israélien." *Le Monde Diplomatique*, December 2023.
Oren, Michael. "The End of Illusions." *Commentary*, February 2024.
Wittes, Benjamin. "Federalism and the Future of Israel-Palestine." *Lawfare Blog*, October 29, 2023.
Wollins, Shlomo. "Federal Zionism: A Path Forward." *Times of Israel*, 2024.
Wollins, Shlomo. "Federal Accommodation and Democratic Resilience." *Times of Israel*, 2024.

V. Legal Documents & Court Cases.

Andhra Pradesh Reorganisation Act, 2014 (India).
Constitution Act, 1867 (Canada).
Constitution of India, 1950.
Grundgesetz für die Bundesrepublik Deutschland [Basic Law for the Federal Republic of Germany], 1949.
In Re: Article 370 of the Constitution, Writ Petition (Civil) No. 1357 of 2019 (India Supreme Court, 2023).
Kesavananda Bharati v. State of Kerala, AIR 1973 SC 1461 (India).
Khalidi, Rashid. *Palestinian Identity: The Construction of Modern National Consciousness*. New York: Columbia University Press, 1997.
Marbury v. Madison, 5 U.S. (1 Cranch) 137 (1803).
Mohd. Ahmed Khan v. Shah Bano Begum, AIR 1985 SC 945 (India).
New State Ice Co. v. Liebmann, 285 U.S. 262 (1932).
Reference re Secession of Quebec, [1998] 2 S.C.R. 217.
S.R. Bommai v. Union of India, (1994) 3 SCC 1 (India).
States Reorganisation Act, 1956 (India).

VI. Author's Works (*The Times of Israel* Articles).

Eger, Frederic. "Is India's Federalism a Model for Israel?" *Times of Israel*, 2025.
Eger, Frederic. "The Federal State of Israel is the Only Possible One-State-Solution." *Times of Israel*, 2025.
Eger, Frederic. "Is India's Federal Model Applicable to Israel?" *Times of Israel*, 2025.
Eger, Frederic. "Israel Influence: The Good, the Bad, the Ugly." *Times of Israel*, April 18, 2025.

Educational & Activism Supplemental

Guide 1

Young Reader's Companion Guide

For Ages 13-18

Welcome, Young Reader!
This companion guide will help you understand the main ideas in *'One-State Solution: The Federal State of Israel.'* The book explores a creative political solution to one of the world's longest-running conflicts. Don't worry if some concepts seem complex at first—that's what this guide is for!

Each chapter summary below explains the key points in simple terms, followed by discussion questions to help you think more deeply about these important issues.

Chapter Summaries

Chapter 1: Ancient History to Modern Times.
This chapter establishes that Jewish people have lived in the land of Israel for over 3,000 years. Archaeological discoveries—like ancient inscriptions and ruins—prove this connection. The chapter explains how Jews maintained their identity even when living in exile for centuries, always hoping to return to their homeland.

Key Takeaway: Historical connections matter when understanding modern conflicts, but they don't determine future solutions.

Chapter 2: Federal Zionism Explained
Here we learn about 'federalism'—a system where different regions share one government but also keep some self-rule (like how the United States has both federal and state governments). The author argues that this model could work for Israelis and Palestinians living together while maintaining their distinct identities.

Key Takeaway: Federalism means sharing power rather than one side winning completely.

Chapter 3: Learning from Other Countries
Switzerland has four official languages and two major religions living peacefully together. Belgium manages French and Dutch speakers. Canada accommodates Quebec's French culture. India governs over a billion people with dozens of languages. These examples show that diverse populations CAN share one country successfully.

Key Takeaway: What works elsewhere might be adapted—not copied exactly—for Israel/Palestine.

Chapter 4: Building Blocks of Federal Government
Every federal system needs clear rules about who decides what. This chapter explains how to divide responsibilities between central government and regional authorities, and how to protect minorities even when they're outvoted.
Key Takeaway: Good rules matter more than good intentions.
Chapter 5: Why Federalism After October 7th
The tragic events of October 7, 2023, showed that the current situation isn't working for anyone's safety. This chapter argues that maintaining the status quo leads to more violence, while federal solutions could provide security for everyone.
Key Takeaway: Sometimes crisis creates opportunity for new thinking.
Chapter 6: Rebuilding After Conflict
Germany transformed from Nazi dictatorship to stable democracy after World War II. This chapter examines how societies heal after terrible violence and build new institutions that everyone can trust.
Key Takeaway: Peace requires not just ending violence but building fair institutions.
Chapter 7: The Abraham Accords
Recently, Israel signed peace agreements with UAE, Bahrain, Morocco, and Sudan. These 'Abraham Accords' showed that regional cooperation is possible—but they didn't address the Palestinian question. This chapter explores both achievements and limitations.
Key Takeaway: Diplomatic progress is possible but incomplete without addressing core issues.
Chapter 8: Economics of Peace
When people have jobs, businesses, and prosperity, they're less likely to support violence. This chapter examines how a federal Israel could create economic opportunities for everyone, making peace more sustainable than any treaty alone.
Key Takeaway: Economics and politics are deeply connected.
Chapter 9: Keeping Everyone Safe
Security is non-negotiable. This chapter explains how a federal system could protect all citizens through unified military command while allowing regional police forces to serve local communities.
Key Takeaway: Security and freedom aren't opposites—good institutions provide both.
Chapter 10: Living Together with Differences
How do schools teach history when different groups remember it differently? How do media represent diverse communities fairly? This chapter explores the cultural challenges of shared citizenship.

Key Takeaway: Institutions can't force people to like each other, but they can create space for coexistence.

Chapter 11: Honest Criticism

Not everyone agrees federalism would work. This chapter presents the strongest arguments against the federal solution and responds to them honestly.

Key Takeaway: Taking criticism seriously makes arguments stronger.

Chapter 12: Step-by-Step Implementation

Big changes don't happen overnight. This chapter outlines how a federal solution might be implemented gradually, building trust at each stage.

Key Takeaway: Process matters as much as destination.

Chapter 13: Transforming the Middle East

Solving the Israeli-Palestinian conflict could change the entire region, enabling cooperation on water, climate, trade, and security that's currently impossible.

Key Takeaway: Local solutions can have regional impact.

Chapter 14: The Path Forward

The final chapter brings everything together, presenting federalism as the best available option—not perfect, but better than alternatives that have all failed.

Key Takeaway: Politics is about choosing the best available option, not waiting for perfect ones.

Glossary of Key Terms

Political Terms

Abraham Accords: Peace agreements signed in 2020 between Israel and several Arab nations.

Autonomy: Self-governance; the right of a group to manage its own affairs.

Bicameralism: A legislature with two chambers (like the U.S. Senate and House).

Canton: A small territorial division with significant self-government (used in Switzerland).

Confederation: A loose association of states that retain most sovereignty.

Constitution: The fundamental laws establishing how a country is governed.

Democracy: Government by the people, typically through elected representatives.

Devolution: Transfer of powers from central to regional government.

Federation: A system where power is shared between central and regional governments.

Federalism: The principle of organizing government as a federation.

Genocide: Deliberate killing of a large group of people, especially an ethnic group.

Governance: The way organizations or countries are managed and ruled.

Hamas: Palestinian militant group controlling Gaza since 2007.

Hegemony: Dominance of one group over others.

Judicial Review: Courts' power to review and invalidate unconstitutional laws.

Legitimacy: The right to rule, accepted by those being governed.

Mandate: Authority given to govern a territory.

Nationalism: Strong identification with one's nation and support for its interests.

October 7th: Date in 2023 of Hamas attack on Israel, killing ~1,400 people.

Palestinian Authority: Governing body for parts of the West Bank since 1994.

Partition: Division of territory into separate states.

Proportional Representation: Electoral system where seats match vote percentages.

Referendum: Direct vote by citizens on a specific proposal.

Self-Determination: Right of peoples to determine their own political status.

Sovereignty: Supreme authority of a state over its territory.

Subsidiary: Principle that decisions should be made at the lowest effective level.

Two-State Solution: Proposal for independent Israeli and Palestinian states.

Unitary State: Country governed as single unit from the capital.

Veto: Power to reject a decision or proposal.

Zionism: Movement supporting Jewish self-determination in Israel.

Historical Terms

Babylonian Exile: Jewish captivity in Babylon, 586-539 BCE.

Bar Kokhba Revolt: Jewish uprising against Rome, 132-136 CE.

Balfour Declaration: 1917 British statement supporting Jewish homeland.

British Mandate: British administration of Palestine, 1920-1948.

Diaspora: Jews living outside Israel.

First Temple: Solomon's Temple in Jerusalem, destroyed 586 BCE.

Green Line: 1949 armistice border between Israel and neighbors.

Hasmonean Dynasty: Jewish ruling dynasty, 140-37 BCE.
Holocaust: Nazi genocide of six million Jews during WWII.
Intifada: Palestinian uprisings (First: 1987-1993; Second: 2000-2005).
Nakba: Arabic for 'catastrophe'; Palestinian term for 1948 displacement.
Oslo Accords: 1993-1995 peace agreements between Israel and PLO.
Second Temple: Rebuilt Temple in Jerusalem, 516 BCE-70 CE.
Six-Day War: 1967 war where Israel captured West Bank, Gaza, Sinai, Golan.
UN Partition Plan: 1947 proposal to divide Palestine into Jewish and Arab states.
War of Independence: 1948 war following Israel's declaration of independence.
Yom Kippur War: 1973 surprise attack on Israel by Egypt and Syria.

Geographic Terms
Gaza Strip: Coastal territory, ~365 km², population ~2 million.
Golan Heights: Strategic plateau captured from Syria in 1967.
Jerusalem: Holy city claimed by Jews, Christians, and Muslims.
Jordan River: River forming part of Israel's eastern border.
Mediterranean Sea: Body of water along Israel's western coast.
Negev: Desert region in southern Israel.
Settlements: Israeli communities in territories captured in 1967.
Temple Mount/Haram al-Sharif: Sacred site in Jerusalem holy to Jews and Muslims.
West Bank: Territory west of Jordan River, captured by Israel in 1967.

Comparative Examples
Belgium: Federal kingdom with Dutch and French-speaking regions.
Bosnia-Herzegovina: Federal state created after 1990s Yugoslav wars.
Canada: Federation accommodating English and French cultures.
Germany: Federal republic rebuilt after WWII.
India: World's largest democracy, governing 1.4 billion diverse people.
Northern Ireland: Power-sharing between unionists and nationalists since 1998.
South Africa: Transition from apartheid to democracy, 1990-1994.
Switzerland: Confederation of 26 cantons with four official languages.

Discussion Questions

Chapter 1-2: History and Concepts
- Why do historical claims matter in political disputes? Should ancient history determine modern borders?
- What's the difference between 'winning' a conflict and 'resolving' it?
- Can two peoples with conflicting narratives share one country? What would that require?

Chapters 3-4: Comparative Models
- What can Israel/Palestine learn from Switzerland? What makes their situation different?
- Why might people prefer self-governance even if unified government would be more efficient?
- How do you protect minority rights in a democracy where majorities rule?

Chapters 5-6: Crisis and Reconstruction
- Does crisis create opportunity for change, or does it make people more defensive?
- How did Germany transform from Nazi dictatorship to democracy? What lessons apply elsewhere?
- What's the difference between 'peace' and 'justice'? Can you have one without the other?

Chapters 7-8: Regional and Economic Dimensions
- Why did Arab countries sign the Abraham Accords? What did they hope to gain?
- How does economic prosperity affect political attitudes?
- Should rich regions subsidize poor ones? Why or why not?

Chapters 9-10: Security and Diversity
- Can you have both security AND freedom? How do democracies balance these?
- How should schools teach contested history?
- What's the difference between 'tolerance' and 'respect'? Which does coexistence require?

Chapters 11-14: Criticism and Implementation
- What's the strongest argument AGAINST federalism for Israel/Palestine?
- Why is gradual implementation important? What happens if you move too fast?
- If you were advising leaders, what would be your first step toward federal solution?

"What Would You Do?" Scenarios

Scenario 1: The Curriculum Committee

You're on a committee designing history curriculum for a federal state where Jewish and Arab students attend the same schools. Israeli history books describe 1948 as 'War of Independence'; Palestinian books call it 'Nakba' (catastrophe). How do you create a curriculum both communities can accept?

- Possible approaches: Teach both narratives? Create 'objective' third version? Let each community teach its own history?
- What are the tradeoffs of each approach?

Scenario 2: The Water Crisis

A federal state needs to allocate scarce water resources between agricultural regions (mostly Arab) and high-tech industries (mostly Jewish). Both need more water than is available. How do you decide fairly?

- What principles should guide resource allocation?
- How do you balance economic efficiency with fairness?

Scenario 3: The Security Dilemma

A terrorist attack occurs in the federal state. Some want to increase security measures that would affect everyone; others worry this unfairly targets Arab citizens. You're a minister who must decide.

- How do you protect security without discrimination?
- What accountability mechanisms would you establish?

Scenario 4: The Language Question

A new federal law requires all government services be provided in both Hebrew and Arabic. Some officials complain this is expensive and inefficient. Citizens in some regions say they need services in their language.

- Is linguistic equality worth the cost?
- What compromises might work?

Scenario 5: The Election

In a federal election, you must vote for candidates representing very different visions: one wants stronger central government, another wants more regional autonomy. Both claim their approach better serves peace.

- What questions would you ask each candidate?
- What information would help you decide?

Recommended Further Reading

For Ages 13-15

- 'I Am Malala' by Malala Yousafzai — A young woman's fight for education shows how individual courage can challenge systems.

- 'The Diary of Anne Frank' — Holocaust perspective essential for understanding Jewish history.
- 'March' trilogy by John Lewis — Graphic novels about civil rights movement and nonviolent resistance.
- 'Persepolis' by Marjane Satrapi — Graphic novel about growing up during Iranian revolution.
- 'A Little Piece of Ground' by Elizabeth Laird — Novel about Palestinian boy's experience during occupation.

For Ages 16-18

- 'Night' by Elie Wiesel — Nobel laureate's memoir of surviving the Holocaust.
- 'The Lemon Tree' by Sandy Tolan — True story of Israeli and Palestinian families sharing one house.
- 'Letters to My Palestinian Neighbor' by Yossi Klein Halevi — Israeli author's attempt at dialogue.
- 'Once Upon a Country' by Sari Nusseibeh — Palestinian philosopher's memoir and peace proposals.
- 'The Birth of the Palestinian Refugee Problem Revisited' by Benny Morris — Academic but accessible history.

On Federalism and Comparative Politics

- 'Why Nations Fail' by Daron Acemoglu & James Robinson — How institutions shape prosperity (accessible version).
- 'The Federalist Papers' (selected essays) — American founders explaining federal principles.
- 'Small is Beautiful' by E.F. Schumacher — Classic on decentralization and human-scale institutions.

Online Resources

- Wikipedia articles on: Swiss political system, Belgian federalism, Indian constitution.
- YouTube: 'CGP Grey' videos on electoral systems and governance.
- Podcasts: 'Conflicted' by Ayman Mohyeldin covers Middle East complexity accessibly.

— End of Young Reader's Companion Guide —

Guide 2

Scholar's Extended Bibliography

Organized by Theme with Annotations

This annotated bibliography organizes scholarly sources thematically rather than by chapter, enabling researchers to pursue specific lines of inquiry. Each section identifies key works, notes research gaps, and cross-references relevant book chapters.

I. Federalism Theory and Comparative Design

Cross-references: Chapters 2, 3, 4, 11, 12

Foundational Works

Elazar, Daniel J. (1987), *Exploring Federalism*. University of Alabama Press.

The essential starting point for federal theory. Elazar's distinction between 'self-rule and shared rule' provides the conceptual foundation for applying federalism to deeply divided societies. Introduces the 'covenant' tradition underlying federal arrangements.

Riker, William H. (1964), *Federalism: Origin, Operation, Significance*. Little, Brown.

Classic rational-choice analysis of federal formation. Argues federalism emerges from military/diplomatic bargains rather than idealistic motivations. Essential for understanding why federations form and what sustains them.

Stepan, Alfred (1999). 'Federalism and Democracy: Beyond the U.S. Model.' Journal of Democracy 10(4): 19-34.

Crucial corrective to American-centric federalism studies. Introduces 'demos-constraining' vs. 'demos-enabling' federalism, relevant for constitutional design protecting minorities.

Comparative Federal Systems

Watts, Ronald L. (2008), *Comparing Federal Systems,* 3rd ed. McGill-Queen's University Press.

Comprehensive comparative analysis of federal systems worldwide. Invaluable for understanding institutional variations and design choices. Tables comparing constitutional provisions particularly useful.

Lijphart, Arend (2012), *Patterns of Democracy,* 2nd ed. Yale University Press.

Extends beyond federalism to consociational democracy. Essential for understanding power-sharing mechanisms in divided societies. Belgium, Switzerland chapters directly relevant.

Burgess, Michael (2006), Comparative Federalism: Theory and Practice. Routledge.
Strong on federal theory evolution and European comparisons. Good treatment of 'asymmetric federalism' relevant to accommodating different regions' needs.
Research Gap
Limited systematic comparison of federal arrangements in post-conflict societies. Most comparative federalism literature assumes peaceful contexts. Need for studies examining federal design under conditions of recent violence and deep distrust.

II. Israeli-Palestinian Conflict: Historical Foundations
Cross-references: Chapters 1, 5, 6
Archaeological and Ancient History
Mazar, Amihai (1990). Archaeology of the Land of the Bible. Doubleday.
Authoritative archaeological survey. Essential for understanding material evidence of ancient Israelite civilization. Balanced treatment of scholarly debates.
Finkelstein, Israel & Silberman, Neil A. (2001). The Bible Unearthed. Free Press.
Controversial 'minimalist' interpretation challenging traditional dating. Important counterpoint to maximalist archaeology. Provoked productive scholarly debate.
Dever, William G. (2003). Who Were the Early Israelites and Where Did They Come From? Eerdmans.
Moderate archaeological interpretation. Good synthesis of evidence for Israelite origins. Accessible to non-specialists.
Modern Conflict Origins
Morris, Benny (2004). The Birth of the Palestinian Refugee Problem Revisited. Cambridge University Press.
Definitive study of 1948 Palestinian displacement. Uses Israeli archives exhaustively. Essential for understanding Nakba/Independence War debates.
Shlaim, Avi (2000). The Iron Wall: Israel and the Arab World. Norton.
Leading 'new historian' interpretation emphasizing Israeli agency. Controversial but influential. Good on diplomatic history through Oslo.
Khalidi, Rashid (2020). The Hundred Years' War on Palestine. Metropolitan Books.
Palestinian-American historian's comprehensive narrative. Strong on Palestinian perspective often absent from Western accounts. Essential for balance.

Research Gap
Insufficient integration of archaeological evidence with modern political analysis. Historians and archaeologists rarely collaborate. Need for interdisciplinary work connecting ancient and modern claims.

III. Constitutional Design and Power-Sharing
Cross-references: Chapters 4, 6, 11, 12
Constitutional Engineering
Horowitz, Donald L. (2002). Constitutional Design for Divided Societies. Journal of Democracy 13(4): 18-38.
Essential overview of constitutional options for diverse societies. Introduces integrative vs. consociational approaches. Directly applicable to Israeli-Palestinian design.
Sisk, Timothy D. (1996). Power Sharing and International Mediation in Ethnic Conflicts. USIP Press.
Practical guide to power-sharing mechanisms. Case studies from South Africa, Northern Ireland. Good on implementation challenges.
Choudhry, Sujit, ed. (2008). Constitutional Design for Divided Societies. Oxford University Press.
Excellent collection covering territorial autonomy, electoral systems, and judicial design. Multiple chapters directly relevant to federal Israel design.
Post-Conflict Constitutionalism
Samuels, Kirsti (2006). 'Post-Conflict Peace-Building and Constitution-Making.' Chicago Journal of International Law 6(2): 663-682.
Surveys constitutional processes in post-conflict states. Identifies success factors and common failures. Practical orientation useful for implementation planning.
Widner, Jennifer (2008). 'Constitution Writing in Post-conflict Settings.' William & Mary Law Review 49(4): 1513-1541.
Empirical study of 194 constitutional processes. Identifies variables associated with durability. Data-driven approach complements theoretical literature.
Research Gap
Limited study of constitutional design specifically for territories transitioning from occupation to shared sovereignty. Most literature assumes either independence or integration, not federal middle ground.

IV. Security Studies and Post-Conflict Stabilization
Cross-references: Chapters 5, 9

Security Sector Reform
Schnabel, Albrecht & Ehrhart, Hans-Georg, eds. (2005). Security Sector Reform and Post-Conflict Peacebuilding. UN University Press.
Comprehensive treatment of security transitions. Case studies from Balkans, Africa. Directly relevant to federal security architecture design.
Brzoska, Michael (2006). 'Introduction: Criteria for Evaluating Post-Conflict Reconstruction.' International Peacekeeping 13(1): 1-21.
Establishes evaluation criteria for post-conflict programs. Useful framework for assessing federal implementation progress.
Israeli Security Studies
Jones, Clive & Murphy, Emma C. (2002). Israel: Challenges to Identity, Democracy and the State. Routledge.
Comprehensive analysis of Israeli security doctrine. Essential for understanding constraints on any federal arrangement.
Byman, Daniel (2011). A High Price: The Triumphs and Failures of Israeli Counterterrorism. Oxford University Press.
Critical assessment of Israeli security policies. Relevant for understanding what federal alternatives must address.
Research Gap
No systematic study of how federal security arrangements might function specifically in Israeli-Palestinian context. Existing security literature assumes either separation or occupation, not integration.

V. Economic Integration and Development
Cross-references: Chapters 7, 8
Economic Peace Theory
Barnett, Michael & Levy, Jack S. (1991). 'Domestic Sources of Alliances and Alignments.' International Organization 45(3): 369-395.
Classic on economic factors in political alignment. Foundation for understanding how economic integration supports political cooperation.
Russett, Bruce & Oneal, John (2001). Triangulating Peace: Democracy, Interdependence, and International Organizations. Norton.
Empirical evidence that trade reduces conflict. Relevant for evaluating economic integration component of federal solution.
Israeli-Palestinian Economics
Arnon, Arie & Weinblatt, Jimmy (2001). 'Sovereignty and Economic Development: The Case of Israel and Palestine.' Economic Journal 111(472): 291-308.

Analysis of economic interdependence between Israeli and Palestinian economies. Essential for understanding integration possibilities.

World Bank (2023). Palestinian Economic Prospects. Various reports.

Regular assessments of Palestinian economic conditions. Data essential for understanding development challenges and potential.

Research Gap

Limited economic modeling of federal arrangements specifically. Need for detailed fiscal federalism analysis addressing revenue sharing, development disparities, and labor market integration.

VI. Identity, Nationalism, and Reconciliation

Cross-references: Chapters 2, 10, 14

Nationalism Theory

Anderson, Benedict (1983). Imagined Communities. Verso.

Foundational text on nationalism as constructed identity. Essential for understanding how national narratives develop and might be transformed.

Smith, Anthony D. (1991). National Identity. Penguin.

Synthesis of primordialist and modernist approaches. Good on relationship between ethnic and national identity. Relevant for understanding both Israeli and Palestinian nationalism.

Reconciliation Studies

Kriesberg, Louis (2007). Constructive Conflicts: From Escalation to Resolution, 3rd ed. Rowman & Littlefield.

Comprehensive conflict resolution textbook. Strong on de-escalation processes. Practical orientation.

Bar-Tal, Daniel (2013). Intractable Conflicts: Socio-Psychological Foundations and Dynamics. Cambridge University Press.

Israeli psychologist's analysis of conflict psychology. Essential for understanding psychological barriers to resolution and how to address them.

Research Gap

Insufficient study of how federal arrangements might transform (rather than merely accommodate) conflicting national identities. Need for longitudinal studies of identity change in federal contexts.

VII. Research Agenda: Gaps and Opportunities

Priority Research Needs

1. Comparative Analysis of Federal Emergence from Conflict

- Systematic comparison of federal arrangements emerging from violent conflict (Bosnia, post-apartheid South Africa, post-war Germany) vs. peaceful federation formation.
- Key question: What conditions enable federal success after violence?

2. Economic Modeling of Israeli-Palestinian Federation
- Detailed fiscal federalism analysis: revenue sources, transfer mechanisms, development equalization.
- Labor market integration scenarios with varying mobility assumptions.
- Trade creation/diversion effects of customs union.

3. Security Architecture Studies
- Comparative analysis of unified federal security forces in divided societies.
- Intelligence sharing mechanisms in low-trust environments.
- Phased transition from occupation to shared security.

4. Constitutional Design Simulation
- Detailed constitutional drafts with alternative provisions.
- Simulation of constitutional processes under various scenarios.
- Public opinion research on constitutional preferences.

5. Identity Transformation Longitudinal Studies
- How do identities change in federal contexts?
- What educational and media policies support identity accommodation?
- Intergenerational transmission of conflict attitudes in federal settings.

Methodological Recommendations
- Mixed methods combining quantitative analysis with case studies.
- Collaborative research involving Israeli, Palestinian, and international scholars.
- Policy-relevant research designs that inform implementation.
- Longitudinal designs tracking change over time rather than static snapshots.

Guide 3

Interfaith Reader's Guide.

This guide offers perspectives from Jewish, Christian, and Muslim traditions on peace, federalism, and coexistence. It is designed to facilitate interfaith dialogue around the book's themes.

Jewish Perspectives on Federalism and Peace.
Textual Foundations.
Jewish tradition contains rich resources for thinking about governance, peace, and coexistence with other peoples:
"Seek the peace of the city where I have sent you into exile, and pray to the Lord on its behalf, for in its peace you will find your peace." (Jeremiah 29:7)
This verse, from the prophet Jeremiah's letter to exiles in Babylon, establishes that Jews are commanded to work for the welfare of the broader community, not just their own. It provides a foundation for participating in shared governance arrangements.
"The world stands on three things: justice, truth, and peace." (Pirke Avot 1:18)
Rabbi Shimon ben Gamliel's teaching reminds us that peace requires justice and truth as foundations. Federal arrangements must address legitimate grievances to achieve lasting peace.
Contemporary Jewish Voices.
Jewish thinkers have long grappled with how to balance Jewish self-determination with ethical obligations to others:
- Rabbi Abraham Isaac Kook emphasized that the return to Zion must elevate humanity, not merely secure territory.
- Martin Buber advocated for Arab-Jewish cooperation throughout his life, believing that genuine dialogue could transcend political divisions.
- Rabbi Jonathan Sacks wrote extensively about 'the dignity of difference' — how diverse peoples can share space while maintaining distinct identities.

Points for Jewish Readers to Consider
- How does pikuach nefesh (preservation of life) apply when evaluating political arrangements that might reduce violence?
- What does 'loving the stranger' (Leviticus 19:34) mean in the context of shared citizenship?
- How do we balance claims of covenant and chosenness with universal ethical obligations?

Christian Perspectives on Peace and Reconciliation.
Textual Foundations.
Christian scripture offers extensive teaching on peace, reconciliation, and the relationship between peoples:
"Blessed are the peacemakers, for they will be called children of God." (Matthew 5:9)
Jesus's beatitude places peacemaking at the heart of Christian discipleship. This calls Christians to actively work for peace, not merely avoid conflict.
"There is neither Jew nor Gentile, neither slave nor free, neither male nor female, for you are all one in Christ Jesus." (Galatians 3:28)
Paul's vision of unity transcending ethnic and social divisions provides a framework for thinking about shared citizenship across religious lines.
Addressing Christian Zionism
Christian Zionism — the belief that supporting Israel is a religious obligation — takes various forms:
- Dispensationalist theology sees Israel's restoration as fulfillment of biblical prophecy and precondition for Christ's return.
- Covenantal theology emphasizes God's enduring promises to the Jewish people without specific political implications.
- Liberation theology approaches prioritize justice for the oppressed, sometimes leading to support for Palestinian rights.

Federal solutions might appeal across these divides: affirming Jewish connection to the land while ensuring justice for all inhabitants.
Points for Christian Readers to Consider
- How does Jesus's command to 'love your neighbor as yourself' apply to all parties in this conflict?
- What does Christian teaching about reconciliation require of those who have harmed each other?
- How should Christians balance support for Israel with concern for Palestinian Christians and Muslims?

Muslim Perspectives on Peace and Coexistence.
Textual Foundations.
Islamic tradition contains significant resources for thinking about governance, peace, and relations with other communities:

"O mankind, indeed We have created you from male and female and made you peoples and tribes that you may know one another." (Quran 49:13)
This verse establishes human diversity as divinely intended for mutual understanding, not conflict. It provides foundation for pluralistic coexistence.
"If they incline to peace, then incline to it also and rely upon Allah." (Quran 8:61)
The Quran commands Muslims to respond positively to genuine peace overtures. This verse has been cited by Muslim scholars advocating for negotiated solutions.

Historical Precedents
Islamic history includes important examples of religious coexistence:
- The Constitution of Medina established by Prophet Muhammad created a multi-religious community with shared governance.
- Al-Andalus (Muslim Spain) achieved periods of remarkable Jewish-Muslim-Christian coexistence.
- The Ottoman millet system, despite limitations, allowed religious communities significant autonomy.

These precedents demonstrate that shared sovereignty arrangements have Islamic historical foundations.

Points for Muslim Readers to Consider.
- How does the Islamic concept of 'maslaha' (public interest) apply to political arrangements that might reduce suffering?
- What does justice ('adl) require in addressing legitimate grievances of all parties?
- How can Palestinians maintain dignity and self-determination within federal arrangements?

Interfaith Dialogue Suggestions.
Shared Principles Across Traditions.
All three Abrahamic traditions share commitments that support peaceful coexistence:
- The sanctity of human life, created in the divine image
- The obligation to pursue justice and righteousness
- The command to care for the stranger and the vulnerable
- The vision of peace as ultimate divine intention.

Dialogue Formats.
Study Circles.
Bring together members of different faith communities to read and discuss the book together. Focus on one chapter per session, allowing time for each tradition's perspective.

Panel Discussions
Invite speakers from Jewish, Christian, and Muslim communities to respond to the book's thesis. Ensure diverse viewpoints within each tradition are represented.

Prayer Gatherings
Organize interfaith prayer services focused on peace. Use texts from each tradition that emphasize peace and reconciliation.

Discussion Questions for Interfaith Groups
- What resources does your tradition offer for living peacefully with those who are different?
- How do your scriptures address the relationship between justice and peace?
- What would your tradition say about sharing sovereignty with others?
- How can religious communities support political solutions without becoming partisan?
- What role should religious leaders play in peacemaking?

Recommended Interfaith Resources
- 'The Faith Club' by Ranya Idliby, Suzanne Oliver, and Priscilla Warner — Jewish, Christian, and Muslim women's dialogue
- 'Abraham's Children' edited by Kelly James Clark — Scholars from all three traditions on shared heritage
- 'Trialogue' edited by Leonard Swidler — Structured Jewish-Christian-Muslim dialogue model
- Scriptural Reasoning movement — Academic and grassroots interfaith text study

Guide 4

Activist's Handbook

This handbook provides practical guidance for advocating federal solutions to the Israeli-Palestinian conflict. It includes talking points, responses to common objections, and resources for organized action.

How to Advocate for Federal Solutions

Know Your Audience

Different audiences require different approaches. Tailor your message accordingly:

For Pro-Israel Audiences

- Emphasize security benefits: unified command, elimination of ungoverned spaces
- Stress that federalism EXTENDS Israeli democracy, not compromises it
- Note that Jewish majority governance continues at federal level
- Highlight economic benefits and regional integration potential
- Frame as victory, not concession: 'peace from strength'

For Pro-Palestinian Audiences

- Emphasize dignity through citizenship vs. endless occupation
- Note that autonomy in regional governments exceeds current PA powers
- Stress that federal citizenship includes FULL political rights
- Acknowledge legitimate grievances while focusing on achievable progress
- Compare to other self-determination movements that accepted federal solutions

For General/Neutral Audiences

- Lead with the failure of current approaches: 'Everything else has been tried'
- Use comparative examples: 'Switzerland manages four languages...'
- Emphasize practical benefits: security, economy, stability
- Acknowledge complexity while stressing that alternatives are MORE complex
- Focus on shared humanity and children's futures

Talking Points by Topic
On Security
Point: Federal arrangement provides BETTER security than occupation.
— Unified federal military eliminates security vacuums terrorists exploit
— Constitutional protections mean security isn't dependent on one government's choices
— Integration creates informational advantages over separation
— Legitimate institutions reduce recruitment for violent resistance
On Democracy
Point: Federalism SOLVES the democracy problem, not creates it.
— Currently, Israel governs millions who can't vote in national elections
— Federal citizenship extends voting rights to all
— Regional autonomy means communities govern themselves on local matters
— Constitutional protections prevent majority tyranny
On Feasibility
Point: Federalism has succeeded in comparable situations.
— Switzerland united hostile Catholic and Protestant cantons
— Germany transformed from genocidal state to stable democracy
— South Africa transitioned from apartheid to shared citizenship
— None of these were 'easy' — but all were achieved
On Identity
Point: Federal citizenship doesn't erase national identity.
— Flemish Belgians remain Flemish while being Belgian citizens
— Quebec remains distinctively French within Canada
— Jews and Arabs would maintain distinct identities within federal framework
— Shared citizenship adds a layer; it doesn't replace existing identities.
Common Objections and Responses
"They'll never agree"
Response: Neither side 'agreed' to the current situation either. The question is what creates better outcomes, not what's currently popular. When conditions make alternatives clearly worse, political positions shift. German post-war transformation wasn't popular initially either.
"The populations hate each other too much"
Response: Federal systems have succeeded between populations with far more recent violent history — post-war Germany, post-apartheid South Africa, post-Troubles Northern Ireland. What

matters is institutional design, not initial attitudes. Attitudes follow institutions more than institutions follow attitudes.

"Demographics would eliminate Jewish majority"

Response: Federal design can protect community interests regardless of overall demographics — see Swiss canton system where small cantons have equal Senate representation, or Belgian linguistic community protections. The question is constitutional design, not numbers.

"Palestinians deserve their own state"

Response: What matters is self-governance and dignity, not flags. Palestinians under federal arrangement would have MORE self-governance than under current PA, PLUS full citizenship rights in federal institutions. Compare: Is a Catalan worse off as Spanish citizen with autonomy than they would be in a struggling micro-state?

"Two states is still possible"

Response: 700,000+ settlers, Jerusalem's indivisibility, infrastructure integration, and water/airspace complexity have made partition physically impossible. Two-state 'solution' is now a diplomatic fiction that prevents serious discussion of achievable arrangements.

"Settlers would never leave"

Response: They don't have to! Federal solution means settlements become part of Palestinian-majority cantons with Jewish residents, just as Arab-majority areas within Israel proper have Jewish residents. Residency and citizenship are separated from ethnic majority status.

Organizations Working on These Issues

Research and Policy

- A Land for All / Two States One Homeland — Israeli-Palestinian federation advocacy
- Institute for National Security Studies (INSS) — Israeli policy research
- Al-Shabaka: The Palestinian Policy Network — Palestinian policy analysis
- Carnegie Endowment for International Peace — Middle East program
- Brookings Institution — Center for Middle East Policy

Dialogue and Coexistence

- Seeds of Peace — Youth dialogue programs
- Parents Circle - Families Forum — Bereaved families from both sides

- Combatants for Peace — Former fighters turned peace advocates
- Standing Together — Jewish-Arab grassroots movement
- Givat Haviva — Arab-Jewish coexistence education

Advocacy and Activism

- J Street — Pro-Israel, pro-peace advocacy (US)
- Americans for Peace Now
- Churches for Middle East Peace — Interfaith coalition
- Foundation for Middle East Peace

Academic Networks

- Association for Israel Studies
- Middle East Studies Association
- International Studies Association — Middle East section

Action Steps

Individual Actions

- Read and share the book — start conversations
- Write letters to elected officials advocating new approaches
- Engage constructively on social media — model civil discourse
- Organize discussion groups in your community, congregation, or campus
- Support organizations working on coexistence

Community Actions

- Invite speakers on federal solutions to community events
- Organize interfaith dialogue sessions
- Create reading groups studying the book
- Develop educational programming for various age groups
- Connect with existing peace organizations

Institutional Actions

- Advocate for academic courses on comparative federalism
- Support research on federal solutions
- Press media for coverage of alternative frameworks
- Engage political candidates on their Middle East positions
- Build coalitions across traditional political divides

Key Message to Remember

Federal solutions represent hope based on evidence — not naive optimism, but practical assessment that everything else has failed. The question isn't whether federalism is perfect (it isn't), but whether it's better than alternatives (it is). We advocate not for utopia but for improvement. As the book concludes: political imagination, properly applied to constitutional design, can resolve even conflicts that have resisted all previous efforts. Our task is to expand that imagination and channel it toward achievable change.

Guide 5

Educator's Toolkit.

This toolkit provides resources for teaching the book in university courses, high school advanced placement classes, or adult education settings. Each section includes lesson plans, discussion guides, and assessment materials.

Course Integration Guide

Suitable Courses

- Middle East Politics / International Relations
- Comparative Politics / Federal Systems
- Conflict Resolution / Peace Studies
- Constitutional Law / Political Theory
- Jewish Studies / Israel Studies
- Modern History / 20th Century History

Suggested Course Positioning

Full Course: Use as primary text with supplementary readings.

Partial Integration: Assign Opening Words + Chapters 3, 4, 11, 14 as federalism case study.

Comparative Unit: Pair Chapter 3 with primary sources on Swiss, Belgian, Canadian federalism.

Lesson Plans by Chapter Group

Unit 1: Historical Foundations (Chapters 1-2)

Duration: 2-3 class sessions

Learning Objectives

- Analyze archaeological and historical evidence for Jewish presence in Israel/Palestine
- Understand the development of Zionist thought and its various streams
- Distinguish between different forms of federalism and their applications

Pre-Class Preparation

- Read: Chapters 1-2
- Watch: PBS documentary 'The 50 Years War' (selected segments)
- Map exercise: Trace territorial changes 1917-present

In-Class Activities

Session 1: Lecture on archaeological evidence and historical claims. Discussion: How should ancient history inform modern politics?

Session 2: Seminar on Federal Zionism vs. other Zionist streams. Small group: Compare Einstein, Buber, Magnes positions.

Assessment

Short paper (1000 words): 'Evaluate the claim that historical presence should determine modern sovereignty.'

Unit 2: Comparative Federalism (Chapters 3-4)

Duration: 3-4 class sessions

Learning Objectives

- Compare federal arrangements across Switzerland, Belgium, Canada, India
- Identify key design variables in federal constitutions
- Apply comparative insights to Israeli-Palestinian context

Pre-Class Preparation

- Read: Chapters 3-4
- Research assignment: Each student studies one federal system in depth

In-Class Activities

Session 1: Student presentations on assigned federal systems (10 min each).

Session 2: Comparative analysis grid exercise — create table comparing divisions of power.

Session 3: Constitutional design workshop — draft provisions for hypothetical federal Israel.

Assessment

Group project: Design and justify a federal constitution for Israel/Palestine, addressing power division, rights protection, and dispute resolution.

Unit 3: Post-Conflict and Security (Chapters 5-6, 9)

Duration: 2-3 class sessions

Learning Objectives

- Understand post-conflict reconstruction challenges
- Analyze security requirements in divided societies
- Evaluate German post-war transformation as precedent

Pre-Class Preparation

- Read: Chapters 5, 6, 9
- Case study: German Basic Law (1949) provisions on federalism

In-Class Activities

Session 1: Guest speaker (if available) on post-conflict reconstruction experience.

Session 2: Security simulation — role-play negotiating security arrangements.

Session 3: Documentary screening and discussion on German transformation.

Assessment

Policy memo (1500 words): 'Design a phased security transition from current situation to federal arrangement.'

Unit 4: Regional and Economic Dimensions (Chapters 7-8)

Duration: 2 class sessions

Learning Objectives

- Evaluate Abraham Accords achievements and limitations
- Analyze economic interdependence and development potential
- Understand fiscal federalism mechanisms

Pre-Class Preparation

- Read: Chapters 7-8
- Data analysis: World Bank reports on Palestinian economy

In-Class Activities

Session 1: Analysis of Abraham Accords texts. Discussion: What explains Arab state normalization?

Session 2: Economic modeling exercise — estimate costs and benefits of integration scenarios.

Assessment

Economic analysis paper: 'Would a federal Israel be economically viable? What policies would be required?'

Unit 5: Critiques and Implementation (Chapters 10-14)

Duration: 3-4 class sessions

Learning Objectives

- Engage seriously with objections to federal solutions
- Understand implementation challenges and sequencing
- Formulate and defend personal position on federal feasibility

Pre-Class Preparation

- Read: Chapters 10-14
- Find and analyze one scholarly article critiquing federalism for Israel/Palestine

In-Class Activities

Session 1: Structured debate — 'Resolved: Federal solution is more feasible than two-state solution.'

Session 2: Implementation timeline workshop — sequence steps over 5, 10, 20 year horizons.

Session 3: Final synthesis discussion — 'What would you recommend if you were advising decision-makers?'

Final Assessment

Research paper (3000-5000 words): 'Evaluate the federal solution thesis, engaging with the strongest counterarguments and reaching a defended conclusion.'

Slide Deck Outlines
Lecture 1: Introduction to the Conflict
- Slide 1: Map — territory from Ottoman to present
- Slide 2: Population demographics over time
- Slide 3: Key dates timeline
- Slide 4: Failed paradigms — why current approaches don't work
- Slide 5: Book thesis introduction

Lecture 2: Federalism Fundamentals
- Slide 1: Definition — self-rule and shared rule
- Slide 2: Federation vs. confederation vs. unitary state
- Slide 3: Why federalism? Historical emergence
- Slide 4: Design variables (power division, representation, etc.)
- Slide 5: Success factors from comparative research

Lecture 3: Comparative Cases
- Slide 1: Switzerland — four languages, one nation
- Slide 2: Belgium — linguistic federalism
- Slide 3: Canada — asymmetric arrangements
- Slide 4: India — scale and diversity
- Slide 5: Lessons for Israel/Palestine

Assessment Questions Bank
Short Answer Questions
- What evidence does the author cite for ancient Jewish presence in Israel/Palestine?
- Distinguish between Federal Zionism and World Federalism as the author describes them.
- Why does the author argue the two-state solution is no longer viable?
- What lessons does the German post-war experience offer?
- What are the main objections to federal solutions and how does the author respond?

Essay Questions
- Compare and contrast the federal arrangements of any two countries discussed in Chapter 3. What design principles might apply to Israel/Palestine?

- Evaluate the claim that 'security through legitimate institutions proves more durable than security through permanent domination.'
- Is the Abraham Accords' approach of 'normalization before resolution' sustainable? Why or why not?
- Design a phased implementation plan for federal Israel. What would be the first step and why?
- Engage with the strongest criticism of the federal solution. Is it fatal to the thesis? Why or why not?

Documentary and Film Recommendations
Historical Background
- 'The 50 Years War: Israel and the Arabs' (PBS, 1999) — Comprehensive documentary history
- '1913: Seeds of Conflict' (PBS, 2015) — Pre-WWI origins
- 'The Gatekeepers' (2012) — Israeli security chiefs reflect on occupation

Comparative Federalism
- 'The Miracle of Bern' (2003) — German reconstruction
- 'Good Night, and Good Luck' (2005) — American federalism context
- Documentary shorts on Swiss and Belgian systems (various YouTube educational channels)

Conflict and Coexistence
- '5 Broken Cameras' (2011) — Palestinian perspective
- 'Waltz with Bashir' (2008) — Israeli memory and conflict
- 'Promises' (2001) — Israeli and Palestinian children's perspectives
- 'The Green Prince' (2014) — Complexity of Israeli-Palestinian relations

Peace Processes
- 'The Oslo Diaries' (HBO, 2018) — Inside the Oslo negotiations
- 'West of the Jordan River' (2017) — Current situation